Encyclopaedia Britalicar

The Story of British Cars & Italian Design

Quiller Print

Encyclopaedia Britalicar

The Story of British Cars & Italian Design

Quiller Print

A catalogue record for this book is available from the British Library

ISBN 978-0-9926651-3-5

Published by Quiller Print, Dorset House, 14 Bowden Road, Ascot, Berks SL5 9NJ, United Kingdom
Web: www.quillerprint.co.uk

Printed in the UK by Short Run Press, Bittern Road, Sowton Industrial Estate, Exeter EX2 7LW
Tel: 01392 211909
Web: www.shortrunpress.co.uk

ABOUT THE AUTHOR

Chris Rees has been writing about cars for almost 40 years. In that time, he has contributed to dozens of car magazine titles, newspapers and motoring websites and has edited a number of motoring publications. He currently edits *Auto Italia* magazine and is Motors Editor for *The Official Ferrari Magazine*, as well as writing freelance for many other publications.

Chris's car ownership has focused mostly on Italian and British marques, with a string of specialist machinery, including – from the British camp – several Caterhams, Bond Bug and Bond Equipe, Trident and Triking, while Italian cars he's owned include a Fiat Panda 100HP, Alfa Romeo 156, 164, SZ and Giulia Quadrifoglio.

To date, Chris has written over 20 motoring books. He lives and works in Berkshire in the UK.

ACKNOWLEDGEMENTS

All work depends on the invaluable contributions of others, especially when you're charting new territory and dealing with little-known subject matter. So it is with this book: without the support of so many people, it simply wouldn't have happened.

Sincere thanks go to all the Italian carrozzerie and designers who contributed archive materials. A great debt is owed to Edgardo Michelotti, who afforded so much time to the project and access to the Archivio Storico Michelotti. I would also like to acknowledge the support of Ares Design, Bertone, Biemme, Paul Breuer, British Motors, Castagna, CECOMP, Fulvio Fantolino at F&F Design, I.DE.A, Italdesign, Paolo Martin, Pilato, Pininfarina, Ercole Spada and Touring. Among British car makers, sincere thanks are due to the PR teams at Aston Martin, Bentley, Ford, Jaguar, Lotus, Rolls-Royce and Vauxhall.

I must also acknowledge many fellow professionals and Italian car enthusiasts, including Richard Heseltine, Simon Charlesworth, Richard Dredge and Gary Axon, as well as the help offered by Alessandro Sannia in Italy. Many thanks also go to Dave Solomon of the Triumph TR Register, and the contributions of Rick Kamen, David Ehrich, Norman Hawkes, Ben Stinson, Richard Wrightson, Vauxford, Stefan Marjoram, Jeroen Booij, Vasileios Papaidis, Darren Lamb, Max Earey, Raphael Belly, Dave Poole, Richard Howard, Adrian Berry, Thomas 039, Mr Choppers, Steven Snoep and Andrew Bone.

In terms of imagery, I would like to acknowledge the support of RM Sotheby's, Bonhams, Historics, Gooding & Co, Classic Motor Hub, Silverstone Auctions, Coys, Osenat, Pendine Historics, RAC, Brightwells, Clark & Carter, Hyman and Christies.

Above all I would like to thank the staff at *Auto Italia* magazine – Claire Prior and the Ward family – for their tremendous help in so many aspects of the preparation of the book, from expert car knowledge to rare imagery. Particular thanks go to Michael Ward for his huge help in terms of photography, design and layout.

Contents

BRITISH MARQUES

18 AC
28 Armstrong-Siddeley
30 Aston Martin
64 Bentley
74 BMC Family
Austin, Austin-Healey, Innocenti, MG, Morris, Riley, Vanden Plas, Wolseley
118 Bristol
130 Daimler
132 DeLorean
136 Elva
139 Ferguson
140 Ford
150 Frazer Nash
154 Frisky
156 Gordon-Keeble
160 Healey
164 Jaguar
194 Jensen
198 Jowett
201 Lea-Francis
202 Lola
204 Lotus
218 Mini
222 Panther
224 Reliant
228 Rolls-Royce
238 Rootes Group
Hillman, Singer, Sunbeam
246 Rover
252 Standard-Triumph
274 TVR
280 Vauxhall

ITALIAN *CARROZZERIE*

282 Allemano
282 Ares
282 Bertone
283 Biemme
284 Boano
284 Boneschi
284 Boniolo
284 Breuer
285 Casale
285 Castagna
285 Cattelan
285 CECOMP
285 Coggiola
286 Drogo/Sports Cars
286 F&F
286 Fiore
287 Fissore
287 Ford Centro Stlle
288 Francis Lombardi
288 Frua
289 FT
289 Garavini
289 Ghia
291 Ghia-Aigle/Italsuisse
291 I.DE.A
291 Indestor
292 Italdesign
294 Michelotti
296 Monviso
296 Motto
296 Opac
296 OSI
297 Pilato
297 Pinin Farina/Pininfarina
298 Schiaretti
298 Sibona-Basano
298 Stabilimenti Farina
299 Tjaarda
299 Touring
300 Vignale
300 Viotti
302 Zagato

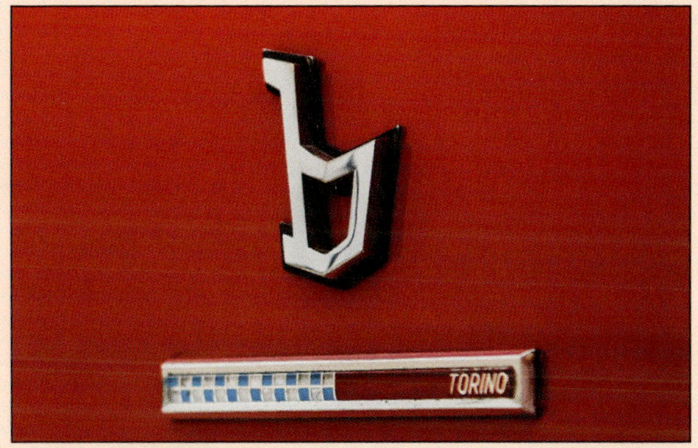

Encyclopaedia Britalicar: The Story of British Cars & Italian Design

Introduction

What have the Romans ever done for us? John Cleese's famous demand in the film, *The Life of Brian*, elicited a deluge of replies about all the benefits that flowed from Rome, from roads to aqueducts. It wasn't just ancient Judeans, however, who came to appreciate 'what the Romans did'. The world owes so much to Italy's cradle of civilisation. The medieval Renaissance was founded on the principles and aesthetics of ancient Rome; it was no coincidence that Shakespeare set one third of all his plays in Italy; and nor that Victorian Britons flocked to Italy in their thousands for the classic 'Grand Tour'.

We may even say there exists a form of 'special relationship' between the United Kingdom and Italy, with many shared links, both strong and varied. We could start with geographical associations: the outlines of Britannia and Italy's 'boot' almost look like mirror images of each other on the European map. Both countries have a mountainous north, and both a central spine of peaks with the same root name: Pennines and Apennines. There's even a geopolitical echo in both countries' famous north-south divides.

The cultural resonances continue with a shared respect for each other's traditions of taste and craftsmanship. For instance, Italy gave the world the sharp-cut Milanese suit; Britain its Savile Row tailoring. Both countries have been preeminent in Formula 1, with Alfa Romeo and Ferrari battling Cooper and Lotus in the 1950s. Both countries had strong car industries in the post-war years but suffered from industrial unrest and significant declines in their car industries as the 20th century progressed.

The contrasts between Italy and Britain are, of course, every bit as strong, and that includes the arena of automotive coachbuilding. While Britain certainly had a thriving industry designing and building car bodywork in the 20th century, it was always much more of a 'cottage' industry than the industrialised design houses that thrived in Italy. The contrasts were stylistic, too. Britain in the 20th century was a country emerging from its days of empire and British car design tended to err towards uprightness, steadfastness and conservatism. Italy, in contrast, was a country reinventing itself and embraced flair, dynamism, optimism and modernity – an attitude summed up by the phrase, *la dolce vita*.

From Italy: elegance, refinement, good taste and fine proportion. From Britain: engineering quality, sporting prowess and an enthusiasm for motoring. These traits commonly – but not always – combined to create some of the world's most desirable cars, such as this Bristol 401 Drophead Convertible by Pinin Farina.

VMG 614

Italian design was rarely modish or flashy, though, instead being imbued with a sense of taste and decorum that only centuries of familiarity with aesthetic etiquette could engender.

Italy consistently produced coachbuilders, or *carrozzerie* in the local parlance, that combined the best artisanry with the best artistry. The scale was also far greater than anywhere else in the world. Hubs formed around Modena, Milan and, in particular, Turin, where any and all skills could be found to create the very best in terms of quality of design and manufacture. Post-war Italy elegantly assumed its role as the undisputed world capital of car design. Indeed, one could argue that Italy became the epicentre of 20th century design, full stop. From fashion to architecture to fine art, the importance of aesthetics has always flourished in Italian culture.

Pretty much all of the great names in car design were Italian. Ask anyone to name a car designer and they'll likely suggest Nuccio Bertone, Sergio Pininfarina, Giorgetto Giugiaro or Marcello Gandini. For each of these storied superstars of design, however, there are a dozen more Italian talents whose names are less well known, but certainly no less accomplished: the likes of Giovanni Michelotti, Federico Formenti and Ercole Spada, many of whom had a significant impact on the British car industry.

Italian designers also enjoyed influence far beyond the boundaries of Italy, as many found work on foreign soil. In France, for instance, two Italians called Giuseppe Figoni and Ovidio Falaschi founded the most flamboyant coachbuilding company of all time (Figoni & Falaschi). And the car that many regard as the most beautiful of all time, the Citroën DS, was designed by an Italian: Flaminio Bertoni, who also styled the 2CV, Ami and H Van. Italians even rocked up in Britain. Dick Burzi left Mussolini's Italy in the 1920s for the UK and joined Austin on the recommendation of Vincenzo Lancia, eventually rising to the position of chief stylist. And one British-born designer – Trevor Frost – even changed his name to an Italian one: Fiore, his mother's maiden name.

It was to Italy that the world's car companies flocked for design work. German manufacturers began their Italian quest in the 1950s with the VW Karmann-Ghia, NSU Sport Prinz and Glas, while BMW imported Italian with its Michelotti-designed 700, 'Neue Klasse' 1500/1800, 2500/2800 saloon and coupe, and the trailblazing 1602/2002 Touring 'hot hatchback'. For his part, Giorgetto Giugiaro had a huge impact on Volkswagen's fortunes with the Passat of 1972, quickly followed by the iconic Scirocco and Golf.

In France, Bertone was responsible for the Simca 1000 Coupe, Frua for the Renault Floride/Caravelle and Michelotti for the Alpine A106/A108/A110. Peugeot's relationship with Pininfarina flourished for many decades, from the 403 of 1955, through the 404, 504, 505 and 605 to the brilliant 205. Marcello Gandini of Bertone also designed two huge sellers for France in the 1980s: the Citroën BX and Renault Supercinq.

Japan and Italy collaborated, too, in post-war car miracles. The Skyline Sport of 1958 and the Hino Contessa Sprint of 1962 were both designed by Giovanni Michelotti, while Pininfarina was involved with the 1963 Nissan Bluebird. But the Italian who truly transformed car design in Japan was Giorgetto Giugiaro, who designed such cars as the Mazda Familia (1963), Mazda Luce (1965), Isuzu 117 Coupe (1968) and Suzuki Fronte Coupe (1971).

The design cross-fertilisation between Italy and the USA has been so wide-ranging that a whole book has been dedicated to it, *Transatlantic Style* by Donald Osborne. Probably the biggest US user of Italian design talent was Chrysler, which got Ghia to help it create a whole litany of concept and production cars in the 1950s. Ultimately, though, it would be Ford that acquired Ghia in 1970.

But it's the rich, deep partnership between the British car industry and Italian design that this book celebrates. Britain's love letter to Italian style has

OPPOSITE PAGE, TOP TO BOTTOM: Battista Pininfarina with Renzo Carli and Battista's son Sergio; Paolo Martin of Pininfarina; Giovanni Savonuzzi of Ghia; Tom Tjaarda.
CLOCKWISE FROM TOP LEFT: Giovanni Michelotti; Giorgetto Giugiaro who founded Italdesign; Elio Zagato; Giovanni and Giuseppe 'Nuccio' Bertone.

ABOVE: Giovanni Michelotti's whimsical 1950s visual take on national design traits. British companies flocked to use his design talents. ABOVE RIGHT: Early sketch by Michelotti for the Triumph 'Barb' (2000) and a cutaway drawing of Bertone's Jaguar E-Type based Pirana.

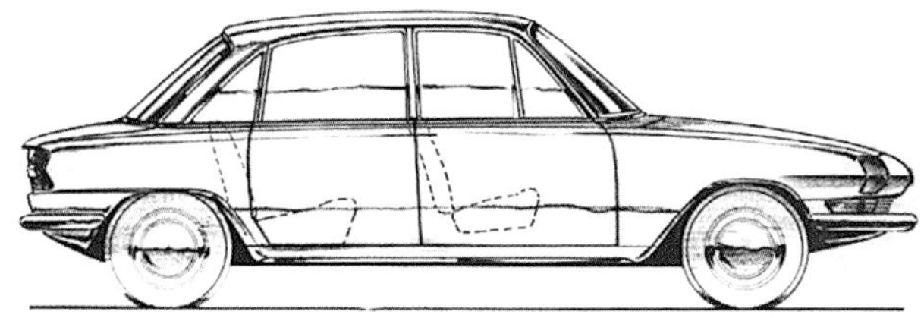

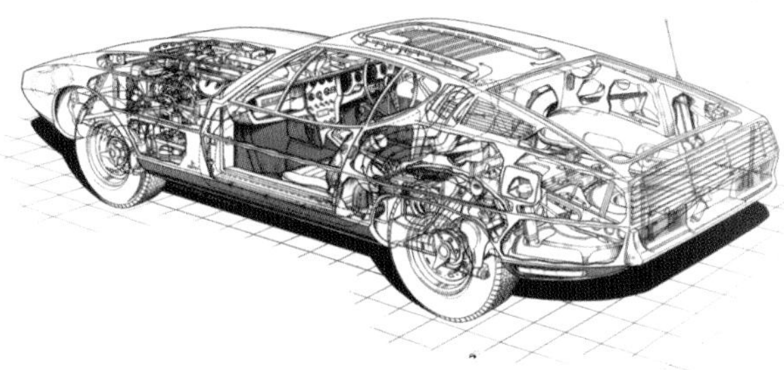

been long and impassioned. So permit me to rephrase John Cleese's question and ask: what have the Italians ever done for the British car industry? Some sense can be gleaned by posing a series of questions in return:

- *Which Italian design house styled Britain's best-selling car of the 1960s? (Pininfarina: BMC 1100/1300)*
- *Which Italian designed every production Triumph model from 1958 to 1975? (Giovanni Michelotti)*
- *Which Italian designed what is widely regarded as the most beautiful Aston Martin of all time? (Federico Formenti of Touring: DB4/DB5/DB6)*
- *Which Italian designed what are now the most collectible versions of both the Aston Martin and Bristol marques? (Ercole Spada of Zagato: DB4 GTZ and 406 GTZ)*
- *Which Italian supercar designer created a critically acclaimed new set of clothes for the BMC Mini? (Marcello Gandini of Bertone: Innocenti Mini)*
- *Which Italian designer invented the 'targa' roof concept, first used on a British car? (Giovanni Michelotti: Triumph TR4)*
- *Who designed the most expensive car in the world in the 1970s? (Paolo Martin of Pininfarina: Rolls-Royce Camargue)*
- *Who designed the longest-running Lotus model of all? (Giorgetto Giugiaro: Esprit)*
- *For which British company did Giorgetto Giugiaro design his very first ever car? (Gordon-Keeble)*
- *Which Italian design house was once lined up to manufacture cars in the UK? (Zagato in 1964)*
- *Which Italian carrozzeria was at one point part-owned by a British company? (Zagato: Aston Martin owned a 50% stake in the mid-1980s).*
- *Which Italian design house probably owed its very survival to rebodying MGs? (Bertone: its Arnolt MG TD of 1952 sold hundreds in the USA)*
- *The very last car ever built by Touring was a British car – which one? (Aston Martin DBS C)*
- *Which British-made car was designed by Pietro Frua and finished off by the designer of the Edsel? (Ford Zodiac Mk3)*
- *Which Italian company made British saloons and sports cars under licence in Turin in the 1960s? (Touring: Hillman Minx and Sunbeam Alpine)*
- *Which British car was the very last design drawn by Giovanni Michelotti? (Reliant Scimitar SS1)*

Broadly speaking, the contents of this book straddle three distinct but overlapping eras. The first arose out of the coachbuilding traditions of the 19th century, when horse-drawn carriage bodywork was crafted entirely by artisans. In the early years of the motor industry, coachbuilders local to car makers typically made car bodywork but it was not long before the fame of Italian artistry spread across the world. Chassis from illustrious British marques such as Bentley and Rolls-Royce found their way to Italy to be bodied by the likes of Pinin Farina, Castagna, Viotti, Zagato and Garavini.

Following World War 2, that process accelerated dramatically. All sorts of prestigious chassis were bodied in Italy, including Bristol, Frazer Nash, Jowett, Jaguar, Aston Martin and MG. This was truly the golden era of coachbuilding, with some of the

CLOCKWISE FROM TOP: Three Italian-designed British icons: Gordon-Keeble (by Bertone), AC 428 (by Frua) and Aston Martin DB4 GTZ (by Zagato).

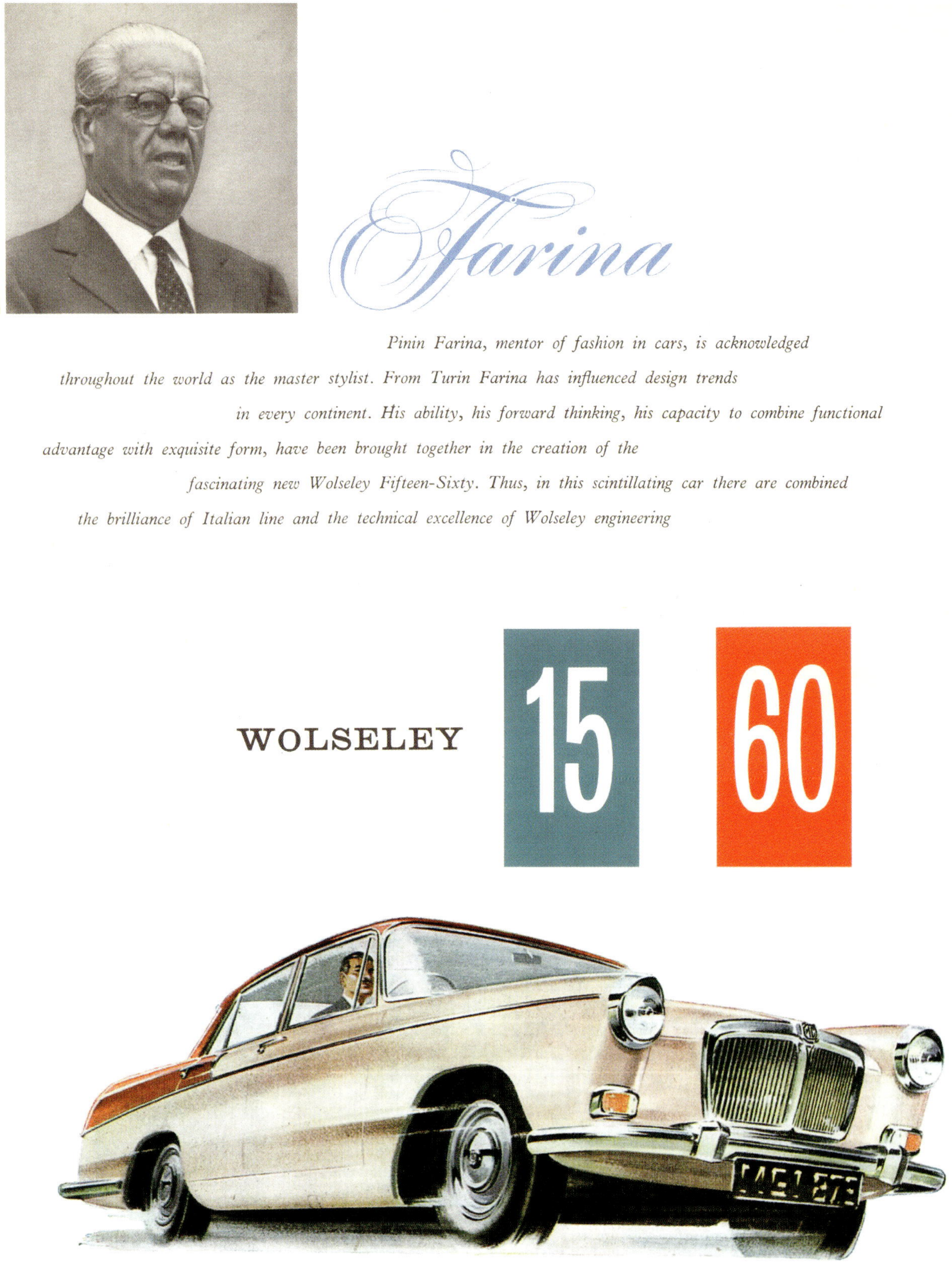

most appealing designs ever created hitting the road during the 1950s. However, this was also a time when car makers eased away from using separate chassis construction towards unitary body/chassis, which made life much harder for coachbuilders who were making original body designs. The coachbuilt era waned dramatically in the late 1950s and early 1960s – although it didn't quite die out.

Italian coachbuilders were very sharp in realising that the nature of their clientele was changing rapidly: it would no longer be wealthy individuals doing the commissioning but big car companies instead. Italian *carrozzerie* reinvented themselves as design houses, creating new shapes that major car marques flocked to, realising that style sold cars. The process began in the 1950s with design houses such as Bertone, Pinin Farina, Touring and Vignale creating critically acclaimed bodywork for regular production cars from Italian companies like Alfa Romeo and Lancia.

British manufacturers soon followed that lead, although it could even be said that Britain actually led the pack in one case. As early as 1947, Don Aldington of Frazer Nash approached Pinin Farina and Touring with a view to offering Bristol models with Italian coachwork. Following that, in December 1955, one of the most fateful encounters occurred when Leonard Lord of the British Motor Corporation (BMC) met the Duke of Edinburgh. The latter criticised the company's stodgy design aesthetic, leading directly to BMC hot-footing it to Italy and into the arms of Pinin Farina. This Turin design house had a huge impact on British car design over the next decade by styling the likes of the Austin A40, Wolseley 15/60 and Austin/Morris 1100/1300.

Italian design had an even greater impact in Coventry, where Standard-Triumph was seduced by the work of Giovanni Michelotti. This prodigiously talented artisan from Turin, mercurially swift in both sketching and realising full-scale creations, was responsible for a whole generation of Triumphs from 1958 onwards, including the Herald, TR4, Spitfire, GT6, 2000, 1300 and Stag.

Over 40 British marques have been involved in some form or other with the Italian design world, including such major companies as Ford of Britain and Rootes. But arguably it was Britain's army of smaller, prestige marques that made the best use of Italian design talent. The most significant of all was Aston Martin, which from 1958 employed the services of Carrozzeria Touring. The company's brilliant designer, Federico Formenti, penned what was possibly the world's most beautiful car at the time, the DB4. Aston Martin also dallied with Zagato, a name with which it has been associated ever since. Italy designed many striking designs for British specialist companies in the 1960s and 1970s, such as the Gordon-Keeble (Bertone), AC 428 (Frua), TVR Trident (Fiore/Fissore), Jensen Interceptor (Touring/Vignale) and Lotus Esprit (Italdesign).

Gradually, though, British companies started to regard car styling as territorial, taking design in-house and severely reducing opportunities for the Italian *carrozzerie*. So it was that a new, third era of British-Italian car design cooperation emerged: the 'concept car'. Most British-Italian designs produced in this era – which stretched from the mid-1960s onwards – were pure art, created solely to wow the public at shows, although they certainly had their use as shop windows for the *carrozzerie*. A whole variety of show concepts based on British cars emerged, including Pininfarina's exquisite BMC 1800 Berlina Aerodinamica and a string of lovely Jaguars by Bertone.

In contrast to other European countries like France, Germany and the UK, whose car design and coachbuilding industries fluttered out in post-war years, the Italian coachbuilding industry proved impressively resilient. But despite the flair and astuteness of these Italian companies, a sunset was coming for the golden era. The casualties started to accumulate: Touring, for instance, bit the dust in

OPPOSITE PAGE: BMC made great play of its fresh Italian design in 1950s brochures. ABOVE: An Italian Ford – the Anglia Torino. BELOW LEFT: Triumph TR3 Speciale by Vignale. BELOW RIGHT: Zagato Zimp.

1966, while Vignale and Ghia were absorbed and then gradually throttled by Ford.

In the 1970s, it was those companies that designed mainstream cars for major manufacturers that thrived – notably Italdesign, Pininfarina and Bertone – and there was even a boom in the manufacture of specialist models at small, specialised factories run by the *carrozzerie* (Rover, Rolls-Royce and Mini all beat a path to Italy for specialist manufacturing). But as the 21st century dawned, the writing was well and truly on the wall. The big car companies were not only designing cars exclusively in-house but also cancelling production contracts for the *carrozzerie*. Italdesign was absorbed into Volkswagen in 2010; Bertone fluttered out of existence in 2014; and Pininfarina was sold to Mahindra in 2015.

But it was still not the end of the line. Perennial survivor Zagato started to put its name to special Aston Martins once again; Ares Design began making special Bentleys; and Italian companies took on the manufacture of special limousine and hearse bodywork on Jaguars and Rolls-Royces.

The reciprocity of the Italo-British relationship

ABOVE LEFT: Pininfarina's last work for Jaguar was the XJ Series 3 of 1979. ABOVE RIGHT: Zagato's Virage Shooting Brake Centennial. BELOW: Aston Martin DB4 GT Zagato with DBS GT Zagato. RIGHT: Coachbuilt traditions remain alive with the Ares Bentley Mulsanne Coupe.

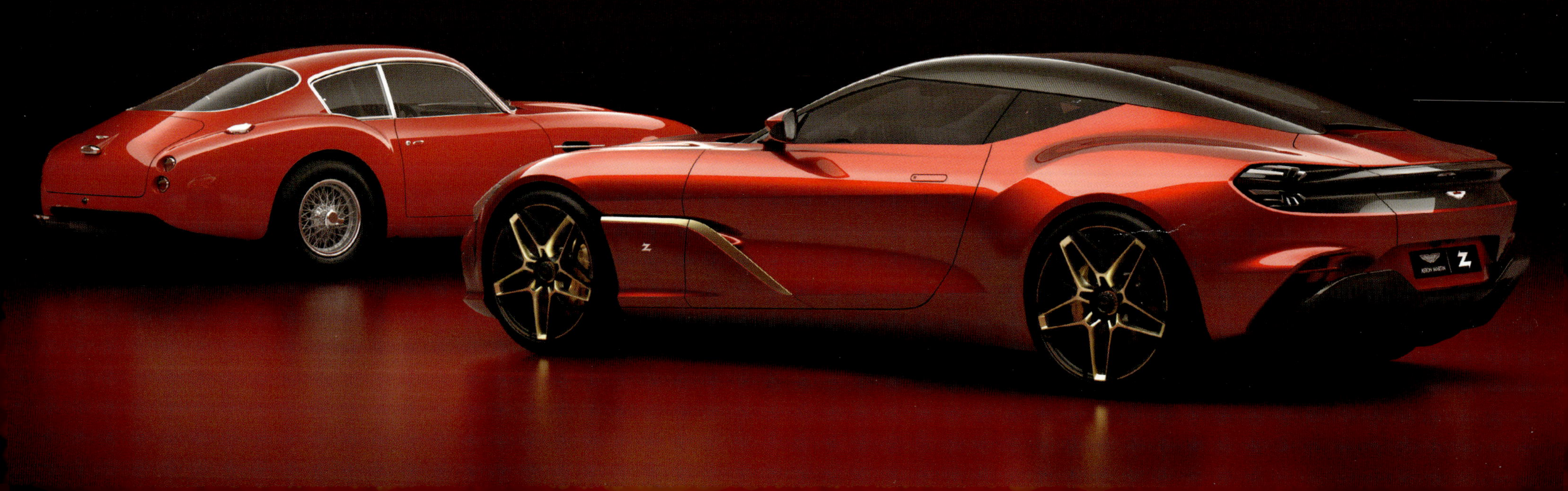

should not be underestimated. The respect that Italians have held for British engineering and design has always been strong. When Ferrari's engineer, Aurelio Lampredi, first drove a BMC Mini prototype in 1959 he famously declared: "If it weren't so ugly, I would shoot myself". And when Enzo Ferrari himself first saw the Jaguar E-Type in 1961, he described it as "the most beautiful car in the world" – quite some compliment considering the competition from Italy at the time. From the 1990s on, Italy ran an annual award called *L'Automobile Più Bella del Mondo* ('the world's most beautiful car') and several British cars received prizes in their respective classes, including the Rover 75, Jaguar XJ, Jaguar XK, MG TF, Bentley Continental GT and Range Rover Sport.

There have even been instances of the British motor industry falling into Italian ownership. For instance, British Leyland's Italian outpost, Innocenti, was acquired by De Tomaso in 1975; the rights to the Mini Moke were sold to the Italian motorbike maker Cagiva in 1991; Lotus was briefly owned in the 1990s by the Italian industrialist Romano Artioli; and Morgan was taken over by an Italian investment group in 2019.

I sincerely hope that, whether you are an enthusiast of British cars, or Italian design, or both, you will enjoy the stories behind the intense, diverse, sometimes surprising and always fascinating links between the British car industry and Italian design. From the characters to the agreements and disagreements, from the sketchbooks to the cars themselves, it's a ride worth celebrating in style.

AC

Beautiful Beasts

Thames Ditton-based AC started life in 1911 as Autocarriers. In the post-war era, AC progressed through a string of ever-more powerful sportscars, culminating in the legendary V8-powered, Shelby-developed Cobra and the Frua-styled 428. By 1973, AC needed a new model and the 3000 ME, with its mid-mounted Ford V6, was shown in 1973 but not actually productionised until 1979, and then in tiny quantities. The project went to Scotland in 1984 and was modified to become the Ecosse but that ended in bankruptcy. Bryan Angliss' Autokraft revived the Cobra and in 1986 showed a new Ace model (scrapped by new owners Ford in 1987). Ford sold out again to Autokraft in 1992 and an all-new Ace model was productionised. The company changed ownership several times thereafter, while manufacturing operations were set up in Malta, Germany and South Africa. The company still exists at the time of writing, making new versions of classic Cobras.

A handful of AC chassis received coachbuilt bodywork in the 1950s and 1960s with Italian design hands behind them. AC joined the list of British companies flocking to Italian *carrozzerie* in 1965, when AC's chief Derek Hurlock forged a relationship with Pietro Frua. It was a productive and rewarding one, with Hurlock enthusing of Frua: "He had a good eye and a great deal of experience in making up parts. He was always very attentive."

ACECA (GHIA-AIGLE)

AC launched its first true sports car, the Ace, in 1954. The chassis was designed by John Tojeiro and notable for being Britain's first post-war sports car chassis with four-wheel independent suspension. Power came from AC's rather asthmatic pre-war 2.0-litre straight-six (75hp) until Bristol's much more potent (125hp) 2.0-litre engine arrived in 1956. A coupe version of the Ace was offered from 1956, called the Aceca. That year a Swiss customer decided to have a special version adapted locally by Ghia-Aigle. Chassis number AEX565 was modified with an aerodynamic front end designed by Pietro Frua. It was originally painted yellow; it survives today, repainted red.

ACE-BRISTOL (ZAGATO)

This one-off was the result of three men's efforts: the Swiss agent for AC, Hubert Patthey; the Swiss racing driver, John Gretener; and the Milanese coachbuilder, Elio Zagato. The latter quoted a price for a special-bodied Ace-Bristol that was not dissimilar to the cost of a new Aceca, tempting Gretener to give the go-ahead.

AC Ace-Bristol chassis number BEX477 was delivered to Zagato in March 1958 and was finished just two months later. Zagato bodied the car in light-gauge aluminium with a trademark double-bubble roof. The rear wheelarches were originally round but were given a squarer shape and flared at some

TOP: Ghia-Aigle's novel front end treatment on an AC Aceca.
ABOVE: Handsome Zagato-bodied Ace-Bristol one-off of 1958.
RIGHT: A British Maserati? Frua's superb AC 428 melded the brutality of the AC Cobra with Italianate beauty.

later date. It was originally painted red with a white central stripe but, having been used as a daily driver with associated damage, it was repainted in 1960 in green with yellow striping.

The petrol tank was twice the original capacity, as Gretener wanted to do long-distance races in it. He enjoyed much success in hillclimbs, sprints and endurance races, including a class win in the 1958 Coupes de Paris at Montlhéry. Ownership of the car passed in 1965 to the celebrated racer, Jo Siffert, who continued to campaign it in many events.

COBRA SPIDER GT (GHIA)

Many British manufacturers began fitting American V8 engines in their sports cars and GTs in the early 1960s, but AC was undoubtedly the most iconic. The heady cocktail of a Ford V8 in an AC Ace chassis was the idea of Texan racing driver and chicken farmer, Carroll Shelby. The resulting Cobra of 1962 instantly hit the headlines with its astonishing acceleration and perhaps inadequate chassis. Initially it was made with 260 and 289 cubic inch small block V8 engines and narrow-wheelarch bodywork; from 1965 that got more absurd with the launch of the AC/Shelby Cobra 427 and its 7.0-litre engine, beefed-up chassis and flared-arch bodywork.

In 1965 Carroll Shelby and Ray Geddes, Ford's liaison man for the Cobra, visited Ghia with the idea to update the Cobra concept with a smart new Italian suit. A prototype Cobra chassis (number CSX 3063) was shipped to Ghia in Italy, whose 96-inch wheelbase was six inches longer than standard (as per Frua's AC 428). Indeed what Ghia created on the chassis was very much an alternative to Frua's 'smart-suited Cobra'.

Ghia's prototype made its public debut at the November 1965 Turin Motor Show, where it was displayed as the 'Cobra Spider GT'. Exactly who designed the car isn't known but it wasn't Giorgetto Giugiaro – he joined Ghia in November 1965, too late to have penned it. The classically curvaceous

shape was undoubtedly attractive. The low, smooth, pointed nose had a wrapround bumper, above which were Perspex covers over the headlamps. As shown at Turin, these lights were oblong but were later changed for double circular lamps. Along the body's flanks was a subtle crease line, below which a triple-vaned air outlet in each front wing served to cool the engine bay. The doors were opened by a recessed push-button, enhancing the smooth look. The rear body sloped elegantly downwards to a low-slung Kamm tail, bisected by a wraparound bumper that distinctively divided the round taillights in two. Only the rather upright windscreen looked at all awkward.

As shown at Turin, the Cobra Spider GT was roofless, but Ghia did also produce a detachable hardtop for it, which had contrastingly sharp lines. The car was finished in metallic blue with natural leather upholstery. Inside was a dashboard of Ghia's own design, symmetrically divided between the driver's and passenger's sides by a substantial centre console sporting minor gauges and switches, while the seats were bespoke, too. Ghia's Cobra was fitted with a big-block (7.0-litre) Ford V8 engine, Halibrand wheels with centre spinners and big Goodyear tyres.

Some sources have suggested that two cars were

TOP: Cobra Spider GT was Ghia's proposal to 'gentrify' the Cobra. MIDDLE: Sharp-edged hardtop contrasted with curvaceous main body. ABOVE: Cabin featured a symmetrical-shaped dashboard designed by Ghia.

made, but it seems more likely that there was only ever one. Shelby American in the US was meant to take delivery of the car for evaluation but whether it actually did so is uncertain, and what happened to the car after its Turin debut is unknown. AC itself showed no interest in Ghia's car and pressed ahead with production of the Frua-designed 428.

WILLMENT COBRA SUPERSONIC COUPE (GHIA)

Giovanni Savonuzzi was the largely unsung design talent who, as design director at Ghia, invented a whole tranche of jet-age styling motifs in the 1950s. Perhaps the most alluring was the so-called Supersonic, which Savonuzzi created in collaboration with Virgilio Conrero. Their Alfa Romeo 1900-based coupe campaigned in the 1953 Mille Miglia, its aerodynamic shape proving ideal for motorsport. As detailed in the relevant chapters, Ghia Supersonic bodywork was also adapted to fit Jaguar and Aston Martin chassis.

Easily the most common version of the Supersonic was applied to Fiat 8V chassis. Launched at the 1953 Paris Motor Show, the Fiat 8V Ghia Supersonic caused a sensation, and some 14 were made, notable customers including designer Virgil Exner and land speed ace, Malcolm Campbell.

The body from one Fiat 8V ended up being fitted to an AC Cobra chassis. Remarkably, racing team sponsor, John Willment, discovered the aluminium body in a scrapyard. He also happened to have a brand new AC Cobra competition chassis (CSX3055) and in 1965 decided to adapt the Ghia shell to fit it. The front end was kept pretty much unchanged but the rear end was altered for its new home. Under the bonnet, the Ford V8 engine was tuned by Holman-Moody and given twin four-barrel carburettors, good enough for 485hp – a huge output for the era. The car was, by all reports, somewhat compromised and never properly finished. Luckily the car survives today, having been restored.

MERCER COBRA (SIBANO-BASANO)

The uniquely bizarre Mercer Cobra was a British-Italian collaboration in one tenuous sense: its chassis was a stretched AC Cobra 289 and its constructor was Carrozzeria Sibona-Basano of Turin. In all other respects, it was a resolutely American concoction.

Virgil Exner, the man behind many successful Chrysler designs of the 1950s, had a lot of contacts in Italy, especially with Ghia. When Exner retired from Chrysler in 1964, he set up his own design consultancy and signed a contract with Ghia to help out in its design department.

Exner was approached by *Esquire* magazine

FAR LEFT: Modified Fiat 8V Ghia Supersonic coachwork was fitted to the Willment Cobra in 1965. LEFT & ABOVE: Peculiar brass-tinged Mercer Cobra was bodied in Italy by Sibano-Basano on a Cobra chassis.

about creating a modern design on a classic theme. The December 1963 issue of *Esquire* featured several modern reinterpretations, including Stutz, Duesenberg and Packard but also a new Mercer Raceabout. A man called George M Hartley, who was president of the Copper Development Association, saw the article and asked Exner if he could have it built to show off the use of copper in cars. Fellow designer Brooks Stevens recommended using Carrozzeria Sibona-Basano; 'Sibona' in the company title was Pietro Sibona, an ex-Ghia metalworker.

The chassis chosen was an AC Cobra (number CSX2451), originally built in 1964. This was specially lengthened in the wheelbase to 108 inches. Exner's design was a classically proportioned, long-bonnet/cab-rearward design but that was about it for conventionalism. The front wings had a curious blade-like shape that ran along the sides of the bonnet to leave the front wheels open. The headlights were mounted on pivots to either side of the front grille, swinging out when illuminated and retracting flush with the nose when switched off. The full-width curved Plexiglas windscreen and chrome-plated side exhausts emphasised a curiously 'antique' feel. Short rear wings straddling the tapered rear end had separate mudguards behind the rear wheels.

The car was designed to show off the colours and textures of copper and brass, chiming with the old-fashioned 'Brass-Era' theme. The classic-style grille stuck out prominently up front was made of brass, as were the taillights. The interior trim, seat backs, door panels and gauges were all in copper, while the 16-inch wheels had multi-piece brass covers. Even the engine bay and brake discs were given the copper treatment. The paintwork was pearl white and the interior was in black leather.

Completed in late 1964, the total cost of the Mercer-Cobra was an eye-watering $35,000. A fully functioning vehicle, it toured many shows internationally. The Copper Development Association kept it for 10 years before selling it on.

428 (FRUA)

In 1965 AC's boss, Derek Hurlock, realised he needed to do something to update his legendary Cobra, which was extremely raw and outdated in terms of driving experience and design. Another factor was that, by 1965, Ford had transferred its allegiance away from the Cobra in favour of the new GT40 project. Hurlock's plan was to create a more sophisticated 'Cobra for the businessman' based on the existing 427 chassis.

Hurlock visited the Geneva Show in March 1965 and met various Italian designers. Nuccio Bertone turned him down because of a lack of capacity, but the Swiss AC importer and racing driver Hubert Patthey introduced him to Pietro Frua, who promised a very fast turnaround of drawings and prototypes. Duly convinced, Hurlock despatched a Cobra 427 Mark III chassis to Frua in May 1965, with a wheelbase extended by six inches (150mm). This provided extra cabin space and an area to fold the convertible's roof away.

The design has often been said to resemble Frua's

LEFT: Frua's 1965 prototype, then still being referred to as an AC 427. ABOVE: Preliminary sketch by Frua. OPPOSITE CLOCKWISE FROM TOP: One-off with pop-up headlamp style; elegant 428 Fastback; open-top version was not quite as popular as the coupe.

UPG 994M

HEXAGON CLASSICS

WYF 91G

TOP LEFT: So-called AC 429 used a discarded Monteverdi bodyshell. ABOVE LEFT: Standard AC 3000 ME. ABOVE & OPPOSITE: Ghia rebodied the 3000 ME with aesthetic success.

1963 Maserati Mistral, but as is so often the case with designers, it is only natural that a well-received shape should find echoes in other designs by the same hand. The Mistral and AC 428 are sometimes confused, with some commentators even stating, incorrectly, that the two cars shared body panels; in fact, the AC was notably wider and the only items that the AC and Maserati actually shared were the front quarter-windows and door handles.

Frua delivered his chestnut red convertible prototype to AC just in time for its debut at the Earls Court Motor Show in October 1965, where it was very well received. However, testing showed that the 428's extra weight meant that changes to the suspension and tyres were needed. After a few more minor changes, it was a full year before the production 428 debuted at the Paris Salon in October 1966. The 428 coupe (dubbed 'Fastback') followed in time for the Geneva Salon in March 1967, shown on Frua's own stand because AC Cars didn't have one. The Fastback's roofline looked every bit as resolved as the open car's.

While the prototype used a Ford 351 V8 engine, and AC's initial plan was to use the Ford 427 engine in production, the latter's peaky power delivery changed minds at AC. After only a few cars fitted with the 427 engine, AC switched to the Ford 428 V8 (7.0 litres and 345hp gross). Performance was exceptional for the time: John Bolster in *Autosport* recorded 0-60mph in 5.4 seconds and a top speed of 145mph. You could choose between four-speed manual or – far more commonly, since in manual guise the clutch required muscles of steel – three-speed automatic transmission.

Chassis were built by AC in Thames Ditton, then shipped over to Frua in Italy where the bodywork was fitted. The first car had aluminium panels but in production all cars were steel-bodied. Once bodied, the cars were returned to England for trimming, wiring and painting. If that sounds like a long-winded and expensive production process, it certainly was, leading Hurlock to try and find a British company to make the bodywork, to no avail. There were more problems with the set-up than merely time and expense, though. The untreated double-skin bodies were left open to the elements during transport; much rectification work was needed back at AC; and delivery dates were erratic.

Unfortunately AC was forced to charge a huge price for the car: £5573 at launch, versus £4229 for an Aston Martin DB6 and £4460 for a Jensen Interceptor. For all the allure of its Italian bodywork, American engine and British construction, the AC 428 lacked appeal for died-in-the-wool AC fanatics. Two factors coincided to sound its death knell in 1973: the energy crisis and the prospect of undergoing crash testing at prohibitive expense. The 428 therefore ended its career in 1973, a mere 81 cars having been built in total, of which 29 were convertibles. One of the very last 428s was given a different front end featuring pop-up headlights. Somewhat sadly, several 428s have been rebodied as AC Cobras.

429 (FRUA)

In 1969, Frua built a four-seat 'saloon' version of the 428 coupe, which has since come to be known as the AC 429. This project actually started life at Frua as that coachbuilder's proposal for a new model for the Swiss specialist car maker, Monteverdi. Frua had designed a new coupe for the fledgling Monteverdi in 1967, called the 375 S.

Then in 1968, Frua proposed a new four-seater Monteverdi prototype, the 375 L, but this version did not reach production (a different design woule be productionised by Fissore instead). Left with an unwanted bodyshell, Frua simply adapted the 375 L prototype unit to fit the AC 428 chassis, at the same time taking the opportunity to change a few details such as the front end (which now featured semi-hooded headlights) and removing the slats on the C-pillars. The rear lights were sourced from the Alfa Romeo 1750 Berlina.

As with the 428, power came from a 7.0-litre Ford V8 engine. The blue-painted 429 was eventually registered in the UK in 1973 but the project did not pass the prototype stage, just the one example being built.

3000 ME (GHIA)

The 428 left production in 1973, in the wake of which AC pursued a novel direction with its 3000 ME model. It bought in a prototype called the Diablo from a design outfit called Bohanna Stables, which AC proceeded to modify. The 3000 ME name signified its layout: 3000cc Mid-Engined, with the 138hp Ford V6 engine being mounted transversely amidships. The two-seater coupe looked good when it was first shown in 1973 but by the time production started fully six years later, in 1979, it perhaps felt a bit tired. Only 82 cars were made up until 1984.

Italian *carrozzeria* Ghia was looking for a mid-engined car on which to produce a concept, and Ghia's owner, Ford, suggested the AC 3000 ME. The thinking at Ford was that it might possibly become a new sports car in its range, or even a rally car conforming to Group B rules. Ford arranged for two cars – one complete, one in chassis form – to be sent to Turin from Thames Ditton in late 1980, leaving four months to finish it for a March 1981 Geneva Motor Show debut.

The new shape, designed by Ghia's Filippo Sapino, was a gentler wedge than the British design, with smoother side profiling and a Kamm tail with a spoiler atop. The bluff front end incorporated low-set fog lights, the main headlamps being concealed pop-ups. The roofline was also elegantly curved, flying rear buttresses angling gently down over the vertical rear window. Ghia's car was smaller than the base AC, at 3810mm long and 1524mm, although its 1168mm height was slightly taller. The standard AC cabin was left untouched, complete with right-hand drive.

The AC Ghia was championed by Ford's Bob Lutz as a potential new Ford sports car but the bean-counters at head office disagreed, as one Ford employee told journalist Steve Cropley in 1981: "The fact is, we're not in business to make sports cars". With Ford out of the equation, AC contemplated a production run itself but decided not to proceed, so that was the end of the project.

As an aside, and closing the Italian theme to the 3000 ME, the original Ford-powered 3000 ME subsequently re-emerged with a new concern, AC Scotland, which intended to sell it with Alfa Romeo V6 power and a redesign by Peter Stevens, but the company sadly went bust before this happened.

FORD/LINCOLN QUICKSILVER (GHIA)

The short shrift afforded Ghia's AC 3000 ME concept did not dissuade the coachbuilder from attempting another effort on the 3000 ME chassis, although the 1983 Quicksilver was hardly recognisable as such. After all, here was a large four-door saloon – how could that possibly be based on a mid-engined two-seat sports car? Good question.

The answer is that Ghia took the 3000 ME chassis and lengthened its wheelbase by fully 290mm (almost 12 inches). It updated the power unit to Ford's 2.8-litre 'Cologne' V6 and mated it to a five-speed manual transmission, the powertrain being positioned just in front of the rear axle. Unusually for a show prototype, this was a fully functioning machine.

The styling was by Filippo Sapino and Delio Meinardi. It resembled a scaled-up version of Ghia's earlier AC coupe at the front, complete with pop-up headlamps. The flanks were almost completely smooth, broken at the rear only by cooling air intakes for the mid-mounted engine. The rear wheels were semi-enclosed, while the back end featured large taillights and curious roof-mounted louvres culminating in a high-mounted spoiler. The glass sat almost flush with the bodywork, thanks to a special window channel frame system invented by Ghia. The result of all this was excellent aerodynamics, the drag coefficient measuring just 0.30.

Very few cars in history have had mid-mounted engines, four doors and space to seat four adults, but the Quicksilver was one. Ghia's design for the cockpit was highly unusual, with a semi-circular array of gauges in front of the driver; the novel radial design was carried over into slab-like panels across the dashboard.

First seen at the 1982 Turin Show, the Quicksilver then did the show circuit for a further three years. Although initially wearing Ford badges, it was latterly given Lincoln badging. The one and only prototype was sold off at auction in 2002, when it fetched $45,825.

378 GT (ZAGATO)

The roots of this project were not British at all, but actually South African. It started at the 2009 Geneva Show when Zagato unveiled, on its own stand, the Perana Z-One. This aggressively-styled coupe was a collaboration with the South African company Perana Performance Group.

Underneath was a tubular and box section steel chassis fitted with a 434hp 6.2-litre Corvette LS3 V8 engine driving the rear wheels. Top speed was claimed to be 185mph, with 0-60mph in less than four seconds.

The dramatic-looking coupe shape was effected

by Zagato's long-standing design chief, Nori Harada. Although large at 173.5in long, 75.7in wide and 48.5in high, it disguised its bulk well with sculpted flanks and a shallow glasshouse. Detail touches included multiple air vents in the front wings, exhaust pipes emerging through the rear valance and Zagato-designed wheels (19 inches up front, 20 inches to the rear). Of course, Zagato's trademark 'double-bubble' roof was present.

Zagato built the first prototype in Milan and the plan was for Zagato to make glassfibre bodies and send them out to South Africa, where Hi-Tech Automotive (a branch of Superformance) would construct the finished cars. The Perana was due to go on sale by July 2009 exclusively within Europe, but it's thought that only about 10 cars were ever built.

Then, after a gap of almost three years, Superformance partnered up with the latest incarnation of AC Cars, and the Perana was reborn as the AC 378 GT Zagato. This was targeted at the UK and German markets, priced at £89,990 and €109,990 respectively.

The new AC debuted at the 2012 Geneva Show but only after missing its press day slot following an altercation with Swiss customs. The new AC Cars was chaired by no less a man than General Sir Jeremy Mackenzie, former Deputy Supreme Allied Command NATO Europe. "Geneva 2012 marks a new beginning for the AC brand", he said. "The company has suffered from a series of false starts in recent years but … all that is firmly in the past". Apparently not. Production was to have taken place in South Africa but it's thought that only one AC-badged car was ever actually made.

OPPOSITE PAGE: The Quicksilver adopted a very odd layout of a mid-mounted engine and four doors.
THIS PAGE: AC 378 GT was a Zagato-designed cast-off from South Africa.

ARMSTRONG SIDDELEY

End of A Tradition

Armstrong Siddeley was founded in 1919, best known for its luxury cars and aircraft engines. This was the first British car maker to launch all-new models following World War 2: the Lancaster saloon and Hurricane drophead coupe of 1945, followed one year later by the Typhoon coupe. These were solid and durable cars that drove in a somewhat staid manner, even with six-cylinder engines fitted; initially these were 2.0 litres, but in 1949 were bored out to 2.3 litres, when a somewhat more dashing Whitley model was launched. A new era for Armstrong Siddeley arrived in 1952 with the Sapphire 346, which boasted a new chassis, more sophisticated independent front suspension and a new 3.4-litre engine. This was also the first ever British car to be offered with power steering as an option. Slightly more sporting saloons followed in 1955 with the Sapphire 234 and 236, with four- and six-cylinder engines respectively. However by the end of the 1950s, Armstrong Siddeley's conservative range was simply too outdated and production ceased for good in August 1960.

WHITLEY TWO-DOOR SALOON (GHIA)

The separate chassis of the 18HP Whitley was seized upon by Carrozzeria Ghia in 1951 as the ideal basis for an imposing new two-door saloon. In style, this was very typical of early 1950s Italian tropes, with bulbous but straightforward lines and relatively few embellishments. It perhaps resembled most Ghia's Ferrari 195 Inter of 1950.

BELOW LEFT: Armstrong Siddeley 18HP Whitley line-up. BELOW: Ghia's 1951 Whitley saloon. OPPOSITE ABOVE: Michelotti Sapphire 234 one-off. OPPOSITE BELOW: 1958 Michelotti sketch for 'Riverside II' saloon.

A version of Armstrong Siddeley's grille was used at the front end, which also incorporated 'whisker' grilles and a strongly-styled lighting set. Presented at the 1951 Turin Salon, this sober saloon – which is sometimes referred to as the Berlina Victoria – remained a one-off.

SAPPHIRE 234 SALOON (MICHELOTTI)

In 1958 Giovanni Michelotti designed, over a Sapphire 234 chassis (number C4230551), a rather more up-to-date suit of clothes than Armstrong Siddeley's own rather gormless saloon. His four-door berlina was built for a client based in Madrid, Spain and remained a one-off. In Michelotti's archive are sketches dated 1958 of a formal, rather Americanesque saloon called the Sapphire Riverside II. This might perhaps have modernised the British marque's image but it seems that Michelotti's proposal never left the drawing board.

ASTON MARTIN

Licensed to Thrill

Aston Martin is not only one of Britain's best-known car brands, but one of the world's favourites. As a paragon of style and desirability, Aston Martin has arguably done it better, and consistently better, than any other British car company. The marque can trace its origins back to 1913, when Lionel Martin and Robert Bamford founded a garage business together. After Martin won a hillclimb at Aston Clinton, his wife proposed joining the two names together to form the agreeable-sounding 'Aston Martin'. Cars started to be made in 1923, which were typically fast and high-class – and also competitive on track, with Le Mans being entered as early as 1928. Despite being expensive, however, the cars rarely made a profit.

British bulldog breed though it may be by reputation, Italian strands have been woven through its DNA almost from the outset. The first of these was the engineer and designer, Augustus Bertelli. Born in Genoa, Italy, he was only four when his family emigrated to Cardiff, South Wales. After working for British manufacturers as diverse as Enfield-Allday, Armstrong Siddeley, Coventry Simplex and Rover, in 1926 Bertelli joined the board of Aston Martin. During his time there, the self-described "head cook and bottle washer" not only contributed to keeping the marque alive but also to designing some of its most famous sports cars. About 620 examples of pre-war 'Bertelli' Astons were built, all with 1.5-litre engines (some supercharged) and typically with wonderfully elongated bonnets. Augustus's brother Enrico also ran a coachbuilding firm, E Bertelli Ltd, next door to Aston Martin's Middlesex works, which built many of the bodies for Aston Martins up until 1937.

That was the point at which Augustus Bertelli left Aston Martin, leaving Gordon Sutherland to take over as design chief. It was Sutherland who eventually sold the company to the tractor and gear manufacturer David Brown in 1947. Brown realised that he needed a better engine than the four-cylinder unit that Aston Martin was making at the time, leading him to acquire the Lagonda marque later in 1947, inheriting its excellent six-cylinder unit that had been engineered by WO Bentley.

Post-war Aston Martins were initially very British in shape and feel. These were the responsibility of the Lagonda stylist, Frank Feeley, whose first Aston Martin design was the Two-Litre Sports (commonly known as the DB1, the 'DB' referring to David Brown), followed by the DB2 and DB3S.

The DB2 had an undeniably Italianate feel to it, not only in its 'Gran Turismo' concept but also its rakish design. This model morphed into the four-seat DB2/4 in 1953, perhaps losing some of its elegance – curiously, Aston Martin referred to its fixed-head models as saloons rather than coupes – but it did provide the perfect platform for coachbuilders, among them several Italian companies: the likes of Bertone, Allemano, Touring and Ghia were all drawn to the DB2/4.

In fact, so impressed was Aston Martin with the work of Touring Superleggera on its chassis that it beat a path to the Italian company for its all-new DB4 of 1958: Touring would not only style the car but also contribute its 'Superleggera' method of lightweight construction. Aston Martin was therefore in the forefront of the British rush to Italian design during the late 1950s and early 1960s, and a very strong relationship with Touring flourished with the subsequent DB5 and DB6, as well as the Lagonda Rapide saloon.

Aston Martin would turn in-house for its new DBS of 1967, employing the skills of British designer William Towns. However, there was another Italian connection with Aston Martin: Zagato. This Milanese coachbuilder styled the DB4 GTZ in 1960, widely regarded as one of the greatest car designs of all time, full stop. The relationship with Zagato would be rekindled several times. In the 1980s the Vantage Zagato made a memorable impact, and Aston Martin would even own a stake in Zagato for a short period. Then in the 21st century, Zagato and Aston Martin resurrected their collaboration with a whole string of limited-production reinterpretations of modern Astons, starting with the DB7 Zagato of 2002. Another Italian connection would be revived by Aston Martin when it began to use Touring's famed Superleggera badge on the 2018 DBS Superleggera.

Ownership of Aston Martin passed to Victor Gauntlett in 1981. Ford acquired its first shares in the company in 1987 and took full control in 1991.

10
1 VEV

Within the Ford empire, Aston Martin sat in Premier Automotive Group alongside Jaguar, Land Rover and Volvo. Ford's Italian styling wing, Ghia, even had a stab at designing a new Lagonda. Ford sold Aston Martin in 2007 and in private ownership there was once again an Italian connection, with investment coming from Investindustrial, which in 2012 took a 37.5% stake in the company.

Early Post-War Coachbuilt Cars

The first coachbuilt Astons in the post-war era were based on the DB2 (1949-1953), but none of these was Italian; Graber of Switzerland and Serra in Spain are believed to be the only foreign firms to have clothed these early cars, although there is a suggestion that Ghia-Aigle in Switzerland might also have bodied a DB2 chassis.

In contrast, the DB2/4 launched in 1953 was bodied by a whole phalanx of Italian design houses. The DB2/4 broadened Aston Martin's appeal by offering 2+2 seating, a higher rear roof section and an opening rear window.

Power came from the same in-line six-cylinder twin cam engine that had been used in the DB2. 125hp was standard but the car's hefty weight blunted performance, cured by expanding the engine to 3.0 litres and 140hp from 1954.

The MkII of 1955 had angular rear wings and a stronger rear axle, plus there was a new model: a notchback hardtop (of which only 34 were made). This and the rare Drophead Coupe (only 24 built) were to special order only from 1956.

The final version of the DB2/4 dropped its '2/4' tag, being simply called the MkIII. This incarnation received a new 'droop snoot' front end, while the engine had a stiffer block, stronger camshaft and larger valves, providing a standard output of 162hp that you could take even higher (up to 202hp with triple carbs). Further novelties were a hydraulic clutch, optional Laycock overdrive and Borg Warner automatic. Girling front discs were optional at first, then standard from the MkIIIB of late 1957. Both saloon and drophead coupe models were offered, and when MkIII production ended in 1959, some 551 examples had been built.

DB2 DROPHEAD COUPE (GHIA-AIGLE)

In a Carrozzeria Ghia-Aigle catalogue of circa 1951, there appeared a mysterious drawing by Giovanni Michelotti entitled 'Cabriolet 2 Posti – Chassis Aston Martin DB2'. This depicted an elegant open two-seater that perhaps prefigured Michelotti's work for Bertone on the DB2/4 (see next page), but the front grille was ovoid rather than the traditional Aston Martin shape. Whether or not any such body was actually built by Ghia-Aigle is unknown.

DB2/4 SPIDER (BERTONE/ARNOLT)

The story of the larger-than-life American, Stanley 'Wacky' Arnolt, is told in full in the Bristol chapter (page 116). Suffice to say here that the Arnolt-Bristol he created in 1953 with the help of Bertone was extremely well received, encouraging Mr Arnolt to replicate that success on a different chassis – namely the Aston Martin DB2/4.

Arnolt purchased the first six DB2/4 chassis that

LEFT: Italian-born Augustus Bertelli was an early Aston Martin board member; rare brochure for the Ghia-Aigle DB2; superb Arnolt DB2/4 Spider. ABOVE: More formal coachwork graced Bertone's luxurious Arnolt DB2/4 Drophead Coupe.

Aston Martin built (LML/502 to LML/507), which are believed to have been made in April 1953. He would also buy a further two chassis – LML/762 and LML/765. All eight were bodied by Bertone but in a variety of different styles.

Easily the most dramatic of these were the trio of Spiders created by Franco Scaglione, whose work was an utter masterpiece. Although clearly looking similar to the Arnolt-Bristol, the fact the Aston Martin engine sat lower in its chassis afforded the shape much greater elegance and cohesion. The wings looked very curvaceous from the side aspect but when seen from a three-quarter angle, superb razor-edged lines atop the wings were revealed. In between, the waistline dipped dramatically at the doors. The nose featured a stylised version of Aston Martin's grille, while the rear end was low and relatively flat, the drama enhanced by rear wheelarch scallops.

Three DB2/4 cars were bodied by Bertone as Spiders for Arnolt: chassis numbers LML/502, LML/505 and LML/507. Each of the three was subtly different. For instance, LML/502 and LML/507 had a stripped-out look, while LML/505 had a full-height windscreen, overriders set into the front grille, quarter bumpers up front and full bumpers to the rear.

The rolling chassis as delivered to Turin probably originally had 2.6-litre power but it seems that all three cars ended up with the larger 2992cc Vantage engine with 140hp.

One of the Spiders featured an 'Arnolt Aston Martin' badge, but David Brown objected to this rebranding. No further Spiders were made beyond this trio; thankfully all three still survive. An indication of the prestige of this model can be gleaned from the 1954 New York Motor Show car (LML/505) being sold at auction in 2016 for a remarkable $3 million.

DB2/4 DROPHEAD COUPE (BERTONE/ARNOLT)

Following the Scaglione-designed Spiders, Wacky Arnolt elected to use some of his allocation of Aston Martin DB2/4 chassis for a rather different Drophead Coupe style. While the coachbuilder remained Bertone (Arnolt was, after all, a director there), the stylist would now be Giovanni Michelotti, working freelance.

The design carried an interpretation of Aston Martin's traditional grille with driving lights neatly mounted within the frame. The bonnet incorporated a cooling scoop, while an ornate vent in the front wings permitted hot engine air to escape.

Two chassis are known to have been bodied in this style – LML/504 and LML/506 – and possibly a third (LML/503, although this chassis is unaccounted for). Chassis LML/504 was given as a Christmas gift in 1953 by the employees of Brown &

Bigelow, a Minneapolis-based greeting card company, to its CEO, Charles A Ward (a colourful character who pioneered the pin-up calendar). LML/504 was painted metallic blue with red leather upholstery and tan carpets, although it was later repainted red. Unique features included a red leather picnic hamper, fitted luggage and a cocktail cabinet under the seat. The purchase price in 1953 was very high at $12,700.

Chassis LML/506 was very similar to LML/504 but lacked grille-mounted driving lights. Sold initially to Edith Field of San Francisco in 1954, it was shown at the 1955 Pebble Beach Concours d'Elegance, where it was awarded third prize in the two-seater sports car class. Much later, this car was owned by the Grand Prix racer Innes Ireland.

DB2/4 DROPHEAD COUPE 'INDIANA' (BERTONE/ARNOLT)

One Aston Martin DB2/4 – chassis LML/762 – was rebodied as a quite distinct Drophead Coupe designed by Franco Scaglione. It carried two unique badges: 'Arnolt Aston Martin' on the nose and 'Indiana' on the front wings.

This elegant car had a sleeker shape than Michelotti's Drophead Coupes, with a lower nose, more compact Aston Martin-style grille, deeply curved windscreen, very little ornamentation and bullet-shaped fins straddling a sloping tail. The bodywork was all-steel except for the bonnet and bootlid, which were in aluminium. Initially painted metallic grey, it was repainted metallic blue some time later. The two-seat interior was unique to this car, too. Underneath were standard DB2/4 mechanicals except for a Vantage engine and Alfin brake drums.

It's thought the car was completed in 1955 and was displayed at the Paris and New York car shows. Only one body to this design was built, retained by Wacky Arnolt for his own personal use. One celebrated later owner was Nick Mason of rock band Pink Floyd.

DB2/4 BERLINETTA (BERTONE/ARNOLT)

The last of the DB2/4 chassis that Stanley 'Wacky' Arnolt bought – LML/765 – was bodied by Bertone once again, but in a unique Berlinetta (or Fixed Head Coupe) style. The designer was once again

Franco Scaglione whose elegant shape reflected changing fashions. For instance, the rear window was an extreme wraparound and the rear end featured sharply-styled fins. Very distinctive highlight lines extended back from the tops of the wheelarches, particularly prominent at the front.

This elegant coupe was commissioned in 1954 by a Parisian mining magnate called Henri Pagezy, to whom it was delivered in 1955, complete with a later-type 2.9-litre engine. Somewhat surprisingly given the age of the car, Bertone borrowed it back to display on its stand at the 1957 Turin Motor Show. It is thought that only one example of this type was built, although it is possible that the 'lost' chassis LML/503 might also have been bodied in this style. Whatever the intentions of the parties may have been, any potential production run was well and truly scuppered when David Brown became reluctant to provide any further chassis for rebodying. Instead Bertone produced a short run of quite similar-looking coupes on Jaguar's XK150 chassis (see page 177).

OPPOSITE ABOVE: So-called 'Indiana' DB2/4 DHC. OPPOSITE BELOW: Distinctive lines for Bertone's Berlinetta. BELOW LEFT: Michelotti designed this handsome berlinetta for Allemano. BELOW RIGHT: Also by Michelotti was Vignale's 1954 DB2/4 Coupe.

DB2/4 BERLINETTA (ALLEMANO)

Only one Aston Martin chassis was ever bodied by Carrozzeria Allemano of Turin, and that was DB2/4 number LML/761. Bought in 1953 from the factory by J O'Hana, a resident of Casablanca in Morocco, the chassis was sent direct from Aston Martin to Allemano in Italy.

While some sources have claimed that the Berlinetta bodywork was designed by Giovanni Savonuzzi, it was in fact the work of another Giovanni – Michelotti. What he created was undoubtedly one of his finest designs, with a profile that in some ways anticipated the work that Carrozzeria Touring would later do for Aston Martin's DB4.

The front end featured a traditional marque grille incorporating spotlamps and very distinctive vertical front light nacelles with a metal plate housing the headlamps and indicators. At the rear there were reverse-angle C-pillars, curved three-piece glass and taillights that echoed the front treatment. Initially the car was bumperless but following an accident, it was rebuilt with bumpers added, as well as two extra seats in the rear (having been a two-seater originally).

Mechanically, the engine was fitted with three Weber side-draught carburettors that boosted power to 180hp, while the suspension and brakes were also upgraded. The car was raced in period by O'Hana in Morocco. Luckily the car survives and, having been restored to its original specification, was sold at auction in 2018 for $671,000.

DB2/4 COUPE (VIGNALE)

Carrozzeria Vignale was responsible for a very pretty one-off fastback coupe body on a DB2/4 chassis (although it did also body a DB3 chassis – see page 37). This was a very special project for the young King Baudouin of Belgium; the Belgian royal family was already a client of Vignale's, having recently taken delivery of a special-bodied Ferrari 250 GT Europa from the Turin-based coachbuilder.

DB2/4 chassis LML/802 was delivered to Vignale's works in September 1954 and completed by March 1955. The gently rounded shape, penned by Giovanni Michelotti, was widely admired at the time. Notable features included an ovoid front grille crossed by metal bars and including driving lamps, bumpers with overriders and 'whiskers', a slightly raised bonnet with a small air intake at its leading edge, and brightwork on the side that gave the impression of air outlets. The flowing fastback had an opening tailgate – a pioneering feature at the time – with a deeply curved screen made of Plexiglas, while the rear wings had two curious cut-outs on each side housing lights.

The finished car was fitted with a 3.0-litre engine and a 1.73:1 final drive ratio. Contemporary images show the car painted both blue, and dark green with a red roof. The car still survives, thankfully.

DB2/4 MARK II SUPERSONIC (GHIA)

Giovanni Savonuzzi remains, to this day, one of Italy's greatest unsung design heroes. His stellar list of credits includes the seminal Cisitalia 202 of 1947, the 1955 Ghia Gilda and the Ferrari 410 Superamerica Gilda. He also famously invented the so-called Supersonic body style – a quintessentially 1950s trope that was a heady thematic mixture of clean aerodynamics and jet-age aesthetics.

The dramatic Supersonic outline debuted with a Savonuzzi-designed, Ghia-built Alfa Romeo 1900 that was created to compete in the 1953 Mille Miglia race, although a fire prevented it from making it there. The Supersonic style would also be used for a series of 14 Ghia-built Fiat 8Vs and three further Jaguar XK120s (page 170).

The very last of the Supersonic series was built by Ghia on an Aston Martin DB2/4 Mark II chassis (number AM300/1132), with bodywork realised in aluminium (and not glassfibre as some reports have claimed). Savonuzzi's design was many things, but subtle was not one of them. For instance, the raised feature that extended from the front to rear wings had a tortured shape that mixed indentations with overlaps. The rear end was particularly fussy with its tailfins and grilled-over rear lights emerging like bullets from the wings. There was never any doubt about how striking it was, though.

Racing driver Harry Schell drove the Aston Martin Supersonic to its public unveiling at the Turin Salon in April 1956, and some have therefore concluded that he was the original owner; however, it seems that the first owner was in fact Richard Cowell, the American water-skiing champion, who paid $15,000 for the car. When Cowell married socialite Gail Whitney Vanderbilt in 1958, one of his gifts to her was the Supersonic.

Originally painted pale green with beige upholstery, the one-off was later restored with a white body, green roof and green interior. In this form, it won second prize in the post-war touring class at the 2011 Pebble Beach Concours d'Elegance; it then sold at auction in 2013 for a remarkable $2,310,000.

ABOVE: Savonuzzi's Supersonic shape launched the 'jet age' of car design. OPPOSITE LEFT: Federico Formenti styled Touring's 'superleggera' Spider. OPPOSITE RIGHT: Superb coachwork graced Vignale's reclothed DB3.

DB2/4 MARK II SPIDER (TOURING)

This striking design marked the historic first association of Aston Martin with Carrozzeria Touring of Milan, a design house that would soon propel the British marque into a new arena of pre-eminence. In 1956, three DB2/4 Mark II chassis were sent to Milan, where Touring used, for the first time ever on an Aston Martin chassis, its patented Superleggera method of lightweight body construction: namely a framework of small-diameter steel tubes covered by hand-crafted aluminium panels.

The design was by Touring's little-known but exceedingly talented designer, Federico Formenti. It was very much a 'barchetta' shape, with small doors, a low waistline and an open top. Much of the detailing was confidently flamboyant, such as the U-shaped rear bumper, a novel interpretation of Aston's grille with curious 'whiskers', sill strips, dual bonnet scoops and curious intakes that fronted prominent fins along the rear wings.

The bodies on all three DB2/4 rolling chassis were completed in 1956, and shown at three major shows that year: Turin (April), Paris (September) and London (October). At the 1956 Earls Court Motor Show, chassis AM300/1161 was offered as a prize in a caption competition in the *Daily Mail* newspaper. The winner was a Scot called Alexander Smith, whose winning slogan for the car was, "Who said a Spyder couldn't fly?" and his prize was duly handed over by the actor, Stanley Baker. This was a substantial prize indeed, valued at £4200 at the time. This car was painted dark green, and although originally left-hand drive, it was later converted to right-hand drive.

The second car (chassis AM300/1162) was shown at the 1956 Paris Motor Show. This became the property of the French Aston Martin distributor and was fitted with uprated DB3S-spec parts. It found its way first to the US and then later to South Africa. The third and final car (AM300/1163) was shown alongside the dark green car at the Earls Court Show in 1956 and was bought off the stand by an American who owned it for the rest of his life.

Sadly, Touring received no further orders for this design. However an historic die had been cast: impressed by Touring's work, Aston Martin would call upon Touring to shape the 1958 DB4. It is even possible to discern a few details of the 1956 design that transferred over to the DB4, such as the forward-thrusting headlights, distinctive grille and vertical rear light clusters.

DB3 (VIGNALE)

Aston Martin conceived its DB3 as a sports racing car in 1951, in which role it enjoyed some success. Only 10 DB3s were made between 1951 and 1953. Five were built as works racers and one of these, the third chassis built, was hit from behind at the 1952 Monaco Grand Prix. It was hastily repaired by the French coachbuilder, Chapron, in time for the 1952 Le Mans 24 Hours (which it failed to finish as a result of a major fire). It then competed in the 1953 Mille Miglia with Reg Parnell

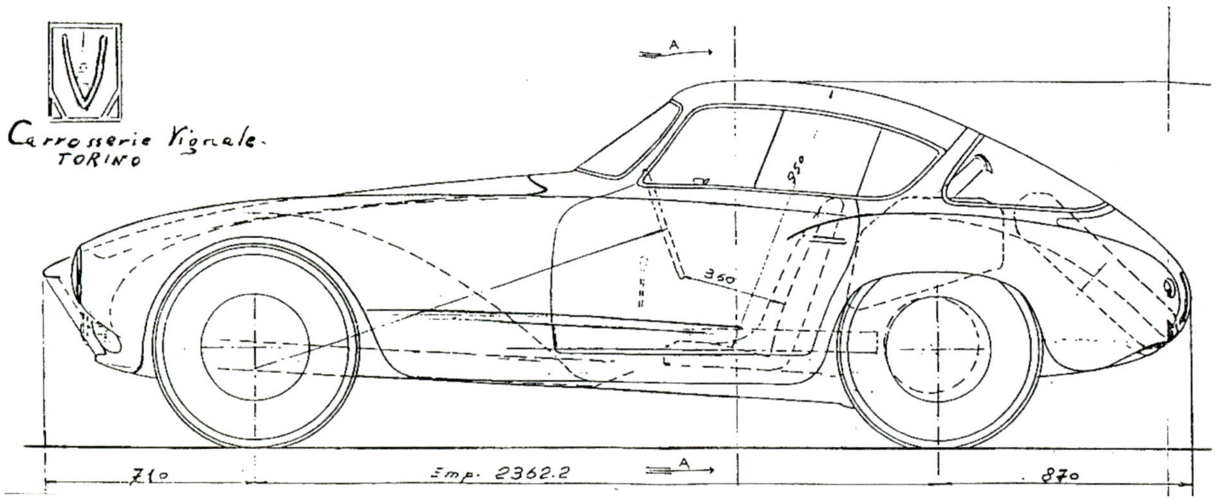

driving and photographer Louis Klemantaski navigating; it finished fifth. The car also scored a class win in the Silverstone 9 Hours.

In May 1953 the car then came into the ownership of the French racing driver, Michel Poberejsky, who competed under the name Myke Sparken. In 1953, he decided to commission Vignale to reclothe the chassis with a unique new coupe body. The Berlinetta bodywork was superbly executed by Giovanni Michelotti, with a very truncated tail that featured a wraparound rear screen. As befitted a body designed for racing, it was not only very lightweight but also incorporated a number of elements to keep the mechanicals cool, including vents for the engine, brakes and rear axle. It measured 3942mm long and 1255mm tall.

Vignale completed the car in time for Sparken to race, with Roy Salvadori as co-driver, in the Casablanca 12 Hours of December 1953, where it finished fourth. The car also raced at Agadir and Dakar in 1954, by which time it had a DB3S engine fitted. In 1955 and 1956 the car continued to compete under new ownership (in order: Cerretti, Boris and Prodiaz). It is believed that the DB3 was dismantled after completing its racing commitments; the fate of the chassis is sadly unknown.

However, the fate of the Vignale bodywork is known. In about 1959, it was taken off the DB3 chassis and transferred over to a Ferrari 340 America chassis (number 0196A), where it remained until 2001. At the time of writing, it is fitted to a 1951 Ferrari 212 Inter chassis.

As an aside, drawings exist of an Aston Martin DB3S Berlinetta with a double-bubble roof designed by Zagato. If it had been built, this would have been the first ever Zagato-bodied Aston but sadly it remained on the drawing board.

The Touring Years

DB4 (TOURING)

"Your car? Preeety car," declares Mafia boss Altalbani to Charlie Croker in the film, *The Italian Job*, as the British crook enters Italian territory in his Aston Martin DB4 Convertible. Pretty the DB4 certainly was: a direct consequence of it being an 'Italian job' in reality, for this car was designed in Milan.

Quintessentially British though Aston Martin may have been, it acquired a distinctly Italian flavour in 1958 thanks to a new love-struck tryst between Newport Pagnell and Touring of Milan. It was undoubtedly a masterstroke to mingle the worlds of Italian design and British engineering into one superlative sum, initiating a happy liaison that persisted for more than a decade.

Aston Martin's respected designer, Frank Feeley – the man who had created both the DB2 and DB3S – produced a proposal for the MkIII's replacement. His DB4 prototype (DP114/2) was, however, ill-liked by the management. Impressed by Touring of Milan's work on the 1956 DB2/4 Spider (see page 37), general manager John Wyatt instead approached the Italian company.

It was Federico Formenti, Touring's designer of precocious but largely shrouded talents, who created the DB4's shape. Many adjectives have been used to describe his sublime creation, among them supple, muscular, seductive and thoroughbred. Its lines were natural and organic, as if carved by the wind, and while its feline shape suggested feminine grace, the DB4 succeeded in coalescing a very masculine character – "a gentleman pugilist in a bespoke Italian suit", as design critic Jonathan Glancey once put it.

Formenti cleverly made the DB4 look like an elegant evolution of the MkIII, creating a masterful amalgamation of British engineering and Italian flair. His work cast the design mould for a whole generation of Aston Martins. The flow of the fastback rear end was, in particular, a masterstroke but there was hardly an element that looked out of place. Early DB4s (dubbed Series 1 in retrospect) had simple bumpers without overriders and a bonnet that hinged at the rear.

It was not just the shape that Touring of Milan supplied, but also its 'Superleggera' (superlight) construction method, which Aston Martin adopted under licence from the Italian company. The Superleggera technique consisted of a framework of small-diameter tubes covered in hand-made aluminium body panels.

Underneath, the DB4 used an all-new chassis,

while Tadek Marek's new alloy six-cylinder engine family took Aston Martin into a completely different performance league. With 240hp in standard form and, from 1962, 266hp in Vantage guise, here was a 140mph grand tourer that handled well and, thanks to servo-assisted brake discs all round, stopped well too. With its luxurious four-seat interior, it was the perfect grand touring machine.

The DB4 was launched at the 1958 Paris Motor Show to huge acclaim but greater things were to follow. One year after the DB4's launch, the DB4 GT of 1959 used a wheelbase shortened by 130mm (five inches) so it was a strict two-seater. Its thinner aluminium bodywork was much lighter, making it perfect for its intended role in competition. The revised proportions suited Formenti's sublime shape even better and its cowled headlamps looked even smoother (the later high-power DB4 Vantage also used the GT's faired-in headlights, albeit with chrome rims). Another Italian touch for the GT was 42-spoke Borrani wire wheels.

The GT weighed considerably less than the DB4 saloon, and with its triple-choke twin-plug engine capable of 302hp, it had fiery

OPPOSITE: Sketch of Vignale's DB3. THIS PAGE: Federico Formenti's work to create the DB4 has long passed into the realm of the iconic. Below is a Series 2 coupe; above and right are images of the sportier Vantage coupe.

performance, capable of 153mph and 0-60mph in 6.1 seconds. The GT was also the perfect choice for coachbuilders, among them Bertone and Zagato, the latter producing the legendary DB4 GT Zagato (see page 45).

The DB4 evolved several times over its production life, grouped into unofficial 'Series' designations. Stylistically, the 1960 Series 2 adopted opening rear quarter-lights with flat glass (rather than curved) and a front-hinged bonnet; the Series 3 of 1961 gained new rear light clusters; Series 4 cars (1961-1962) replaced the previous eggbox-style grille with a new design with vertical bars and a smaller bonnet scoop; the Series 5 was lengthened by 90mm and its roof raised slightly to boost passenger space.

A convertible version of the DB4 arrived in 1961, once again styled by Formenti of Touring, and commentators noted that its look echoed his Maserati 3500GT and Lancia Flaminia designs. The DB4 Convertible driven by Michael Caine in the 1969 film *The Italian Job* was – apparently – pushed over a mountain pass; in fact, it was a converted Lancia Flaminia that was destroyed, the film crew realising that it looked convincingly similar to the DB4.

The DB4 was an instant success right from the word go, despite its steep pricing. Up to the end of production in 1963, some 1110 were built, of which 1040 were fixed-heads and 70 were convertibles.

DB5 (TOURING)

From the outside, the DB5 of 1963 looked very much like the DB4, except that it now adopted cowled headlamps as standard. For some people, this is the most beautiful Aston Martin of all.

The main evolution was the new 4.0-litre engine with 282hp, or 314hp in Vantage form. This made it a genuine 150mph car; 155mph in the case of the Vantage. The earliest cars had four speeds or optionally five, but within three months five became standard, while there was also an automatic option.

OPPOSITE: *Sean Connery very much made the DB5 James Bond's own.*
TOP: DB5 was a masterpiece of understated refinement.
ABOVE & BELOW: DB6 in saloon and Volante convertible guises, distinctive for its kicked-up rear spoiler.

There were both fixed-head and Convertible models, the latter evolving in 1965 to become the DB5 Volante, using many DB6 parts such as split bumpers front and rear, a larger oil cooler opening and Triumph rear light clusters. Some 1021 DB5s were made in all.

Of course, it was James Bond who made the DB5 so iconic in films like *Goldfinger* and *Thunderball*. Ian Fleming had actually intended Bond to drive a DB Mark III, but by 1963 when *Goldfinger* was being produced, the DB5 was nearly ready and Aston Martin allowed the prototype DB5 to be used in the film.

DB6 (TOURING)

Launched at the 1965 London Motor Show, the DB6 took Touring's seminal work in a somewhat new direction. The major difference was under the skin – or perhaps we should say the skin itself, since the DB6 was no longer constructed according to Superleggera principles. Instead, more conventional steel underpinnings lay underneath the aluminium outer panels. The Superleggera bonnet badges that had graced previous DBs were now absent.

The shape also evolved, with a longer wheelbase than the DB5's and a higher roofline providing more room for passengers in the rear. The windscreen was made more upright, while other glasswork changes included opening front quarterlights and new rear quarterlights. Also new were split front and rear bumpers.

Easily the biggest stylistic change, though, was the new truncated tail with its upswept 'spoiler'. This was quite a novel idea for 1965; and while it enhanced stability and reduced aerodynamic drag, not everyone was convinced that it improved the DB5's elegant appearance. Arguably the Kamm tail suited the DB6 Volante power-roof convertible better than the coupe.

By the time the DB6 MkII arrived in June 1969, Aston Martin had already introduced its DBS, a model that severed the Italian design connection entirely, being created in-house by William Towns. The MkII did borrow a few items from the DBS, like its wider wire wheels, hubs and seats. The extra width in the track meant that the wheelarches were now flared. Other changes included power steering and optional fuel injection. With the DBS trailblazing a new era for Aston Martin, the DB6 was retired in 1970, after a total of 1567 fixed-heads and 215 Volantes had been built.

LEFT: As gawky as the DB4 was elegant, the Rapide failed to hit the mark, stylistically or commercially. RIGHT: The very last model built by Touring was this very successfully realised coupe, the 'DBS C' of 1966.

LAGONDA RAPIDE (TOURING)

Touring had done such a widely admired job with the Aston Martin DB4 that it was only natural to return to Italy for the company's new four-door saloon, planned for launch in 1961. This was to be badged as the Lagonda Rapide.

The new saloon used a modified version of the DB4 chassis lengthened by 16 inches and fitted with a de Dion rear axle, which improved rear passenger space. The construction followed Touring's traditional Superleggera principles of aluminium panels over a tubular framework.

Given this promising set-up, why was it that Federico Formenti's design for the Rapide was so poorly resolved, and so poorly received? Seen from the rear, the design wasn't bad, resembling Formenti's work on contemporary Maseratis. Even though the glasshouse looked a little small, the main issues lurked at the front end. The upright main grille looked heavy, while the horizontal inlets flanking it did it no favours; nor did the clumsy bars bisecting each of the grilles. Compounding a miserably overwrought frontal aspect were double front lights set in oddly shrouded nacelles. Some commentators unfavourably compared the general mess with Ford's ignominious Edsel. Overall, this was a rare case of Italian style missing the mark badly.

Even powered by the 4.0-litre Tadek Marek-designed straight-six engine (the first car ever to receive it), the Rapide was so heavy (1715kg) that performance suffered: for instance, its top speed was merely 130mph. Another problem was its huge price tag of £4950; even so, Aston Martin is thought to have lost money on each car made. Between 1961 and 1964, a paltry 55 Rapides were built.

DBS C (TOURING)

The DB6 was launched in 1965, but already Aston Martin was planning other models. The first was code-named MP220, a two-door, four-seat coupe designed to be powered by the forthcoming Aston Martin V8 engine. The second was the MP226, a more sporting two-seat coupe based on the DB6 chassis.

It was only natural that Aston Martin should return to Touring to design these projects. However, Touring was in a parlous state at the time: it had entered receivership in 1964, and while it was revived, the writing was on the wall. According to some reports, David Brown had provisionally accepted Touring's ideas for the 'MP' projects but Aston Martin now had a new and talented young designer within its ranks, the British-born William Towns, who had penned an alternative MP220 proposal. This eventually got the nod instead of Touring's to become the new DBS, launched in 1967.

This was not the end of the line for Touring, however. While Aston Martin put its efforts into getting the Towns-designed DBS into production, the MP226 two-seater was put on ice. In 1966 Touring went ahead and built Federico Formenti's coupe, which featured attractively sharp lines that evoked his earlier design for the Lamborghini

350GT. The form of the front grille was traditional Aston Martin but very narrow, with half-bumpers cutting in at each side. The low nose was set off by headlamps mounted in angular nacelles, behind transparent cowls. A swage line ran all the way around the car at mid-body level, while grilles in the lower front wings and rear roof pillars performed cooling functions. The angular rear end featured circular taillights in cut-outs and a novel hatchback.

The basis was a DB6 chassis modified to use de Dion rear suspension (as would appear on the production DBS). While the DB6 wheelbase was retained, the engine (a Vantage-spec six-cylinder) was mounted 10.5 inches further back in the chassis. The result was almost 7 inches shorter and a substantial 5.5 inches lower than the DB6. It also weighed 180kg less.

Touring's coupe did the motor show rounds in 1966, appearing in Paris, London and Turin in September, October and November respectively. Any chance of this model being manufactured alongside Aston's other models was scuppered when Touring went bust for good at the end of 1966. Two examples were built by Touring, one right-hand drive and the other a left-hooker (chassis 266/1/R and 266/2/L), the former with a 365hp Vantage 'C'-spec engine, the latter with 325hp. These cars were the very last ever built by Touring. Although badged DBS at the time, they are usually referred to retrospectively as DBS C to avoid confusion with the production DBS of 1967.

DB4 GT JET (BERTONE/GIUGIARO)

In December 1959, Bertone bravely hired a 21-year old Giorgetto Giugiaro, a decision that would prove spectacularly successful. The very first car he ever designed while at Bertone was for a British company – Gordon (see page 156) – but very soon after he turned his design talents to another British chassis: the Aston Martin DB4 GT.

Giugiaro's design, suitably named Jet, was sleek and low-slung, with a very slender glasshouse. The front end featured prominent headlights either side of a hexagonally patterned grille, with chromed half-bumpers above grilles for brake cooling and an oil cooler inlet in the centre. The bonnet's large power bulge incorporated distinctive vanes for extra cooling; more cooling vents behind each front wheel were enveloped by swage lines along the body flanks. Other design details included very slim roof pillars, a sharply raked rear screen and an elegant tail with stylised half-bumpers and unique faired-in lights. Inside was a bespoke cabin with a body-coloured facia, black vinyl dash top, wood-rim

THIS PAGE: The lithe 1961 DB4 GT-based Jet was the work of a very young Giorgetto Giugiaro. OPPOSITE: Zagato's seminal DB4 GT is widely regarded as the most desirable Aston Martin of all time.

steering wheel, twin main dials, six extra central gauges, leather seats and electric windows.

Bertone took delivery of DB4 GT chassis number 0201/L in December 1960 and on this basis built its new bodywork mostly of steel, a choice of material that made it heavier than Touring Superleggera's aluminium-bodied DB4 GT (the only aluminium panels on the Jet were the sills and front and rear aprons).

The DB4 GT Jet made its debut at the March 1961 Geneva Salon and reappeared at the Turin show in November that year. Originally painted light green with a grey interior, it was soon repainted blue for Turin.

This one-off was restored at the factory in 1988 and went on to win first prize in the Italian Coachwork class at Pebble Beach in 1989 and Best in Show at Villa D'Este in 2001, among many other concours trophies. It was sold at auction in 2013 for the remarkable sum of £3,249,500.

The Jet name would be reprised by Bertone twice in the 21st century with the V12 Vanquish-based Jet II (2004) and Rapide-based Jet 2+2 (2013), which are detailed on pages 62 and 63 respectively.

The Zagato Years: Part 1 – 1960s

DB4 GT ZAGATO

Proudly on display on Zagato's stand at the 1960 Geneva Show was a splendid coupe based on a Bristol chassis: the 406S Zagato (detailed on page 124). Surely it was no coincidence that the contract for what would become the Aston Martin DB4 GT Zagato (GTZ) – conceptually similar in so many ways to the Bristol Zagato – was signed between Aston Martin and Zagato at the very same show.

Conceptually similar? Indeed. Aston Martin's plan was to build a car to challenge the Ferrari 250 GT SWB on track. Zagato's proven track record in creating lightweight, aerodynamic versions of cars like the Alfa Romeo Giulia (and indeed the Bristol) made it the ideal candidate to take the DB4 GT and turn it into a road race and circuit contender.

Remarkably, it took Zagato just seven months to complete the new car, which was unveiled at the London Motor Show in October 1960. All the history books state that this car was designed by Ercole Spada, then a 22-year old apprentice at Zagato, although Andrea Zagato has recently told a somewhat different story, citing Spada as merely one of the people involved, the others being Celeste Gobbi and Gianni Zagato.

Zagato's DB4 had a completely different body shape to its neighbour Touring's. It felt more

'essential', with shorter overhangs and a more muscular stance, enhanced by the short (2360mm) wheelbase of the DB4 GT chassis. It wasn't an especially radical design, but was simply a very fine, balanced expression of classical themes. As per Zagato's modus operandi, non-essential elements like bumpers and almost all brightwork were dispensed with. As much as possible of the new bodywork was made from ultra-thin aluminium, keeping overall weight down to 1250kg, about 45kg less than the regular DB4 GT.

The DB4 GT's 3.7-litre twin-cam straight-six was given a higher 9.7:1 compression ratio and extra power (314hp), endowing the GTZ with blisteringly quick pace: 0-60mph could be accomplished in just 6.1 seconds and the top speed was 154mph.

Rolling chassis were dispatched to Milan where they were clothed by Zagato. Initial plans called for a limited run of 25 DB4 GTZs but perhaps because the price was exceedingly high – £5470, almost £1000 more than the regular DB4 GT – takers were few. Between 1961 and 1963, just 19 GTZs were made (although since two of them shared the same chassis number, that total has now been revised to 20).

The DB4 GTZ's competition career was somewhat stymied by Ferrari developing its all-conquering 250 GTO. A GTZ was entered in the 1962 Le Mans 24 Hour race with Mike Salmon and Ian Baillie driving, but it was forced to retire with a holed piston. GTZs did claim wins in many other events, however, notably in the hands of Roy Salvadori and Jim Clark.

Zagato's DB4 GT is today widely regarded as one the most beautiful cars of all time and almost certainly the greatest ever road-going Aston Martin. As much is recognised by the classic car market: at auction, genuine examples have fetched in excess of £10 million.

DB4 GT ZAGATO SANCTION II

There is some irony in the fact that, by consensus, the most desirable Aston Martin ever made should

THIS PAGE: Zagato's approach was to make its DB4 GT as lightweight as possible. Ballooning values inspired a string of 'continuation' models. OPPOSITE: Gianni and Elio Zagato standing next to their V8 Vantage.

have fallen short of its original intended production total. Of the original tranche of DB4 GT Zagatos scheduled for build, not all were sold, leaving a delicious possibility open. With values of original DB4 GTZs reaching astronomical levels in the late 1980s, a plan was hatched to build new cars using the remaining four unused chassis numbers (0192, 0196, 0197 and 0198). These would be known as the 'Sanction II' – a brilliant idea that has since been adopted by several other manufacturers.

The cars were not actually made at the factory and Victor Gauntlett described them as "works approved replicas" with full backing from both Aston Martin and Zagato. Using original DB4s, and in one case a DB5, as donors, replica chassis were built by Richard Williams (RSW) at his Cobham, Surrey workshop, and then despatched to Italy for bodywork to be fitted – but not by Zagato itself, which by that stage had given up building cars in its factory. Instead the Sanction II cars were made at the workshop of ex-Zagato employee Mario Galbiatti, who used Richard Williams's own DB4 GTZ as a template to ensure exact replication. The only external differences over the 1960 original were the wheels and tyres, while one example had a single bonnet bulge (the others had three). The four chassis were shipped out to Italy in 1989 but the finished cars would not be completed until July 1991, all of them painted RSW Green.

DB4 GT ZAGATO SANCTION III

In 1998, RS Williams received permission to build a further two DB4 GT Zagatos from Aston Martin chairman, Walter Hayes, under the Sanction III banner. These were all but identical to the earlier Sanction II, with Hayes insisting that genuine DB4s be used as the basis (chassis 344/R and 424/R). As before, chassis were shipped out to Italy to be rebodied. These were very much 'under the radar' with no publicity surrounding them. Both cars were finished in 2000, painted RSW Green.

DB4 GT ZAGATO CONTINUATION

A number of car makers realised that, with the market for classics reaching heady new heights in the 21st century, there was a market for so-called 'continuation' cars – newly made cars that carried on where production had ended decades before. Aston Martin duly created brand new GTZs under the designation DB4 GT Zagato Continuation. Sold as part of a two-car Centenary Collection (the DBS GT Zagato was the other), and priced at £6 million, 19 Continuation cars were made, starting in 2019.

The Zagato Years: Part 2 – 1980s

V8 VANTAGE ZAGATO

Aston Martin's owners, Victor Gauntlett and Peter Livanos, both attended the 1984 Geneva Show, which was notable for the furore surrounding Ferrari's sensational new GTO. Aston Martin's stand happened to be close to Zagato's and when Zagato's chief finance officer, Guidi Cantele, suggested that the coachbuilder design a new limited-production, high-priced Aston to Gauntlett (himself an owner of a DB4 GT Zagato), he was immediately enthusiastic, and with Elio and Gianni Zagato, a plot was quickly hatched for a new Zagato Aston.

Just one month later, in April 1984, Livanos and engineering director Michael Bowler visited Milan to finalise ideas. Three months further on, Zagato's chief stylist Giuseppe Mittino flew to the UK to present his sketches. He looked at the V8 Vantage chassis and realised that by shortening the car, making it a two-seater, reducing weight, tweaking the engine and improving aerodynamics, this could be not only the ultimate Aston but also one of the fastest cars in the world.

A styling rendering was released to the press in

March 1985, resulting in £5 million worth of orders for what Aston Martin declared would be a production run limited to 50 cars. It would be another full year before the V8 Vantage Zagato was unveiled at the 1986 Geneva Show in the flesh. However, things were not all rosy, with two big factors displeasing customers who had placed orders. First, the car's looks did not compare favourably with the original rendering. Second, interminable delays set in, caused to a large degree by Zagato's perilous finances. Gauntlett reluctantly agreed to take a 50% stake in Zagato to get the cars built – a stake that would last until May 1987.

The Zagato's wheelbase was the same as the V8 Vantage but overall it was shorter by almost 12 inches and a fraction narrower, too. Very short overhangs gave it an aggressive stance and the Aston Martin grille was well integrated but the overall shape was widely viewed as disappointingly bland.

In an attempt to achieve aerodynamic efficiency, complex new flush-fitting glass was used. The main front windows were fixed with small, separate drop-down panels. A modest tail spoiler was added to boost downforce, too, while sleek-looking Zagato wheels also reduced turbulence. However, the targeted Cd figure of 0.29 was missed – it ended up being 0.32 (still respectable).

Weight was saved by using aluminium bodywork with composite front and rear sections, the bodies in white being made by Opac in Turin. The Zagato-designed interior was pared down by Aston standards, with lightweight seats borrowed from the Lancia Delta S4.

One controversial aspect was the 'power bulge' in the bonnet needed to clear the airbox for the four carburettors. The original sketch had shown a much flatter bonnet because fuel injection had been planned, but power demands scuppered that; the production engine eventually made 410hp (optionally 437hp with even larger carbs). One thing the car did achieve was astonishing performance. Magazine testers achieved a top speed of over 185mph and 0-60mph in 4.7 seconds.

Priced at £95,000, Aston Martin did not, in the end, have trouble shifting slightly more than the 50 cars originally planned. Some 52 fixed-head coupes were made, the 'extra' two owners being Gauntlett and Livanos themselves.

V8 VOLANTE ZAGATO

So successful had the V8 Vantage Zagato proven that demand remained for more. Victor Gauntlett conceived a plan to sell more while keeping his word about maintaining exclusivity for existing buyers: make a drophead Volante version.

Zagato's Giuseppe Mittino once again did the design work, using a structure suitably strengthened to cope with the loss of the roof (Michael Bowler would claim it was in fact even stiffer than the coupe). Weight was up by 132kg.

Another way in which the V8 Volante Zagato

OPPOSITE: Charming Italian sketch of the V8 in a 'typical' British setting. THIS PAGE: Some thought the V8 Vantage Zagato's look was 'challenging' back in 1986 but time has treated it pretty well.

differed was that it received the less powerful fuel-injected V8 engine (305hp versus 410hp). Since the bulky airbox was not needed, the Volante did without the awkward power bulge. The other main change over the coupe was a new, more enclosed front grille and pivoting covers for the headlamps.

The roof was a power-operated soft-top with a plastic rear window. Once folded, it was covered by an old-fashioned tonneau. The side windows were full-sized and, along with the rear side windows, could be wound down fully.

Performance was well down on the V8 Vantage, with a claimed top speed of 160mph and 0-60mph in 6.0 seconds. However, some cars were later converted to have more power by the factory's Customer Services Division.

The Volante was displayed at the March 1987 Geneva Show, the prototype actually being Gauntlett's own coupe that had been converted to drop-top spec. The original announcement said that only 25 Volante Zagatos would be built, but by the time production ended in 1989, some 37 cars had been completed at a cost of £125,000 apiece.

ABOVE: Zagato's ill-advised Rapide of 1988 was frankly a bit of a shocker. ABOVE RIGHT: This entirely speculative sketch for a new Aston Martin was created by Zagato in the 1990s.

LAGONDA RAPIDE (ZAGATO)

While the V8 Zagatos were still a live project, in 1988 Zagato took it upon itself to create a vision of a new Lagonda Rapide. Since Aston Martin was still making the Towns-designed Lagonda saloon at the time, this was a bold move indeed, but Zagato differentiated its proposal by making it a two-door four-seater coupe rather than a four-door saloon.

Newport Pagnell supplied Zagato with a Lagonda chassis shortened by 7.9 inches. On this base, Marco Pedraccini, with assistance from Gianni Zagato, designed a three-box shape that, according to Aston Martin's Michael Bowler, was meant to evoke Frank Feeley's work of the 1950s.

The design was notable for its ungainly waistline kink, giving the car, in Bowler's words, a "broken-backed look". Zagato claimed the dropped front quarter-light base improved visibility, although ironically most onlookers shielded their eyes when they saw it. The extremely long overhangs unbalanced the proportions, while a height raised by 4.3 inches compared to the Lagonda saloon amplified the overall unhappiness. More controversy surrounded the stainless steel front grille, whose design was a departure from Lagonda traditions.

This was very much a mock-up, with no mechanicals fitted, wooden wheels and no interior (the 'windows' were painted opaque). The press certainly wasn't kind to it, *Car* magazine calling it "the ugliest car on display" at the Geneva Show of March 1988 – its one and only public appearance.

Aston Martin boss Victor Gauntlett took the unusual step of distancing his company from anything to do with the car. Despite Zagato contemplating a convertible version of the Rapide as well, there was clearly no production future for the new car and it was quietly dropped.

At the request of Victor Gauntlett, independent designer Tom Tjaarda also proposed his own Lagonda Coupe in 1991, as well as a replacement for the 'wedge' Lagonda, but neither went further than the scale model stage.

The Zagato Years: Part 3 – 2000s

DB7 ZAGATO

Aston Martin having been acquired by Ford in 1991, the British marque had ready access to design resources from within the corporation, notably at Ghia (which created the Lagonda Vignale in 1993 – see page 59). It's no surprise that it felt no compunction to collaborate with Zagato at the time, although Zagato did do some Aston Martin design sketches during the 1990s, while in 1995 a Virage chassis was sent to Zagato in Italy, ultimately with no outcome.

However with Ghia's influence waning, a new Zagato affiliation would be born in 2002. The choice of car was one of the most successful Aston Martins of all time: the DB7, originally launched in 1993. In many ways, Aston's DB7 was an unlikely confection, conceived in partnership with Tom Walkinshaw

THIS PAGE: DB7 Zagato was a happy marriage that kick-started a whole new era of Italo-British cooperation.

Racing (TWR) and using the Jaguar XJ-S as its basis. It certainly helped that Ian Callum's design was so sensationally good. Throughout its life it got better and better, the biggest upgrades being a V12 engine to replace the original straight-six. By the end of DB7 production, over 7000 examples had been made, making it the mainstay of the company during difficult times.

The story of the DB7 Zagato started in August 2001, when Aston Martin's CEO, Ulrich Bez and Andrea Zagato were both judges at the Pebble Beach Concours d'Elegance. They got talking and had soon agreed a new association between the companies. As Bez would later state, the move "shows the confidence we place in the value of combining the Aston Martin and Zagato names". Work began very quickly: following a press announcement in April 2002, the new limited-production Zagato supercar was unveiled in August 2002 at Gieves and Hawkes, the gentlemen's outfitters in Savile Row, London.

The design was by Norihiko Harada of Zagato, overseen by Henrik Fisker, Aston Martin's Head of Design. Although the silhouette was reminiscent of the DB7, the only items kept from the donor bodywork were the windscreen and front lights. The design very much had its own personality, in part due to the wheelbase being shortened by 60mm, but also by reducing the overhangs front and rear. The classic grille was somewhat deeper than the DB7's, while distinctive bulges on the front and rear wings extended into the doors.

The rear end was the most striking aspect of all, with a deeply indented double-bubble roofline extending into the rear screen glass. The circular rear lights added a distinctly Italian flavour, too, while the boot lid dropped down to access the luggage space. The overall effect was perhaps not the happiest-looking Aston Martin, it must be said.

The cabin was a strict two-seater and, while it used the DB7's steering wheel and switchgear, most of the interior was reconfigured. This was the first Aston Martin to use quilted aniline leather rather than pigmented leather.

Mechanically, the 5.9-litre V12 was upgraded to produce 435hp, while the suspension and brakes were also uprated. Since the DB7 Zagato weighed 60kg less (1740kg), it was very fast, capable of 190mph and 0-60mph in under five seconds.

The new bodywork was made of steel (roof and wings), aluminium (all opening panels) and composites (front and rear bumpers). Zagato did not make the panels; instead these were done by another Italian company, Opac of Turin. Completed shells were then sent to Aston Martin's Gaydon plant to be painted and then dispatched to the Bloxham facility.

Priced at around £166,000, this was an expensive machine indeed and Aston Martin expected to sell between 75 and 99 cars. In the end it received some 200 orders, but decided to cap production at 99, although the factory did make one further example which it retained itself. Customer deliveries began in mid-2003 and had been completed by 2004. So successful was this project that it ignited a whole new era for Zagato and Aston Martin.

THIS PAGE: DB AR1 Zagato was more than a simple DB7 Zagato chop-top. OPPOSITE TOP: Vanquish Roadster Zagato was a trend-setting one-off. OPPOSITE BELOW: Unusually, the V12 Zagato began life as a racer and was then transformed into a road car.

DB AR1 ZAGATO

It would be unfair to say that the DB AR1 Zagato was simply an open-topped version of the DB7 Zagato, despite appearances and despite the fact that it was built to assuage the disappointment of those who had missed out on the chance to buy its fixed-head predecessor.

The biggest difference between the two projects – apart from the total lack of a roof, not even a rudimentary soft-top – was the fact that the AR1 was built on an unshortened DB7 Vantage chassis, the reason being that it could therefore pass American Type Approval regulations. The AR1 remained a two-seater, however, the area behind the cockpit being filled with double-bubble-shaped hard panelling. In other respects, the DB AR1 replicated the DB7 Zagato's shape and lines. Once again the design was by Norihiko Harada of Zagato and body assembly was by Opac.

Two specifications were offered: six-speed manual with a 435hp V12, and (more popularly) five-speed automatic with a 420hp engine. The former could do 184mph and 0-60mph in 5.0 seconds, whereas the automatic was limited to 165mph and took 0.1sec longer to reach 60mph.

As for the AR1 name, this deliberately evoked the DBR1 racing car of the 1950s, while 'AR' stood for 'American Roadster' since this was a car intended for US consumption alone. The public unveiling took place at the Los Angeles Auto Show in January 2003, with a limited run of 99 cars planned. Within three months, all 99 had been sold – but not, in the end, to American customers only; eight were delivered to European buyers and a single further example with right-hand drive was sold within the UK. A 100th example was also retained by the factory. The DB AR1 is historic in another way: it was the very last Aston Martin built at the company's Bloxham factory before it closed in early 2004.

VANQUISH ROADSTER ZAGATO

In 2004, the same year that Bertone showed its Jet II coupe concept based on the V12-engined Vanquish, Zagato produced its own Vanquish-based convertible concept. Unlike previous Zagato-badged Aston Martins, this creation was merely an open-topped version of an existing model, the Aston Martin Vanquish coupe.

That's not to say it didn't have its own unique features, though. The "modular cover system" included a hardtop for winter use, and for hot days a transparent hardened glass rear cover (with a curvaceous 'double bubble' form) plus a soft cover. The only other difference over the coupe was at the rear end, with its round light clusters, tapered tail and new bumper. This was strictly a two-seater with a luggage compartment behind the seats.

This design cooperation between Norihiko Harada at Zagato and Peter Hutchinson (Design Manager at Aston Martin) was described by Zagato as a "provocation" and despite around 100 customers trying to place orders, the car remained strictly a one-off.

V12 ZAGATO

The Aston Martin V12 Zagato was, highly unusually, born as a racing car and then morphed into a production road car. It was based on the existing V12 Vantage, which Aston Martin had launched in 2009, a very successful concept that mated V12 power with a very compact bodyshell.

Zagato's take would be an even more dramatic and exclusive affair. It was a design collaboration between Norihiko Harada at Zagato and Marek Reichman, Aston Martin's English-born designer. The bodywork was handcrafted in aluminium using

ABOVE: Grandly proportioned Centenntial in coupe form.
OPPOSITE: The Centennial was also built as a Spyder and as a Shooting Brake.
OPPOSITE BELOW: Vanquish Zagato Coupe.

traditional-style bucks, with some carbon elements and classic design cues like a double-bubble roof and short body overhangs.

Mechanically the car was essentially a V12 Vantage but in its eventual full race spec, it was fitted with a big rear wing, uprated brakes and race wheels, while its engine power output would be slightly raised.

The new car was unveiled at the May 2011 Concorso d'Eleganza Villa d'Este in concept form as a race car, painted red and nicknamed 'Zag'. It even received the Design Award for Concepts and Prototypes at the show.

Just one week later, a second car, painted green and known internally as 'Zig', debuted at the Nürburgring as a precursor to its appearance in the June 2011 Nürburgring 24 Hour race, where it raced alongside Zag as a two-car team. The cars finished fifth and sixth in the SP8 class.

Following the success of the V12 Zagato Corsa, a Stradale (road-going) version was announced just before the Frankfurt Show in 2011. The plan was to make no more than 150 examples but this was subsequently scaled down to no more than 101. The V12 Zagato Stradale entered production at the Gaydon facility in 2012, each example taking an incredible 2000 hours to build (five times longer than the regular V12 Vantage). Priced at £396,000, the first deliveries occurred in the autumn of 2012. In the end only 65 examples were made up until mid-2013, including the two Corsas.

DBS COUPE ZAGATO CENTENNIAL

The 'Centennial' part of the DBS Coupe Zagato Centennial's name alluded to what this very special project celebrated: the 100th anniversary of Aston Martin in 2013. The new car made its debut at an official celebration at Kensington Palace in July 2013.

The styling was the work of Zagato's chief designer, Norihiko Harada. The look was very low and sleek, perhaps resembling a stretched-out version of Zagato's Lancia Hyena of 1992. Of course there was a double-bubble roof, which was emphasised by the roof's curves continuing over the rear screen and on to the bootlid. Also adding to the drama was a swooping aluminium strip that stretched from the bonnet right back to the C-pillar, where it arched right over the double-bubble rear window. The full-width satin alloy grille echoed that of the 1960s DBS and housed projector headlights. The heavily sculpted rear end was finished off by unique light clusters, a rear diffuser and trapezoidal exhaust tailpipes.

The running gear was all taken from the DBS V12, including its 510hp AM08 engine, wheels and ceramic brakes. The interior was also essentially standard DBS V12, making this the very first Aston Martin Zagato to have rear seats. There were never any plans for a production run, however: this was a strict one-off commissioned by an anonymous Japanese customer.

DB9 SPYDER ZAGATO CENTENNIAL

Debuting alongside the DBS Zagato coupe at Kensington Palace in July 2013 was a very similar-looking car in convertible form, called the DB9 Spyder Zagato Centennial, a one-off built for an American collector called Peter Read. There were a few differences, in addition to the folding soft-top, such as side strakes/vents (which were absent on the coupe). The main difference, however, was the basis: the DB9 Volante rather than the DBS, fitted with an AM11 V12 engine with 510hp. The paint finish was Aston Martin Racing Green with a Sahara Tan leather cabin.

VIRAGE SHOOTING BRAKE ZAGATO CENTENNIAL

The third and final Centennial model was the Virage Shooting Brake Zagato Centennial, although its existence was not confirmed until 2014, one year after the coupe and convertible. Norihiko Harada's rear end was a dramatic new shooting brake (estate) style, complete with a hatchback. Arguably this was the most accomplished of the trio in design terms. The mechanical basis was different again: this time the Virage with its AM25 V12 490hp engine, Touchtronic transmission and carbon brakes. The Shooting Brake one-off was built for a European customer who remained anonymous. Its public debut was in September 2014 at the Chantilly Art & Elegance Concours d'Elegance in France.

VANQUISH ZAGATO

The four variants of the Vanquish Zagato series – Coupe, Volante, Shooting Brake and Speedster – kicked off at the Concorso d'Eleganza Villa d'Este in May 2016, when the Vanquish Zagato coupe was first shown in 'concept' form.

This was a collaborative design effort between the Aston Martin Design team (led by Marek Reichman) and Stephane Schwarz of Zagato. The concept had

classic Aston Martin proportions and emphasised a forward-thrusting stance. The new body was realised entirely in carbonfibre. Side strakes ran from the front wheelarch into the door and the door mirrors were inspired by those of the Aston Martin One-77, while a muscular crease in the rear wings gave the car highly accentuated haunches. The roof featured Zagato's double-bubble, which extended into the rear window glass. The shape of the rear end drew on the DB11's profile, featuring a retractable spoiler and an opening tailgate. Four exhaust pipes nestled in carbonfibre sills that appeared to run around the whole lower body. Unique circular taillights used 'bladed' LED technology, as debuted on the Aston Martin Vulcan supercar. The 2+2 cabin featured certain elements like the air vents and switchgear picked out in gold, while the seats had special 'Z' stitching.

The engineering and build were done at Aston Martin's headquarters at Gaydon, with the Vanquish's naturally aspirated V12 engine being uprated to 600hp, its exhaust made louder and its suspension firmed up. One month after the concept's debut, a production run of 99 cars was announced, starting in autumn 2016 and continuing into the summer of 2017.

VANQUISH ZAGATO VOLANTE

Even before production of the Vanquish Zagato coupe had started, Aston Martin announced the open-roof Vanquish Zagato Volante version at the US Pebble Beach Concours in August 2016. The shape was essentially the same but the roof was a soft top using a mechanism derived from the Vanquish Volante's. The double-bubble effect was hinted at by twin rear headrests blending into the bootlid. Inside was a signature 'Z' quilt pattern stitch on the seats and doors, as well as 'Z' emblems embossed on the headrests and the centre console. Once again, production was limited to 99 examples, following on from the end of coupe production in late 2017.

VANQUISH ZAGATO SPEEDSTER

Monterey Car Week in August 2017 saw the unveiling of the final two Vanquish Zagato models: the Speedster and Shooting Brake. The Speedster was basically a reworked two-seat iteration of the Volante offering an "uncompromising roofless design". The boldest design aspect was the so-called 'Speed Humps' that formed streamlined cowls flowing from the seats backwards, hinting at Zagato's 'double-bubble' profile. As with all members of the Vanquish Zagato family, the body panels were made of carbonfibre. The Speedster would be the rarest Vanquish Zagato model, with a production run of just 28 units, all of which were pre-sold prior to production starting in 2018.

VANQUISH ZAGATO SHOOTING BRAKE

The Shooting Brake was perhaps the most appealing of the quartet of Vanquish Zagato designs. Its extended roofline appeared to float above the glasshouse and incorporated Zagato's signature 'double-bubble' surfacing, but with glass inlays to make the cockpit airier. Although a strict two-seater, it was conceived as a practical GT car; hence a powered tailgate offered access to an opulently trimmed boot, complete with a tailored luggage set.

The Vanquish Zagato Shooting Brake entered production in 2018, with a total build run of 99 cars, all pre-sold. That meant the four-strong Vanquish Zagato family totalled 325 units in all. Prices were never announced but it's thought the cost of the Vanquish Zagato family was in the region of £525,000 to £650,000 each. Even at such elevated figures, some customers ordered a full set of four cars.

DBS GT ZAGATO CENTENARY

The first Zagato model to be based on Aston Martin's so-called 'second century platform' (which underpinned the DB11), the DBS GT Zagato Centenary was based on the DBS Superleggera model, Aston Martin's most potent series production car.

The design was inspired, said Aston Martin, by the original DB4 GT Zagato and was created by Aston Martin and Zagato designers in tandem. Up front was a unique grille featuring 108 individual diamond-shaped carbonfibre pieces that were flush to the body when stationary but swivelled open on start-up to allow the 760hp twin-turbo V12 engine to breathe. The full-length gloss carbonfibre roof extended down in one piece to the bootlid. There was no rear screen because a camera-based rear-view mirror obviated any need for one.

A new colour called Supernova Red was exclusively reserved for the DBS GT Zagato Centenary. In addition to black-and-gold machined wheels, solid 18-carat gold badges were applied front and rear, while the side strakes and centre-lock wheel nuts were gold anodised. Inside, Zagato 'Z' seat quilting was joined by a world-first 3D-printed interior finish, in one of three materials: carbon,

OPPOSITE: Three of the four Vanquish Zagato variants – Volante, Speedster and Shooting Brake.
THIS PAGE: The DBS GT Centenary was only sold as part of a pair including a DB4 GT Continuation, priced at a cool £6 million.

aluminium or gold PVD.

The DBS GT Zagato was announced in March 2019 and unveiled in October 2019, with production starting in 2020. It could only be bought paired with the DB4 GT Zagato Continuation (see 47) as one half of the so-called 'DBZ Centenary Collection', 19 of which were available priced at £6m for the pair – and that was excluding tax.

V12 ZAGATO HERITAGE COUPE & SPEEDSTER

A new partnership between Aston Martin, Zagato and British specialist manufacturer, R-Reforged, resulted in a new pair of Aston Martin-approved Vantage V12 Zagato Heritage 'Twins' – Coupe and Speedster. R-Reforged was part of the Swiss-owned AF Racing Group, which worked closely with Aston Martin.

Although the designs were all-new, they had definite echoes of the Vanquish Zagato family of 2016. The bodywork was all in carbonfibre, incorporating active aerodynamics with a deployable rear wing. Other design tweaks included centre-locking 19-inch alloy wheels by APP Tech and 100th anniversary gold 'Z' badging to celebrate Zagato's 100th anniversary (2019). Both Coupe and Speedster had double-bubbles, the former in its roof, the latter in its dual cowls behind the rear headrests.

Each pair of cars was based on the Aston Martin Vantage V12 Zagato of 2011 using a reworked version of the 5.9-litre naturally aspirated V12 producing 600hp (85hp more than the original).

R-Reforged announced in 2019 that it would hand-build 19 pairs of Twins (38 cars in total), with most pre-sold. Owners could specify each element with R-Reforged designers based at Aston Martin St Gallen in Niederwil, Switzerland. Production started at the R-Reforged factory in Warwick in November 2020.

Other Modern Coachbuilt Astons

LAGONDA VIGNALE (GHIA)

The Vignale name has great historic resonance as one of Italy's most celebrated coachbuilders, even if its independent status ended in 1969 when it was acquired by Ghia. Just one year later, Ghia (and therefore Vignale) was acquired by Ford. The feeding frenzy at Ford continued with its 1991 acquisition of Aston Martin Lagonda, after which Ford decided to revive its old Vignale trademark for the 1993 Lagonda Vignale – the first and only melding of the British and Italian names.

Here was a bold new concept for a four-door super-luxury car, reviving the Lagonda badge that had disappeared when the William Towns-designed version left production in 1990. Although designed in Italy, the new Lagonda Vignale was, somewhat ironically, the work of a British designer. This was because Ford gave the design work to Ghia's studio in Italy where the head of design at the time – and the man whose exterior styling proposal was eventually chosen – was a Briton: Moray Callum, the brother of Ian Callum (who designed the Aston Martin DB7 contemporaneously). Moray had previously produced a full-size mock-up of a large Aston Martin coupe proposal back in 1990, so he was a known and trusted figure within the company. Another Brit, David Wilkie, was put in charge of interior design, while materials were chosen by Sally Erickson Wilson.

Ghia's Lagonda Vignale was an imposingly vast machine, measuring fully 5236mm long, 1955mm wide and 1449mm tall. In stark contrast to the 1976-1990 Towns Lagonda, which was characterised by almost painfully sharp razor-edged lines, a low wedge-shaped profile, ultra-slim front grille and

OPPOSITE: V12 Zagato Heritage Coupe and Speedster of 2020.
THIS PAGE: Ghia's imposing Lagonda Vignale, seen above with designers Moray Callum, David Wilkie and Sally Erickson Wilson.

digital electronic dash, Ghia's 1993 proposal was almost the polar opposite. It had no straight edges at all, as well as a rather tall stance with a high waistline and a much more conventional grille. The drooping tail was particularly noteworthy, highlighted by slender light clusters extending almost the whole length of the rear wing, connected right to the front of the car by a jutting waistline strip. This strip was a rare example of ornamentation on the car, realised in nickel, extending along each flank, around the side windows and on the nose. The main bodywork was in aluminium.

Wilkie's interior design featured retro-look analogue instruments and a preponderance of circular shapes. There was a single piece of beechwood for the dashboard, a wood-lined boot, leather-and-beech steering wheel and Parchment leather seats that incorporated curious circular metallic control panels. Rear passengers were treated to power-operated desks.

Another irony was that the underpinnings of the prototype had absolutely nothing to do with Newport Pagnell: the basis of the car was an extended Lincoln Town Car chassis, complete with its 190hp 4.6-litre V8, automatic gearbox and de Dion rear axle – hardly the stuff of exotic coachbuilt dreams, it must be said. It would have been different in production, though, as the intended chassis was to have been an aluminium modular unit with all-independent suspension, while a 5.9-litre V12 engine was mooted (effectively two Ford Duratec V6 units joined together).

The car debuted at the 1993 Geneva Show to gauge its potential as a new model, which was intended to sell for $225,000 in its biggest market, the USA. Ghia's managing director, Filippo Sapino, described the design as "timeless" but expert reactions were more equivocal: it was described as "trend-setting" and "marvellous" by some, but also "the ugliest car around" by one magazine title. The mixed reception, coupled with the relatively unknown Lagonda name, consigned the car to an early grave, and CEO Bob Dover later called the project "a blind alley".

In addition to two prototypes built by Ghia (one painted grey, the other dark blue), a third car was constructed in 1995 by Aston Martin at Newport Pagnell. This was intended as a more producible version of the Lagonda and had a different platform, smaller dimensions and numerous subtle changes to the design, including larger headlights and front grille, plus a lightly revised interior. This third car was painted dark red and fitted with a V12 engine. But despite being viewed as a serious candidate for production, with a launch date of 1997 suggested, ultimately the project was cancelled and the red V12 car was sold on to the Brunei royal family for £1.3 million. This marked the end of the line for the Vignale name – until 2015, that is, when it was revived, somewhat ignominiously, as an up-market Ford trim level.

AM3 & AM4 (PININFARINA/COGGIOLA)

In the 1990s, Aston Martin forged a strong link with Prince Jefri of Brunei. Via Aston Martin's Customer Service Division (later renamed Works Service), it

created a string of coachbuilt cars for the Brunei royal, among them four-door saloons and shooting brakes based on the Virage and Vantage.

During the same period, Pininfarina had also been designing unique bodywork for Prince Jefri on many prestige chassis, including Bentleys and Rolls-Royces (see respective chapters in this book). When the prince asked Pininfarina to create a special Aston Martin for him, the Italian company approached Kingsley Riding-Felce at Newport Pagnell with a proposal to collaborate. An agreement was duly reached and Pininfarina was supplied with five right-hand drive Vantage rolling chassis with upgraded suspension and 600hp engines, plus one standard Vantage, all between May 1996 and July 1997.

Pininfarina created five different design proposals for its royal customer, numbered AM1 to AM5. Of these, two were approved – AM3 and AM4. The AM3 was quite a radical design, especially at the front. Any notion of a traditional grille was lost, replaced with a black composite nose section that housed the lights. Bizarrely, a shape like an Aston traditional grille did make an appearance – but at the back of the car! – with another composite panel housing the rear lights. Also unique to the car were its six-spoke alloy wheels and its 2+2 interior. Indeed, just about the only part of the car that was recognisably an Aston, apart from the badges, was the cooling cut-out in each front wing.

The AM4 was rather soberer in appearance, but also absolutely bespoke. The front end was much more conventional, with DB7-style lights and a traditional grille, while the same grille shape was echoed in the rear light panel, albeit inverted. Again the interior was bespoke.

A finished prototype was extensively tested with the help of Aston Martin engineers, and proved to be an extremely fast grand tourer, capable of 205mph. Pininfarina arranged for a nearby coachbuilder, Coggiola, to build all of the cars, of which there were six examples in all (three AM3s and three AM4s), constructed during 1997 and early 1998.

OPPOSITE: *Pininfarina's pretty AM3 and AM4 coupes were built in secret for the Brunei royal family.*
THIS PAGE: *Highly unusual design approach for Italdesign's DB7 Vantage Volante-based Twenty Twenty of 2001.*

TWENTY TWENTY (ITALDESIGN)

In 1961, a very young Giorgetto Giugiaro designed the Aston Martin DB4 Jet for Bertone (see page 44). So when a new Giugiaro Aston Martin was set to appear at the 2001 Geneva Show, there was tremendous anticipation, especially since it had the blessing of Aston's boss, Ulrich Bez. The Twenty Twenty that ultimately appeared, however, certainly courted controversy.

A DB7 Vantage Volante chassis was despatched by Aston Martin to Italdesign Giugiaro, to be rebodied in a joint design effort by Giorgetto and his son, Fabrizio. It was the latter who suggested an exposed exoskeletal structure for the car, a design path that Italdesign had already explored with another concept car, the Structura of 1998. The exposed extruded aluminium frame had echoes of the Smart Fortwo about it, as did the non-stressed body panels (variously made of carbonfibre and composite materials). A feature was made of the external door hinges, the upper one forming part of the classic-style Aston front wing vent. The targa-

THIS PAGE: Handsome Jet II by Bertone. OPPOSITE TOP: Jet 2+2 was a five-door shooting brake version of the Rapide. OPPOSITE FAR RIGHT: Peculiar EG was a joint effort by Boniolo and Quality Cars.

style roof could be removed and stored in a special housing. Other design details included a grilled fairing in the bonnet, elongated rear lights and aluminium front and rear bumpers.

Inside, there was space for two adults and, if you removed a bulkhead, two small children behind. The dashboard was completely symmetrical, with instruments grouped together on the steering column (in theory making a switch between left- and right-hand drive easily achievable). The trim was a mix of brushed aluminium and terracotta-coloured leather.

The 'Twenty Twenty' name supposedly derived from when Aston Martin management viewed the car (in October 2000) and said that the style could be understood in 2020. Looking back with '2020 vision', this feels more of a design dead-end than anything forward-looking; more bizarre than beautiful. Although the Twenty Twenty was a fully functional car, powered by an uprated version of the DB7 Vantage 5935cc V12 with 500hp, Aston Martin showed no interest in pursuing it further and it remained a one-off.

JET II (BERTONE)

We have already covered the 1961 Giugiaro-designed Bertone Jet in this chapter. Some 43 years later, at the 2004 Geneva Motor Show, Bertone unveiled its new 'Jet II' design, this time based on the Aston Martin Vanquish. With support from the UK factory, Bertone started work in 2003 using a V12 Vanquish aluminium-and-carbonfibre chassis lengthened by 210mm.

The design really had very little to do with the 1961 Jet, nor indeed with the Vanquish. Although it retained the Vanquish's structure and windscreen, every body panel was unique to this car. Its shooting brake design theme was created by Bertone's design director, Giuliano Biasio, overseen by the managing director, Roberto Piatti. The front end featured a classic Aston grille but was flanked by unique headlamps and air ducts to cool the brakes. The rear aspect also reflected Aston's grille shape, outlined in the rear window and lighting bank. The panoramic transparent T-bar roof was made of Plexiglas.

The interior was designed by the same man who'd done the Vignale Lagonda, David Wilkie, mixing Vanquish and DB9 parts along with unique elements like the switchgear and wood-veneer centre bar, inspired by classic boats, as was the luggage area which was covered in wood and aluminium ribbing.

Reputedly the prototype cost $1.8 million to build and while Aston Martin praised the concept, there was never any thought of a production run. It did make a surprise reappearance at the 2013 Geneva Show alongside Bertone's new Rapide-based Jet 2+2 (see next page), where it was repainted gold from its original light silver sage green and had a retrimmed interior.

JET 2+2 (BERTONE)

When in 2012 UK-based Aston Martin enthusiast Barry Weir asked Bertone if it could create a shooting brake version of the four-door Rapide, it readily agreed. Barry's ideas were realised in Italy, with the cooperation of Aston Martin: the Bertone design team got full approval of its design from the Gaydon factory, which considering this was such a well-resolved conversion came as little surprise.

A donor Rapide was sent to Bertone in Turin in December 2012, and it took only three months for the car to be completed in time for an unveiling at the March 2013 Geneva Show. The so-called Jet 2+2 left much of the Rapide untouched, including its 470hp 5.9-litre V12 engine. New panelling was created by hand in sheet metal and carbonfibre. The main difference was the estate car rear end, featuring a tailgate that gave access to a sliding boot floor with foldable rear seats, which also offered better headroom than the standard saloon.

Inside were newly designed front seats, above which was a panoramic glass roof that could change colour from clear to blue, an early example of a dimmable glass roof. Unique wood, two-tone leather and glazed aluminium featured in the cabin.

The weight was almost the same as the Rapide, at around 1990kg, leading to a claim that this was the world's fastest shooting brake with a top speed of 200mph and 0-60mph in 5.3 seconds.

The Jet 2+2 was the very last car that Bertone built before the famous *carrozzeria* closed down for good in 2014. That scotched apparent plans for a further production run of 10 cars, leaving the Jet 2+2 a one-off.

EG (BONIOLO/QUALITY CARS)

The Aston Martin EG (named after the initials of the owner who commissioned it in 2007) was a one-off shooting brake conversion based on a Vanquish. The coachbuilder was Quality Cars, a little-known outfit founded in 1990 and based in Vigonza, but the car's designer, Francesco Boniolo, was slightly better known because his company, Boniolo Advanced Design, had been working since 1975 with some big names, including Ford and Volvo.

The shooting brake rear end lengthened the Vanquish by some 600mm; overall it measured 4700mm long, 1950mm wide and 1318mm tall. Not only was this a four-seater but also a four-door car, the rear doors neatly following the line of the rear wheelarches. The entirely new body was made in aluminium and carbonfibre over a steel tube frame. The panoramic 'Isolite' glass roof could be darkened at the touch of a button, while a neat tailgate provided access to a luxuriously trimmed luggage area. The cabin was strikingly trimmed by Pineider in pink leather (described as "lobster-coloured") with bamboo for the door cappings and dashboard.

BENTLEY

Coachbuilders' Choice

If Rolls-Royce is the quintessentially aristocratic, establishment British marque, then Bentley is its more raffish, dashing alter ego: the sort of car chosen by the well-heeled gentleman who also has a passion for driving, rather than being driven. The two marques circled each other like twin suns in their early years, before collapsing into a single star with their merger in 1931, and then spinning off again in 1998 into new orbits around German solar systems – BMW in Rolls-Royce's case and VW in Bentley's.

Bentley Motors began life in 1919 when Walter Owen (WO) Bentley founded the company in Cricklewood, London. His intent was, "to build a good car, a fast car, the best in class" and the Bentley 3-Litre was certainly that, famously scoring victory in the 1924 Le Mans 24 Hours. Larger-engined models followed in the 1920s, culminating in the stupendous 8-Litre of 1930.

While one Italian coachbuilder – Viotti – did clothe a pre-war Bentley chassis, it was not until the MkVI (1946-1952) that the Italians really 'discovered' the British marque, Pinin Farina notably creating a series of elegant bodies. Both Pinin Farina and Bertone would also body the later R-Type Continental chassis but the Italian Bentley coachbuilt era effectively ended in the 1950s (except for Pininfarina's lone Bentley T coupe of 1968).

Pininfarina was given a more official task for the 1995 Bentley Azure, designing its soft-top and building it in Italy. Pininfarina also made several special-bodied Bentleys for the Brunei royal family during the 1990s. In more recent years, three further Italian couturiers have offered their own Bentley interpretations: Touring, Zagato and Ares.

3-LITRE (VIOTTI)

One of the very first British chassis ever rebodied by an Italian coachbuilder was a Bentley 3-Litre 'Blue Label', chassis number 650, manufactured in 1924 to a standard-length wheelbase. Viotti rebodied it in about 1933 with an unusual sports touring body to a 'double phaeton' style with separate front and rear passenger areas. This could possibly have been a body made some years previously for a Lancia Dilambda chassis and simply substituted. The Bentley was registered in the UK with the number plate XU 5160 but the car eventually found its way to the USA. Its current whereabouts are unknown.

MKVI CRESTA (PININ FARINA)

Bentley's first post-war effort was the MkVI, a traditionally constructed luxury car with a sturdy chassis, independent front suspension, servo-assisted brakes, six-cylinder engine and four-speed gearbox. The regular four-door bodywork was made in steel by Standard Steel but there were innumerable special bodies, mostly in aluminium, made on the MkVI rolling chassis by such British coachbuilders as Park Ward, HJ Mulliner and James Young.

The only continental coachbuilder known to have designed coachwork for the MkVI chassis was Pinin Farina (there is some question over whether Ghia

TOP: Viotti created this 3-Litre sports tourer phaeton body in about 1933. ABOVE & RIGHT: MkVI-based Cresta perfectly expressed Pinin Farina's characteristic cleanliness of line in the immediate post-war period.

XBV 230

might have done a MkVI, too, but there is scant evidence for this). In 1947, Pinin Farina produced sketches for a dual phaeton convertible but this was never built (although a MkVI drophead coupe would soon be built by Farina – see below). In 1948, the Turin *carrozzeria* was approached by Frenchman Jean Daninos, the owner of Facel Métallon which manufactured special bodywork on the basis of Simca, Ford and Panhard models. Keen to branch out into the luxury car market, his request to Pinin Farina was to design two-door coupe bodywork for the Bentley MkVI chassis.

Pinin Farina duly designed a very attractive, modern and aerodynamic shape that, considering the long wheelbase (120 inches), worked very well. Its straight-through wing line was in stark contrast to the traditional style of most Bentleys. Also resolutely modern was the grille, which was recessed rather than being proud of the bodywork as was the usual Bentley way; in fact, Bentley would subsequently insist that Pinin Farina alter the grille to a much narrower shape that better echoed its heritage. Only the chrome sills and oversized bumpers seemed a little heavy-handed.

The prototype (chassis number B323CD) was made by Pinin Farina in Turin and displayed at the 1948 Paris Salon, painted black with a blue interior. Bentley was sufficiently impressed – after its concerns about the radiator grille had been addressed, at any rate – to approve a production run in France, undertaken by Facel-Métallon. Bentley delivered special MkVI chassis suitable for the Cresta's more raked steering column and low radiator header tank and scuttle. A higher final drive ratio was also fitted. A special 'ff' badge was applied to the door, signifying the collaboration between Facel and Farina.

Following a second appearance at the 1949 Geneva Salon, the first customer car completed (chassis B447CD) was delivered to Count Manuel Matos. The exact production tally of Bentley Crestas is not precisely known, but it is something between 10 and 17 cars.

Another Facel-bodied Bentley, the so-called Baby Cresta, was subsequently shown at the 1951 Paris Salon but this was a quite different project that had no design input from Pinin Farina; this would form the kernel of the future Facel Vega.

The Cresta's significance extended beyond its limited production run. Gerald Palmer, the designer at the British car group, Nuffield, happened to visit the 1948 Paris Salon and was so impressed by Pinin Farina's work on the Bentley that he was directly inspired by it when he designed the Wolseley 4/44 of 1952, as he later admitted. And in 1956, Pinin Farina was hired by BMC directly to design its new era of saloon models.

MKVI DROPHEAD COUPE & COUPE (PININ FARINA)

In 1947 a Swiss doctor called Willi Spieler, based in Zurich, visited Pinin Farina to commission special new drophead coupe coachwork. This was to be effected on a right-hand drive Bentley MkVI chassis (number B435CD), which was built in May 1948.

The designer of the new coachwork was Battista 'Pinin' Farina himself. Paolo Pininfarina would later declare this car to be one of his grandfather's personal favourites. The shape was quite unlike the Cresta, featuring much more traditional lines with a prominent upright grille and free-standing foglights. The bespoke aluminium coachwork made the car significantly lighter than the standard steel-bodied Bentley saloon and

BELOW: MkVI Cresta's original wide front grille would be altered. BOTTOM: 1948 Drophead Coupe by Pinin Farina. RIGHT: Two speculative sketches by Pinin Farina for MkVI bodywork. BOTTOM RIGHT: Elegant one-off MkVI Coupe built by Pinin Farina in 1951.

therefore a much sprightlier performer.

The new design broke cover at the March 1949 Geneva Salon, where Farina exhibited two versions: drophead coupe and fixed-head coupe. The former was delivered to Dr Spieler in April 1949; it eventually ended up in Canada, before being sold at auction in the USA in 2005. It is believed that Pinin Farina bodied one further chassis as a two-door coupe, making a total of three examples in this style (two fixed-heads and one drophead).

MKVI COUPE (PININ FARINA)

The last of the Bentley MkVI chassis rebodied by Pinin Farina was completed in October 1951 and made its public debut at the March 1952 Geneva Show. This one-off was built for a Swiss customer and featured a high waistline, low roofline, wraparound rear screen curving into the wings, flowing tail and thin roof pillars. Some of the styling details were perhaps a little gimmicky, such as the chromed teardrop-shaped headlamp pods and two-tiered rear light clusters, but overall this was a well resolved design. Its life involved ownership in Switzerland, the USA, UK and Japan, and thankfully it survives to this day.

R-TYPE CONTINENTAL (PININ FARINA)

Bentley's 1952 replacement for the MkVI was the R-Type, the vast majority of production being Standard Steel four-door saloons. However, the most celebrated version was the Continental R by HJ Mulliner, whose glorious fastback shape was perfectly proportioned and probably the pinnacle of Bentley's post-war production.

Pinin Farina's effort on the R-Type chassis was a Bentley factory commission undertaken in November 1953 on chassis number BC49C. The design was clearly influenced by Pinin Farina's 1951 rebodying of the very similar Rolls-Royce Silver Dawn (see page 230), the main differences being the position of its headlights (on the edges of the wings) and a wraparound rear screen (accomplished in sections). While restrained and tasteful – *The Autocar* remarked

ABOVE: Pinin Farina's restrained 1954 effort on the R-Type chassis.
ABOVE RIGHT: So-called Arnolt-Bentley was by Bertone on an R-Type chassis.
OPPOSITE PAGE: Paolo Martin's pretty T Coupe Speciale of 1968 ultimately led to a commission for Pininfarina to design the Rolls-Royce Camargue.

on its "restrained lines of great beauty" – it lacked the ultimate grace of the HJ Mulliner fastback. Rear wing bulges were a nod to tradition; decorative sill plates were stylised but unobtrusive; the rear lights were very simple; and the front 'flying B' motif was stylised.

Despite its grand proportions, this was a strict two-seater, the area behind the seats being turned over to a carpeted surface to carry tailored luggage, secured by straps. The plush interior featured Bentley gauges that were now chrome-bezelled in a leather-lined dash.

Launched at the April 1954 Turin Show and also seen at the Paris Salon later that year, the R-Type was despatched to Bentley in the UK where it was registered OUK 999 and eventually sold on to a private customer. It remained a one-off.

R-TYPE CONTINENTAL SALOON (BERTONE)

In 1953, the flamboyant American car wheeler-dealer 'Wacky' Arnolt commissioned a special body from Bertone using a Bentley R-Type Continental chassis (B43LSP). Created for his wife, this was unique among Continentals in having four doors, arranged in 'clap-hands' fashion, the rear ones being hinged at their rear edge.

Giovanni Michelotti did the design work and in profile there were definite echoes of his contemporary Arnolt-MG (see page 80), albeit scaled up. It was notable for its flat-sided body, high waistline and relatively small glasshouse. The huge expanse of the flanks was broken up by a swage line that started at the front end, swept around the wheelarches and extended straight back and then changed direction dramatically half way through the rear doors. The front end featured a Bentley radiator grille that was narrower than normal, emphasising its height. The notchback rear end marked a stark contrast to the regular Continental's swooping fastback design. The luxurious interior was also bespoke.

Bertone's R-Type Continental saloon is often referred to as the Arnolt-Bentley, referring to its customer. Bertone displayed this one-off machine at several motor shows during 1953, including Paris, London and Turin, before delivering it to its owner in the USA.

T COUPE SPECIALE (PININFARINA)

What do you do when you're an industrialist with a penchant for expensive cars and enough wealth to be dubbed 'Lord Moneybags' in the press? For the future knight of the realm, James Hanson, it was to ask Sergio Pininfarina to rebody a Bentley T Series saloon, the badge-engineered version of the Rolls-Royce Silver Shadow that was launched in 1965.

Bentley T Series chassis number CBH 4033 was duly despatched to Turin where the brand new car was completely stripped. Pininfarina gave it the project code PF 917 but it would eventually be named the 'Coupe Speciale'.

Apart from a stipulation to create a modern version of the Bentley Continental, Pininfarina was essentially given a free design hand. The man chosen for the job was Paolo Martin, who in 1968 had just arrived at Pininfarina from Bertone as its new head of styling. Paolo Martin later recalled of the Bentley: "It was built by hand in the workshop from simple sketches – there were no technical drawings. It was necessary to use existing lights: Opel Admiral

headlamps and Fiat Dino Spider rear lights, which partially influenced the final result."

The eventual two-door fastback's lines suggested both stateliness and sportiness. A neat swage line broke up the body sides visually, while the gracefully tapering roofline recalled Pininfarina's Ferrari 365 GT 2+2. The shape of the radiator grille was clearly Bentley-esque but it was considerably cut-down compared to the T Series item. The car was painted in a shade of green so dark that it was often mistaken for black. Inside, the bespoke four-seat cabin was finished in black leather upholstery with champagne carpeting.

The new car was shown at several shows in 1968 – Paris, London and Turin – before Hanson took delivery in May 1969. It remained a one-off but there were hopes within Pininfarina that further examples would be made, as Lord Hanson revealed to *Thoroughbred & Classic Cars* magazine in 2000: "[Sergio Pininfarina] got quite excited about the idea and agreed to do it at cost price because he felt he would be able to persuade Rolls-Royce to use his prototype as the new Bentley Continental." That cost was reputedly £14,000, about twice the price of a Bentley T Mulliner Park Ward two-door.

However, Crewe was not persuaded that production was a good idea. Perhaps, though, the car did influence Rolls-Royce's decision to award the contract to design the Camargue coupe to

ABOVE: The transformation of the Continental coupe into the Azure convertible was done by Pininfarina – and it was also built in Italy.

ABOVE: Extremely rarefied Brunei specials designed and built by Pininfarina. From top to bottom: B2, B3, Spectre and Phoenix.

Pininfarina (for which, incidentally, sketches were also made for a Bentley version). The Coupe Speciale was the only Bentley T ever to receive a coachbuilt body. In 1979, the one-off was updated to later Bentley T2 running gear by Jack Barclay, although it retained its original 6230cc V8 engine. It still exists today, now painted metallic grey and featuring a completely revised interior.

AZURE (PININFARINA/OPAC)

It was in 1991 that Rolls-Royce management realised that its Bentley subsidiary could and should return to having an identity of its own, rather than simply making do with rebadged Rollers. That year saw the revival of the Continental badge for a handsome and imposing new Bentley two-door coupe.

The coupe's design was strictly an in-house affair but for the convertible version of the Continental – the Azure – Bentley turned to Pininfarina for assistance. The Italian coachbuilder undertook a two-year engineering process to transform the Continental R into a drophead. The soft-top was not only designed by Pininfarina but the *carrozzeria* was also contracted to provide complete bodyshells, built up from floorpans and sub-assemblies supplied by Park Sheet Metal in Coventry. In this task it was assisted by Opac of Turin, which made the bodies in white. Final assembly was by Rolls-Royce in Crewe.

The Azure was launched in 1995 and lasted in production till 2003. Despite being the most expensive British car ever made at the time, costing £215,000, it sold very well: 1403 were made in total.

B2, B3, SPECTRE & PHOENIX (PININFARINA/COGGIOLA)

Extravagance was the byword of Prince Jefri of Brunei, the independent Sultanate on the island of Borneo. Fuelled by huge riches from oil extraction, he amassed a collection of thousands of luxury cars that simply defied belief. In terms of Bentleys alone, Prince Jefri owned an estimated 380 examples.

In addition to dozens of regular and customised production models, he also ordered many unique coachbuilt versions exclusive to him. Several European coachbuilders were called in to build these very special cars, perhaps the most prestigious being Pininfarina in Italy.

In 1994 the prince asked for the first of a line of coachbuilt Bentleys, awarding the commission to Pininfarina in great secrecy. Two distinct models were developed alongside each other: the B2 (a rebodied Azure convertible) and the B3 (a rebodied Continental R coupe). Since the Azure was already a Pininfarina project, the B2 was constructed at its works. However, Pininfarina was so overwhelmed with other work at the time that the manufacture of the B3 was sub-contracted out to a local coachbuilder, Coggiola (although the B3 was still designed by Pininfarina).

The B2's central body echoed that of the 'donor' Bentley Azure; the main differences were at the front and rear. The styling was entirely different between the B2 and B3. The B2 had unique bumpers, swoopily shaped headlamps and an inclined front grille. In contrast, the B3 was a complete reskin of the Continental R, with more rounded lines, more conventional headlamps and a more upright grille. The interiors, too, were realised to specific requests from Brunei. Some 17 examples of the B2 were made between 1994 and 1996, while 13 examples of the B3 were produced from 1994 to 1995.

Following the B2 and B3, two follow-up models were designed by Pininfarina in 1995: the Spectre and Phoenix. Both were convertibles based on the Bentley Azure. Each had quite different front and rear end treatments: the Spectre was swoopier (somewhat like the B2), while the Phoenix was more traditional (again similar to, but not the same as, the B3). It is thought that the wheels, brakes and exhaust were also upgraded. Between 1995 and 1996, nine examples of the Spectre were made by Pininfarina, plus a further nine of the Phoenix.

CONTINENTAL FLYING STAR (TOURING)

In 2004, Bentley created an internal Continental GT shooting brake proposal, led by Raul Pires Jr, codenamed BY 612, but this didn't go ahead. Then in 2005, the Italian coachbuilder Castagna proposed its own Continental GT-based shooting brake but this was merely a digital rendering and was never built in the metal.

Essentially the same idea was eventually brought to reality by Carrozzeria Touring Superleggera, whose chief designer, Louis de Fabribeckers, developed an estate version of the Continental for launch at the Geneva Show in March 2010. Its name – Continental Flying Star – referenced Touring's Lamborghini Flying Star which had originally trailblazed the shooting brake supercar concept in 1966.

Starting with a Continental GTC (convertible) as a donor, all the bodywork from the A-pillars backwards was changed for new panelwork, which was hand-shaped in steel. The new panels included a unique roof, wider rear wings and reinforcement for the rear chassis. Also new were the rear bumper, brightwork and tail lights. The chief change, however, was the electrically operated tailgate realised in aluminium (the same material being used for the door skins). Inside was an all-new rear compartment with folding rear seats and a flat luggage platform with optional bespoke luggage set.

Each conversion took six months to complete at the eye-watering cost of 590,000 euros. Engineers at Bentley signed off every car before it was delivered. Touring said it would make a maximum of nine examples of the Continental Flying Star, which remains available at the time of writing.

CONTINENTAL GTZ (ZAGATO)

When Andrea Zagato met Bentley's boss, Dr Franz-Josef Paefgen, at the 2006 Pebble Beach Concours d'Elegance, the latter asked if there had ever been any Zagato-bodied Bentleys. On discovering that the answer was no, Paefgen immediately said he'd like to commission one.

The result was launched at the March 2008 Geneva Motor Show. The Continental GTZ retained all the 'hard

LEFT: Zagato's Continental GTZ offered a sharper style than GT coupe. LEFT BELOW: Touring's Flying Star brought shooting brake style to the Continental. BELOW: Ares Design's two-door Bentley Mulsanne Coupe.

points' of the original Bentley Continental GT but the bodywork was entirely new – only the headlights were retained. Zagato's Norihiko Harada designed the striking new set of clothes to a much more flamboyant shape than the original. The front grille was elongated, the haunches were accentuated and the tail made longer and more flowing. Zagato's trademark double-bubble roof was incorporated, the swoopiness flowing into the rear window and boot lid. The upper part of the body could optionally be painted in a contrasting colour. The cabin was left largely standard apart from 'Z' motifs on the seats and a full leather headlining.

Customers would supply their own car and hand it over to Zagato, based just outside Milan. The transformation to GTZ was effected in around four months at a cost of £400,000 on top of the donor car. Production was limited to nine examples in all.

MULSANNE COUPE (ARES)

Ares Design was set up in 2014 by Danny Bahar (ex of Ferrari and Lotus) as a modern Italian coachbuilder. From its base in Modena, it offered a range of special-bodied cars, including – from 2018 – the 'Coupé for Bentley Mulsanne', a two-door version of Bentley's four-door saloon. Since Bentley had ceased production of its own Brooklands two-door coupe in 2011, Ares aimed to exploit this gap in the market.

The Mulsanne's standard wheelbase was retained but extensive work was done to turn it into a two-door coupe. The B-pillars were moved backwards to allow the fitment of longer front doors, while new rear quarter panels were fabricated in aluminium. The new doors and roof panel, meanwhile, were made of carbonfibre. A more flowing roofline and reprofiled C-pillars were integrated into the rear wings. The angle of the rear screen was adjusted and a new section added between the base of the screen and the original boot lid, while bespoke glass with new chrome surrounds was fitted.

Inside, special front seats were needed to permit entry to and egress from the rear seats, while extensive modifications were also carried out to the rear trim panels. At a cost of around £650,000, any Mulsanne made from 2014 to 2017 was suitable for conversion, with Ares claiming its two-door conversion was both lighter and more aerodynamic than the original saloon.

BMC FAMILY

Conglomeration to Collapse

The story of the post-war British motor industry is a roller-coaster ride of spectacular successes, catastrophic failures, economic booms and busts and ultimate implosion. Particularly internecine was the interplay of a multitude of brands that started off in competition with each other but found themselves thrust into often painfully awkward alliances. Economic and governmental pressures forced an era of unmanageably distended amalgamations.

It all started with the April 1952 merger of two of the largest and most significant companies in the UK car industry – Morris Motors and the Austin Motor Company – to form the British Motor Corporation (BMC). This was not just two marques coming together but a whole host of familiar names, since Morris Motors also owned the Nuffield Organisation, which included MG, Riley and Wolseley. Austin would also, in 1952, launch a new sub-marque, Austin-Healey, following a fruitful collaboration with Donald Healey.

Even before the BMC merger, there was evidence of the influence of Italian design thinking within the British motor industry. In his autobiography, Nuffield's British-born designer Gerald Palmer freely admitted this Italian influence in his own penwork. He cited a visit to the 1948 Paris Salon as a pivotal moment: on seeing Pinin Farina's Bentley Cresta, he was inspired to mimic many of its design tropes in his Wolseley 4/44, launched in 1952, while his first thoughts on a replacement for the MG TF sports car were also very Italian-influenced.

In the wake of the 1952 merger, BMC set up the Amalgamated Drawing Office (ADO) as its design and engineering hub. Numbers were assigned to each project under an ADO designation system, which lasted well into the late 1970s, beyond the transmogrification of the company into British Leyland (although the ADO codes were never used for former Leyland Motors marques such as Rover and Triumph).

The tension that exists in almost all car companies between design and engineering departments was particularly acute at BMC. Designers wanted a particular shape; engineers wanted particular characteristics; and often the two did not coincide. There may have been strong arguments from both sides, but compromise was almost inevitable. At BMC, it was hard to ignore the impact of one particularly strong-minded figure: Alec Issigonis. This brilliant Greek-born engineer joined BMC in 1955 from Alvis, having previously designed the iconic Morris Minor in the 1940s. Issigonis's attitude to styling can be appreciated from an interview he did with *Time* magazine in 1962: "My job is not to design fashion accessories or status symbols, but motorcars – things that travel as efficiently as possible from A to B. A car should take its shape from the engineering that goes into it."

This puritanical attitude had a major impact on how cars at BMC developed. Having said this, Issigonis did have a good working relationship

Innocenti was BMC's Italian manufacturing partner and outpost for 15 years. Innocenti's Coupe was a handsome reinterpretation of the Austin-Healey Sprite.

with his styling wing man, Dick Burzi, who had been Chief Stylist at the Austin Motor Company before the 1952 merger. This Argentinean-born designer of Italian parentage had fled Mussolini's Italy in the 1920s and joined Austin on the personal recommendation of Vincenzo Lancia. Burzi's Italian descent led to his internment on the Isle of Man during World War Two, although Austin's boss Leonard Lord intervened to have him freed in the early stages of the conflict.

Although Burzi occupied a styling role right up until 1968, his heyday was undoubtedly the 1950s. His most celebrated work was the so-called 'Counties' range of Austins, while he also designed Austin's flying 'A' bonnet ornament and was behind the ostentatious but ill-fated A90 Atlantic. He also 'Austinised' several other models, including Raymond Loewy's and Tucker Madawick's A40 Somerset and Holden Koto's A30.

The first project that Issigonis and Burzi tackled together was ADO15, the Mini, a car that was hardly 'styled' at all, its look being largely dictated by its novel packaging. At its launch in 1959, there was a certain market resistance to its radical appearance, and the next model that Issigonis worked on – the larger ADO16 – would be designed with the help of Pinin Farina.

The era of Italian influence at BMC and then British Leyland (BLMC/BL) lasted from 1956 well into the 1970s, although it did progressively wane. In 1968, BMC hired a tranche of stylists from Ford, including Harris Mann, who was Chief of Exterior Styling from 1969 to 1983.

By this stage, BMC was bloating. In September 1965, it took control of Pressed Steel, the bodywork supplier, and one year later BMC merged with Jaguar Cars. Then in May 1968 there was another amalgamation with the truck maker, Leyland, which owned Standard-Triumph. A new entity was thus formed: the British Leyland Motor Corporation. BLMC continued to elicit the help of Italian studios for design proposals, including Michelotti, Italdesign and Pininfarina, but by the 1970s design at British Leyland was a largely in-house affair. A new generation of cars, such as the Austin Maxi, Morris Marina, Austin Allegro and Princess 1800/2200, took the company in new, and not always entirely happy, directions.

PININ FARINA & BMC

How Pinin Farina became involved with Austin dates back to a visit to the factory on 8 December 1955 by the Duke of Edinburgh. The story, as reported in the Leonard Lord biography, *Brick by Brick*, goes that Prince Phillip asked Lord whether he "had ever thought of employing an outside designer". On being asked who such a designer might be, the Duke suggested Pinin Farina. Another account says that the Duke opined that Dick Burzi's work wasn't "up to the foreign competition" and that Farina was invited to come to Britain the very next day.

Whatever the story, it is certainly true that mid-1950s design at BMC was looking stuffy and dated. A new fillip was needed and Farina was a natural. His work was already well known in Britain, since his expertise had previously been used for the Nash-Healey. Very soon after the royal visit, Farina signed a contract to design a whole range of new Austins. Work began on the first designs as early as 1956, with three projects in the initial phase. The first to reach the market was the Austin A40 (ADO8) in 1958. Soon after came Farina's new range of mid-size BMC saloons (ADO9). This was the era

when 'badge-engineering' really got into its swing at BMC, with each marque receiving subtly different versions of the same design: Wolseley 15/60, Riley 4/68, Austin A55 Cambridge, MG Magnette and Morris Oxford. Then in 1959 came the third Farina family for BMC, the large ADO53 (Austin A99 Westminster, Vanden Plas Princess 3-Litre and Wolseley 6/99).

Perhaps Pininfarina's most successful and impactful work was on ADO16, the BMC 1100/1300 family. This grew out of an Alec Issigonis project for a larger version of the Mini, and despite the irascible engineer's opposition to stylists, he made an exception for Battista 'Pinin' Farina, whom he regarded as a friend. ADO16, launched in 1962, was a great example of a successful engineer/stylist collaboration, it was an exceptionally clean design that survived the test of time and became Britain's best-selling car for many years. Pininfarina was also entrusted with designing the larger ADO17 (BMC 1800/2200), as well as the MGB GT and a couple of other MG projects that never saw production.

Perhaps Pininfarina's greatest work for BMC was, ironically, a project to which BMC showed singular indifference: the 1800 Berlinetta Aerodinamica of 1967. By this stage, Pininfarina had begun to lose favour in Britain, a process accelerated by the agglomeration of BMC with Leyland and the favouring of another Italian, Giovanni Michelotti, who was Triumph's darling. While Pininfarina was tasked with a few BL design proposals, including for the Morris Marina, Triumph SD2 and ADO88 (the Mini replacement), all were rejected on grounds of cost, as development engineer, Ron Nicholls, recalled: "You could never productionise Farina's stuff without making lots of changes". Pininfarina would only regain favour within BL on one further occasion: the Jaguar XJ Series III of 1979.

BMC's promotional artwork made much of the Italian styling connection, explicitly citing Farina (below) and imagery of Italian architecture (opposite page), although the Austin A40 (far left) was illustrated in a quintessentially British manner as a 'shooting brake'

MICHELOTTI & BMC

While Pininfarina's proposals were increasingly rejected on the grounds of cost, in contrast the services of Giovanni Michelotti were viewed as extremely good value by the British. The full story of Michelotti's association with Standard-Triumph is told in the relevant chapter but suffice to say that he was very much Triumph's design guru when it merged with the British Motor Corporation and Jaguar to form BLMC in 1968. Michelotti's grand touring car, the Triumph Stag, caused big waves at its launch in 1970 but despite this, the Michelotti partnership waned in the new BLMC regime.

Michelotti was called on to make proposals for some non-Triumph cars in the BLMC era, including the Morris Marina (ADO28), Rover P10 (a pre-Rover SD1 project) and ADO74 (Mini replacement), but all were rejected. Michelotti also designed the Leyland-Crompton electric car prototype, and built a Mini-based sports car proposal called ADO70, but the days of Italian design holding sway in British mass-market car industry were over.

Michelotti ADO74

ZAGATO, BERTONE AND ITALDESIGN AT BMC

Zagato assayed some designs on British cars in pre-BMC days, notably the MG Y-Type Panoramica of 1949 and various Jaguars in the 1950s. The BMC Mini Gatto of 1961 was perhaps its most serious contribution to a potential BMC-based production car.

Bertone had comparatively little to do with BMC. The design house did create a successful sports car based on the MG TD in the early 1950s (giving birth

Zagato Mini Gatto

to the Arnolt-MG). Bertone was also a great fan of the Mini, creating his own bespoke 'Mini VIP' in 1965, while the design house's services would be called upon by BL's Italian arm, Innocenti, to create the sharp-suited Mini 90 and 120 in the 1970s.

Italdesign was even less involved; despite the fact that the Morris Ital was named after the design house, Giugiaro helped only with the production engineering and had zero input on the design side.

Coachbuilt MGs

MG Y-TYPE PANORAMICA (ZAGATO)

American businessman, film maker and racer, Roger Barlow, was the man behind the US-based car dealership, International Motors Los Angeles. He was keen on commissioning a run of special MGs to sell to US customers. In 1948, he visited MG's Abingdon works to talk with chief planning engineer, Syd Enever, about modifying the MG Y-Type to his needs. His ideas included lengthening the steering column, lowering the steering wheel, having an optional higher final drive ratio, boosting power to MG TC specification and possibly even adding a supercharger.

Barlow then hotfooted it off to Italy to talk with three coachbuilders – Castagna, Pinin Farina and Zagato – about creating a range of new sports car and touring bodies on the MG chassis, which he would then sell in the USA; the plan was to import around 70 such cars.

Zagato duly created a two-door coupe to its newly-patented 'Panoramica' style. This featured curved Plexiglas cut into the roof at the sides and above the split flat windscreen, the idea being to enhance visibility. Such curved surfaces were quite revolutionary for the time; whether it enhanced the aesthetics is more open to debate. Zagato's MG was rounded to the point of being dumpy; while reasonably successful when viewed from the front, the rear end looked less happy and the lack of a boot lid didn't ease practicality. A cut-down MG grille was used up front, with Zagato's 'Z' badge prominent on the bonnet.

The new car was proudly displayed at the 1949 Lugano Salon in Switzerland, with MG's sales and service manager, John Thornley, in

attendance. However, it seems that neither MG at Abingdon nor Barlow in Los Angeles were sufficiently taken with Zagato's effort to pursue it further, and the car remained a one-off.

MG Y-TYPE (CASTAGNA)

Quite some time after his visit from California to tour Italian coachbuilders in 1948, Roger Barlow commissioned a sports car from one of Italy's most noble coachbuilders, Castagna. This would be the very last chassis ever bodied by the Milanese *carrozzeria*.

Barlow arranged for a 1952 MG Y-Type chassis to be delivered to Italy for Castagna to reclothe as a drophead coupe. It did so in a mixture of steel and aluminium bodywork in a fairly contemporary style, although the standard MG grille was used unaltered, giving the car a traditional flavour. Borrani wire wheels injected a more Italian element, with a fifth wheel mounted on the rear deck as a spare. Twin fuel tanks were installed up front, just ahead of the scuttle. The car was painted red with a black soft top, while the 2+2 cabin was upholstered in black.

The car was picked up personally from Castagna by Barlow in 1954, just after the coachbuilder had gone into receivership. The 1250cc engine was reportedly somewhat asthmatic to drive, leading Barlow to fit a supercharger on its return to the USA.

MG TD BARCHETTA (MOTTO)

Carrozzeria Motto was based in Turin, specialising in making bodywork for racing cars as well as road machinery. Motto became known to an American racing driver called Dave Ash, who also happened to be the East Coast importer for T Series MGs (Inskip Motors). In 1951 he commissioned Rocco Motto to build him a barchetta body on an MG TD chassis. The new panelwork was made of lightweight aluminium to a smart shape that owed much to Italian racing practice.

ABOVE: Motto's smooth aluminium-bodied MG TD barchetta of 1951. LEFT: Castagna MG Y-Type. BELOW: 1956 Schiaretti MG TD. OPPOSITE PAGE: Zagato's 'Panoramica' MG Y-Type.

Motto built two further MG-engined sports cars using special tubular chassis made by Gilberto Colombo (Gilco). Syd Enever of MG provided the 1.25-litre engine, transmission and suspension to Gilco.

All three cars were raced extensively in the USA, not only by Dave Ash but also Fred Allen and Martin Block. Allen and Gus Ehrman finished eleventh overall and fifth in class at the 1954 12 Hours of Sebring, ahead of significant rivals such as Oscas, Porsche 550 Spyders and Kieft MGs.

MG TD (SCHIARETTI)

MG TD chassis number 20325 was originally imported to Italy in December 1952 by Fattori & Montani, the Rome-based MG concessionaire, and sold to Edward Petot, an American soldier who was stationed in Italy. He asked a coachbuilder called Virgilio Schiaretti, based in Parma, to reclothe this MG chassis in the style of an Italian racing barchetta.

Handsome doorless aluminium bodywork was duly constructed, the car being completed in 1956. Modifications from standard included Borrani wire wheels, Andex lever arms at the front end, Alfin drum brakes and an uprated engine (twin Weber carburettors, alloy sump and high-lift camshaft). The one-off returned with Petot to the US in 1959.

THIS PAGE: The car that saved Bertone? MG TD-based coupe and convertible were commercialised in the US by Stanley 'Wacky' Arnolt in 1952. OPPOSITE: Michelotti-designed Ghia-Aigle MG TD at Geneva 1952.

ARNOLT MG (BERTONE)

There can be no doubt of Bertone's status as one of the greatest names in coachbuilding. But had it not been for a pair of cars that Bertone built on MG TD chassis in 1952, the *carrozzeria* could well have sunk without trace. That's not hyperbole, but the genuine situation at the time, as Nuccio Bertone himself stated to the American journalist, Griffith Borgeson. On its knees financially, Bertone asked the Italian MG importer in Rome (Fattori & Montani) to lend him two MG TD chassis to rebody, one as a coupe and the other as a convertible.

Some sources attribute the design to a very youthful Franco Scaglione, then newly employed at Bertone. However, the designer was in fact Giovanni Michelotti, whose creations on the TD chassis were elegant, original and quite unlike the base MG. The enveloping bodywork was handsome, disguising its tall and narrow profile well, even if the MG grille was a dead giveaway of the mechanical basis.

The cars' debut came at the 1952 Turin Show, and on the opening day a certain American approached Bertone asking if he could buy them. Bertone explained that the chassis were not his to sell, but when the man explained he actually wanted to buy 100 of each, Bertone reacted with astonishment and delight – his company was effectively saved.

This American was Stanley Harold 'Wacky' Arnolt, who had made his fortune in World War Two with the Sea-Mite engine and had since formed SH Arnolt Inc in 1950 to import British cars, starting with Morris Minors. Eventually he would represent Rolls-Royce, Aston Martin, Riley and – significantly for this story – MG.

Not only did Arnolt provide the finance to build the cars, he was also appointed a director at the Italian *carrozzeria*. Chassis were bought from MG, shipped by boat to Genoa and transported to Bertone's works in Turin, where the new bodywork was fitted, before being exported to the USA. Here they were marketed as the "family car with sports car styling" from 1953. The prices were $2995 for the coupe and $3145 for the convertible – about a third more than the MG TD.

The main steel body was welded to the chassis rather than being bolted, while the doors, bonnet and boot were made of aluminium. Since all the bodies were hand made, they differed from each other in detail. The cabin made use of an inverted MG TD dash cluster and overall the feeling was much plusher than the regular MG. The cars were fitted with many accessories that Arnolt was selling for MG TDs as standard, including wire wheels.

The Arnolt MG proved to be rather heavy – about 10kg heavier than the base MG TD in open form, and 20kg in coupe guise – and the 1250cc, 55hp MG engine was only sufficient for a top speed of 75mph. A small number of cars used the larger 1.5-litre MG TF engine.

Over the next three years, just over 100 Arnolt MGs were built in all – a lot less than the planned 200. Estimates of the exact split vary between 65 and 67 coupes, and 33 and 35 convertibles, plus the two original prototypes. Wacky Arnolt died in 1963 at the age of 56.

MG TD (GHIA-AIGLE/MICHELOTTI)

In 1952, the Swiss MG distributor, JH Keller, approached the local Swiss branch of Ghia, known as Ghia-Aigle, about creating more modern bodywork on the MG TD chassis. Giovanni Michelotti was tasked with the design work.

The new design broke cover at the 1952 Geneva Show. Unlike the very traditional feel of the TD 'Midget', Michelotti's design was resolutely modern, with full-width bodywork and a well-proportioned elegance. If there were a traditional element, it was the upright MG-badged grille, either side of which sat cowled headlamps. The sharp-edged rear wing line flowed all the way down to the full-width bumper.

As well as the convertible, Michelotti also designed an MG TD coupe for Ghia-Aigle with a completely different shape to the drop-top. In addition to its fixed roof with rear quarter-lights, the coupe had a taller waistline and reshaped front and rear wings. The nose was also new: out went the upright grille of the convertible and in came a wider, flatter affair that incorporated curious

foglights. Small headlamps were positioned at the front end of the wings, while the lower, flatter bonnet featured a small air scoop.

Some sources say that Ghia-Aigle was supplied with six MG TD chassis but exactly how many TD-based cars were actually made is not certain. It seems that, in addition to the 1952 Geneva car (chassis TD-22878), at least one more convertible was built: chassis TD-25580, painted red with a blue interior and blue roof, which debuted at Geneva in 1954. This was later converted to a hardtop coupe in Switzerland, featuring a wraparound rear screen.

MG TD (VIGNALE)

In 1953, one year after Giovanni Michelotti's Ghia-Aigle MG TD, he designed another MG TD body, this time for Vignale. MG sent a TD chassis out to Turin, on to which a steel structure was added to support the doors, scuttle and windscreen.

This was a much more flamboyant design altogether, a very glitzy affair that was laden with chrome adornments. The high-waisted side profile was quite elegant but many aspects appeared heavy-handed. The front end looked particularly awkward with its inset egg-crate grille, over the top of which the front bumper appeared to snake; below was a body-colour valance bearing the MG logo. The body sides had a big chrome flash running down them, while an odd 'porthole' motif appeared on the front wings. The main body was painted red but the roof was in black.

The very luxurious interior featured wood veneer and was trimmed in light brown and black. The leather front bench was split to seat two, with the area behind reserved for a cocktail cabinet with space for two bottles and four glasses.

The bodywork was entirely of aluminium so that, despite the extra chrome, coupe roof and luxurious appointments, it weighed only 950kg, some 50kg more than the MG TD. With 65hp from the TD engine, a top speed of 85mph and 0-60 mph in 19.4 seconds were claimed.

Only one MG TD 'Midget' appears to have been made by Vignale, which ended up in Switzerland, but Vignale did build a very similar body to this one year later on a Fiat 8V chassis.

TOP LEFT: Ghia-Aigle coupe and convertible had quite distinct shapes. TOP: Monviso's pretty MG TF Everest. ABOVE: Vignale-bodied MG TD of 1953 was styled by Michelotti. OPPOSITE PAGE: Pietro Frua penned the handsome MGA-based EX205/2. Scale model shows EX205/3 coupe.

MG TF EVEREST (MONVISO)

Stabilimento Monviso of Turin was one of Italy's lesser-known coachbuilders, making special bodywork on Fiat 1100 chassis under the name Stella Alpina. It aimed higher with the Everest of 1954, which was a pretty convertible body on an MG TF chassis (number 5014). The TF basis was only really revealed by the front grille, which came straight from the MG.

Probably the most striking design feature was the prominent 'Everest' lettering on the front wings. Other details included an upward-sloping nose and headlights, oblong foglights, small rear fins and squared rear wheelarches. It was painted light green with a dark blue interior. After winning a prize at the Enghein concours in Belgium, it is thought that the car was sold to a Moroccan, possibly the King of Morocco.

MGA EX205/2 (FRUA)

When MG launched its new MGA sports car in 1955, it was extremely well received. BMC very quickly began to think about a successor – indeed MG at Abingdon was working on what would become the MGB as early as 1957. MG's Syd Enever also decided to send an MGA chassis to Carrozzeria Pietro Frua of Turin, to see what it could do.

Under the project designation EX205/2 (not EX214 as is sometimes quoted), Frua created a particularly attractive roadster that had echoes of contemporary Maseratis. Design features included a profoundly concave grille, ornate U-shaped front bumper, panoramic windscreen, waistline crease with a chromed accent and modest tail fins with integrated rear lights.

The aluminium bodywork was painted red with red-piped cream leather upholstery and a white soft-top. A hardtop was also developed for it, also in white. The cabin used standard MGA instruments and controls in a plush new setting.

In spring 1957 Frua's prototype was delivered to MG in Abingdon for assessment. Later that year, an alternative fastback shape was suggested in a 1:4 model built by Harry Herring (the so-called EX205/3). However it seems that Frua's design was not well received at MG. Various objections have been suggested as the reason for its rejection: its design was too ornate; it weighed too much; and it would have been too expensive to produce in series. Whatever the reason, MG pursued its own in-house path for what would become the MGB. Later in 1957, Frua's prototype was apparently destroyed with acetylene torches in front of a customs officer in order to avoid import duties.

Coachbuilt Rileys

Riley became part of the Nuffield Organisation, alongside Morris and MG, in 1938. Its chassis were never as widely rebodied as MG's but a handful of cars, mostly Riley RMs, were coachbuilt in Italy.

It is thought that Stabilimenti Farina may have built its own convertible body on an RM chassis but no images have ever emerged. Bertone definitely did create bodywork on the RM chassis. This was very similar in style to the Nardi-Danese built by Bertone for Marco Fabio Crespi in 1947. Designed by Mario Revelli di Beaumont, it was an imposingly large four-seat drophead convertible whose elegance of line was somewhat curtailed by its lengthy wheelbase. The Bertone Riley was first seen at the 1947 Triennale Exhibition in Milan and later appeared in a 1952 Italian movie, *Cinque Poveri in Automobile*. It is thought that the car was eventually rebodied in the UK in the late 1950s to a completely different style.

One further RM was rebodied in Italy, by Vignale. Seen at the April 1951 Turin Show, this was a sports saloon designed to a style typical of Vignale in that era. The Riley upright grille was clearly employed, with a striking highlight line stretching from the side grilles around the main grille and alongside the bonnet.

It is thought that Giovanni Michelotti designed one further Riley for the Swiss-Italian coachbuilder, Ghia-Aigle, in the 1950s but sadly no hard information on this project has ever come to light.

THIS PAGE, TOP TO BOTTOM: 1947 Bertone Riley RM; Vignale Riley RM of 1951; front and rear views of Cattelan's one-off Austin-Healey 100. OPPOSITE PAGE, TOP TO BOTTOM: Motto's reworked Healey front end; same for Ghia-Aigle Sprite; Healey 3000 GT-based Firrere of 1962.

Coachbuilt Austin-Healeys

AUSTIN-HEALEY 100 (CATTELAN)

While posted with the US Air Force in Tripoli, Libya in 1954, David S Ehrich Jr bought a brand new Austin-Healey 100. After being transferred to Italy in 1955, the pilot took the car with him but while there it was badly damaged in a crash. He decided to take the wreck to Fratelli Cattelan, a coachbuilder based in Udine. Cattelan's heyday as a coachbuilder was prior to World War Two, but it was still operating after the war, mostly making commercial vehicle and light bus bodywork. Excited by the prospect of creating a new sports car body, it designed all-new panelwork for the crashed car.

The task took five months to complete. The resulting roadster had a completely different, and very Italian, look compared to the Austin-Healey. The low nose featured a Ferrari-like 'eggcrate' grille straddled by quarter bumpers and lightly hooded headlamps. Behind squared-off rear wheelarches was an all-new tail with low-set upright lights and small bumperettes. A wraparound windscreen replaced the original fold-down item and Cattelan also made a removable hardtop for the car. Mechanically the Healey remained unchanged.

The car was completed in May 1956 and driven by its owner to the UK, from where it was shipped back to New Jersey in the USA. Sadly the car's current whereabouts are unknown.

AUSTIN-HEALEY 100 (MOTTO)

Carrozzeria Motto was tasked, in 1957, with creating a new front end for an Austin-Healey 100 owned by a US army officer based in Italy. Only the front end was changed but the effect was striking: a very smooth, rounded new nose featuring cowled headlamps and a low-set grille, suiting the look of the Healey quite well.

AUSTIN-HEALEY SPRITE (GHIA-AIGLE)

In around 1959, Ghia-Aigle (via Pietro Frua) restyled the characteristic 'frogeye' front end of the Austin-Healey Sprite with a rather more conventional look. This featured a deeply inset oval grille and wider-set headlamps located in nacelles. The bodywork aft of the new glassfibre bonnet was left untouched.

AUSTIN-HEALEY 3000 GT FIRRERE & ADO30 (PININFARINA)

In late 1961, the Swiss motoring annual, *l'Année Automobile*, launched a competition to celebrate its tenth anniversary. Open to all, the brief was to design "an automobile which allows at least two people with luggage to make long journeys in all weathers with speed, comfort and safety" – in other words, a feasible production prospect rather than a 'dream car'. It had to be based on one of these production chassis: AC Greyhound, Alfa Romeo 2000, Austin Healey 3000, BMW 3200, Bristol 406, Ferrari 250 GT, Lancia Flaminia, Maserati 3500GT and Triumph TR4 – note the preponderance of British cars here.

The winning entry came from Germany, specifically the Hochschule für Gestaltung in Ulm. Three students here – Henner Werner, Pio Manzoni (aka Manzù) and Michael Conrad – collaborated on a coupe based on the Austin-Healey 3000. Manzù, incidentally, would go on to become an eminent car designer, famously penning the Fiat 127.

Their design was graceful, resolved and mature. The front end was formed as a single piece, with the horizontal slits of the grille simply stamped out. Boosting the sense of smoothness were Plexiglas coverings over the headlights and indicators, while the door handles were sunk into the bodywork behind the doors.

A thin bonnet bulge gave it a spine-like feel and a subtle waistline crease began on the front wings and wrapped right around the car to the rear end. The fastback roof profile did not preclude a small boot opening. The overall effect was sharp yet aerodynamic, and, said Manzu, "coherent with the history and traditions of the famous British marque". Manzu later released drawings of a convertible version of the car, which looked very elegant.

L'Année Automobile arranged for Pininfarina to build the car ahead of exhibiting it at major international motor shows (in October 1962 at the London Earls Court show, the month after at Turin, and again at Geneva in 1963). It was painted metallic green with an ivory leather interior, and on its nose was a badge inscribed with the car's name: 'Firrere'.

The sole prototype was immediately acquired by BMC. To the outside world, that was that. But within BMC, minds were feverishly working. In the Firrere, BMC's chairman and chief executive, George Harriman, saw a potential Austin-Healey-badged rival for the Jaguar E-Type.

A new project was set up – ADO30 – with high hopes. This was to be a technological tour de force, featuring Hydrolastic suspension and a Rolls-Royce 4.0-litre six-cylinder engine. This powerplant was chosen for the simple reason that BMC had committed to buying a lot of engines from Rolls-Royce to use in the Vanden Plas Princess 4-Litre R, but slow sales of that model left BMC with a stockpile of engines and nowhere to use them.

The new sports car was nicknamed Fireball XL-5 at the factory (after the spaceship in Gerry Anderson's science-fiction TV series) but the plan was to launch it as the Austin-Healey 4000. But that never came to pass. The handling was reportedly woeful, the Belgian racing driver Paul Frère recalling that "it was too heavy and Hydrolastic wasn't really right for a sports car". The Jaguar/BMC merger of July 1966 should really have put an immediate stop to the project but development was allowed to progress. However, when feasibility studies showed that the 4000 would have cost more to produce than the E-Type, it was finally abandoned in 1967. Sadly no images exist to show us how ADO30 might have looked.

BMC Farinas

ADO8: AUSTIN A40 (PININ FARINA)

ADO8 represented the first phase of BMC's collaboration with Pinin Farina. Only a matter of months after signing a deal with the Italian design house, Pinin Farina's first mock-up was ready to be delivered to Longbridge in 1956. Its clean, unadorned styling marked a total contrast with the car it was replacing, Dick Burzi's Austin A35. Flat panels and crisp wing lines were Farina's signature at that time, in the wake of its hugely influential Lancia Florida concept. This being the mid-1950s and an era dominated by Americanesque fins, the A40 had a sharply finned rear wing treatment with vertical light clusters.

Farina's original mock-up went on to be adopted virtually unchanged in production. The prototype had thin roof pillars that were thickened up, while the window frames were simplified to cut costs. An in-house BMC attempt to fit a small grille was thankfully rejected in favour of Farina's full-width original.

Farina worked to strict packaging requirements, which meant keeping many elements of the A35 untouched. For instance, it used the same 948cc A-Series engine, very similar suspension and steering, even the same instrument panel. Farina's extended roofline cleverly created a 'two-box' shape with the rear window almost at the same angle as the bootlid. This was a stylistic innovation of great significance, for here was the template for the future: the two-box design would eventually be adopted almost universally for small cars.

The shape gave birth to another significant innovation: the possibility of making the boot much more accessible by hinging the rear window at the top – what we now call a hatchback. In the 1959 A40 Countryman's case, it was a horizontally-split tailgate, the lower half hinging down and the upper half upwards, supplemented by a fold-down rear seat. When BMC's Italian licensee, Innocenti,

produced its own version of the A40 (see page 107), it took the next logical step and developed a single bootlid hinged at the roof – the world's first full mass-produced hatchback.

The importance Pinin Farina felt for the project can be judged by the fact that both Battista and his son Sergio attended the 1958 launch of the new model at Longbridge. Reciprocating the gesture, BMC actually suffixed the A40 with a 'Farina' sigil.

The A40 MkII of 1961 was updated slightly: it had a four-inch longer wheelbase, while Pininfarina added a wider front grille and different headlamps. The A40 was a storming sales success: between 1958 and 1967, some 342,280 examples were built.

ADO9: 'BIG FARINAS' (PININ FARINA)

Hot on the heels of the A40, Pinin Farina rushed in a replacement for the ageing Austin A55. This was codenamed ADO9 at BMC, while contemporary Farina documentation refers to it as the Austin A50.

Unsurprisingly, perhaps, the new saloon picked up on many elements of the Austin A40's design, including its wide grille, crisp surfaces and rear fins.

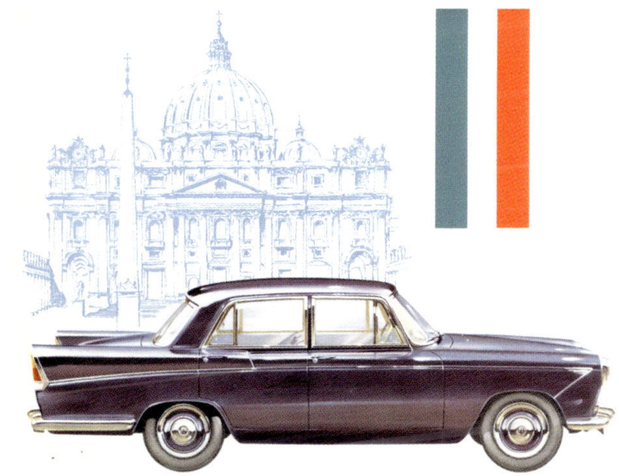

As with the A40, Farina's prototype was accepted by BMC with very few changes for production – only the original reverse-angle front end squared-off windows were revised.

Undoubtedly the ADO9 saloon was less successful, stylistically speaking, than the A40. Many commentators compared it to the Peugeot 404 and Fiat 1800 that Farina did contemporaneously – and unfavourably, since the French and Italian efforts indisputably received a crispness of line that the British car lacked. ADO9's narrow track and short wheelbase didn't help, making it look dumpy and over-bodied. As with the A40, the new suit of clothes hid somewhat archaic underpinnings, too: the 1489cc B-Series engine was carried over from the old Austin Cambridge, for instance.

Pininfarina's design was publicly revealed in December 1958 as the Wolseley 15/60. Battista's personal image was widely used in publicity for the new Wolseley 'Farina', even though the Italian had in fact created only the Austin version (the so-called A55 MkII that launched in January 1959); all detail alterations for the many badge-engineered BMC versions were done in-house by Dick Burzi and Sid Goble. After the Wolseley and Austin came the MG Magnette MkIII (February 1959), Morris Oxford V (March 1959) and Riley 4/68 (April 1959). As well as the saloon, estate versions (named Countryman and Traveller) also proved popular.

In 1960, Farina was asked to perform a facelift, codenamed ADO38, which duly reached the market in 1961. Most members of the family lost their now-unfashionable rear fins (only the MG Magnette and estate body styles persisted with them). Other changes included a slightly extended wheelbase and a new grille. Most models in the range were renamed (as the Austin A60 Cambridge, MG Magnette MkIV, Morris Oxford VI, Riley 4/72 and Wolseley 16/60).

Production lasted until 1969 for the most part, although the Wolseley limped on until 1971 as the very last of BMC's rear-wheel drive medium saloons. Honest, tough and reliable, but ultimately rather dull, the ADO9 family was nevertheless very popular, with over 1.5 million sold.

OPPOSITE PAGE TOP TO BOTTOM: A40 in production form; Leonard Lord and George Harriman with Battista and Sergio Pininfarina at 1958 launch; 1956 prototype. THIS PAGE, CLOCKWISE FROM TOP: Farina's 'Austin A50' prototype; early ADO9 mock-up; production A55; Italian-themed Wolseley 15/60 brochure.

ADO53: 'FULL-SIZE FARINAS' (PININ FARINA)

Pinin Farina started work on the largest of BMC's new family of cars, codenamed ADO53, at about the same time as it did ADO8 and ADO9. Stylistically this was intimately related to ADO9, sharing essentially the same three-box profile, upright glasshouse and kinked rear wing line with small fins. Somehow the larger dimensions seemed to suit the style better.

Farina itself referred to the prototype as the Austin A90, and once again this was very little altered in production form. The new car reached the market in 1959 in three badge-engineered versions: the Austin A99 Westminster, Wolseley 6/99 and (codenamed ADO37) the Vanden Plas Princess 3-Litre.

The Austin A99 had its own plain grille, while the Wolseley received a more traditional upright grille, sculpted bonnet, foglamps, chrome side strip and luxury trim. The posh Vanden Plas had its own unique grille and hubcaps, no bonnet scoop, extra sound deadening and leather and wood aplenty. There was even a Touring Limousine option.

Powering all three versions was a BMC C-series six-cylinder engine bored out to 2912cc and fitted with twin carburettors. An all-synchromesh three-speed gearbox had double overdrive and was controlled from the steering column; automatic was optional. One innovation was servo-assisted disc front brakes, a first for an Austin saloon.

In 1961 a revised range was presented: Austin A110, Wolseley 6/110 and Vanden Plas 3-Litre MkII. All featured a longer wheelbase, extra power, more luxury and the option of power steering and air conditioning from 1962, with four speeds standard from 1964. That year also saw the launch of a new variant (codenamed ADO66): the Vanden Plas 4-Litre R. That unassuming 'R' was BMC's way of saying that under the bonnet sat a Rolls-Royce engine: a twin-carburettor 3909cc straight-six. The body was identical to the 3-Litre except for cut-down tail fins, a longer and flatter roofline, horizontal tail lights and built-in foglamps. Rolls-Royce also briefly considered making its own version. Production of all Austin, Wolseley and Vanden Plas variants ended in 1968.

THIS PAGE: Largest of the 'Farina' BMC family was ADO53. Prototype 'Austin A90' (left) was taken almost unchanged into production as the A99. OPPOSITE PAGE: Farina's early ADO16 prototype (top left) was only mildly altered for the production version.

ADO16: BMC 1100/1300 (PININ FARINA)

What became the ADO16 started life in 1958 as the XC9001, itself a front-wheel drive evolution of an even earlier project called XC9000 that started off with rear-wheel drive, a car that represented Alec Issigonis in his most rationalistic, anti-styling phase.

The XC9001 project eventually split into XC9003 – which evolved into the Mini, a car with no Italian design influence at all – and XC9002. Issigonis's original XC9002 shape was effectively an enlarged Mini in looks. Indeed, BMC judged that it looked too similar to the Mini, so in early 1958 Leonard Lord invited Pinin Farina to come up with its own proposal for XC9002.

What Farina effected was a perfect transformation from ugly duckling to swan. Engineering imperatives firmly took the lead, and considering the restrictions imposed on the Italian designer – pared-down overall length, minimal overhangs, short bonnet – the Italian designer did an excellent job.

Pinin Farina delivered its full-size design mock-up to BMC as early as October 1958. The initial proposal had a very bluff front end and some complex-to-manufacture aspects like the glasshouse, so BMC asked the Italians to tweak the shape. By July 1959 – with the project now known as ADO16 – the essential shape for the forthcoming Morris 1100 was fixed.

BMC's designers in Britain widened Farina's shape somewhat to provide space in the back for three adults. One clever trick employed was curved front side windows – a first for a British car

– to make the most of the interior space. The cabin was designed by the Longbridge Styling Department, headed by Dick Burzi.

Morris was the first of BMC's marques to launch with the new small saloon, the Morris 1100 arriving in August 1962, a full year before the Austin 1100. As with ADO9, it was BMC's in-house team that tweaked Farina's template to create a bewilderingly wide variety of badge-engineered versions. The MG 1100 arrived later in 1962, sporting an MG grille, hub caps and badges, plus a twin-carb engine. It was followed by the Austin 1100 and the plush Vanden Plas Princess in 1963, then the Riley Kestrel in 1965. Larger-engined 1300 models followed, giving rise to the commonly used term BMC 1100/1300 for this sprawling model range.

This was a very advanced car for its time, offering Hydrolastic interconnected suspension, front disc brakes and sharp front-wheel drive handling. Several body styles were offered: two- and four-door saloons and a three-door Traveller estate, and even a sporty-looking GT from 1969. The MkII of 1967, meanwhile, had its tail fins trimmed down.

Without its crisp, sleek looks, ADO16 would probably not have become such a success, emerging as Britain's best-selling car for years; a total of well over two million were made in Britain up until 1974. Many regard the 1100/1300 family as the best-looking small saloon car of the 1960s, perfecting the two-box look that would sweep the design world in the following decades. In Japan, it achieved a surprising cult status due to its clean design.

This was definitely a case where good design overcame weaknesses: for instance, it was hardly a paragon of reliability, with sagging Hydrolastic suspension and rampaging rust all too common. Despite its shortcomings, this was perhaps the most successful car of the whole BMC era.

ADO16: AUSTIN APACHE & VICTORIA (MICHELOTTI)

In South Africa, the local BL outpost (called Leykor) was looking for a new mid-sized saloon to complement its range. It was allowed to pick up a design that Michelotti had proposed for an ADO16 three-box saloon. Its rear end was extended to allow for a saloon boot to be added but the car was also substantially restyled front and rear, aping the look of Michelotti's Triumph 2000.

The new car entered production as the Austin Apache in December 1971. Some 21,665 were made between 1971 and 1977, making this the very last ADO16 variant to be made anywhere.

In Spain, BL's subsidiary Authi also built a slightly modified version of the Apache under the name Austin Victoria at its Pamplona plant between 1972 and 1975. The standard Victoria had rectangular headlights, while the upmarket TC and Deluxe versions had four round front lights.

ADO17: BMC 1800/2200 (PININ FARINA)

Yet another offshoot of BMC's original XC9001 proposal was an even larger car designed to slot in above the 1100/1300, codenamed ADO17. Pinin Farina again got the nod to develop this model's styling but the long wheelbase that Issigonis insisted on using was a real constraint. ADO17 would eventually emerge as a triumph of space over style.

Farina's initial proposal, submitted in 1959, had a four-light glasshouse and looked very much like a larger version of ADO16 – in fact, far too much like it. BMC asked Farina to have another go and its next proposal went in the opposite direction, with an ostentatious front end featuring quad headlamps and a very wide front grille, similar to other Farina efforts such as the 1957 Buick Lido and 1959 Fiat 2100 Coupe. The front end was soon toned down with a more conventional grille and single headlamps, but the proposal had already established the six-light window arrangement that would be adopted on the production model.

By 1960, the shape had pretty much been finalised, even if Alec Issigonis did fiddle with the Farina shape in detail, for instance ditching the chromed window surrounds. The end result was nowhere near as well proportioned as ADO16 and adjectives such as 'sturdy' and 'robust' were used, rather than elegant. Pundits nicknamed it the 'Landcrab'.

ADO17 would be presented to the public as the Austin 1800 in September 1964, with a badge-engineered Morris variant following two years later and the Wolseley 18/85 in 1967. It was quite well received at the time, even being voted European Car of the Year for 1965, and had many advanced features like front-wheel drive and cosseting Hydrolastic suspension. However, few look back on it with any fondness from a design point of view. This would be the last complete car designed by Farina for BMC.

OPPOSITE PAGE: Michelotti altered ADO16's front and rear for the Austin Apache and Victoria saloons.
ABOVE & BELOW: BMC 1800 'Landcrab' was a triumph of substance over style.
RIGHT: XC9001 prototype looked dowdy.

BMC 1800 BERLINA AERODINAMICA (PININFARINA)

In the 1960s, Pininfarina had a small but waning foothold in the BMC organisation. Aiming to re-establish a liaison, it decided to create, on its own initiative, a show-stealing shop window of its design capabilities using the BMC ADO17 (Austin/Morris 1800) as a basis.

During 1967, drawings and models were created. While some people have credited the car's design to Leonardo Fioravanti, it was in fact Paolo Martin who was the chief architect, as evidenced by a number of contemporary design sketches that bear his name.

An example of an Austin 1800 De Luxe arrived at Pininfarina's works on 10 August 1967 and the prototype was built up into a fully functional car in just nine weeks. It was first shown at the Turin Motor Show In November 1967 as the BMC Berlina Aerodinamica (incidentally the only car ever to have been badged 'BMC').

The shape was as smooth and svelte as the BMC 1800 'Landcrab' was stodgy and frumpy. The elegant two-box shape was a four-door saloon with a hinged tailgate – a somewhat revolutionary idea at the time. As its name suggested, this was an exercise in aerodynamism. The front end was low and rounded with headlamps behind cowls and a hidden cooling grille. The profile was a gentle wedge, culminating in a cut-off 'Kamm' tail. The roofline was continuously curving, the roof pillars were thin to enhance interior light and visibility – even the apparently chunky C-pillars actually had slanted louvres to give the impression of strength without blocking the view out. The windows were frameless, while ribbed rear light clusters were designed to avoid dirt building up. The claimed drag co-efficient (Cd) was radically improved from 0.45 to 0.35. Pininfarina suggested it could reduce this even further by making the wheels sit flush with the bodywork.

Inside, the adjustable electric seat mechanisms and electric windows were derived from Rolls-Royce, while the door handles, steering column and stalks all came from Ferrari.

The prototype was mechanically standard ADO17, except for a slight tweak to the engine's rocker cover so that it would fit under the low nose. During test drives on the Turin-Ivrea autostrada, the car exceeded 106mph, compared to 94mph achieved by Sergio Pininfarina's own standard

OPPOSITE PAGE & LEFT: Pininfarina BMC 1800 Aerodinamica of 1967 was truly ground-breaking in design terms. ABOVE & BELOW: 1100 version was stubbier but still very attractive. BOTTOM: Paolo Martin's wild initial sketch.

BMC 1800, and it was reportedly very stable in a straight line. The prototype weighed in at 1360kg (3000lb), but Pininfarina estimated that a production version would be 136kg (300lb) lighter.

The prototype was sent to Longbridge for assessment. Alec Issigonis was positive but his view held less sway by this time than men like Harry Webster (who preferred Michelotti) and Roy Haynes, who didn't like the idea at all. At a time when the British Leyland merger was looming, there was no appetite for such a model, which was rejected as too expensive and complex for mass production. That may well have been true; and for this reason perhaps we should not lament too much that BMC missed a major opportunity to enter production with such an advanced machine.

The shape was widely admired – and indeed widely copied. It strongly influenced the styling of the 1970 Citroën GS and a string of other cars of the 1970s, such as the Citroën CX, Rover SD1 and Lancia Gamma. After being used extensively by chief engineer Harry Webster, Pininfarina's BMC 1800 prototype (which was nicknamed the 'Yellow Peril') was, tragically, destroyed in the late 1970s.

BLMC 1100 BERLINA AERODINAMICA (PININFARINA)

Pininfarina revisited the two-box saloon formula in 1968, using BMC's smaller ADO16 (1100/1300). Paolo Martin also styled the 1100 version, doing a great job of scaling down the shape. Its profile looked somewhat similar, if visually taller because of the shorter length. The main differences were an indented rib along the body flank and door handles that were cleverly hidden in the chromed window surrounds. Reflecting the morphing of

LEFT: 1100 Aerodinamica could have been a BMC world-beater. LEFT BELOW: Three-door '1000' mock-up. BELOW: Bertone Mini-Cooper 'VIP' had a new nose and plush cabin. OPPOSITE PAGE: Zagato's Mini Gatto of 1961 had unresolved styling.

BMC into BLMC, the prototype wore a BLMC badge on its nose. Had this car made production, it would have been a sure-fire contender in the popular medium-sized hatchback market epitomised by the Volkswagen Golf. But BLMC had just as little interest in Pininfarina's ADO16-based car as it did in the 1800. The prototype survives at the British Motor Museum at Gaydon.

A very similar-looking three-door mock-up was also built by BLMC at Longbridge as an extrapolation of Pininfarina's Aerodinamica idea. This was based on a long-wheelbase Minivan platform and had 10-inch wheels. Sometimes referred to as the 1000 Aerodinamica, it could have become a radical new version of the Mini. Sadly, it suffered the same fate as the other two Aerodinamica concepts and had no production future.

MINI VIP (BERTONE)

As the Mini was in its final stages of development, BMC presented its ideas to Battista Pinin Farina, asking for his opinion about what needed to be changed, design-wise. Farina is reputed to have said: "Leave it. It is unique." That was why, unusually for a BMC product of the late 1950s, the Mini had zero input from the Italian designer. The Mini certainly had its admirers in Italy, though: Enzo Ferrari personally owned no fewer than three Mini-Coopers, while Ferrari's engineer Aurelio Lampredi is reputed to have declared on driving a Mini for the first time, "If it were not so ugly, I would shoot myself".

Perhaps his words were still ringing in Nuccio Bertone's ears when, on John Cooper's instigation, Bertone bought a right-hand drive Austin Mini-Cooper 1275 'S'. After being spirited off to Turin, Bertone converted it to a very luxurious specification in 1965. From the outside, the so-called Mini VIP was discreetly upgraded: extra indicators on the front wings, Bertone badging, Riley Elf bumpers, Fiat 500 rear lights and metallic blue paint. In its initial guise, the front end featured a controversial upright centre grille and mustachio side grilles but this was later

changed by John Cooper to a more conventional Mini-shape grille, albeit lightly modified.

The cabin received a lot of attention, including reclining front seats with headrests, electric windows, angled quarter-lights, a clock and fully trimmed doors. The facia was all-new, featuring a sizeable aluminium instrument binnacle with an angled switch panel and no fewer than seven dials. A sweeping centre console housed items like the radio and electric window switches. In the rear, the bench was heavily sculpted for two, while bizarre rear headrests dangled down from the roof.

Back in the UK, where luxury Minis were all the rage (via companies such as Radford and Wood & Pickett), the Cooper Car Co offered Bertone's VIP conversion in 1966. The price was a substantial £500 over and above the Cooper S's £818 price tag; but in the event, production of the VIP never started because of objections from BMC.

MINI GATTO (ZAGATO)

The Mini's use of subframes meant that rebodying was fairly straightforward and Zagato of Milan was one of the very first coachbuilders to tackle such a project in 1961. The instigation came from a British-based, Italian-born engineer called Vincenzo Piatti, the creator of the Piatti motor scooter brand, which was active between 1948 and 1956. The project was given the name Mini Gatto (Mini Cat).

This was one of Ercole Spada's earliest designs at Zagato. Over the long-wheelbase floorpan of the Minivan, he created a three-box shape that never really escaped the limitations of its donor vehicle, particularly the tall engine, and the end result was not exactly pretty. The cowled headlamps gave the car its 'Mini Cat' name, as they reminded Spada of a cat's eyes, but perhaps the most striking aspect of the design was a single keyline extending right the way around the body at waist level.

The 3680mm overall length was over 600mm longer than the Mini saloon and while it was exactly the same width (1397mm) as the Mini, it was quite a bit lower (1220mm versus 1346mm). The bodywork was realised in aluminium, attached to the floorpan via steel strips. This kept weight down to 610kg (about 16kg less than a Mini). That in turn enabled top speed claims of over 80mph using standard Mini 850 mechanicals, or 93mph if a Mini 1000 engine were used – significantly faster than the regular saloons.

The United Kingdom concessionaire for Zagato at the time was Anthony Crook Motors, which exhibited the car at the Earls Court Motor Show of 1961. Here a price of £1200 was announced, with production scheduled to take place in Britain at a rate of 30 per week, using glassfibre rather than aluminium bodywork. However that never came about, almost certainly because BMC wasn't at all keen on the idea. Only one Mini Gatto was ever built, a right-hand drive car with Mini-Cooper 1000 mechanicals, which Piatti used himself, and which survives to this day. The basic idea of the Mini Gatto would soon be resurrected for Zagato's Hillman Imp-based Zimp (see page 242).

ADO34/ADO35: MG MINI SPORTS CAR (PININFARINA)

It had initially been in BMC's plans to make an MG-badged version of the Mini called the MG M-Type. Styling sketches were done and two prototypes were built in 1963, but the project never came to fruition, more than likely because the Mini-Cooper fulfilled the role of the sporting Mini so flawlessly.

However, BMC also contemplated a small MG sports car based on the long-wheelbase Minivan platform. Conceived in 1959 by MG's Syd Enever, project ADO34 was to be a small open-topped front-wheel drive sports car. The original Abingdon-designed proposal looked like a scaled-down MGB but it never progressed beyond the mock-up stage, as it was effectively killed off by the arrival of the Midget, MG's adaptation of the Austin-Healey Sprite.

The idea was revisited in 1964, when the ADO34 project – by now based at Longbridge – was given to Pininfarina to design a completely new version. The main design challenge was the Mini's tall engine, which Pininfarina got around quite elegantly by using a straight-through waistline. The soft-top was an object lesson in simplicity and functionality, and overall the design perhaps had hints of Pininfarina's Peugeot 204 Convertible about it.

Pininfarina eschewed the previous Minivan floorpan basis in favour of a new steel chassis into which Mini subframes were bolted, while a Cooper 1275 'S' engine was fitted to make it a runner. Pininfarina's prototype, painted pale green, was delivered to MG in Abingdon for assessment. The car reportedly drove just like a Mini, which was nothing but positive news, while some of the Mini's faults, like the lack of legroom and bus-like steering wheel angle, were resolved in the two-seater.

MG stylists then had a stab at an MG-badged coupe version of the ADO34, which was given the project number ADO35 – essentially no more than the ADO34 with a fastback roof added – while an Austin-Healey-badged variant (ADO36) was also mooted. It's thought that at least one version of the ADO35 coupe was built by Pininfarina, supplied as a non-runner and then given an engine in Abingdon. ADO34/ADO35 came quite close to getting the green light for production but Issigonis was dead against any idea of making a two-seat Mini derivative – and so, ultimately, was BMC's management.

Luckily the ADO34 prototype survives, currently residing at the British Motor Industry Heritage Collection at Gaydon. The ADO35 coupe also survives in the hands of a private enthusiast.

BELOW, TOP TO BOTTOM: MGB-style ADO34 by Syd Enever; ADO35 coupe; Pininfarina's ADO34 MG convertible.

ADO70: CALYPSO (MICHELOTTI)

In a similar fashion to ADO35, ADO70 (also called Calypso) was to be a new Mini-based sports car. Conceived in 1969, it was to be targeted principally at the US market and might well have replaced the MG Midget and possibly the Triumph Spitfire and Mini-Cooper as well.

The design is sometimes attributed to Michelotti but in fact the Italian *carrozzeria* merely built the prototype. The design work was all done in-house in the UK by Robin Owens and Paul Hughes. With the design approved by BLMC's Harry Webster, a Mini 1275GT was sent to Michelotti in Italy and suitably adapted (for instance, the steering wheel was repositioned). Michelotti finished building the car in a mere two months. Innocenti was given the task of making the car driveable and the prototype successfully returned to the UK under its own steam in the summer of 1970.

The targa roof was specified because US safety legislation for soft-tops was becoming more stringent, but it didn't help the overall aesthetics. Indeed, in contrast to the clean and elegant lines of Pininfarina's ADO35, the Calypso looked rather fussy. It also proved to be somewhat overweight.

BLMC's board originally thought it could sell 80,000 Calypsos a year, probably badged as an MG, but there were too many objections: the look wasn't well received, the front-wheel drive platform was judged wrong for the US market and the capital investment required to put it into production was simply too great. The prototype has now been restored and is currently on display at the British Motor Museum at Gaydon.

9X (PININFARINA)

After successfully seeing the BMC 1100 and 1800 into production, Alec Issigonis put plenty of thought into replacing the Mini. In 1968 he pursued the 9X project, an almost completely independent effort since Issigonis was now heading up his own separate R&D department.

The crisply modern styling was mostly done in-house by Fred Boubier and Syd Goble and featured a hatchback – something of a pioneering idea at the time. It was even shorter than the original Mini (9ft 8in, as opposed to just over 10ft) yet was both roomier and airier inside. Its basis was an entirely new platform with conventional McPherson front struts and a beam rear axle, while even the engine and gearbox were new.

The 9X's Italian connection is that the prototype was sent to Pininfarina. The Italian design house may perhaps have had some input on its design but it certainly built it into a working car. Sadly the BLMC merger effectively put an end to the 9X project, which many people see in retrospect as a great missed opportunity, since the European market in the 1970s was dominated by 'supermini' hatchbacks.

SPIAGGETTA (MICHELOTTI)

Giovanni Michelotti designed a beach car called the Shellette (or Spiaggetta) in 1968. This was made in a series of some 80 units by Michelotti at its own factory, using the Fiat 850 as a mechanical basis. The design was adapted for Morris mechanical parts for the Australian market but the project never left the prototype stage.

ADO74: 'LADYBIRD' (MICHELOTTI)

ADO74 was the first of BL's corporate efforts to replace the Mini. Although given the project code ADO74, it was always a fluid project with many faces: as well as being potentially a Mini replacement, it was also mooted as a new 'supermini' in the Fiat 127 class. Under the codename 'Ladybird' it would have been between 380mm and 500mm longer than the Mini and 60mm wider, and powered by an engine between 900cc and 1100cc in size.

A whole variety of styling exercises was produced, mostly in-house. Harry Webster decided to reignite his link with Giovanni Michelotti in Italy, asking him to design a Ladybird proposal. Michelotti produced a quite attractive small hatchback with an angular glasshouse, an original-looking nose and quirky character lines extending from the wheelarches front and rear.

However, British Leyland management quickly discounted the Italian's ideas in favour of a Harris Mann version of the same car. In the end, ADO74 never reached production, being cancelled in 1973 as the £130 million cost to productionise it was adjudged too great.

ADO88: MINI REPLACEMENT (PININFARINA)

Almost as soon as ADO74 had been cancelled in 1973, BL turned its thoughts to another potential Mini replacement: ADO88. Beginning in 1974, this would eventually lead to the Mini Metro of 1980 – which ironically failed to replace the Issigonis Mini. While the Metro was definitively a British design, along the way BL sought the input of at least one Italian design house, in 1975 asking Pininfarina to come up with a proposal. Its effort certainly had character, with large wraparound 'floating' bumpers front and rear, trapezoidal headlamps and angular lines highlighted by raised edges on the front and rear panels on each flank. As with so many Pininfarina designs, it was rejected because the production costs would have been too high.

LEYLAND-CROMPTON ELECTRIC (MICHELOTTI)

In 1948 Austin bought a 50% share in an electric vehicle manufacturer, AEVM, and renamed it Austin Crompton Parkinson Electric Vehicles, famed for its Morrison-Electricar milk floats. After the BL merger of 1968, the electric vehicle business was renamed Crompton Leyland Electricars.

In 1971 it was decided to make a small electric research vehicle using Mini underpinnings. The design was farmed out to Michelotti and despite the significant design constraints imposed by the tiny dimensions, the result was surprisingly modern and crisp, with a wedge-shaped outline, low nose, four headlamps, characterful rear pillars and a small glass tailgate. It anticipated some of the design elements of Michelotti's ADO74 (previous page). Intriguingly, the two-seat cabin incorporated a squared-off steering wheel – the first iteration of the infamous BL 'quartic' wheel soon to be adopted by the Austin Allegro.

On board were 24 lead-acid batteries and two 3.9hp electric motors. The mass of these batteries made the prototype 33% heavier than the Mini, despite its lightweight glassfibre body. Its top speed was only 32mph and its range was a mere 40 miles but BL estimated that its running costs were around half a penny per mile at the time. The car appeared at the March 1972 Geneva Motor Show but later that year British Leyland sold its electric car business to Hawker Siddeley. The Leyland-Crompton electric car was retired into BL's historic collection and it remains on show in the British Motor Museum collection to this day.

OPPOSITE PAGE, CLOCKWISE FROM TOP LEFT: Spiaggetta by Michelotti; Leyland-Crompton Electric (front and rear views); Pininfarina's ADO88 'new Mini'; Michelotti's ADO74 'Ladybird'. BELOW: Pininfarina effected MGB's conversion from roadster to GT coupe.

MGB GT (PININFARINA)

The MGB started to be developed as early as 1958 under the codename EX205. Its unitary structure, replacing the old separate-chassis construction of its MGA predecessor, made it a truly modern sports car. The design was resolutely British, MG's Abingdon HQ being preferred to BMC's new-found love affair with Pininfarina – at least for the MGB roadster launched in 1962.

When it came to making the fastback MGB 'GT' version, Italian help was called upon. Abingdon had designed an initial proposal but management was not entirely happy with it. At this time, Pininfarina was still in its honeymoon period with BMC and the coupe was sent to Turin with a request to tidy it up.

Exactly what Pininfarina tweaked is the subject of some debate. Some contend that it raised the level of the glasshouse, to the benefit of aesthetics, while others say that this idea had already been implemented before being sent to Italy. Whatever the exact details of the changes, the revised MGB

GT design submitted by Pininfarina was given the nod by BMC management virtually without change, entering production in 1965 to great acclaim and market success.

ADO76: MGB FACELIFT (MICHELOTTI)

When thoughts of a replacement for the MGB came about, Giovanni Michelotti was approached to update its design. In about 1968, he created a sketch for an MGB with a longer front end, new front grille and lamp surrounds, more steeply raked windscreen and all-new rear styling. The B-pillars were designed so that the roof could be either a removable targa top or hinged glass panels. Sadly the project never saw the light of day; instead the MGB would go on to be mildly facelifted with its infamous rubber bumpers.

MG EX234 (PININFARINA)

In 1964, MG started to contemplate a possible replacement for the MGB, codenamed EX234. Syd Enever and his team constructed the mechanical side of a prototype, which used a 1275cc A-Series engine and independent rear suspension (something that had been rejected for the first 'B' as too expensive), as well as Hydrolastic damping and disc brakes all round.

The rolling chassis was sent to Pininfarina in Turin for bodywork to be created. The look that the *carrozzeria* created somewhat resembled its work for Italian car makers, such as the Fiat 124 Sport Spider and Alfa Romeo Spider, notably its sharp-edged Kamm tail. Despite being shorter than the

MGB, room inside was superior and there was even space for a couple of small rear seats. The dashboard used a clever symmetrical design so that it would have been easy to make left-hand and right-hand drive versions (the prototype was RHD). Pininfarina's working car had not only a folding soft-top but also a hardtop, since a GT version was planned, too.

EX234 was returned to the UK where the car was well received: it looked good, drove well and had a nice cabin with excellent visibility. When it was tested by journalist John Sprinzel, he declared it to be "beautifully flat and smooth through the corners, with none of the usual lurch".

EX234 could have been fitted with the larger B-series engine, as well as the A-series, and so had the potential to replace both the MG Midget and MGB in one fell swoop. However, no production future awaited. MG's existing sports cars were doing well in the marketplace, so the need for a replacement was not pressing. The merger of BMC with Leyland in 1968 did the EX234 no favours, either. It survived and was acquired in 1977 by the MG dealer, Syd Beer, eventually being sold at auction in 2016 for £63,100.

OPPOSITE TOP LEFT: MGB GT prototype as delivered by Pininfarina. OPPOSITE TOP RIGHT: Michelotti's sketch for ADO76 (facelifted MGB GT). LEFT & THIS PAGE: Delicately styled MG EX234 had different brightwork on left and right sides, and even a hardtop.

LEYLAND P76 (MICHELOTTI)

Sometimes described as Australia's Edsel, since it was such a catastrophe in the marketplace, the Leyland P76 is only tangentially a British-Italian project, as it was conceived not in the UK but down under by Leyland Australia, as a local-market rival for Holden and Ford. The Italian connection was Giovanni Michelotti, for he was the car's designer. Development of the P76 actually took place both in Australia and the UK, the British side headed by MG engineer Roy Brocklehurst. British Leyland also had plans (albeit never realised) to sell the P76 in the UK.

The managing director of BLMC's Australian branch, together with its director of development and production, David Beech, visited the UK in November 1968 and got the go-ahead to develop this new large car. The original plan was to use Italdesign to style the car, but reportedly Beech and Giugiaro did not get on. With very little budget to play with, Harry Webster of Triumph recommended using Michelotti, who was duly commissioned in February 1970. His shape was clean and elegant, an impression boosted by

ABOVE: Ill-fated Leyland P76 saloon was styled in Italy and co-engineered in Britain for the Australian market. BELOW LEFT: Force 7 coupe. BELOW & ABOVE RIGHT: Leyland P82 coupe sketches by Michelotti. OPPOSITE BOTTOM: Leyland P82 saloon model.

features such as hidden windscreen wipers, while its rising profile line from front to rear earnt it the nickname 'The Wedge'. This was not a 100% Michelotti design, though, as the shapes of the front and rear were tweaked in Australia.

Launched in June 1973, the P76 could be had with either a 2.6-litre in-line six-cylinder engine (derived from BL's E-series unit) or a 4.4-litre V8 (an expanded Rover V8). It was well received by the press, even being crowned Car of The Year by *Wheels* magazine in 1973. But production delays, poor quality control and the oil crisis squashed sales and forced the P76 to be axed in November 1974 after only 12,525 cars had been sold. Leyland abandoned manufacture in Australia in 1975.

One twist in the P76 tale is the two-door coupe version, called the Force 7. Michelotti was the designer once again; he created a well-resolved shape with a pleasing fastback profile. Features included a large glass hatchback, air vents that echoed muscle car tropes and pillarless side windows. It got very close to production: tooling was created for it and 58 examples were built in late 1973 for a planned launch in February 1974. But the plug was pulled and all but 10 were scrapped. A Force 7 was even sent to the UK, where BL Chairman, Lord Stokes, used it as his personal transport.

LEYLAND P82 (MICHELOTTI)

In the late 1960s, Leyland Australia had accepted the idea of manufacturing the Morris Marina down under but it very much wanted the Marina's successor, due in 1977, to be a design targeted at and exclusibe to the Australian market.

In 1972, several designers were approached to come up with suggestions for the so-called P82, including Bertone, Giugiaro and Michelotti. Eventually Michelotti got the nod to develop his proposals, producing many sketches and several quarter-scale models. The model line-up would have comprised a four-door saloon, two-door van and two-door coupe. A P82 prototype was reportedly built and flown to Longbridge in the UK for approval but the project had been canned by late 1974.

ABOVE: ADO28 Morris Marina proposals by Michelotti (left) and Pininfarina (right). BELOW LEFT: Michelotti-designed Condor was a putative Ford Capri rival. OPPOSITE PAGE: Infamous Morris Ital. BOTTOM RIGHT: MGF had Pininfarina engineering input.

ADO28: MORRIS MARINA (MICHELOTTI/PININFARINA)

Following the merger of BMC with Leyland, there was an urgent need to come up with a rival for the Ford Cortina. With nothing in development, a new project – ADO28 – was set up. As well as an in-house design, developed by Roy Haynes, two Italian design houses were asked for their proposals: Pininfarina and Michelotti.

All the designs were presented to a British Leyland committee in August 1968. Pininfarina's low-waistline design was rejected partly because its extensive glasshouse would have made it too expensive to build. Triumph stalwart Harry Webster reportedly said it was "like sitting in a bloody goldfish bowl".

Webster preferred Michelotti's effort, which he described as "perky", and it featured a small spoiler on the boot, which was innovative for the time. But it was Haynes' designs for a saloon and coupe that were given the go ahead to become the new Morris Marina, launched in 1971.

ADO68/28: CONDOR (MICHELOTTI)

The ADO68 Condor project was intended to be BL's rival for the Ford Capri. The project was instituted in December 1969, although ADO68 was quickly split into three distinct projects: ADO68/28 (earmarked for basis on ADO28, the Morris Marina); ADO68/14 (front-wheel drive based on ADO14, or Austin Maxi, components, potentially using an E-series six-cylinder engine) and ADO68/67 (Austin Allegro based).

Only one of these projects had Italian input: the Marina-based ADO68/28, for which Michelotti was asked to explore design ideas. He came up with a creditable two-door fastback that featured a rear hatch. The shape shared hints of the two-door Marina's and featured double headlamps and a stylised front grille flourish. Michelotti's design was, during 1970, altered in-house at BL, when it was renamed ADO68/28-2, with single headlamps and a flatter rear three-quarter window shape. However, the Condor project never proceeded any further than the styling stage.

ADO73: MORRIS ITAL (ITALDESIGN)

Ask Giugiaro about the Morris Ital today and his eyes will roll. Carried within that 'Ital' name was the suggestion that Italdesign had done the styling for this made-over Morris Marina for the 1980s. It remains the belief among many that Giugiaro did indeed do the design work – not surprising since official advertising declared it was "Styled in Italy. Built in Britain". However, the first part of that statement was resolutely untrue.

By the end of the 1970s, the Morris Marina – always a stop-gap model, even at its launch – was looking very tired indeed. Under the project

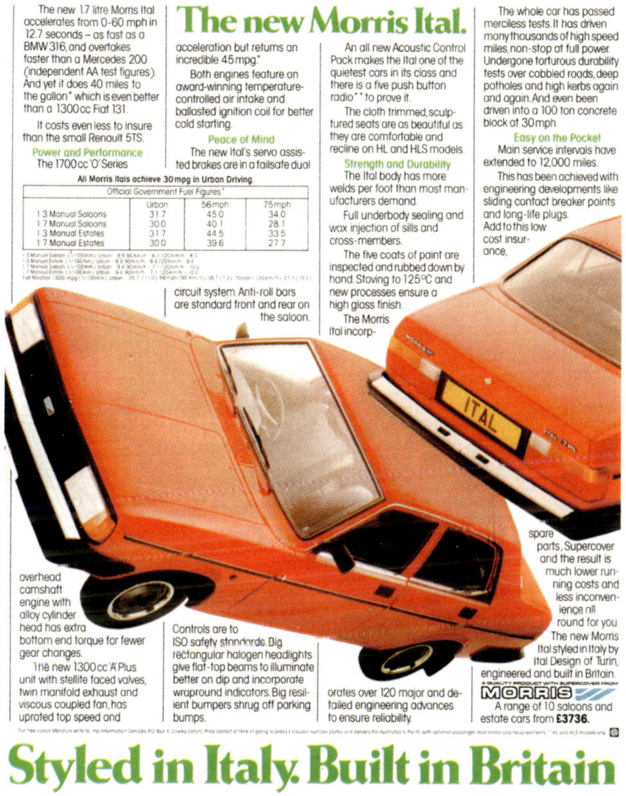

name ADO73, Longbridge's drawing office, headed by Harris Mann, effected a reasonably successful facelift, updating the front and rear ends of the car, the latter receiving a higher boot line and larger wraparound lights. No changes were made under the skin.

So why, if this was an in-house job, was Italdesign given the credit? At the time, Austin Morris was busy with the new Metro, so it gave the job of readying the car for production to Italdesign. Perhaps foolishly, Giugiaro allowed Austin Morris to film its television advert for the car on Italdesign premises, with a Turin-registered car seen screeching past a Maserati Merak. It was clearly in Austin Morris's interests to perpetrate the misconception that Italians had designed the new car, much to the chagrin of Giugiaro.

The original plan had been to call it Marina Ital, but boss Michael Edwardes insisted that the somewhat tarnished 'Marina' name be dropped, and when it was launched in June 1980 it was called simply Ital. It stumbled on until 1984, when it was replaced by the Austin Montego.

MGF (PININFARINA)

Project Phoenix was conceived as a modern-day MGB. Very much *not* a throwback to an antique age, it was designed as a cutting edge, affordable sports car, which was duly launched as the MGF in 1995. Parent company MG Rover opted for a mid-engined format and the MGF was widely praised for its impressive handling. The shape was unambiguously modern, too, done completely in-house.

Pininfarina's name is associated with the MGF for two reasons. First, it was on the shortlist of two companies to manufacture the car in series (the other one being the UK company, Mayflower, which eventually got the contract). The second reason is that the shapely soft top was engineered at Pininfarina's Turin facility. Fatefully, this was to be the very last occasion on which Pininfarina had any involvement with MG Rover.

BMC in Italy: The Innocenti Story

Italy became a very important manufacturing site for the British Motor Corporation, thanks to Innocenti – or to give its full name, Innocenti Societa Generale per l'Industria Metallurgica e Meccanica SpA. Founded by Ferdinand Innocenti in 1933, the company started off producing machine tools and steel tubing but really made its name with the Lambretta scooter, named after the company's factory in Lambrate, Milan.

Innocenti branched out into the manufacture of car components and body presses for Fiat, Lancia and Alfa Romeo but it would soon become a car maker in its own right after signing an accord with the British Motor Corporation in 1959. The alliance began with licensed production of the Austin A40 Farina from 1960. A variety of BMC models would soon be licence-built in Italy, including ADO16, the Mini and even the Austin Allegro, while Innocenti also produced its own Austin-Healey Sprite-based sports cars.

Six years after the death of Ferdinand Innocenti, his company was sold to British Leyland in May 1972 and renamed Leyland Innocenti SpA, with Geoffrey Robinson installed as the new chairman. His chief achievement was bringing a Bertone-styled update of the Mini to production but BL's tenure of Innocenti would be short-lived. Facing significant, indeed terminal, problems in its home market, BL's involvement with Innocenti ended in the summer of 1975 as its Italian branch went into liquidation. The remains were acquired by the mercurial Alessandro De Tomaso in April 1976, and a new company – Nuova Innocenti SpA – was formed. At the end of 1981, the deal to buy A-series engines from the UK expired, effectively severing all connections with the alma mater. Fiat bought De Tomaso out in 1990 and finally axed the Bertone-styled hatchback in 1993.

INNOCENTI AUSTIN A40 (PININ FARINA)

As the 1960s dawned, BMC was keen to expand in Italy whose protectionist taxation policies made imports very expensive. It found a perfect partner in Innocenti, signing an agreement in 1959 for the Italian company to build the Austin A40 for local consumption. That was almost a coming home for the model, since it had originally been designed in Italy, by Pinin Farina.

Production started in November 1960, initially using CKD kits supplied from Britain, but soon using Innocenti's own pressed panels. The A40 was priced to undercut the best-selling Fiat 1100 and proved very popular. The Italian market version had a few subtle differences and both Berlina (saloon) and Combinata (estate) versions were offered. In February 1962, a Series 2 model was introduced with the same extended wheelbase as the British-built MkII, plus local market additions Isuch as rectangular indicators and additional side repeaters.

In December 1962, when Innocenti's A40 got the 1098cc A-Series engine to become the A40S, the old split-tailgate Combinata was revised to feature a single-piece tailgate hinged at the top – a true pioneer of the hatchback supermini form. The Berlina was dropped in 1965 but the Combinata lasted until February 1967, by which time some 67,706 A40s had been built by Innocenti.

OPPOSITE: Innocenti factory in Lambrate was a major enterprise. THIS PAGE: Innocenti's A40 was offered as the 'Combinata' with a very early interation of the hatchback.

AUB
334E
WSJ 750

OPPOSITE: Handsome Spider and Coupe were unique to Innocenti.
BELOW: Early Tom Tjaarda proposal.
RIGHT: Spider was essentially a prettified Austin-Healey Sprite.

INNOCENTI SPIDER & COUPÉ (GHIA)

Innocenti asked BMC if it could make its own version of the Austin-Healey Sprite to suit local tastes, featuring a new body design. BMC agreed and various styling houses were canvassed to design what was called Project AX1. Ghia won the contract, and the man charged with the design work was the American-born Tom Tjaarda. This would mark his car design debut in a stellar career that would later encompass the De Tomaso Pantera and Ford Fiesta Mk1.

Innocenti's 950 Spider was launched at the 1960 Turin Motor Show, where it was very well received; Gordon H Jennings of *Road & Track* magazine said it was, "a substantial improvement over the original. Apart from the obvious upgrading in appearance, there are also slightly better accommodations for driver and passenger and, best of all, there is a proper trunk compartment with a lockable lid."

Manufacture started in 1961, with body construction subcontracted out to an offshoot of Ghia's, Officine Stampaggi Industriale (OSI). Early cars had 948cc BMC A-series power and by the end of the year, upgrades included a close-ratio gearbox and a power hike to 46.5hp. In February 1963 came a new 'S' version with a 1098cc engine and front disc brakes.

While mainly a domestic product, the Innocenti Spider was sold in some overseas markets, including the USA, but it cost about one-third more than a Sprite. BMC even considered selling the car in the UK but its high cost and potential impact on BMC's own Sprite precluded this.

A new version arrived in 1965 in the form of the Coupé (or simply 'C'). A substantial redesign was done by Sergio Sartorelli of Ghia, giving the new fixed-roof car its own distinct identity. The Coupé was six inches longer and two inches wider than the Spider, while the front bulkhead was moved forwards to allow for longer doors and extra room in the footwells. The cabin used a mix of Alfa Romeo and Ferrari trim parts. As for paint, the Coupé was offered in any colour you liked as long as it was green, white or red – the colours of the Italian tricolore flag. Just 794 Coupés were made up until 1968, making it substantially rarer than the Spider, of which 6800 or so were built.

THIS PAGE: Delicate Innocenti Spider. OPPOSITE PAGE, CLOCKWISE FROM TOP: Michelotti's three-box saloon version of the Innocenti Austin I4; Regent brochure claimed the styling was Italian (it wasn't); Morris IM3; Boneschi's unique IM3 built to show the Duke of Edinburgh around the Innocenti plant in 1965.

INNOCENTI MORRIS IM3 & AUSTIN I4/I5 (PININFARINA/BONESCHI/MICHELOTTI)

Innocenti's next licence-built BMC product was the Morris 1100 – after the Austin A40, another case of a Pininfarina design 'coming home' to Italy. Launched in spring 1963, it was called the Morris IM3 because it was the third Innocenti-Morris joint venture. As with the A40, it had its own Italianate differences: unique upright headlamps, a different grille and a revised interior featuring a more upright steering wheel. The IM3 was fitted with an MG 1100 twin-carb engine with 58hp, while a lightly revised version was sold as the IM3S from 1966 until 1970.

The IM3 was joined in 1964 by a more basic model, badged Austin I4. Unlike the restyled Morris, this looked identical to the UK Austin 1100 and was fitted with a less powerful 50hp single-carburettor engine. The Austin I4S followed on as a downmarket version of the Morris IM3S, while the Austin I5, sold from 1970 to 1973, was facelifted with a redesigned fascia and wider grille.

Two other interesting variants are worthy of note. To transport the Duke of Edinburgh around the Innocenti factory during an official visit in 1965, a special IM3 was built by the coachbuilder Boneschi with its rear roof made of Plexiglas to allow a better view. The interior was also plusher and the front passenger seat was reversed.

Another Innocenti proposal was a unique three-box saloon reinterpretation of the Austin I4. In 1969, Giovanni Michelotti was tasked with designing it and he came up with a quite successful and well resolved shape. Not only was there a longer boot with a horizontally-mounted lid but the front and rear ends were substantially restyled with a more squared-off shape. The front now incorporated dual headlamps mounted within a black grille and the bumpers were new, too. While Innocenti was not in a position to put the prototype into production, the idea of a three-box ADO16 did see the light of day when the Austin Apache was productionised in South Africa (see page 90).

INNOCENTI REGENT

Voted on many occasions as one of the worst cars of all time, the Austin Allegro was at best a mediocre replacement for the BMC 1100/1300, at worst a lemon of the sourest variety that hastened the demise of the UK car industry. The Allegro was not only made at Longbridge in Britain but also in Italy. To replace the locally made Morris IM3, it was decided to manufacture the Allegro in Italy as the Innocenti Regent; in fact, this would be the first new Innocenti model following the company's takeover by British Leyland.

The Regent range comprised 1300, 1300L and 1500L models, sporting a few differences over the Allegro. While it retained Austin's baffling 'quartic' (squared-off) steering wheel design, the centre boss was unique, while the road wheels on plush 'L' models featured unique squared-off centres. Other differences included an all-black grille with a silver stripe and an offset badge; separate front quarter-lights that swivelled open; and side indicators on the front wings. The instrument pod was also larger than the Allegro's.

Perhaps the Regent's biggest point of difference was that all versions boasted twin-carb engines, in contrast to the mostly single-carb Allegro range. The 1275cc A-series engine (borrowed from the Innocenti Mini Cooper 1300) boasted 66hp; the 1485cc E-series had 79hp.

Launched in January 1974, the Regent lasted barely 18 months in production as the whole company went into liquidation in summer 1975. Just 11,213 units had been sold by then. BL did offer the Allegro in Italy as an Austin thereafter but with little success.

INNOCENTI MINI

Italy enjoyed a true love affair with the Mini. It suited the narrow city streets of Rome, Milan and Turin and sold tremendously well there; indeed, by the 1970s, the Mini was the most popular non-Fiat car sold in Italy. In September 1965, Innocenti started to make the Mini locally, initially using engines and gearboxes imported from the Coventry engine plant, while many body parts were also imported. Local content included trim, electrics, wheels, glass and some body pressings.

The first model was the Innocenti Mini-Minor 850 of 1965. Italian Minis always boasted a level of trim that far outclassed British-built Minis, with standard opening rear quarter-lights, lever-pull door handles, ribbed vinyl trim, rubber mats, three-gauge oval dial, unique grille and extra indicators on the front wings. For the MkII of 1968, a higher compression ratio saw power rise to 48hp, making it livelier than the UK Mini, too. A new Mk3 Innocenti Mini arrived in January 1970, again with more power than UK Minis. The estate body style was also made in Italy.

Arguably the best Italian Minis were the Innocenti Mini-Coopers, built from March 1966 onwards. The initial 998cc engine had a special camshaft to give 56hp, as well as uprated Cooper 'S' driveshafts, brakes and wheels. In September 1968 came the

Innocenti's version of the 'Issigonis' Mini had many features unique to the Italian-made model, from windows to lights, dashboard to power outputs.

MkII with 60hp and a top speed of 93mph. The MkIII of February 1970 had winding windows that were quite different to the UK Mini's, as they had front quarter-lights. The 998cc Cooper lasted until 1972.

Years after the Cooper name was axed in the UK in 1971, it continued going in Italy, latterly in Cooper 1300 form with a 71hp 1275cc engine shared with the Austin 1300 GT. Special wheelarch extensions and a full-width plastic dash with six dials marked out this delectable Italian Cooper. As the Cooper 1300 Export, it lasted until 1976, by which time nearly 450,000 Minis had been built in Italy.

INNOCENTI MINI (BERTONE)

Innocenti had considered a roomier, updated version of the Mini as early as 1969. Michelotti and Bertone were approached to come up with mock-ups in 1970 – the latter's being penned by Marcello Gandini – but a lack of finances caused the programme to be halted. When British Leyland took over Innocenti in 1972, the project was revived and Bertone was asked to develop it further.

Gandini came up with a superbly clean-looking new set of clothes. His all-new bodywork was an exercise in angularity and he pulled off the difficult job of realising excellent proportions in a very small car. The wheelbase was marginally longer and the car grew in length by 2.6in (66mm) and in width by 3.5in (89mm) compared to the Mini. Weight did increase, though, to 1600lb (725kg).

Innocenti's newcomer offered more space for passengers and, because the rear seats folded, practicality was greatly enhanced. The rear hatchback still represented something of a novelty in the early 1970s. However, it suffered from a very high loading lip, limited rear headroom and problems with body rigidity.

Two models were offered at launch: the Mini 90 (998cc engine with 48hp, good for 87mph) and Mini 120 (1275cc Cooper engine, 64hp, 96mph). Mechanically, most of the car was pure Mini: front subframe, rubber-cone suspension, A-series engines, steering and brakes. But there were mechanical differences such as a wider rear subframe, larger fuel tank, bigger brake discs, new exhaust and resited radiator. Inside, everything was different, with an all-new dashboard, notably featuring peculiar square dials in the 120 model. The Mini 90 had matt black bumpers, the 120 chromed ones.

The 'Bertone' Mini was launched in 1974 and was well received from the off. *Autocar* tested it in 1975 and concluded that, "as a replacement for the ubiquitous Mini, the Innocenti 90 and 120 models are a success".

Although assembled in Italy, many of the body pressings and most of the mechanicals were actually made in Britain. The Mini 90 and 120 were sold in several markets outside Italy (usually badged Leyland Innocenti) but were never offered in Britain. That can perhaps be seen as a missed opportunity. Plans were mooted to assemble the car in the UK, but costings concluded it would more expensive to make than the Mini, and in any case the Mini Metro was already in development by then.

In 1976, after Innocenti was bought by Alessandro De Tomaso, a sporty Mini De Tomaso was added to the range, with a 71hp or 74hp 1275cc A-series engine and a more purposeful look. Another

OPPOSITE PAGE: Michelotti's proposal for the new Innocenti Mini hatchback (top); production Mini 90 and 120 (below). THIS PAGE: Marcello Gandini's Innocenti Mini was a masterpiece of clean design, seen here in hot hatch De Tomaso form.

evolution came in 1980 when Gandini facelifted the car to become the Mini Mille, consisting of new glassfibre bumpers and an updated interior. In all but name, Innocenti severed its Mini connections when, in April 1982, it launched the new Mini 3 with a Daihatsu three-cylinder engine. By that time, Innocenti had made over 230,000 new-shape Minis. Eventually even the name changed to Innocenti Small, limping on in production until 1993.

ITALY'S MOKE

The Moke made by BMC at Longbridge in the 1960s found a new manufacturing home in both Australia (1966-1981) and Portugal (1983-1989). In April 1990, Rover put the Moke project up for sale and found a buyer in the form of Italian motorbike maker, Cagiva. A new company called Moke Automobili SpA was set up in Bologna and Rover transferred the 'Moke' title to the new company. Production continued in Portugal until the end of 1993, when all tooling was apparently transferred to Italy, where Cagiva hoped to restart production in early 1995. In fact, that never happened.

BRISTOL

The Elegance of Eccentricity

It is impossible to think of a car marque that better embodies the essence of a particular type of Britishness than Bristol: a vanishing kingdom of eccentricity, derring-do and gracious manners. It does not even seem out of keeping that the cars produced by this iconoclastic concern owed their origins to German engineering, since even this fed into a British trope of sorts – namely that Bristol's automobiles were the spoils of war, even if this claim is perhaps tenuous.

The Bristol Aeroplane Company was, at the end of World War 2, one of the world's largest manufacturer of aeroplanes and aero engines. Facing uncertain prospects for the aircraft industry in post-war years, proprietors George White and Reginald Vernon-Smith had the foresight to repurpose the company's expertise in engineering and aerodynamics to launch a car making enterprise.

BMW cars were certainly known to Bristol and a chance conversation between Bristol's Eric Storey and DA and HJ Aldington of AFN (the company behind the Frazer Nash-BMW in pre-war years) put the marque firmly on Bristol's radar. Drawings for BMW's six-cylinder engine also found their way into Bristol's hands, enabling the creation of the Frazer Nash-Bristol in September 1946 – one of the very first new British car models following WW2. However, the Aldingtons and AFN soon parted company from Bristol to make their own cars under the Frazer Nash name (see page 150), even if AFN continued to act as Bristol agents.

The first 'pure' Bristol was the 400, launched at the 1947 Geneva Motor Show. Here began a dynasty of robust, luxurious, high-concept sporting models and a car marque that would endure longer than almost any other comparable British company.

It was Don Aldington of AFN who first formed ties with Italian design, as he courted Carrozzeria Touring when a new model to succeed the 400 was in development. After Aldington's departure, Bristol's future would be much more inwardly focused, as historian Rainer Simons summed up: "By involving such Italian coachbuilders as Touring and Pinin Farina, Aldington hoped for a chance to give the planned Bristol car a decidedly sporting nature. It was precisely for this reason that George White resisted any involvement on the part of the Italians. He continued to prefer the concept of a respectable tourer because he believed this corresponded much better to the tastes of his countrymen." There is no question, however, of the debt owed by Bristol to Carrozzeria Touring, which set not only the style but also the 'superleggera' construction method of the Bristol 401.

After many years persisting with pre-war BMW-derived straight-six engines, Bristol started to develop its own six-cylinder unit (which was ultimately canned). In searching for an automatic gearbox for it, Chrysler's Torqueflite was suggested, which arrived at Bristol with a V8 engine attached. When it was bolted in, it proved the perfect choice. In 1961 Bristol duly launched its first Chrysler V8-powered model, the 407.

ABOVE: Tony Crook – seen here with a model of the 401 – was 'Mr Bristol' for many decades. RIGHT: Pinin Farina's very elegant cabriolet body on the Bristol 400.

SMT 259

It was the right move, and the potent combination of North American power and European design was enduring: indeed Bristol outlived every other enterprise offering such hybrids, including Jensen and Gordon-Keeble, despite – or perhaps because of – its insistence on hand-building cars with aluminium bodies and separate chassis.

One man was central to the Bristol marque's perseverance from the 1960s onward: Antony Crook. At first a Bristol agent, Crook took a minority shareholding in September 1960 when Bristol was sold back to the marque's founder, George White. Crook increasingly concentrated his focus on Bristol, eventually assuming sole ownership of the company in 1973. It was Crook who forged a new tryst with Italy in the form of Zagato. Having met Gianni Zagato in Italy, he acquired not only the UK concession for Zagato but also, incidentally, the Abarth UK concession (some Abarth parts would even fleetingly be used in Bristol engines). Thus followed a gloriously quirky partnership between Bristol and Zagato. Both 406 and 407 models would receive Italian coachwork in the early 1960s, while Zagato was later called on to design the 412 in the 1970s. This would be the last Italian-designed Bristol for many years, finally leaving production (as the Beaufighter) in 1992.

The Bristol marque, meanwhile, became ever more marginal as its clientele of well-heeled, old-school eccentrics withered on the vine. Crook divested himself of all interests in Bristol in 2007 and sadly Bristol entered administration in 2011. It was then bought by a new investor, Kamkorp (which also owned Frazer-Nash Research), and in 2012 the services of another Italian designer, Fulvio Fantolino of F&F Design, were secured. He penned several new designs for Bristol but only one of these – the Bullet – was ever shown publicly. The venerable British marque of Bristol finally succumbed to a winding-up order in 2020.

400 CABRIOLET (PININ FARINA)

Bristol launched its new 400 model, a cutting-edge two-door saloon, at the 1947 Geneva Motor Show. This looked somewhat like a pre-war BMW 327, and under the skin resemblances to BMWs continued, for the 400 was based on a BMW 326 chassis and used

BELOW: Pinin Farina's tasteful 401 Drophead Convertible. ABOVE RIGHT: One of Touring's designs for the Bristol 401 saloon. BOTTOM RIGHT: Felice Bianchi Anderloni of Touring pictured next to the design that greatly influenced the production Bristol 401 (extreme right).

a BMW 328 2.0-litre six-cylinder pushrod engine. With a top speed of nearly 100mph, it was successful in rallying and time trialling.

As well as the home-built saloon, Bristol also courted Italian coachbuilders to body its 400 chassis in alternative body styles. Pinin Farina was one such *carrozzeria*, clothing three Bristol chassis in its typically clean style, closely resembling the elegant coachwork it was then creating for the Lancia Aprilia and Alfa Romeo 6C 2500.

The first chassis (400/1/102) was delivered to Pinin Farina in Turin in December 1946. The car was originally intended to be sold as a Frazer Nash-Bristol, and indeed Frazer Nash's brochure illustrated it as such, but with the relationship between Bristol and Frazer Nash falling apart, the new car would be called a 'Bristol 2-Litre'. It was delivered in 1947 to HJ Aldington (the Frazer Nash director) and successfully rallied by him, for instance at the 1949 Alpine Rally. No doubt its fitment of a competition-spec engine helped its chances in racing.

Another chassis (400/181) was delivered to AFN at Isleworth in December 1947 as a left-hand drive car destined for Drenowatz, the main BMW agent in Switzerland. This chassis was fitted with a convertible body by Pinin Farina, to a very similar style as the earlier chassis but differing in some details, such as lighting and brightwork. AFN subsequently converted the car to right-hand drive and updated the engine for a new owner in 1950, the British racing driver Peter Bolton.

401 (TOURING)

Befitting Bristol's origins as an aircraft manufacturer, it was entirely appropriate that, for its second model, the company should turn to a company known for super-lightweight construction methods that shared much in common with aeronautical concepts. That company was Italian: Carrozzeria Touring Superleggera, whose patented construction method of light alloy panels over a multi-tubular frame hit the spot perfectly.

In 1947 Bristol invited Touring Superleggera to design and engineer the bodywork of its forthcoming 401. The

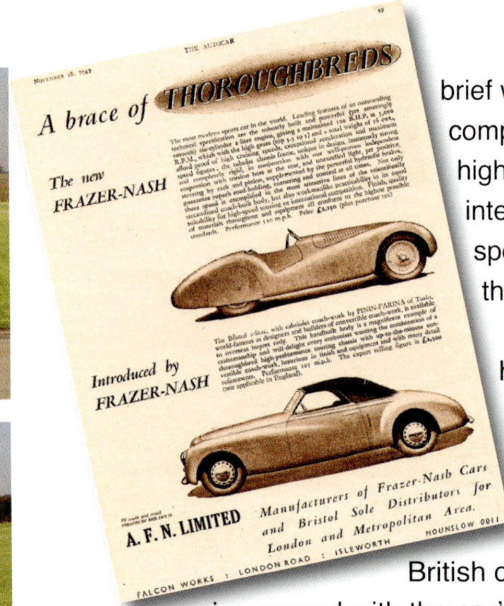

brief was to create a compact, lightweight, high performance international sporting car for the family.

The initial plan had been for Touring also to make the bodywork for Bristol but the British company was not impressed with the car's finish and dismissed Touring's proposal. It's thought that Touring did make seven or eight cars in Milan with aluminium-panelled bodywork over a steel tubular frame. A Touring proposal to make a four-door version was also rejected.

Bristol ultimately chose to pursue an in-house route for its 401. The design work was done by Dudley Hobbs and Dennis Sevier, who made full use of Bristol's aeronautical wind tunnel to finesse airflow on the car. Undoubtedly, however, a big debt was owed to Touring, whose general profile was clearly visible in the 401, although the British model lost some of the handsomeness of Touring's 401, as well as details such as the ridges on the wings and the tiny, teardrop-shaped rear lights. Of equal significance was Bristol taking out a licence for Touring's *superleggera* construction method. All in all, the 401 was a big step forwards compared to pre-war-derived Bristols.

The 401 was notably aerodynamic: wind tunnel testing was conducted and a drag coefficient of less than Cd 0.36 was recorded, exceptionally good for the time. The headlights were positioned close in to the narrow 'kidney' grille, which looked a little less BMW-like than the 400's. One advanced feature was the flush door furniture; a simple button on the door was pressed to open it. Another novelty was flush-fitting rubber spring-mounted bumpers. The spacious cabin could seat five in comfort, too. The chassis and mechanicals were essentially the same as the 400: a 2.0-litre in-line six-cylinder engine, four-speed gearbox, hydraulic brakes and telescopic dampers.

The Bristol 401 was launched in October 1948 at the Earls Court Motor Show and was also joined by the 402 convertible. In 1953 it was replaced by the 403 with an uprated 2.0-litre engine, remote gearchange, Alfin drum brakes, a front anti-roll bar and better damping. The 403 had the distinction of being Bristol's first 100mph car.

401 DROPHEAD CONVERTIBLE (PININ FARINA)

An advert in the 26 November 1948 edition of *Autocar* magazine described the new Bristol 401 Drophead Cabriolet by Pinin Farina as a: "fine example of hand craftsmanship and possesses the beautiful lines, exceptional attention to detail refinements and luxurious finish throughout, which have distinguished Italian coachbuilders' exhibits at Brussels, Geneva and Paris. The combination of coachwork by leading Italian designers on this latest version of a thoroughbred high-performance chassis provides the perfect car for the discriminating enthusiast."

The design was quite similar to Farina's earlier 400-based convertibles, featuring sober lines for a car with sporting intent, but this was undoubtedly one of the most stylish of all Bristols. The bumpers were unadorned; the chromework was restrained; and the narrow grille contrasted with the headlights mounted far out on the wings, lending the car an impression of imposing width. The lightweight all-aluminium bodywork helped to deliver a top speed of 105mph, impressive for the time.

The number of 401 chassis sent to Pinin Farina for Drophead coachwork is unclear, but probably between three and six. The first of these was despatched as early as July 1948, some months before the 401 made its official debut. Although listed in AFN's UK press adverts priced at £2500, Pinin Farina's convertible was never actually available in Britain, but offered in export markets only. Bristol

OPPOSITE: Although advertised by AFN, Pinin Farina's 401 Drophead Convertible was never sold in the UK.
OPPOSITE BELOW: Ghia-Aigle 401 at the 1953 Geneva Motor Show.
ABOVE: A true masterpiece of taut sporting style – Bertone's Arnolt-Bristol.

would offer its own 401-based convertible as the 402 to a very different style.

401 COUPE (GHIA-AIGLE)

Ghia in Italy bodied not a single Bristol chassis but its Swiss offshoot, Ghia-Aigle, did produce a one-off coupe. The styling was a rather sober affair of straight-through waistlines and a simple roof. The only unusual facet was the front end with its stylised upright kidney grille, large quarter-bumpers and insets at the leading edge of the front wings containing minor lights. The Ghia-Aigle Bristol 401 was shown at the Geneva Motor Show in March 1953, painted white with a red roof.

ARNOLT-BRISTOL (BERTONE)

The full background of Stanley Harold Arnolt II, nicknamed 'Wacky', is told in the chapter on BMC, which details the Bertone-bodied Arnolt MG TD (page 80). With the MG TD leaving production, Arnolt was in need of another sports car to sell to his American customers. In April 1953, he met James Watt, sales manager of Bristol, in New York and expressed an interest in representing Bristol in the US. At the time, Bristol was shortly to introduce the new 404, a two-seat coupe on a shorter wheelbase than the 403 from which it derived. Dubbed the "businessman's express" in the press, it was elegant, fast and expensive. In fact, too expensive in Arnolt's view. Could Bristol perhaps supply 404 chassis for Arnolt that could be rebodied in Italy by Bertone, he asked? Watt concurred with the plan and made an initial agreement to deliver 250 chassis (later revised down to 140). Watt visited Bertone at the end of April 1953 with chassis drawings in hand, and within a month Bertone had received its first chassis.

What Bertone conjured up was nothing short of miraculous. Designer Franco Scaglione crafted a true masterpiece. A beautiful crease line started at the front grille and swept over the front wings, vanishing briefly over the doors before re-emerging over the rear wings. This clever feature emphasised the height of the wing and distracted from the rather high bonnet line that was dictated by the tall Bristol engine. The overall effect was superbly understated, with almost no adornment whatsoever – only some badging and an air vent in each front wing. The windscreen was ultra-low; the grille was restricted in size and incorporated the headlights so that the front end was exceptionally clean. The same comment also applied to the interior, with a dashboard that was a plain, painted affair.

The bodywork was mostly made of steel, although three bodies would be made of light alloy. The car weighed substantially less than Bristol's 404 and was also more aerodynamic – as validated by Bristol itself, doing airflow tests using wool tufts.

The car debuted at the 1953 Earls Court Motor Show, described as "for export only". Its 1971cc six-cylinder engine was tuned to give 130hp, good for 112mph and 0-60mph in under nine seconds. A handful of cars were later fitted with Corvette V8 power for even more spectacular performance.

The new model warmly reviewed in the press. *Sports Cars Illustrated* declared: "In terms of performance, the Arnolt-Bristol is a thoroughbred racing car fit to be stabled with Ferrari and Mercedes". The racing car analogy was apt, since the Arnolt-Bristol promptly went racing, first winning the E-modified National Championship in 1954 and then taking part in the Sebring 12 Hours the following year

OPPOSITE ABOVE: Arnolt-Bristol with cut-down screen. OPPOSITE BELOW: Good-looking Coupe; only three were made. ABOVE TOP: Weather gear was optional. ABOVE: Unusual scalloped front wing design featured on some cars. LEFT: Franco Scaglione (standing) talks with his boss, Nuccio Bertone (in car).

with a three-strong team (securing first, second and fourth places in the 2.0-litre class). For several years following, there would also be strong showings at Sebring from the Arnolt-Bristols.

The brochure somewhat immodestly described it as "the world's most distinguished sports car", going on: "American ingenuity envisioned this dashing sports car. British engineering skill and Italian artistry helped to bring it into being". It was keenly priced considering that Bristol's own 404 retailed for $9946. The $3995 base model (sometimes called the Bolide) had a cut-down windscreen and no weather gear. For $650 more you got the DeLuxe version with a soft-top, side windows and quarter-bumpers. There was also a coupe version with winding windows and a fixed roof; only three of these were made, one of which was bought by the actor, Lee Marvin. Being hand-built, individual cars differed in detail, with a variety of lighting, wheel and wheelarch treatments, for instance. While only 46 examples of Bristol's own 404 were made between 1953 and 1955, the coachbuilt Arnolt version can be judged a triumphant success, since 142 were sold, even though it took over 10 years to shift them all.

406 GT ZAGATO [LWB] (ZAGATO)

Bristol's 406 of 1957 cut loose from its Italian origins, receiving a completely new notchback body which looked staider but at the same time more modern. The construction was now steel-framed but mechanically it was almost identical to earlier Bristols, except for an enlarged 2216cc version of the existing 'six', giving better torque but the same 105hp power output. The 406 came with standard disc brakes all round, a Watt's linkage for the rear axle and electronic overdrive. Up until 1961, some 161 examples of the 406 were made.

In 1959, Anthony Crook asked his new-found friend in Italy, Gianni Zagato, to rebody a standard 114-inch wheelbase 406 chassis, coded 406/L/P1. What Zagato came up with was still recognisably a Bristol, with cowled headlamps flanking a hole-in-the-wall grille, but quite distinctively Zagato. The waistline was effectively straight-through but with a characteristic, strong kick in the rear wing line. The cabin and glasshouse were also rather upright in style, while the roof was of course a double-bubble, or perhaps more accurately a sunken channel through the centre of the roof.

Since weight (3009lb/1365kg) definitely counted against the regular 406, Zagato's specialism in reducing weight was a significant attraction. The new car, described as the "Bristol Zagato Grand Touring Model", was some 450lb (204kg) lighter than the regular 406 saloon. In uprated '110S' form, the 2.2-litre engine had a hotter camshaft and Abarth manifolds, increasing power to 130hp. The result was Bristol's most rapid six-cylinder model of all time, easily topping 120mph. Following its launch at the 1959 Earls Court Motor Show, just six examples of the 406 GT Zagato were made between 1959 and 1961. It's thought that a further three Zagato bodies were subsequently fitted on to older Bristol 400 chassis.

406S ZAGATO [SWB] (ZAGATO)

Right at the start of the 406's life, in 1957, Bristol had made two chassis with a shortened 102-inch wheelbase (a full 12 inches less), referred to as the 406S. One of these chassis was bodied to a unique style at the Filton works, while the other chassis was left unused and put aside – until Anthony Crook had it delivered to Zagato in Milan.

The car that Zagato created is usually referred to as the 406S Zagato or 406 GTZ SWB (short wheelbase). This was a handsome two-seat coupe. Who designed it? A fresh-faced 22-year old designer called Ercole Spada had just joined Zagato and the 406S Zagato is widely credited as being his first ever design for the company, although Zagato itself has stated that the car was jointly designed by Gianni Zagato and Celeste Gobbi. The styling was far sportier and more fluid than the LWB 406 Zagato. The bodywork sat very low but the tall engine meant that a bonnet bulge was required (curiously, in transparent Plexiglas). Zagato's

THIS PAGE: Zagato's square-roof 406 GT long-wheelbase (LWB) coupe. OPPOSITE TOP: Line-up of 406 LWB Bristols outside Zagato's Milan works. OPPOSITE BELOW: Despite its elegance, the 406S Zagato short-wheelbase remained a one-off.

trademark double-bubble roof was present, too.

Zagato's 406S was presented at the March 1960 Geneva Motor Show, painted metallic grey (it was later repainted red). Built as a gift from Crook to his daughter Carole, the car remained a one-off. However, it can be said to have directly inspired one of the greatest sports cars of the day, by a quite different manufacturer. David Brown of Aston Martin saw the new Bristol at its Geneva debut and reputedly asked Tony Crook to loan the car to him. This was a fateful request since, suitably impressed, Brown signed a contract with Gianni Zagato for a rebodied version of his Aston Martin DB4 GT. By October 1960, Zagato had designed and delivered the new DB4 GTZ – a car that arguably owes not only much of its design to the Bristol but also its very existence.

407 GT ZAGATO (ZAGATO)

In 1961 came a sea-change for Bristol. With its cars becoming heavier and its rivals more powerful, it stopped fitting the old BMW-derived six-cylinder engines, swapping over to V8 power sourced from Chrysler in Canada. The new 407 at last had sufficient power (around 250hp from the 5130cc unit) to take on Jaguar in terms of performance.

Tony Crook asked Zagato to do a lightweight coupe version of the new V8 Bristol, something that the Milanese coachbuilder completed in just 10 weeks.

LEFT: While Zagato's 407 GT looked somewhat similar to its earlier 406-based coupe, in fact it had an all-new and quite distinct style.
BELOW: Viotti's simple yet well-proportioned shape was designed by Pietro Frua; only the convertible version was ever built.
OPPOSITE: Zagato's 412 of 1975 was a peculiarly slab-sided concoction.

The elegant new coupe bodywork looked somewhat like the short-wheelbase 406S Zagato of one year previously – notably its swoopy waistline, wraparound rear screen and cowled headlamps – but it was in fact all-new and quite different in proportion, since it was based on the longer 114-inch wheelbase chassis. Its lines were somewhat softened and the proportions perhaps better resolved. Many details were different, too, such as the flush front grille (rather than recessed), quarter-bumpers (rather than full-width ones), metal sill covers and a smooth roof rather than a double-bubble.

Launched at the Earls Court Motor Show in October 1961, the 407 GT Zagato appeared on Zagato's own stand, rather than Bristol's (alongside the Zagato Mini Gatto – see page 95). Zagato's 407 was significantly lighter than Bristol's own saloon and was therefore capable of a higher top speed (125mph). However, the heavy V8 engine in such a lightweight car drew criticism from some road testers, as its unfavourable weight distribution unbalanced the handling. While Crook had hoped to sell the 407 GT Zagato in series, priced at about $9500, ultimately it never reached the market and remained a one-off.

407 (VIOTTI)

While Zagato had tackled a 407 in coupe form, it was to another coachbuilder – Carrozziere Esercizio Stabilimenti Viotti – that Bristol turned for a convertible 407. Designer Pietro Frua sketched both a coupe and a drop-top but only the convertible was realised.

A right-hand drive 407 chassis was duly despatched to Viotti. Frua's shape was an exercise in tasteful restraint, resolutely clean and modern. The front grille and headlights had a hint of Lancia Flavia about them but most of the 'character' lay at the rear end: the waistline crease kicked up aft of the doors to run along below the tops of the raised rear wings, while three small circular lights graced each side of the tail.

Viotti's Bristol debuted at the 1962 Turin Motor Show as the only coachbuilt car with a non-Italian chassis. A small production run was announced but this never happened and the car remained a one-off. The design clearly had one big fan in the actor Peter Sellers, who asked to buy the prototype to accompany the 407 saloon that he also had on order (Anthony Crook of Bristol also owned the Viotti concession for the UK). Once fully finished, the convertible was registered in 1963 in Sellers' name – although it was usually driven by his wife, the actress Britt Eklund.

412 (ZAGATO)

Convertibles had not appeared in Bristol's price lists for two decades when, in 1975, the eccentric car maker returned to Zagato to design an all-new drop-top model. The resulting 412 was a radical departure for Bristol. The styling borrowed from the same playbook as Zagato's contemporaneous Lancia Beta Spyder. The shape – attributed to Giuseppe Mittino – was a real contrast to the curvaceous Bristol 411 on which the 412 was based, with startlingly sharp-edged lines, to the point of being brick-like.

The challenge – not altogether successfully enacted, it must be conceded – was to make the

proportions work on a chassis whose roots could be traced back to the pre-war BMW 327. The 9ft 6in wheelbase was long but the track was far too narrow for a balanced look. Another constraint was the need for a long nose to permit the stowage of the spare wheel and battery in special bays in the front wings. There was, in consequence, no angle from which the 412 could be regarded as pretty. Journalist Giles Chapman summed the awkwardness up well by describing the 412 as, "one of the ugliest inducements ever made to the sybaritic community". The 412's largely flat aluminium body panels were at least easy to form, allowing Bristol to manufacture it in-house rather than rely on an outside coachbuilder.

The 412 did feature some nods to modernity, including rectangular headlamps, wraparound bumpers, flush-fitting door handles and Avon alloy wheels. The echoes of Lancia Beta Spyder were all too real in the rear lights, which were purloined directly from the Italian car. Also echoing the Lancia was the convertible concept: steel rollover bar, folding rear roof and removable centre targa roof. The latter was made of steel on Zagato's prototype but on production cars the roof panel was glassfibre. Later cars also had a removable rear hardtop in addition to the fabric hood, while the Beaufort variant was an export-only full convertible that dispensed with the rollover bar.

In its initial guise, as launched in 1975, the 412 had a 6.6-litre Chrysler V8 engine but the S2 of 1977 switched to a smaller 5.9-litre engine. The rapid 140mph Beaufighter of 1980 had an American Rotomaster turbocharger bolted on (making it a contender to be Britain's first ever turbocharged car), beefed-up gearbox and restyled double-headlamp front end. The Beaufighter remained in production until 1992.

Priced at over £14,500 at launch in 1975, the 412 cost more than a Jensen Interceptor but less than a Rolls-Royce Corniche. Production numbers were tiny: a mere 20 Series 1 cars, 19 Series 2s, 19 Beaufighters and a single Beaufort – 59 cars in total.

THIS PAGE: Inspired by a 1960s speedster prototype made by Bristol, the Bullet was designed in Italy by Fulvio Fantolino. Modern cabin featured a large touchscreen.

BULLET (F&F DESIGN)

With a whole swathe of new models secretly waiting in the wings (see below), Bristol decided to launch a new model as a first step in re-establishing the marque. This was the Bullet, announced in 2015 under the working title 'Project Pinnacle', whose brief was to be a new flagship Bristol with modern design and mechanicals.

The inspiration for the car was the discovery of a one-off prototype hidden under a dust sheet at Bristol's headquarters, a curious roadster made in the 1960s and named Bullet. Other design inspirations were taken from Bristol's 1951 404 Coupe and the later 405 Drophead Coupe.

At the time, the design was ascribed to "an eminent Italian designer who chooses to remain anonymous" but the identity of the mysterious designer was later revealed to be Fulvio Fantolino of F&F Design based in Turin, Italy.

The two-seat, roofless sports car was characterised by its long bonnet and that extended front-to-bulkhead ratio so typical of Bristol. The retro-themed front end had one very modern element – LED lighting – while the rear end was a throwback to the days of tailfins. A very low windscreen was matched by low head fairings whose profiles extended into the bootlid, while roll-over bars were also provided. Gill-like slits sat below extensions to the wheelarches on the front wings, while the flush-fitting door handles were inverted Fiat Barchetta units. The interior was trimmed in leather with CNC-milled details and a large touchscreen.

This was to be the first Bristol ever to use carbonfibre in its construction (in the form of exterior panels and some interior components), mounted over a Morgan Aero 8 bonded aluminium box-section chassis with all-independent suspension. Overall weight was very low at only 1130kg. The Bullet was intended to be the very last Bristol powered by internal combustion before the marque switched to range-extender electric power. It used a BMW 4.8-litre V8 producing 370hp – a choice that was not accidental, since the link between Bristol and BMW existed at birth of the British car company. The 0-62mph claim was 3.8 seconds.

The Bullet made its dynamic debut at the Goodwood Festival of Speed in 2016, and a production run limited to 70 units was scheduled to start in 2017, priced at £250,000 each. However, production never started in earnest; it is thought that eight chassis and five bodies were made but only one complete car – the prototype – was ever built (by F&F Design in Turin, along with partner companies in the Piedmont region).

FIGHTER SPORT COUPE (F&F DESIGN)

The last car made by Bristol in series was the Dodge Viper V10-engined Fighter, produced between 2004 and 2011, of which only around a dozen were completed. When Bristol came under the ownership of Kamkorp, it planned for the Fighter badge to be revived on an all-new coupe model designed to compete with the Aston Martin DB9 and Bentley Continental GT.

Italian design house F&F Design was called in to design and build a running prototype in 2014. Fulvio Fantolino stated: "We wanted to design a Gran

Turismo coupe on classic English proportions, highlighting the historicity of the Bristol brand. From the Bristol logo, we traced its history and the medieval context of the city helped us in designing the main lines of the car, to which we added very strong details that recalled hand-beaten pieces. We wanted to pay homage to the craftsmanship and great dexterity of the British builders."

This would have been the first of Bristol's new era of range-extender electric hybrid models. The prototype used a Jaguar XF chassis and V6 engine combined with Kamkorp's hybrid battery power system. However, the project did not progress beyond the running prototype stage.

BLENHEIM (F&F DESIGN)

Bristol planned to revive the Blenheim badge on a new four-wheel drive luxury SUV. Described as a 'hyper SUV', it was conceived in 2016, just as Bentley was launching its Bentayga (which would have been its closest rival). The design job was given to F&F, which said: "Blenheim was a project that wanted to go against the trend towards the sporting aspect. The Blenheim was characterised by massive proportions, like a military vehicle, and an almost fragmented style with plates that hid the hybrid platform." The Blenheim was fully designed using 3D computer software but in terms of a physical car, only the hybrid platform, based on the Ford Edge, was ever completed.

HOT ROD (F&F DESIGN)

The Hot Rod would have been a highly surprising departure for Bristol, had its plans come to fruition. This was to have been Bristol's first luxury panel van, based on the platform of the Metrocab Taxi that Kamkorp had also developed (see page 153). The preliminary design work was conducted by F&F in 2016, which described it as "a young vehicle, with a different flavour from the usual vans" and cited as inspiration vintage delivery vans and even the Ford Transit Supervan. The Hot Rod was a purely 2D concept research project that never left the computer screens.

As an aside, between 2006 and 2010, Fantolino also oversaw some IED student design projects in collaboration with another British company, McLaren.

TOP: Highly distinctive detailing featured on F&F's Fighter Sport Coupe, which was based on a Jaguar XF patform with hybrid power.
ABOVE MIDDLE: Blenheim would have been Bristol's first ever SUV model.
ABOVE: Hot Rod "luxury panel van" remained on the drawing board.

DAIMLER

Blue Blooded Bolides

One of the very oldest names in the British car industry, Daimler was founded in 1896 in Coventry by H J Lawson. From a very early time – 1902, in fact – Daimler secured a Royal Warrant to produce cars for the British monarchy, cementing its place as a purveyor of august and robust machinery, specialising in limousines. It never really shook this image, even when it dabbled in more sporting cars in the 1950s, such as the Conquest Roadster and SP250 – the latter a car of peculiar ugliness that stands as a prime example of the stark contrast between the gawky British design aesthetics of the time and the much more cutting-edge approach of the Italians.

Daimler was subsumed by Jaguar in 1960, which ultimately – apart from the DS420 limousine – demoted the Daimler marque to a mere badge-engineering exercise. The very last car to wear a Daimler badge was the Super V8 (1997-2003). Daimler chassis were not commonly adopted by coachbuilders abroad, with Michelotti the only Italian designer creating anything in the metal.

REGENCY COUPE (GHIA-AIGLE)

First revealed in 1951, the Daimler Regency was a substantial piece of machinery indeed: a portly, upright saloon with V8 power. It was relaunched in 1954 as the Regency II with a 3.5-litre V8 engine in place of the original 3.0-litre unit. In the UK, Hooper offered the stately Empress on this chassis but all other coachbuilders shied away – all except Ghia-Aigle, at any rate.

BELOW: Low-slung, smoothly styled and sporty coupe bodywork by Michelotti belied the rather august Daimler Regency underpinnings.

ABOVE: Giovanni Michelotti's original sketch for the Ghia-Aigle Daimler shows he was considering rear wheel spats. RIGHT: This Trevor Fiore design for a Daimler project proved abortive.

The Swiss company decided to rebody a right-hand drive Regency II chassis with a sporty coupe body designed by its Italian 'house' stylist, Giovanni Michelotti. The Regency grille and front lights were retained but in all other respects this was a fresh design. The body was barrel-shaped with smooth sides, other than a kick in the rear wings that began in the doors, and a curious raised section with chrome bars just in front of the rear wheels, presumably to allow cooling air in. The glasshouse was quite small, but then the interior was formatted to seat only two people.

Unveiled at the March 1955 Geneva Show, the Ghia-Aigle coupe was painted light blue with a beige leather interior. The Swiss magazine *Revue Automobile* reported that it weighed 200kg less than the regular Regency, but since that still meant it tipped the scales at 1.8 tonnes, it was hardly a lightweight. Ghia-Aigle's coupe failed to sell at the Geneva Show but was eventually registered in Switzerland.

The ultimate fate of this one-off is unrecorded.

A Ghia-Aigle brochure from the mid-1950s also advertised a 'Gran Sport' coupe to a very similar design based on a Daimler Conquest chassis with a six-cylinder engine but this was never actually built.

ROADSTER (FIORE)

Sketches exist by the English-born but Italian-based designer, Trevor Fiore, from the early 1960s showing a sharply-styled two-seat roadster proposal with Daimler badging. These were merely speculative sketches, however, with no future in the metal.

DELOREAN

DE LOREAN MOTOR COMPANY

The Dream That Failed to Take Off

The John Z DeLorean story reads like a highly implausible Hollywood drama. The son of a car factory worker, DeLorean's rags-to-riches career started out at Packard in research and development before he became a real high flyer at General Motors. Notably, he helped create a Pontiac that shared its name with a Ferrari (the GTO) and rose to the position of vice-president at GM.

In 1973 he left GM with a grand vision to set up his own car company, which he duly did in 1974: the DeLorean Motor Car Company (DMC). He imagined a whole range of DMC-badged models, starting with a sports car to build brand image. As well as being dramatically styled, he also wanted it to be made in high volumes. A convoluted search for financial backing – even involving comedian Johnny Carson – saw him knocking on the doors of several different national governments. Eventually the UK authorities took the bait in 1978, offering grants and loans totalling more than £80 million if DeLorean would set up shop in economically-disadvantaged Northern Ireland. It wasn't a difficult decision for the American.

For design, DeLorean turned to Italdesign's Giorgetto Giugiaro, whose work he had admired at the Turin Motor Show in 1974. Giugiaro also had a proven track record in production sports cars with the Lotus Esprit, which had a backbone chassis, a format that DeLorean also wanted to use.

Giugiaro penned his first proposal for the DMC-12 as early as July 1975, the shape being typical of the Italian's clean, angular approach. The low front end had four square headlamps and an integral bumper and spoiler. The rear was equally avant garde with its latticework lights and louvred screen, while the

ABOVE: John Z DeLorean with the stylist of the DMC12, Giorgetto Giugiaro.
LEFT: Overall shape was very typical of Giugiaro's 'folded paper' school of design.
RIGHT: Gullwing doors and brushed steel bodywork felt like novelties rather than well thought-through ideas.

NTH
347X

turbine-style spoked alloy wheels were very striking. But easily the most arresting aspect of the design was the gullwing doors – a great novelty on a production car. The design did not allow for full wind-down windows, so instead small 'ticket' apertures were engineered in. The eventual production interior was lavishly equipped with 'glove leather' upholstery, tinted glass, air conditioning and electric locking.

One other aspect marked the DeLorean out as unique: its brushed steel body finish. Giugiaro said that this was chosen because DeLorean wanted to avoid the expense of painting his cars, but it was also a nice selling point: the exposed metal look certainly carried showroom appeal. However, it also attracted dirt and scratches like chalk in the real world. The construction method was unique, with the steel outer panels bonded on to a composite understructure.

The first running prototype was ready for its press presentation in October 1976 but it still had some way to go in terms of development. Originally designed around a four-cylinder powerplant, the eventual choice of engine – a 2.8-litre V6 sourced from Peugeot/Renault – meant that the architecture had to be altered, with the engine sited further back than originally planned. Lotus was called in to help with engineering the backbone chassis and did a good job of sharpening up the handling, even if the 145hp engine never delivered the performance that the car's looks promised.

The idea was to market the DMC-12 exclusively in the American market with a keen projected price of $25,000, and 345 US dealers were duly appointed. Initially, production was scheduled to begin in June 1979 but that got delayed until early 1981 due to problems with regulations compliance and funding. Early plans to build 30,000 cars per year were vastly over-ambitious and production rates were slashed by early 1982. The car's reputation was tarnished by significant problems, such as leaking gullwing doors and a poorly finished cabin.

In October 1982, two catastrophic events occurred. Firstly, John DeLorean was arrested by the FBI for racketeering and drug dealing (for which he was eventually acquitted in court). Secondly, the UK Government decided to close the business in the wake of a string of financial irregularities. By then, only 8583 examples of the DMC-12 had been built.

With the demise of the DMC-12, another Giugiaro-designed DeLorean – a four-seater saloon, also with gullwing doors – was dragged down as well. Designed in 1979, Giugiaro completed a full-size mock-up in 1981, with the hope that it would reach the market by 1984 (up to 10,000 units per year being talked about). Following the demise of the whole DeLorean empire, Giugiaro reworked the mock-up he'd built and presented it at the 1982 Bologna Motor Show as the Lamborghini Marco Polo.

LEFT ABOVE: Backbone chassis was developed with Lotus help.
LEFT BELOW: Original Italdesign prototype differed in many details.
BELOW: Cabin leaks were a problem.
BELOW RIGHT: Four-seater gullwing proposal for DeLorean was repurposed as the Lamborghini Marco Polo in 1982.

ELVA

She Goes... To Italy

The Elva Engineering Company was set up by Frank Nichols, under the umbrella of London Road Garage Ltd (or LRG), a company that Frank and a small team had formed to deal in second-hand cars from the early 1950s. The Elva brand name came from the French 'elle va' ('she goes'). Nichols started out making inlet-over-exhaust conversions for the Ford E93A sidevalve engine, which were used in various road and race cars by the likes of Lotus, Morgan and Dellow.

Elva's earliest car-making years were dedicated to racing machinery. The first Elva racing car was built in 1955: this was an aluminium-bodied sports racer that was soon being offered to enthusiasts at £120 for the chassis or £350 in full kit form. Several dozen examples were sold, from the first MkI of 1955 to the MkIII of 1958.

Egged on by his American importer, Chuck Dietrich, Nichols launched a new roadgoing Elva, the Courier, in 1958, from a base in Bexhill, Sussex. This was not only handsome but also a very effective machine on the road. It scored notable commercial success, establishing a strong following in America – more so, in fact, than in its native Great Britain.

The Courier went through several evolutions, right through the 1960s, as did the company itself. Elva Engineering went into liquidation in 1961, whereupon it was bought by Trojan Ltd of Croydon, a company that was then making the Heinkel bubble car. Trojan sold out to Ken Sheppard Customised Sports Cars based in Shenley, Herts in 1965. Two years later Courier production drew to a close and by 1968 all car manufacturing had ceased. Elva Cars still exists as a company, based in Arundel, where Roger Dunbar runs Elva Cars and Elva Racing Components.

The Italian connection with Elva can be traced to Peter Agg, the owner of Trojan, who in the 1950s had become the UK importer of Lambretta scooters. In 1964, he hatched a plan for Elva to produce an all-new mid-engined sports car – what would eventually become the Elva-BMW GT160. When it came to finding a company to design and build it, Frank Nichols wanted to employ Ogle – a rare example of a UK-based car design company – but he was overruled by Agg, whose Italian connections led him to select Carrozzeria Fissore of Savigliano.

However, the new car would actually be designed by an Englishman: Trevor Fiore, who was only 27 years old at the time. His birth name was Trevor Frost but he decided to change it to Fiore, which was his Italian mother's maiden name, as he thought it lent greater credibility in design circles. From 1964, Fiore worked in continental Europe, both in Paris and in Turin. The Elva-BMW GT160 was Fiore's first ever design job for a British car maker that reached reality (he had penned something for Lea-Francis in 1963 but that never got built).

The GT160 was an extremely low car, measuring just 40 inches (1016mm) high. The nose was almost shovel-shaped and featured novel swivelling headlamps. Between humped wheelarches, the central body section had an almost dead-straight

ABOVE: Trevor Fiore (left) with Mario Fissore (right) and the Elva-BMW GT160. RIGHT ABOVE: Speculative sketch drawn by Fiore labelled Elva SPR 950. RIGHT BELOW: GT160 shape penned by Fiore was widely praised at the time and has clearly stood the test of time.

waistline, the lower body interrupted only by vented cooling intakes that mirrored the shape of the rear quarter-lights. The roofline swooped elegantly down almost to the tail, which was punctuated by half-bumpers. The cockpit was a cramped affair, since each sill contained a fuel tank, and the focus was very much on performance rather than luxury.

Fissore built the aluminium body in Italy over an Elva Mk7S racing chassis. The overall weight was claimed to be under 600kg, although when the car was weighed at its appearance in the Le Mans 24 Hour race in 1965, it actually tipped the scales at 762kg.

The GT160 used a tuned BMW 1800 engine fitted longitudinally amidships, reputedly developing 185hp; one of the cars was later fitted with a 3.5-litre Buick V8. A top speed of 140mph was quoted. The choice of a Hewland manual gearbox proved problematic, as it was simply not up to the job; indeed, it was transmission failures that would scupper the GT160's competition career.

Only three GT160s were ever made: one red, one white and one blue. The car – or rather two cars together, the blue and white ones – debuted at the 1964 Earls Court Motor Show. A further showing came shortly after in Italy at the Turin Show, where the GT160 appeared on Fissore's stand alongside the new De Tomaso Vallelunga. The Elva was extremely well received, *Style Auto* magazine declaring: "the Italian maestro has produced his most attractive work", also opining that Fiore had come up with "a completely new, almost geometric line". The *Daily Mail* was even more effusive, naming the GT160 "the most beautiful car in the world".

Elva announced its intention to offer the GT160 to the public at a projected price of £4500, which was extremely high. Fissore was set to manufacture the bodies on chassis supplied by Elva, but when the *carrozzeria* admitted that it had got its sums wrong and needed to triple its price, the GT160's fate was sealed. In January 1965, *Autocar* magazine reported that Trojan had abandoned all production plans. When Ken Sheppard acquired Elva in 1965, he considered producing the GT160 using glassfibre rather than metal bodywork, but that never came to anything.

The GT160 raced in several international events in 1965, the most notable being Le Mans. Despite being feted as the fastest British car there that year, that was not really saying much since so few British cars raced at Le Mans in 1965.

A second Elva design was penned by Trevor Fiore: a fastback coupe with the designation SPR 950, but it appears that only sketches of this project ever existed.

Very low roofline, horizontal waistline, raised winglines and chiselled nose all gave the GT160 a sense of race-bred drama.

FERGUSON

Fanatical for Four-Wheel Drive

In the 1950s Harry Ferguson – part of the Massey Ferguson tractor empire – developed a four-wheel drive system for cars, called Ferguson Formula (FF). This was famously fitted to the Ferguson P99 Formula 1 racer built in 1960 and raced during the 1961 season.

Several prototypes of a road-going 4x4 project were also built, starting with the R2. By the time the R4 saloon had arrived in 1954, it boasted highly innovative Dunlop Maxaret anti-lock disc brakes. This evolved into the R5 estate car, finished in 1959 and powered by a 2.2-litre horizontally-opposed four-cylinder engine, with four-wheel independent suspension.

Initially the shape was functional and ungainly but the Italian connection arrived when Giovanni Michelotti was tasked with designing a more attractive body to an estate format ('giardinetta' in Italian). He came up with several three-door and five-door proposals, the one eventually chosen looking somewhat like his contemporary work for Triumph. This was a not altogether successful mishmash of unusually angled panels, fussy chromework and tortured lighting.

The FF system was touted around several car makers, including Standard and Rover. BMC showed the most interest in productionising Ferguson's ideas but did not ultimately proceeed. Only a handful of prototypes were built, to a rather different and somewhat bland body design, in 1965.

Harry Ferguson died in October 1960 before seeing his innovations ever reach production. That's a shame because his FF system did enjoy an important legacy, being fitted to experimental Ford Zodiac police cars in Britain and to several Formula 1 racers in the late 1960s. Most significantly, it was also fitted to the world's first ever four-wheel drive performance car, the Jensen FF. That came about because Richard Jensen of Jensen Motors had seen the Ferguson R5 and maintained contact with the Ferguson enterprise, eventually buying the technology for his Jensen FF – which, since it was designed by Touring and built by Vignale, is described in the relevant chapter of this book (page 194).

Michelotti designed this somewhat gawky body to demonstrate Ferguson's pioneering four-wheel drive system.

FORD

Anglian Cousins in Italy

Ford might be a marque of American origin but in the UK it became something quintessentially British. For decades Ford dominated the British market, consistently lodged as number one in the sales charts. And for decades, Ford's offerings in Britain were unique to that market.

The Ford Motor Company (England) was founded in 1911 and a factory set up soon after in Trafford Park, Manchester, to build the Model T. By 1928, a new entity, Ford Motor Company Ltd, had been formed and a new plant was built in Dagenham, Essex, becoming Europe's largest car factory. It would not be until 1960, however, that Ford in Dearborn, USA bought all the shares in its British arm.

As well as offering US-designed models, Ford in Britain created many models of its own specifically suited to British customers, starting with the 1932 Model Y, which was the very first Ford specifically designed for sale outside North America.

Like many other British car makers, Ford courted Italian designers during the 1950s. while BMC snapped up Pinin Farina and Standard-Triumph allied with Michelotti, Ford beat a path to Bertone and Pietro Frua, the latter conceiving not only the essential outline of the Zephyr Mk3 but also proposing several other Ford designs during the 1960s and 1970s. While design at Ford of Britain always remained essentially an in-house affair, the Italian connection did persist in one aspect: Ford chose to name several of its models after Italian locations, such as Cortina and Capri.

While the French and German arms of Ford also developed their own unique models in post-war years, there was increasing pressure from Ford HQ to share resources in Europe. This resulted in the creation of Ford of Europe in 1967, merging the Ford Motor Company in Britain with Ford-Werke in Germany. From that moment on, the independence and significance of Ford's British arm diminished by steady degrees. In 1976, production of the Ford Granada devolved entirely to Germany, followed by the Capri and eventually all other models, leaving the UK's Ford factories making commercial vehicles and engines only. All Ford vehicle production ceased in the UK in 2013.

Italy continued to carry significance for Ford. The American parent company had begun a relationship with the Italian sports car maker De Tomaso, whose Pantera of 1970 was Ford-powered. In 1967, De Tomaso had also acquired the troubled Italian coachbuilder Ghia; three years later, the design house was sold on to Ford. Gradually Ghia became the European styling and prototype wing of Ford globally. Plenty of Ford prototypes were built by Ghia during the 1970s and 1980s, but these can rarely be regarded as British projects, since they were almost all coordinated from Ford headquarters in Cologne, Germany or in Detroit, USA. In this book, only those Ghia designs with a specific connection to Ford of Britain are included.

ABOVE: Italy thought it could do a better styling job of the Ford Anglia; Italy was probably right, even though the resulting Anglia Torino was hardly the handsomest car on the planet. RIGHT: The very last Anglo-Italian Ford project was the RS200 rally car, which was styled by Filippo Sapino of Ghia.

C74 BNX
HISTORY OF RALLYING
Mobil

The Ghia name would also be used, somewhat ignominiously, as the top trim level on Ford models, starting in January 1974 with the Granada Ghia and continuing well into the 21st century. Via its purchase of Carrozzeria Ghia from De Tomaso, Ford also inherited another Italian coachbuilding name: Vignale. This led to preliminary discussions about potential coachbuilt Vignale models for the UK market but nothing concrete ever came of this. Vignale would, in 2016, be adopted as the name of Ford's plushest trim level; a little bit of Ghia history repeating, perhaps, but this was certainly far from a glorious use of the once-great Vignale badge.

Ford's Advanced Vehicle Operation (AVO) department, which operated from 1970 to 1975 at South Ockenden in Essex specialising in Ford's RS models, had some Italian connections, for instance working with Frua on prototypes. In 1974, AVO even considered starting production of the De Tomaso Pantera in the UK, possibly fitted with an Essex 3.0-litre V6 engine – a format that Vignale had already trialled in a Pantera – but Ford's senior management judged, probably correctly, that this would be a commercial distraction.

ZODIAC MK2 (BERTONE)

Ford's Consul/Zephyr range of saloons was the quintessential choice for families and businessmen during the 1950s. The Mk2 shape (1956-1962) was designed in-house by the British stylist, Colin Neale, consisting of a three-prong family: entry-level Consul, mid-range Zephyr and plush Zodiac, the latter having a snazzier front grille and altered rear styling. With the late 1950s rush of British companies to Italian styling houses, Ford asked Bertone, in 1958, to rework the Zodiac's brightwork, the idea being to move it further upmarket from lesser models. The Italian company created a new front grille, some fancy body trim and different hubcaps, but the Italian proposals were not adopted in production.

ZEPHYR MK3 (FRUA)

When it came to replacing the Zephyr/Zodiac Mk2, Ford initially asked the designer of the Mk2, Colin Neale, to come up with ideas. Neale's proposals were based around themes he'd explored with the Anglia 105E, notably its idiosyncratic reverse-backlight treatment. This direction wasn't widely liked within Ford, so Ford summoned designer Elwood Engel over from the USA to come up with alternatives that were notable for their rear fins. Neale then performed a sleeker interpretation but the management rejected both as being too Americanesque.

So in 1959 Ford UK approached Frua to design its Zephyr Mk3. The Italian design house came up with a very crisp shape that was distinctly European, and which cleverly hid the car's bulk (almost a foot longer than its predecessor). Ford liked it so much that it formed the basis of the new car's style. However, it was not adopted untouched; as one employee was quoted to have said, somewhat sardonically: "One could not expect the US board to approve anything reflecting such good taste and sophistication".

The man tasked with reworking the Frua design was Ford's Canadian-born stylist, Roy Brown Jr, who had been one of the main lights behind the doomed Edsel, and would later go on to design the Ford Cortina. Frua's ostentatious quad-lamp front end and fussy side detailing were duly reworked, but the main shape – including the mildly befinned, razor-edged rear end and the simple glasshouse – was left pretty much as Frua had conceived it.

Called Zephyr 4 (with a four-cylinder engine), Zephyr 6 (with a 'six' and a full-width grille) and range-topping Zodiac (with quad headlamps), the range was launched in April 1962 and lasted until 1966, some 292,144 Mk3s being made.

Frua delivered one further proposal for Ford in the early 1960s: a clay model for the Ford Cortina that featured exaggerated fins, but this wasn't adopted. Another Italian design house, Zagato, is known to have created sketches for a two-door coupe based on the Cortina; again this never came to anything.

TOP TO BOTTOM: 1958 Zodiac facelift by Bertone; Frua Zephyr; befinned Frua Cortina buck; Zagato sketches for a Cortina-based coupe. OPPOSITE: Open-topped Anglia Spider sports car was sadly stillborn.

auto italiana

20 GIUGNO 1963 - NUMERO 25 - ANNO 44 - L. 100

L'ANGLIA SPIDER

PER LA PATENTE DI GUIDA

DIO SULL'AUTO A TURBINA

SITA DI CLARK IN BELGIO

ANGLIA SPIDER (FRUA)

When Ford introduced its Anglia 105E saloon in 1959, it was widely praised for how well it drove, if not necessarily for how good it looked. In Italy, Pietro Frua thought the new Anglia had strong possibilities as the basis for a new sports car and in 1962 designed a 'Spider' version of the Anglia.

From the front, its Anglia basis was clear, as it retained the British Ford's grille and headlamps. Everything aft of this, however, was completely new. The overall shape was fairly innocuous, although the pronounced wheelarch edges were an unusual feature. The interior had two seats, a three-spoke wood-rim steering wheel and a new dashboard with rev counter, tachometer and water/oil gauges.

Auto Italiana magazine featured the new car on its cover in June 1963, reporting that the prototype belonged to Ford of Italy, and that the Anglia Spider might possibly reach production in limited numbers. However, it's thought that only one prototype was ever built. In 1964 Frua presented a very similar Spider design based on the Opel Kadett.

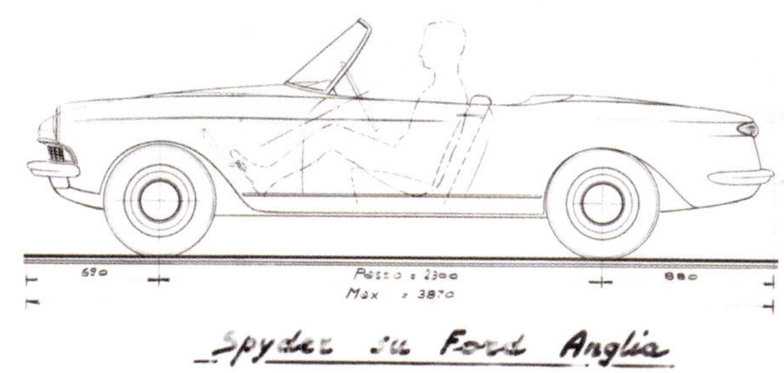

ANGLIA TORINO (MICHELOTTI & OSI)

Some historians have stated that the Anglia Torino was born because Italian buyers disliked the UK-made Ford Anglia 105E. That's simply not true: the Anglia was actually the number one best-selling imported car in Italy in the years 1960 and 1961. The trouble was, the Anglia was the very epitome of a faddishly styled car. Its 'breezeway' reverse-angle rear window and Americanesque tailfins may have looked cutting edge at launch in 1959 but those fads quickly faded.

The man in charge of Ford's Italian import operation at the time was an American, Filmer Paradise – the very man who, in 1963, spooked Ford's deal to buy Ferrari when he reputedly asked Enzo Ferrari: "Do you expect to sell the company and still remain in charge afterwards?" A furious Signor Ferrari ejected Mr Paradise from his office, and the deal was off.

Back to the Anglia, and the unshakeable Mr Paradise sought permission from his Ford bosses to restyle the British-styled Anglia in Italy, which was duly granted. The man given the task of restyling the Anglia was Giovanni Michelotti. The instruction

OPPOSITE: Body-wise, the Anglia Torino shared only its floorpan, doors and windscreen with the British Anglia 105E.
BELOW: Giovanni Michelotti stands alongside his handiwork.
BOTTOM: The Torino debuted, suitably enough, at the 1964 Turin Show

was to retain not only the floorpan and mechanicals from the Anglia, but also the doors and windscreen. Otherwise Michelotti had a free hand to create a crisp new set of clothes. He dispensed with the Anglia's Z-form C-pillars, replacing them with a more conventional profile that featured a somewhat BMW-like kink in them. The tail fins were also eradicated, as were the hooded headlights and sloping grille, replaced with much more sober styling, while new circular taillights were made locally by Altissimo (and shared, incidentally, with various exotic Italian cars). While undoubtedly clean, the overall shape was perhaps too anonymous to have much impact, while the high wing line made it look narrow and top-heavy.

The task of building the new car was given to Officine Stampaggi Industriali (OSI) of Turin, so the new model's name of Anglia Torino was entirely fitting. The 1964 Turin Show also provided the backdrop for the car's launch and the car's instigator, Filmer Paradise, was presented with a silver-painted example.

The manufacturing process consisted of complete knock-down (CKD) kits of parts being shipped over to Turin from Ford's Halewood plant. The underpinnings of the Anglia 105E were left unchanged, including the Kent 997cc overhead valve engine and four-speed gearbox. However, alongside a regular 41hp Torino, Ford Italiana offered a more powerful (52hp) Torino S version that sported a twin-choke Weber carburettor and four-branch exhaust manifold.

The Anglia Torino was sold principally in Italy, but Belgium, Luxembourg and the Netherlands also imported the model. In 1965, production was running at 60 units per day at OSI's factory but reports of poor build quality didn't help sales and production lasted only a couple of years. Some 10,007 units were sold in Italy in total, although it took until 1969 to shift them all. OSI also produced another special-bodied Ford, the 20M TS Coupe, but this was based on a German-made model, the Taunus.

ESCORT MONTE CARLO GT (FRUA)

The Escort may have been conceived as a European car – it was the first post-war Ford built simultaneously in Britain and Germany – but its design was wholly British. A tremendous success, it sold well over two million examples from 1968 to 1974 and sired a whole string of legendary high-performance versions, including the GT, Sport, Mexico and more.

There might also have been an Escort sports coupe, had coachbuilder Pietro Frua's plans come to fruition. Reviving his links with Ford, he produced a prototype of a new Escort-based two-door coupe for the November 1970 Turin Show. This Escort 1600-engined car was called the Monte Carlo GT, sometimes also referred to as the Fruaway.

This was a fairly attractive notchback (three-box) shape with a sloping nose, indented headlamp nacelles and a bonnet cooling vent. At the rear end were taillights borrowed from the Alfa Romeo 1750 Berlina, while the cabin offered 2+2 seating. The prototype remained a one-off but Frua revived the idea two years later with its Escort Mexico-based coupe (see below).

ESCORT MEXICO COUPE (FRUA)

A refreshed version of Frua's previous Escort coupe was created in 1972. The main difference was new fastback styling, recalling Frua's work many years earlier for German company, Glas. Other changes included squared-off rear wheelarches, a black tail panel and a wraparound rear bumper, although the Alfa Romeo 1750 Berlina rear lights were retained.

In 1972, Frua approached Walter Hayes of Ford with a proposal to enter production. The idea was to have Escort Mexico floorpans shipped from the UK to Turin, where new bodywork would be built, trimmed and painted, then returned to Ford's Advanced Vehicle Operations (AVO) division in South Ockendon, Essex.

LEFT: Escort Monte Carlo GT by Frua. LEFT BELOW: Handsome Escort Mexico Coupe of 1972, also by Frua. BELOW & OPPOSITE: Ford of Italy's studio created its own restyled GT70 (shown in standard form top right).

Frua's right-hand drive, red-painted prototype was shipped over to Ford in Britain, where it was UK-registered and tested on the road with Escort RS1600 wheels fitted. However, Ford's AVO division judged the design to be too 'feminine'; at the time, AVO was much more interested in a testosterone-charged, motorsport-orientated clientele. There were other objections, too: Ford was simply not used to such a coachbuilt set-up; dealers would have had to keep a stock of unique parts for the car; and the production process was judged to be prohibitively costly. Frua's coupe was briefly considered as a potential rally car, in the wake of the failed GT70 (see opposite), but not taken forward. The one and only car made was eventually exported to New Zealand.

GT70 (FORD OF ITALY)

Before Bertone conceived the Lancia Stratos, Ford seriously considered making its own mid-engined rally car: the GT70. In the wake of Ford's Le Mans-conquering GT40, a mid-engined rally machine looked like a promising bet, especially as the front-engined Escort was being challenged on the rally stages by out-and-out sports cars like the Porsche 911 and Alpine A110.

The GT70 was the brainchild of Ford's competition director, Stuart Turner, fresh from his success with BMC's rally Minis. GT40 guru Len Bailey was drafted in to engineer the new GT70 in 1970. The body design was done at Ford's Research and Engineering Centre in Dunton, Essex, under the direction of Joe Oros (the American designer responsible for the original Ford Mustang). The glassfibre body featured a sharp edge curving around the nose and sweeping around to the cut-off tail, manually-activated pop-up headlamps and a black-louvred engine cover. Overall the shape was smooth but perhaps somewhat bland.

When Henry Ford II saw the GT70, he loved it. Developed in just nine months, it made its public debut at the January 1971 Brussels Motor Show, and looked all set to be made in series. As a road car, 500 units would need to be sold at a price of £2500 apiece to make it viable, but such a prospect seemed unlikely. In addition, the GT70's disappointing performances in rallies cut short any hopes of a competition career for the new car.

The GT70 was extensively tested during 1971 but a mere six GT70 chassis were built in total. One of these was dispatched to Italy where, in September 1969, Ford had set up a little-known styling studio at Bruino near Turin, headed by Filippo Sapino and Ercole Spada. The Italian team set to work on an alternative vision of the GT70 during 1971. Its shape was largely realised by Spada, who later said that he did not get prior sight of the Dunton body design before starting work on it. A full-size model was built in Styrofoam covered with Epowood (an epoxy resin).

The Italian shape was much more sharp-edged than the Joe Oros original; indeed, when he saw it, Oros asked for it to be made less severe, as Sapino later recalled: "Joe Oros came down and said [our original model] was too sharp. We rounded it off to please him. This was a big help by Joe Oros. If we'd come out with our super-sharp design, it wouldn't have lasted."

Design features included flying rear buttresses behind a distinctive rollover bar, concealed windscreen wipers and two NACA air ducts in the front lid. Pop-up headlamps were flanked by slender sidelights, while foglights sat either side of the front grille. The long tail was good aerodynamically speaking but also provided room for luggage.

The full-size model was shown at the Turin Motor Show in November 1971 in a striking metalflake orange colour. There was no interior in the car, although one was planned by Ford's UK studio, featuring a pistol-grip gear lever, stowage space behind the seats and warning lights mounted in the roof.

The sole, non-running Ford of Italy GT70 prototype was the only project ever publicly shown by Ford's secretive Bruino studio, which was closed down in July 1973 after being merged with Ghia, where Sapino took up the design reins.

RS200 (GHIA)

In many ways the Ford RS200 was a very British project. Conceived and produced by Ford Motorsport in Boreham, it was a mid-engined, four-wheel drive car designed for rallying in Group B. Assisted by Gordon Murray and Keith Duckworth, Ford Motorsport assessed a number of engineering designs, the winning contender being that of ex-Lotus F1 designer Tony Southgate. This consisted of an aluminium monocoque on to which tubular steel spaceframes were bolted, while power came from a 250hp Ford RS1700T engine.

It was in Italy that the RS200's body was styled, by Filippo Sapino of Ghia. He was given just a few constraints: the windscreen, cut-down doors and rear lights all had to come from Ford's Sierra, to lend the RS200 a tad of family resemblance, while the hinged sections front and rear had to allow easy access to the mechanicals. Post-testing, Ford's

engineering department at Dunton made some alterations to Sapino's design, revising the front end and adding a large rear aerofoil. The prototype's body was made of a composite of carbon, aramid and glassfibre but eventual production bodies were all-glassfibre. The interior was designed by Ford at Dunton and executed by Tickford.

The RS200 was revealed in 1984 at both the Belfast and Turin Motor Shows. A road-going version was needed for FIA homologation, which called for 200 cars to be produced. After six pre-production prototypes were built by ART of Woolaston, the remaining 194 were built by Reliant in Staffordshire. Sadly the rush to manufacture the required 200 cars meant that build quality was quite poor, especially considering the car's elevated £50,000 price tag. Some experts believe that far fewer than the homologation requirement of 200 units were in fact built.

The RS200 was very much a British-engineered project intended to beat all-comers in rallying. Its shape was created in Italy by Filippo Sapino of Ghia.

FRAZER NASH

Sporting Intent

Archibald Frazer-Nash set up a sports car manufacturing company in his own name (Frazer Nash without a hyphen) in 1922, initially based in Kingston-upon-Thames. After going into receivership in 1927, it re-emerged as AFN Limited, in which form it was acquired in 1929 by Harold J 'Aldy' Aldington and run by him and his two brothers.

Having been the UK concessionaire for BMW pre-war, Frazer Nash relied on these links after the war and the company formed strong links with Bristol, launching the Frazer Nash-Bristol in September 1946. Aldington was going to market a Pinin Farina-designed 1947 convertible as a Frazer Nash but the two companies had fallen out by the time it was finished and it ended up being badged as a Bristol 2-Litre instead (see the Bristol chapter for more). Frazer Nash made a string of sports car models in the 1940s and 1950s, its last in 1957. By then it had become the UK concessionaire for Porsche, a role it fulfilled until 1965. A tiny handful of Frazer Nash chassis received Italian coachwork, as detailed in this chapter.

The Frazer Nash name made a surprise comeback in the 1990s as a research and development company specialising in electric and hybrid powertrains. It developed electric car and golf buggy designs and co-operated with Malaysian car makers. In 2001, parent company, Kamkorp, bought the taxi maker, Metrocab, while in 2009 it cooperated with Italdesign-Giugiaro to create the Namir supercar prototype. In 2011, Frazer Nash was even reunited with its erstwhile partner, Bristol Cars, when the latter's assets were bought by Kamkorp. However, in July 2018, Frazer-Nash Research (written with a hyphen) was wound up, followed less than two years later by Kamkorp (and therefore Bristol).

2000 SPYDER (TOURING)

As the UK concessionaire for BMW in pre-war years, Frazer Nash relied on these links for its first production sports car, which was developed during 1946-1947 by engineer John Perrett. A BMW 328-style twin-tube chassis was designed and fitted with a BMW 1971cc six-cylinder engine.

An early chassis – only the second-ever built (421/E2) – was sent to the Italian coachbuilder Carrozzeria Touring, probably in late 1947. This was duly built up as a Spyder using Touring's 'Superleggera' principle of body panels wrapped over a framework of thin steel tubing.

The style clearly reflected the BMW origins of the underpinnings. The front grille was a BMW-style 'kidney' shape, flanked by two sets of lights and half-bumpers over additional air inlets. Flares over the wheelarches, front and rear, extended backwards to ape the upper wing lines. There was a small windscreen with no top bar and no roof at all.

Launched at the March 1948 Geneva Show, the car was finished in cream paint with green upholstery. When the Shah of Persia (today's Iran) visited the Bristol works to peruse the Brabazon aeroplane, he also saw the Spyder and bought it on the spot for

ABOVE: Touring's 2000 Spyder was a true work of art; tragically only one was made and its ultimate fate is unknown. RIGHT: Giugiaro was the styling hand behind this 21st century reinvention of the Frazer Nash marque.

SKODA
BENTLEY MOTORS
LOTUS
SPYKER
PAGANI

TOP: This Fiat 8V rebody replaced the original Frazer Nash bodywork in 1953. ABOVE: Motto's coupe on a Le Mans chassis looked neat, if unspectacular. RIGHT: Namir was the name given to this hybrid supercar in 2009.

£2584, an enormous sum at the time. After being dispatched to Teheran in October 1948, sadly all trace of this very special one-off was lost.

FIAT 8V REBODY (FIAT CARROZZERIE SPECIALI)

In 1951, Giovanni Lurani famously won the Targa Florio race in Sicily in a Frazer Nash (chassis number 421/100/109). His victorious car remained in Italy but by 1953, it had been rebodied with a new steel coupe body, which was taken directly from a Fiat 8V, as designed by Fabio Luigi Rapi of Fiat's Carrozzerie Speciali department. The car was painted in British Racing Green with red fabric upholstery.

LE MANS CA-MO (MOTTO)

In 1949 Frazer Nash's 'Competition' model was renamed the 'Le Mans Replica' after its famous success at the French 24-hour race. An early example (chassis number 421/100/112) was delivered to Frazer Nash's Italian distributor – Ital Clarco of Milan – in April 1950, and was duly shown at the Turin Motor Show.

Apparently the car proved impossible to sell. Possibly as a result, its body was removed in May 1954 and replaced by new coupe bodywork by Carrozzeria Motto (Ca-Mo), Rocco Motto's celebrated coachbuilding company based in Turin. This was a pretty, if fairly typical fastback style realised in aluminium. The Frazer Nash grille was kept intact.

In August 1954, Ital Clarco sold the car to Emilio Vicentini of Milan. In 1976, it was passed on to a British enthusiast but sadly its coupe bodywork was removed in the UK and in 1982 the chassis was returned to Le Mans Replica specification; in this form the car was subsequently owned by Victor Gauntlett, the head of Aston Martin. The Motto body was then used to build a home-made special by David Brown, using a Rolls-Royce 4.0-litre engine.

NAMIR (ITALDESIGN-GIUGIARO)

The Frazer Nash name was revived in the 1990s as Frazer-Nash Research (FNR), specialising in

developing electric and hybrid drivetrains. In 2009, Italdesign-Giugiaro chose the 2009 Geneva Show to launch a new supercar in collaboration with FNR, using joint Frazer-Nash and Giugiaro badging. The car was dubbed the Namir, the Arabic word for 'tiger'.

The styling was by Giorgetto Giugiaro's son, Fabrizio, who was inspired by the Frazer-Nash diamond logo to create a starkly geometric shape. Among the most dramatic aspects of the design were a V-shaped windscreen, angular criss-cross volumes to the sides and a roof that flowed into a windowless rear end which had cooling slits forming a capital letter 'M'. The scissor doors allowed access to a two-seat cabin that was "a homage to British tradition", featuring leather, tweed and brushed steel.

The prototype was built at Italdesign-Giugiaro's Turin base. It had a carbonfibre monocoque chassis with honeycomb panelling, weighing just 110kg. An FNR-developed hybrid powertrain consisted of a transverse rear-mounted 814cc petrol rotary engine and two electric motors, one on each axle, giving the car four-wheel drive. With a combined power output of 370hp, claimed performance was certainly in the supercar league: 0-62mph in 3.5 seconds, 0-124mph in 10.4 seconds and a top speed of 187mph. This was in fact claimed to be the fastest hybrid electric car in the world at the time. Yet it was also eco-friendly with a claimed fuel consumption of 160mpg and CO_2 emissions of 60g/km.

Two versions of the Namir were shown at Geneva: a road car (painted orange) and a racer (painted green, black and white). While the racer was a non-running mock-up, the orange car was a fully functioning prototype that made its dynamic debut up the hill at Goodwood Festival of Speed in 2009. The Namir's hybrid system was also due to underpin Bristol's new era of models (page 128) but that never happened.

PERDANA (F&F DESIGN)

As the new owner of the Frazer Nash and Bristol marques in the 21st century, Kamkorp had big plans for both. It courted consultancy roles, one of which was for the Malaysian national car maker, Proton, which in 2012 wanted to make a big statement with a new Perdana limousine.

Kamkorp approached Fulvio Fantolino of F&F Design in Turin to come up with the design. Fantolino created a very British-looking limousine – quite Bentley-esque in fact – with an upright front grille, circular headlamps, classical swage line and raised boot. F&F built a fully running prototype in 2012 but this was never revealed publicly, the project only coming to light when F&F released images of the car in 2020.

METROCAB (F&F DESIGN)

The archetypal London taxi was, seemingly for an eternity, the Austin-based FX4. However, in 1987 the Metrocab was launched as a direct rival for the classic taxicab, being manufactured until 2006, latterly by Kamkorp. After several years of hiatus, the Metrocab name was once again given life by Kamkorp, which tasked its Frazer-Nash Research division (now hypenated) to develop an all-new London taxi. The Metrocab was battery-powered with an additional small range extender petrol engine fitted. In this respect it was very like its main rival, the LEVC TX, which it beat to launch, making the Metrocab the first ever authorised electric-powered London 'black cab' when it was unveiled in 2014.

Despite the quintessential Britishness of the London taxi concept, the Metrocab's bodywork was actually designed in Turin, Italy by Fulvio Fantolino of F&F Design. It was styled with what Fantolino described as a "vintage look" that some ventured to suggest aped the design of the famous TX London taxicab. Indeed the London Taxi Company even took the case to court in 2015, claiming that the Metrocab infringed its trademarked shape, but the judge dismissed LTC's claims in favour of the Metrocab's creators. Sadly, despite promotions involving London's then mayor, Boris Johnson, the Metrocab never reached production.

TOP: F&F Design created the Perdana limousine for UK-based Kamkorp. ABOVE: The hybrid-powered Metrocab of 2014 may have looked quintessentially British but it was actually designed in Italy.

FRISKY

Economy With Style

Microcars were a major part of the motoring scene in the 1950s and early 1960s, typified by the 'bubble car', a genre that originated in Italy in 1953 with the Iso Isetta. The Italian designer Giovanni Michelotti would migrate much of the Isetta's style and concept to the BMW 600 microcar, but that's another story. In the meantime we need to wind our story back to the Anglo-Italian theme and another small detour, this time to Cairo in Egypt. Here we find three brothers – Raymond, Neville and Derek Flower – who held the Nuffield Group franchise for Egypt. They attempted to make a sports car based on Morris mechanicals but this was scuppered by the Suez crisis of 1956, when all the Flower family's possessions were seized and the brothers were expelled from Egypt.

Undeterred, the Flowers reasoned that a very small and economical two-seat car would be the perfect riposte to the challenges that followed in the wake of the Suez oil crisis. Back in the UK, Captain Raymond Flower forged a partnership with the British engineering company Henry Meadows Ltd, which agreed to provide space and facilities at its Wolverhampton works to develop a brand new microcar: the Frisky.

A prototype was duly completed in December 1956. This was designed by Gordon Bedson, who had previously worked at racing car maker, Kieft, and at the aircraft company, Vickers; assisting him was another ex-Kieft engineer, Keith Peckmore. Unfortunately the team lacked styling experience and the resulting gullwing-doored prototype, nicknamed 'The Bug', had a rudimentary appearance to say the least.

On the recommendation of the motoring journalist Gordon Wilkins, it was decided that Neville Flower should fly to Turin to seek the assistance of Carrozzeria Vignale. On his arrival, Alfredo Vignale greeted him personally and invited his favoured designer, Giovanni Michelotti, to meet the Englishman. Within 24 hours Michelotti had sketched a promising-looking proposal for Flower, complete with handsome gullwing doors. Flower returned to Britain with the sketches under his arm and Vignale's promise of a built-up prototype within three months.

Now Raymond Flower needed a mechanical basis for his new microcar. He arranged to meet Harry Webster, technical director of Standard Cars, with a view to securing the rights to use Standard mechanicals. That meeting would be a fateful one, but not really for Flower, who failed to get the permission he was after; instead, this would be the moment when Webster first saw the handiwork of the extraordinarily talented Signor Michelotti, which would have long-lasting consequences for Standard Triumph (a story

ABOVE: Gullwing doors were a real novelty among economy cars of the 1950s. This prototype, designed and built in Italy, debuted at the 1957 Geneva Motor Show.

This new design made its debut, as the FriskySport, at the October 1957 Earls Court Motor Show, with production starting in March 1958. In September 1958, the convertible was joined by a hardtop Frisky Coupe. Initially a 249cc Villiers two-stroke engine was used but a 324cc Villiers engine was soon offered as an option. The FriskySport lived up to its name by the standards of the day, capable of 65mph. Frisky continued to make cars, latterly in Kent, up until 1964.

LEFT: Giovanni Michelotti's sketch was used in Meadows' publicity for the Frisky, along with the Vignale logo. BELOW: The eventual production FriskySport was redesigned back in the UK.

told fully on page 252 of this book).

Back to Michelotti's design for the Frisky; this was quickly built up on a ladder chassis with a narrow rear wheel track so that no differential was required. The car's shape had certain styling similarities with the Abarth 750 Vignale 'Goccia' that Michelotti had designed in 1956, including a smooth front end, teardrop rear end and gullwing doors.

The new Frisky 'Gull Wing' prototype made its debut, proudly sporting Vignale badges, at the prestigious Geneva Motor Show in March 1957, where it garnered a huge amount of interest. Well received though the design may have been, the body was judged to be simply too complex and too expensive to manufacture in series. Michelotti's design was therefore rejected, or rather transformed. Gordon Bedson turned it into something quite different, with conventional doors, small tailfins and a soft-top in place of the fixed roof, the whole thing being much easier to make in glassfibre.

GORDON-KEEBLE

A Tortoise To Outpace Rival Hares

The origins of Gordon-Keeble can be traced back to Peerless Cars, the Slough-based company that had made the Peerless GT coupe from 1958 until its bankruptcy in 1960. While the Peerless was revived as the Warwick by one of the former company's directors, Bernie Rodger, another ex-director of Peerless, John Gordon, would do his own thing: make the Gordon-Keeble.

The idea was inspired by a one-off that garage owner Jim Keeble was asked to build for an American pilot called Rick Neilson, who requested the installation of a Chevrolet Corvette V8 engine into a Peerless GT chassis. John Gordon of Peerless was approached and he gave the project the green light, as long as the work was carried out at the company's headquarters in Slough.

Shortly before the V8 one-off was completed, Gordon resigned from Peerless and suggested that he and Keeble make a brand new V8-powered road-going GT car, and together they formed the Gordon Automobile Company in 1959.

Keeble designed a new multi-tubular spaceframe chassis with an independent front end using wishbones and coils, plus de Dion rear suspension. The big news, though, was the installation of an American V8 engine – a pioneering move in Britain at the time. The prototype had a 283 cubic inch (4.7-litre) V8 but eventual production cars would use the larger 327 cubic inch (5355cc) Chevrolet V8, taken direct from the Corvette Sting Ray and good for 300hp. Legend has it that General Motors' Ed Cole agreed to supply 1000 of these engines to Gordon after driving the prototype and being suitably impressed.

When it came to designing the bodywork, Gordon turned to Italy, having lived for some time beforehand in that country. His chosen design house was Bertone, where he had the extreme good fortune to take advantage of its most recent hiring: a 21-year old Giorgetto Giugiaro. This prodigiously talented newcomer was given the design brief, a historic move since it was the very first Giugiaro design to be shown publicly (although he had designed the Alfa Romeo 2600 Sprint for Bertone before the Gordon – incidentally a car that shared a very similar profile – it was the British coupe that broke cover first). It took Bertone just one month to construct the prototype after the chassis had been delivered to Turin. The new car was presented as the Gordon GT at the March 1960 Geneva Show, where it had the distinction of being the only all-new car displayed at that year's show.

The Gordon GT attracted much favourable comment, mostly thanks to its excellent proportions, understated elegance of line, generous glasshouse and evocatively curvaceous body sides. Double headlamps were all the rage in the early 1960s and to make the Gordon-Keeble look distinctive, these were arranged on a slant, with oblong indicators set below. Tail fins were subtle both in size and shape, with the rear lights arranged in a vertical cluster along their trailing edge.

The Gordon drove extremely well, too. The

One of Giorgetto Giugiaro's first ever designs for Bertone, the Gordon-Keeble somewhat resembled the Italian stylist's Alfa Romeo 2600 Sprint coupe.

FEW 555D

prototype was road-tested by *Autocar* magazine, which enthused that it was, "the most electrifying vehicle we have ever tested". The V8 engine ensured formidable performance – 142mph and 0-60mph in 7.7 seconds – although the clutch pedal and gear lever required firm pressure, and the steering suffered somewhat from bump-steer. Cornering was reportedly very good, while powerful and progressive disc brakes hauled the car up confidently.

Initially, a manufacturing partner was sought. Armstrong-Siddeley showed interest, while fridge and microcar manufacturer, Renzo Rivolta, made moves to build the car under licence in Italy (in fact, Rivolta would launch his own American V8-powered Iso Rivolta grand tourer in 1962 – also designed by Giugiaro). Instead, Gordon and Keeble decided to do it independently, a process that took fully four years under the auspices of Gordon-Keeble Ltd of Eastleigh, Hampshire. At the car's March 1964 press unveiling at London's Savoy hotel, it had now been renamed the Gordon-Keeble GK1. On its nose sat a badge in the form of a tortoise, apparently chosen after one strolled

Contemporary advertising played heavily on the Italian design connection, as well as the car's British engineering and American-sourced V8 power.

in front of the car during a photo session – despite Keeble thinking it was bad luck. Williams & Pritchard created an aluminium body plug for the car, with production bodies being moulded in glassfibre to an extremely high standard.

A true grand tourer, the Gordon-Keeble had full seating for four adults. Although the upholstery was mere vinyl rather than leather, the cabin was otherwise very well equipped, with electric windows, Britax inertia-reel seatbelts, fire extinguisher and push-button radio.

The launch price was £2798, which compared very favourably with its main rivals (for instance, Ferrari's cheapest model cost twice as much). In fact, the GK1 was simply too cheap to make a profit and just one year into its life, production ceased. The model was revived in 1966, renamed the IT (standing for International Touring), but only a handful of additional cars were produced. There was one final revival in 1968, when a US Ford agent called John de Bruyne displayed a slightly redesigned version at the New York Auto Show, but only two such cars were built. 100 cars had been made in total by the end.

HEALEY

Sportsman's Choice

Cornish-born Donald Mitchell Healey was precociously talented both as a driver and an engineer. In motorsport, he won the 1931 Monte Carlo Rally and the 1932 Alpine Trial. As an engineer, he took up positions at Riley and Triumph, rising to become technical director at the latter, and was responsible for designing all of Triumph's cars during his spell there, including the Dolomite sports car.

In 1945 he formed the Donald Healey Motor Company based at an old RAF hangar at Warwick. He developed a series of mostly Riley-engined sports cars, which achieved notable racing successes at such events as the Mille Miglia, Targa Florio and Le Mans. As road cars, Healeys were expensive but always acknowledged to be of very high quality.

While only one Healey chassis was bodied by a coachbuilder in Italy (Bertone), a 1951 liaison with the American car maker, Nash, led to the Anglo-British Nash-Healey, which was given a fresh suit of Italian clothes in 1952 by Pinin Farina. By 1954, it was all over for Healey as an independent car maker. By then, however, Donald Healey had given his name to one of the world's most famous sports cars: the Austin-Healey. For Italian coachbuilt Austin-Healeys, please see the chapter on BMC (page 84).

HEALEY CABRIOLET (BERTONE)

Launched in 1946, there was no faster British four-seater in the immediate post-war period than the Healey. Light weight (under a ton) and a tuned Riley 2443cc six-cylinder engine gave the newly-launched Healey range a top speed of 105mph. Three models were offered by the factory: Westland (roadster), Elliott (saloon) and Sportsmobile (drophead coupe).

Healey's stiff box section chassis with its coil-sprung suspension front and rear was a natural choice for coachbuilders, among them Duncan in the UK. Bertone was the only Italian *carrozzeria* to clothe Healey's chassis, which it did in 1947, the result being displayed at the 1947 Triennale exhibition of carrozzieri in Milan.

The design work for the cabriolet body was by Count Mario Revelli di Beaumont. This was fairly typical of Bertone's immediate post-war output, displaying an undeniable American influence and borrowing from similar work by Bertone on Stanguellini and Nardi-Danese chassis. The front end was somewhat ornate, with a wide-mouthed grille, decorative bonnet flash, ovoid headlamp surrounds and curvaceous bumper. From the side, prominent wheelarch blisters and long doors dominated the view, while the rear end featured a large overhang.

NASH-HEALEY (PININ FARINA)

The Italian/British/American Nash-Healey had its origins in a chance meeting in late 1949. Donald Healey was returning home aboard the Queen Elizabeth ocean liner after an unsuccessful attempt to strike a deal for the supply of Cadillac engines for his Healey Silverstone sports car. While on the ship, he happened to meet the boss of Nash-Kelvinator, George W Mason. The pair hit it off to such an extent

ABOVE: Bertone-built body on Healey chassis was an Americanesque affair. RIGHT: Pinin Farina's reworking of the original Nash-Healey consisted of nothing but positive changes.

NASH-HEALEY

LEFT: *Battista 'Pinin' Farina leans into the Nash-Healey cockpit where George W Mason, Nash's boss, sits.* BELOW: *The original 1950 Nash-Healey looked neat but rather dowdy.* BOTTOM: *Neat badging; early sketch.*

that by the end of the journey they had formed a bond to make a new British-American sports car together: the Nash-Healey.

Things moved very fast; by the autumn of 1950, a prototype was ready to be shown at the London and Paris Motor Shows. When the production version of the Nash-Healey was launched in the US in February 1951, it was claimed to be America's first new mainstream sports car since the 1920s.

The chassis was a widened, reinforced Healey Silverstone box-section ladder frame with independent front suspension and a Nash rear beam axle located by a Panhard rod and using coil springs. The original model was designed by Gerry Coker, a Healey regular, and had aluminium bodywork by Panelcraft of Birmingham. Capable of seating three abreast, it suffered from a somewhat anonymous look. Since Nash was getting its whole range worked over by Pinin Farina for 1952, the Turin *carrozzeria* was also asked to give the Nash-Healey a major facelift, the refreshed version making its debut at the 1952 Chicago Auto Show.

Pinin Farina gave it a new front end with a distinctive and harmonious grille that incorporated headlights mounted low down and close together – a configuration described as 'Safety-Vu', since it was claimed to provide superior vision in foggy conditions. Instead of smooth body sides, there were strong character lines, culminating in small tailfins that housed fake vents, while a curved windscreen replaced the previous two-piece flat screen. Most of the panelwork was in steel but weight was kept down by making the bonnet, bootlid and dashboard in aluminium. While the pre-1952 car used a Nash-supplied 3.8-litre in-line six-cylinder engine with 125hp, the revised model had a 4.1-litre Nash 'six' producing 140hp.

The production process for the Farina-designed

BELOW: Roadster mixed American engine, British chassis and Italian design to good effect.
BOTTOM: Le Mans coupe version was launched for the 1953 model year with a longer wheelbase and fresh styling.

Nash-Healey was dauntingly convoluted. Nash despatched engines and drivelines from Kenosha, Wisconsin to be installed into the chassis at Healey's Warwick factory in England; the rolling chassis were then sent to Turin in Italy, where Pinin Farina added the bodywork and did final assembly for export back to the USA. As a result, the $5908 price tag was very high – way above, for instance, the $3513 Chevrolet Corvette.

For the 1953 model year, a new coupe joined the existing convertible, called the Le Mans after the racing successes of Nash-Healeys in the famous French endurance race. The Le Mans was also designed by Pinin Farina and differed from the open topped model not only by having a steel roof but also a continuous high-level wing line from front to rear. The 108-inch wheelbase was also six inches longer than the drop-top's. The Le Mans was well received, being awarded first prize in the 1953 International Concours d'Elegance held at Stresa in Italy.

For the 1954 model year range launched in June 1953, the convertible was discontinued and the Le Mans coupe was lightly redesigned with a three-piece rear window instead of the previous single piece. The 1954 movie *Sabrina*, starring Audrey Hepburn and Humphrey Bogart, featured a Farina Nash-Healey that certainly enhanced the coachbuilder's status in the USA.

However, two factors ultimately conspired against the model. Donald Healey's attention was now diverted to the much more significant Austin-Healey 100, while Nash's focus was on merging with Hudson to form the American Motors Corporation, which was concluded in May 1954. Production of the Nash-Healey ceased in August 1954, after a total of 402 Farina-bodied cars had been made (150 in 1952, 162 in 1953 and 90 in 1954).

JAGUAR

Grace and Pace Augmented

From humble origins in 1922 as the Swallow Sidecar Company (a simple maker of motorcycle sidecars), it seems improbable, even today, that Jaguar should have grown to become such an international giant of luxury and sports cars. Founded by William Lyons in Coventry, in pre-war years the company chose the name SS Cars, but switched to Jaguar Cars in 1945 for obvious reasons.

Its advertising slogan, 'Grace, Space, Pace', perfectly summed up what the company's products were all about. The Mark V of 1949 retained pre-war looks but used an all-new chassis and exclusively six-cylinder engines. It was with the Mark VII of 1950 that Jaguar moved to become Britain's pre-eminent luxury car maker. This reputation was cemented with the 1955 2.4-Litre saloon (retrospectively 'Mark I'), Jaguar's first car with monocoque construction. Further successful saloons included the Mark X, S-Type and – perhaps most notable of all – the XJ of 1968.

Yet Jaguar is probably best known for its sports cars, starting post-war with the spectacular XK120 (1948-1954), followed by the XK140 (1954-1957), XK150 (1957-1961) and then the all-conquering E-Type (1961-1975). Jaguar succeeded where numerous other high-class car makers had failed by offering excellent value for money alongside impeccable engineering and exceptional design integrity. It also helped that, on the world's race tracks, Jaguar sports cars such as the C-Type and D-Type reigned supreme.

Jaguar's industrial story is one of constantly shifting mergers and sell-offs. It bought rival Daimler in 1960 and then merged with the British Motor Corporation in 1966 to form British Motor Holdings (BMH). In turn, BMH merged with Leyland in 1968 to become the British Leyland Motor Corporation (BLMC). After an ill-fated spell under nationalisation from 1975, the marque became newly independent again in 1984, before being bought by Ford in 1999. Ownership changed again in 2008 when Ford sold out to the Indian giant, Tata.

In the post-war era, Jaguar's impressively engineered, good value chassis proved tempting to many clients who wanted coachbuilt cars, and Italian companies flocked to offer bodywork on such chassis as the MkVII and, in particular, the XK series. A few independently made concepts were created by Italian design houses, some with a view to tempting Jaguar's custom. The British company did indeed invite Italian *carrozzerie* to submit design proposals for some models during the 1970s but only one – Pininfarina – was ever given a contract for a production model (the 1979 XJ Series 3). In truth, Jaguar's own exceptional pool of design talent, including William Heynes and Malcolm Sayer, was held in such high esteem internationally that it hardly needed outside help. Jaguar unquestionably produced some of the world's most beautiful cars, among them the XK120, E-Type and XJ.

Not that Jaguar's founder was unappreciative of Italian design. After attending the 1967 Turin Show, Sir William Lyons asked to visit Bertone's facilities. There he espoused the thought that, had he been 25 years younger, he wouldn't have chosen to be a car maker but instead run his own *carrozzeria*.

Jaguars provided the perfect basis for some stupendous coachwork – none more so than that produced by the Italians. Pictured right is one of the best: the Bertone XK150-based XKE of 1957, skilfully penned by Franco Scaglione.

MkVII Coachbuilts

The new generation of post-war Jaguar saloons arrived in 1950 with the MkVII, a true landmark model. Its XK six-cylinder twin overhead camshaft engine was capable of a genuine 100mph, while the MkVIIM of 1954 and MkVIII of 1956 offered even more power. With its separate chassis and modern mechanicals, the MkVII was an excellent choice for independent coachbuilders.

MKVII METEOR & GOLDEN ARROW (STABILIMENTI FARINA)

After WW2, a flamboyant heiress by the name of Joska Bourgeois was awarded the Jaguar concession for Belgium, something she liked to celebrate by carrying her pet jaguar cat around with her. After forming the Anglo-Belgian Motor Company, she concocted a plan to body Jaguar's MkVII chassis with two-door coachwork, and in 1951 turned to Stabilimenti Farina of Italy, with whom she had close personal ties.

Two designs were duly created, each given exotic names by Joska Bourgeois: the coupe was called 'Meteor' while the cabriolet was dubbed 'Golden Arrow'. Both cars shared very similar designs, other than their roofs, with a typically clean early-1950s Italian enveloping look. Only the bluff front end with its upright grille seemed at all inelegant. The designer is said to have been Franco Martinengo (who would leave Stabilimenti Farina at the end of the 1951 to join Pinin Farina); however if it was Martinengo who designed it, he must have taken at least some inspiration from Giovanni Michelotti, whose signed sketches clearly prefigured the cars' shape. Stabilimenti Farina realised the bodywork in steel with aluminium opening panels, using the long MkVII chassis untouched.

The first Meteor, painted green and originally fitted with Borrani wire wheels, was shown at the January 1952 Brussels Show, alongside the Golden Arrow (which would also be shown at the 1952 Turin Show). The latter was based on chassis 731715 and was, appropriately enough, originally painted gold. It's thought that, while the Golden Arrow was unique, a second example of the Meteor was built later on, making the total number of Farina-bodied MkVIIs three. Farina also made an XK120-based version of the Meteor coupe, the 'Flying Jaguar' (page 169).

BELOW: MkVII Meteor coupe and Golden Arrow convertible, both by Stabilimenti Farina. OPPOSITE PAGE, CLOCKWISE FROM TOP: 1952 Ghia-Aigle Coupe; Ghia-Aigle cabriolet (chassis 730659); Pinin Farina's 1956 coupe built for George Embiricos; two images of the third and final Ghia-Aigle MkVII – a pretty car.

MKVII COUPE & CABRIOLET (GHIA-AIGLE)

The Swiss-Italian coachbuilder Ghia-Aigle made three cars using Jaguar MkVII chassis, all of them the work of designer Giovanni Michelotti. The first was a coupe that arrived in 1952. The long Jaguar wheelbase perhaps compromised its overall elegance but it was a neat shape featuring smooth body sides that were broken up by a swage line running from the door to the end of the rear wing. A large, upright grille headed a somewhat ornate front end with odd 'whiskers' extending out from auxiliary lights and a baroque bumper with overriders.

The coupe was shortly followed by a cabriolet to a rather different style, featuring a more curvaceous waistline and a cut-down upright grille that was flanked by auxiliary lights housed in curious nacelles, from which swage lines emanated right to the tail of the car. Built on chassis number 730659, it was painted red and owned by Michael Urban.

The third and final Jaguar MkVII made by Ghia-Aigle was a more resolved affair to another quite different style. Its front end abandoned the upright grille for a lower, more Americanesque full-width interpretation, flanked by driving lights and, above, hooded headlamps. These 'hoods' were the starting point for long chrome strips that extended down the sides of the body, incorporating door handles and air intakes on the rear wings (which had squared-off wheelarches). Inside, the original Jaguar instruments were retained.

The commission came in December 1954 from a Swiss surgeon called Dr Jean Rein and was built on chassis number 721420. Ghia-Aigle wanted to show the car on its stand at the 1955 Geneva Motor Show but Rein apparently refused permission. The car was eventually bought by the noted Jaguar collector, Roland Urban.

MKVII SALOON & COUPE (PININ FARINA)

Pinin Farina first tackled Jaguar's MkVII saloon in 1953, when it presented a lightly retouched version at the Geneva Show. This merely had extra louvres on the bonnet and a reshaped rear end with lights housed in protruding nacelles. A one-off, it was sold to the Greek shipping magnate, George Embiricos.

Three years later, Pinin Farina made another Jaguar MkVII-based car, this time a completely new coupe. A huge and imposing car, it looked as modern as Pinin Farina's contemporaneous XK-based coupe (page 171) looked traditional. Design features included a triple front grille, elaborate double bumpers up front, a bonnet scoop, swooping body swage lines and triple-tone paintwork.

Farina's MkVII coupe was first shown at the 1956 Geneva Show, from where it was sold to Embiricos and driven to Monaco. It was entered in the concours d'elegance in Cannes in August 1956, where it won the Grand Prix d'Honneur. By the end of the 1950s, an extra pair of driving lights had been added to the grille and front bumper overriders had been fitted, but the car disappeared from trace after that.

ABOVE: Standard XK120 (shown left) was lightly restyled by Ghia-Aigle (top right). RIGHT: Motto's XK120 barchetta was designed to resemble a C-Type as closely as possible. OPPOSITE PAGE: The so-called 'Flying Jaguar' built by Stabilimenti Farina in 1952.

XK120 Coachbuilts

The sensation of the 1948 London Motor Show was undoubtedly Jaguar's XK120, a two-seat roadster with dramatic bodywork (initially in light alloy, then steel). Starring under the bonnet was Jaguar's new XK engine, which fathered all of Jaguar's six-cylinder engines well into the 1990s, and meant that the sports car could reach 120mph (hence the XK120 name).

In 1954 Jaguar upgraded its model to become the XK140, whose larger 3.4-litre engine provided an extra 30bhp (or even more in SE specification), while rack-and-pinion steering became standard and overdrive on the four-speed gearbox was offered. A badge on the bootlid celebrated the XK's victory at Le Mans.

Closed coupe and drophead coupe versions were offered in addition to the roadster, all of them extraordinarily elegant, but there was nevertheless considerable demand for coachbuilt bodywork, often by Italian *carrozzerie*.

XK120 (GHIA-AIGLE)

A number of Jaguar XK120s had bodywork lightly modified by Ghia-Aigle of Switzerland. For instance, chassis number 660562 was a cabriolet, painted olive green, exhibited at the March 1951 Geneva Show with a number of differences to Jaguar's coachwork, while chassis number 660063, in right-hand drive, was delivered to Jean-Pierre Bellorini of Lausanne and competed in the Rallye de Sestrière of February 1951.

Chassis 660095, dating from 1950, was another right-hand drive XK120 delivered to Switzerland, painted cream with tan hood and two-tone light brown interior. In around 1952, it was converted by Ghia-Aigle to a semi-fixed-head coupe with a removable hardtop; also modified were the doors which had external flush-fit handles.

XK120 BARCHETTA (MOTTO)

Carrozzeria Motto was founded by Rocco Motto, who soon invited his bothers, Ernesto and Clemente, to join him. Motto's first involvement with a Jaguar came in 1951 when he created a one-off body for the famous Italian driver, Clemente Biondetti, who raced XK120s. After being turned down by Jaguar for a C-Type to use in Italian events, Biondetti decided to do his own thing. He created a tubular chassis based around a Ferrari 166 as a starting point and installed a Jaguar XK120 straight-six engine. He then got Rocco Motto to design and build a new body that looked as much like a C-Type as possible. The resulting barchetta ran in the 1951 Mille Miglia but Biondetti failed to finish. As similar fate awaited a new driver pairing for the car in the 1952 Mille Miglia.

XK120 FLYING JAGUAR (STABILIMENTI FARINA)

The very last car made by Stabilimenti Farina before it closed its doors in 1953 was the so-called Flying Jaguar. As with Farina's Jaguar MkVII cars (page 166), the commission came from the Belgian Jaguar importer, Joska Bourgeois.

XK120 chassis number 660922 was despatched to Stabilimenti Farina in 1951. Franco Martinengo designed the coupe bodywork, which had particularly elegant lines. While the overall shape very much replicated the look of Farina's MkVII designs, the proportions were far better resolved since the resulting car was the same size as an XK120 (around 500mm shorter than the MkVIIs). The lower, shorter, more flowing fastback roof was particularly pretty. The car was painted dark red with a white roof. The four-seat interior, meanwhile, was trimmed in tan leather to a unique design, although the dashboard housed regular Jaguar dials.

The car starred on Bourgeois' Jaguar stand at the January 1952 Brussels Show, alongside the MkVII-based Meteor and Golden Arrow, and it also appeared at the 1952 Turin Show. Despite hopes that a production run might ensue, the Flying Jaguar never 'flew', remaining a one-off. Luckily it still exists today and was shown to great effect at the Goodwood Festival of Speed concours in 2018.

XK120 SUPERSONIC (GHIA)

There is no question that Ghia's 'Supersonic' designs of the 1950s rank as some of the most radical and important car designs of that decade. In picking up themes of the aircraft 'jet age', the Supersonic anticipated a whole new form that would soon sweep the USA. It was also a true progenitor of the notion of the 'concept car', while also being commercially available to the well-heeled buyer.

The Supersonic shape began in 1953 when Ghia created an Alfa Romeo 1900-based coupe. A similar form was then applied to a number of other chassis, including Aston Martin (see page 36). It was particularly successfully applied over the Jaguar XK120 chassis in 1954. The drama of Giovanni Savonuzzi's coupe shape included such highlights as a raised, crenulated styling line extending from front to rear wings, tiny tailfins and jet-themed circular rear lights and curious bumperettes.

Three XK120 Supersonics were built. Two were delivered, via the Jaguar importer in Paris (Royal-Elysées), to a colourful businessman based in Lyon, France, called Malpelli; one was painted red, the other blue. The third car, painted white, was sold to a Swiss owner. Ghia's Jaguar Supersonic was displayed to great acclaim at the 1954 London and Paris Shows, while a concours event in Cannes brought all three examples together for the first and only time. While the whereabouts of two cars are currently known, all trace of the third (Swiss, white) car has been lost.

XK120 SE COUPE (PININ FARINA)

This car owes its existence to the well-known American-based, Austrian-born importer of European luxury cars, Max Hoffman. In April 1954, he bought a brand new Jaguar XK120 in SE (Special Equipment) specification (180hp 3.4-litre engine, firmer suspension, wire wheels and twin exhaust) and had it shipped to Pinin Farina in Turin in May 1954.

Under the project name PF471, Pinin Farina used some of the original Jaguar steel bodywork during a radical rebodying exercise. Some elements may have hinted strongly at the XK120 basis, such as the front grille and headlamps, but in most ways this was a distinctively Italian design. The wing line was almost a straight-through shape, with only the gentlest of falls to the tops of the front wings and a very slight upward kink just aft of the doors. The brightwork was on the ornate side, especially the hockey-stick front bumpers, thick chrome sill lines and body side accents, although the rear end was quite restrained. The bonnet and bootlid were both realised in aluminium.

It has been reported that this car attended the March 1955 Geneva Motor Show but there is no evidence that it actually did. It was delivered to its new owner in the US. This car – which is believed to be a one-off – was fully restored in 2015 using its original colour scheme of a green exterior with ochre Connolly leather upholstery. It won the runner-up prize in the Post-War Closed Class at the 2017 Pebble Beach Concours d'Elegance, and also appeared at the 2018 Goodwood Festival of Speed.

OPPOSITE PAGE: This spectucular jet-age creation – dubbed Supersonic – could only be the work of Giovanni Savonuzzi of Ghia. THIS PAGE: Imposingly styled XK120 SE coupe was the work of Pinin Farina.

XK140 COUPE (GHIA)

Ghia of Turin built three aluminium-bodied XK140s in 1955-1956 for the Lebanese Jaguar distributor, Robert Trad. The design of these cars was in stark contrast to Ghia's earlier Jaguar XK120 Supersonic, which isn't surprising since the designer was not Giovanni Savonuzzi but a different Giovanni – Signor Michelotti.

The three cars were recognisably related but differed in detail. At least two cars featured hockey-stick front bumpers and an oval front grille aperture sporting a central trilobed motif, while one had a bonnet air intake, and at least one had small air intakes just fore of the rear wings. All three featured tailfins of slightly differing sizes and profiles. Celebrity owners of these cars included the Aga Khan and Mexican actor Ricardo Montalban.

line was blade-like but a downward-sloping character line and hockey-stick swage lines recalled vintage car design tropes. The glasshouse was compact, with curved screens front and rear and polished metal B-pillars. At the rear end, the very low tail was flanked by fins.

The Loewy XK140 was exhibited at the Paris Salon in October 1955. It was then shipped to the USA in 1956 but was sadly destroyed in a fire the following year. Loewy also later modified a Jaguar E-Type but that had no connections with Italy.

XK140 COUPE (ALLEMANO)

Carrozzeria Allemano produced a two door coupe on the XK140 chassis in 1956. The designer was Giovanni Michelotti, who reinterpreted sketches he'd previously come up with for the Fiat 1100 TV and Maserati A6G54. It was not, perhaps, his most resolved piece of design: the profile was smart enough, with a high waistline and compact glasshouse, but it was over-adorned with too many details such as awkwardly prominent cooling vanes on the front wings, a bonnet scoop with a central vane running through it and fussy front lights. The sole example built was finished in white with a blue roof.

XK140 COUPE (BOANO/MICHELOTTI)

The designer of this highly unusual Jaguar one-off was an American of French extraction: the celebrated designer Raymond Loewy, who had made his name styling not only Studebakers but also the iconic Coca-Cola bottle. Wanting to create a special coupe based on a Jaguar XK140, he had chassis number 814096 despatched to the Italian coachbuilder Boano, which built it to a very distinctive design during 1955. A drawing in the Boano archive shows that Giovanni Michelotti was involved in the design phase along with Loewy.

The shape was 'different', to say the least, especially the front end with its very low, narrow nose and low-set faired-in headlamps. A huge sloping grille appeared to form a cascade down from the bonnet, which had a cooling scoop in it. The front wings were carefully shaped to allow cooling air to reach the front brakes. The wing top

OPPOSITE PAGE: Two of the three XK140 coupes built by Ghia, which differed in detail. ABOVE: Overwrought XK140 coupe built by Boano for Raymond Loewy. RIGHT: Michelotti's somewhat unusual XK140 was designed for Allemano.

XK140 COUPE (GHIA-AIGLE)

At the March 1956 Geneva Motor Show, Ghia-Aigle displayed a Jaguar XK140-based coupe that was something of a half-way house between Ghia of Turin's XK120 Supersonic and 1955 XK140 coupes (see pages 170 and 172). Undoubtedly inspired by the Supersonic were the raised styling lines along its flanks. At the front end were half-bumpers and a relatively plain grill with imbedded spotlamps. At the rear were tailfins so beloved of the period. Despite the similarities with Savonuzzi's Supersonic, the designer of this one-off was in fact Giovanni Michelotti.

XK140 COUPE (ZAGATO)

Zagato's second post-war design on a British chassis – following its unhappy MG Y-Type of 1948 (see page 78) – was based on a Jaguar XK140, which had been ordered by a Milanese playing card manufacturer, Guido Modiano. He managed to smash the car up fairly soon after taking delivery and decided that his best course of action to get back on the road was to take it to Zagato, based in his home city of Milan, for a rebody.

It has been suggested that the designer of this car was Luigi Rapi but Andrea Zagato has recently stated that it was in fact styled jointly by Gianni Zagato and Celeste Gobbi. The shape was a complete departure from Jaguar's original, somewhat resembling Zagato's contemporary Ferrari 250 GTZ, with a front end characterised by an inverted U-shaped main grille straddled by rather crude-looking rectangular grilles either side. It was certainly lighter than the regular XK. However, unlike the racing-orientated, ultra-lightweight ethos of the Ferrari, Zagato placed more emphasis on the Jaguar's role as a road car, working hard to give it a high-quality finish. According to those who drove it, it felt more like the later E-Type than an XK150. It was painted dark green with an unusual full suede interior, covering not just the seats but the dash, doors and headlining, too.

OPPOSITE TOP: Ghia-Aigle XK140 by Michelotti. OPPOSITE BOTTOM & BELOW: Zagato's first Jaguar body was on an XK140 chassis. BOTTOM TWO IMAGES: The unique XK140 as rebodied in 1957 by Giovanni Michelotti. BOTTOM RIGHT: Jaguar's XK150 provided the perfect basis for bespoke, hand-built coachwork.

Jaguar was persuaded to display the car on its own stand at the 1957 Paris Salon, where it was warmly received. Elio Zagato hoped that a limited run of cars could be built and indeed Zagato did build two further Jaguars to a similar style but these were based on the XK150 (page 177). The sole XK140 Zagato built survives today in the USA.

XK140 (MICHELOTTI)

In May 1955, a cream-coloured XK140 SE coupe (chassis number S814286) was delivered to France, where its first owner was Mme Jeanne Gaymard of Paris. In 1957, it was involved in accident so severe that its body was beyond repair, so the XK was dispatched to the famous Giovanni Michelotti to be rebodied in aluminium. This was a highly unusual scenario as Michelotti was a freelance stylist without his own *carrozzeria*; the car bore the very rare badge 'MAG Torino'.

The shape was unusually clean, with a sweeping waistline and an elegant fastback. The headlamps were unusual for the period in being oblong-shaped, while unique front half-bumpers and side cooling vents added character. A bonnet scoop was required to clear the engine, which was taken from a Jaguar C-Type. The interior was also changed to Michelotti's own design.

Several sources have claimed that this car was once owned by the actress, Brigitte Bardot, but apparently without any shred of evidence. The one-off sold at auction in 2018 for 365,000 euros, despite needing extensive restoration.

XK150 Coachbuilts

Despite suffering a factory fire in 1957, Jaguar was ready to present a successor to the XK140 that year: the XK150. The exotic styling of previous XKs gave way to a mellower design with less pronounced wing lines and a one-piece windscreen. In terms of roadholding and comfort, the XK150 was a significant advance. Between 1957 and 1961 some 9398 examples were made – roadsters, coupes and drophead coupes – providing an excellent basis for coachbuilders to produce striking new bodywork.

XK150 COUPE (MOTTO)

The coachbuilder Motto only ever produced two bodies on Jaguar chassis. XK150 chassis number 824166 was manufactured in December 1957 and delivered in chassis-only form to Carrozzeria Rocco Motto in 1958, to the order of the Jaguar distributor in Lyon, France.

The bodywork was in light alloy over a steel structure to a sober design that looked almost Bristol-like, especially the front grille. Inside was a new cabin with leather upholstery, sculpted seats, fitted seatbelts and a padded dashboard. A second XK150 was subsequently built by Motto to a very similar design, although with a slightly different, less pronounced grille design.

XK150 SE (ZAGATO)

Zagato had first brushed with a Jaguar XK in 1957, when it rebuilt an XK140 into an elegant coupe (see previous page). Jaguar having showed it on its stand at the 1957 Paris Salon, Zagato pressed ahead with offering further bodies, but now using the XK150 chassis. Its first custom came via the Jaguar dealer in Geneva.

Browns Lane assembled a rolling chassis (number S834369) in August 1957 and despatched it to Milan. Zagato then constructed an alloy coupe body over it that was very similar to its earlier XK140, although it was slightly wider and the front end differed had a wider main grille and a full wraparound bumper.

This car was finished in time to receive its debut on the Zagato stand at the Geneva Show in March 1958, and was apparently originally painted dark bronze. Elio Zagato was so confident of the car's prospects that he had a brochure printed, calling it the Jaguar XK150 SE Zagato.

However, nothing like a full production run ever ensued. It seems that just one further XK150 Zagato was built, in 1960. The current whereabouts of this second car are unknown but the first example made its way to the USA in the early 1960s.

ABOVE & LEFT: 1958 Motto XK150 coupe. BELOW & OPPOSITE TOP LEFT: Jaguar XK150 SE Zagato coupe of 1958. FAR RIGHT: Superb XK150 'XKE' by Bertone was undoubtedly one of the high points of Italian design during the 1950s.

XK150 XKE (BERTONE)

As Bertone's star designer during the 1950s, Franco Scaglione was tasked with reclothing a Jaguar chassis in 1957 when an XK150 was rebodied. In outline, it very much resembled Scaglione's Aston Martin DB2/4 Berlinetta for Bertone (see page 34) and indeed the two cars appeared alongside each other at the 1957 Turin Show. The Bertone Jaguar wore 'XKE' badges – a prescient move as it turned out, since Jaguar would later adopt the XKE moniker for its forthcoming E-Type.

The design was, although not especially ground-breaking by Scaglione's standards, a very successful one. The front end managed to retain a certain elegance among the chromed fussiness, while the flowing wings, kicked-up rear wings and slim tail lent it a classically exotic Italianate air. The design was certainly acclaimed at the time, inspiring a further two to be built.

The first car was based on a 3.4-litre XK150 chassis and featured unusual scallops behind the wheelarches of the front wings, triple wipers and sharp corners on the rear window. As seen at the 1957 Turin Show, it was painted green; sadly its fate is unknown.

The second chassis was a 3.8-litre XK150 S one (S834365). This looked quite similar to the first one but had no scallops in the front wings. This example had many changes of paint colour over the years, including green and then red, but following a restoration in 2020, it is currently black. This is the only known survivor of the three Bertone XK150s built and was restored for presentation at the Concours of Elegance at Hampton Court Palace in 2020.

The third and final chassis (S824439DN) was supplied to Tony Hubbard, heir to the Woolworth fortune. This car was also based on a 3.8-litre XK150 S chassis and was the only one made in right-hand drive. It could be readily identified by its round-cornered wraparound rear window. When displayed at the 1958 Turin Show, it was painted in a dramatic gold-tinged opalescent candy red but it was later repainted silver.

The dealer who dealt with the order was racing driver, John Coombs, who arranged for the car to be taken to the Jaguar factory where, reputedly, it was assessed by management as a prospect for production as an official model; they ultimately rejected the notion. It is believed that this chassis was scrapped in the 1960s.

XK150 COUPE (GHIA-AIGLE)

By 1958 the Swiss-Italian concern, Ghia-Aigle, was on its last legs as a coachbuilder. Indeed, its Jaguar XK150 coupe of 1958 was probably the last car Ghia-Aigle ever made. Pietro Frua was the designer and his styling had hints of contemporary Frua Maseratis. The eggcrate front grille was very prominent, flanked by distinctive teardrop-shaped nacelles that housed the lights. Other styling highlights included squared-off flared wheelarches, an upright glasshouse, extensive chrome trimming and kicked-up rear wings with tailfins ending in sharply-angled taillights.

Jaguar XK150 3.4S chassis number S834831DN (the DN signifying it had an overdrive gearbox) was shipped in December 1957 to the Swiss Jaguar distributor, Emil Frey. At one point the car was converted to use Mercedes SL headlamps but it was later restored to the original set-up. It's thought that Ghia-Aigle may have built one further example of this coupe, possibly on the Paris-supplied right-hand

drive chassis S824166DN. Ghia-Aigle continued to run advertisements until 1964 that included its Jaguar XK150 but in practice the company was by then a simple repair shop.

XK150 COUPE (ALLEMANO)

Following Allemano's not terribly successful XK140 rebody of 1956, the coachbuilder tried again in 1958 on an XK150 chassis.

Once again the design was by Giovanni Michelotti, who created a slightly better resolved shape, even if some of the detailing was still somewhat fussy, such as the split reinterpretation of the traditional upright Jaguar grille, sectioned bonnet scoop and hockeystick-shaped brightwork strip along the body sides, which acted to break up the smooth lines.

Once again this was to be a one-off, believed to have been built for a Swiss client, with white paint and a contrasting dark roof.

D/E-Type Coachbuilts

Having enjoyed huge racing success with its C-Type, Jaguar launched the much more aerodynamic D-Type in 1954 as its contender in events such as Le Mans. A pure racer – even though Jaguar also offered it in road-going trim as the XKSS – only one D-Type chassis was ever rebodied in Italy, by Michelotti.

Unquestionably the star of the 1961 Geneva Show – and quite possibly the whole of the 1960s – was Jaguar's E-Type. This seminal machine completely redefined how a sports car should be. A William

FAR LEFT: Pietro Frua designed the ornately decorated Ghia-Aigle XK150 of 1958.
LEFT: Allemano's second stab at a Jaguar coupe – the XK150 of 1958.
THIS PAGE: Giovanni Michelotti's extraordinary rebodying of a D-Type Jaguar.

Lyons/Malcolm Sayer design masterpiece, it achieved 150mph in road tests, all for a price of just over £2000. Initially it was powered by a 3.8-litre XK engine, which was a better performer than the 4.2 that replaced it in 1964. The E-Type was appealing both as a roadster and as a coupe, but perhaps less so in its third body style from 1966: the 2+2 with its extra length, height and weight.

Over 38,000 Series 1 E-Types were made up until 1968, when the Series 2 arrived with its cowl-less headlamps, bigger bumpers and lights, and redesigned bonnet. In 1971 came the Series 3 with V12 power, a model that lasted until 1975.

D-TYPE LE MANS (MICHELOTTI)

To rebody a Jaguar D-Type racer may seem an unlikely scenario but Giovanni Michelotti did indeed do so, although not until some years after D-Type production had ended. The chassis in question was

OPPOSITE PAGE: Michelotti D-Type Le Mans was beautifully proportioned. ABOVE: Frua's truncated nose and fussy grille did little for the E-Type's looks.

XKD513, which had been sold to a Frenchman, Jean-Marie Brussin, in 1955. He finished third in the car at the 1957 Le Mans 24 Hours with co-driver Jean Lucas. Tragically Brussin crashed in the following year's Le Mans race, with fatal consequences.

How this car eventually ended up at Michelotti's workshops in Turin in 1960 is lost in history but the damaged panelwork was cut away there, leaving relatively intact underpinnings. On this basis a coupe body was fabricated using all-new steel bodywork designed by Michelotti. The main D-Type components – engine, transmission, subframes and suspension – were bolted into the new car.

The beautifully proportioned shape had elements of other Michelotti designs, including Maserati 3500GT and Triumph Spitfire. The wing line was notably low, with a pronounced kick just aft of the doors. At the low-set front end was a large wraparound bumper, while character features included a small bonnet bulge and twin cooling vents in each front wing. A distinctively cut-back rear end incorporated large half-bumpers and horizontal taillights, while the badge on the boot lid read 'Jaguar Le Mans'.

The Le Mans-spec final drive ratio reportedly made this car difficult to drive at low speeds; other compromises of its racing heritage included a lack of passenger foot room, a narrow cockpit and considerable heat soak from the engine.

Michelotti's coupe made its first public appearance at the Geneva Show in March 1963, painted light metallic blue (it was later painted red, before being restored to its original colour). After spending some time in the USA, the car made its way to the UK, where its original D-Type parts were stripped out in the 1970s in order to build another D-Type. Lynx Engineering then installed Jaguar E-Type parts into the Michelotti car, including a 4.2-litre engine. The car still exists today in Belgian ownership.

E-TYPE (FRUA/ITALSUISSE)

British racing driver and Jaguar dealer John Coombs asked Frua to give his E-Type coupe an Italian look. Short on time, Frua didn't do the full rebody that perhaps he should have, instead modifying only the front and rear ends. The nose was truncated by five inches (12cm) and a rather curious traditional-style grille added, blending in with grandly dimensioned chrome bumpers. The headlamps were resited further back and a small cooling duct was added to the bonnet bulge. The rear was even more controversial: a very heavy-handed piece of design with a preposterously sized bumper that housed Alfa Romeo rear lights.

The build-up was actually done by a small coachbuilder in Geneva, Switzerland called Italsuisse, which had been set up in 1959 by an ex-Ghia-Aigle director, Adriano Guglielmetti. The E-Type debuted alongside Frua's S-Type at the 1966 Geneva Show.

Coombs tried to market this 'improved' E-Type as a conversion in the UK for £2500 but it was surely sheer ugliness that deterred any interest from potential buyers and the car remained a one-off (which survives to this day). At least this wasn't the worst E-Type converted in Italy; that accolade belongs to Drogo.

E-TYPE (CARROZZERIA SPORTS CARS/DROGO)

Once seen, never forgotten, the Jaguar E-Type rebodied by Carrozzeria Sports Cars (often called 'Drogo') is one example where Italian design definitely did not improve on the British original. That was perhaps surprising since Drogo's history was infused with some of the most beautiful cars of all time, among them some very special Ferraris and Bizzarrinis. So ugly was Drogo's E-Type rebody that it has even been blamed for the Italian coachbuilder's ultimate demise.

This car was built for a wealthy French businessman who had crashed his 1962 E-Type (chassis 886294). Keeping the Jaguar monocoque and all the mechanicals intact, Drogo built a new body in steel, a process that took 2700 hours.

The design was by a man called Tadini. The harshly angular lines were in stark contrast to the original Jaguar's curvaceous profile. Some elements were well realised, such as the front wing vents and a rear end that looked somewhat like a Maserati Ghibli. However, many aspects were crude and ineffective, such as the clumsily overhung front and rear ends, jarringly angular glasshouse and peculiar oblong front bumper that almost surrounded the grille. There was frankly no cohesiveness to the design.

The existence of the Drogo Jaguar was first reported in the Italian press in May 1968. It was painted silver with a black interior, which was also reworked with a symmetrically split effect. The car remained a one-off – most would say mercifully – but Drogo did build two further similar-looking bodies on Ferrari chassis, which did the company absolutely no favours.

Other Coachbuilts & Concepts

S-TYPE COUPE (FRUA)

In 1963, Jaguar launched its S-Type saloon, using a modified version of the platform and centre hull of the old Mark 2. Three years later, Pietro Frua produced his own interpretation of a modern Jaguar saloon using a rolling chassis that Jaguar had supplied through its Turin dealer, Fattori e Montani, in December 1965. This was a left-hand drive 3.8-litre manual (chassis number 1B78869DN) that was strengthened prior to being rebodied.

In a remarkably short timescale of just three months, Frua prepared the car ready for its debut at the March 1966 Geneva Show. The design work was rather formal and upright but resolutely Italian, drawing inspiration from other Frua creations such as the Maserati Mexico and Glas 2600 V8. The shapely grille featured inset driving lights and was flanked by the original Jaguar's hooded headlights employed in a stylised form. At the rear was a long but sharply cut-off tail with horizontal lights. The body flanks were simple yet elegant and the tall, square glasshouse was in stark contrast to the Jaguar S-Type's curvaceousness. Most of the interior was bespoke, except for the dashboard, which was pure S-Type.

After its Geneva debut, Frua's opalescent light blue coupe was delivered to its first owner, Francesco Respino. Since Jaguar had launched its E-Type 2+2 at the precisely same show, it had no interest in pursuing another coupe and the Frua car remained a one-off. Luckily it remains in existence, beautifully restored.

OPPOSITE PAGE: Frua's ungainly E-Type (top) appeared masterful alongside Drogo's appallingly ill-conceived effort (below). ABOVE RIGHT: There were Maserati echoes in Frua's 1966 S-Type Coupe.

ABOVE: Trevor Fiore of Fiore Design did some styling sketches for Jaguar four-door saloons in around 1965. This one, labelled 'S-Type', had echoes of the E-Type. Sadly nothing concrete ever came of it.

FT (BERTONE)

Bertone's first Jaguar since its XK150 of 1958 was the 1966 FT. This was commissioned by the Jaguar importer for Northern Italy, Giorgio Tarchini, who asked for a two-door, five-seat coupé based on the Jaguar S-Type saloon. The 'FT' name came from the initials of the importer's founder, Ferruccio Tarchini.

The car's designer was Marcello Gandini, then quite new at Bertone, who tackled it not long after he'd finished the Lamborghini Miura. Sadly the FT lacked the poise and drama of that supercar; it was not an entirely happy design. Despite a Jaguar MkX-style radiator grille and MkX side lamps and indicators being used, the front end resembled an Alfa Romeo more than a Jaguar. That was even more the case at the rear end, where Alfa Giulia Berlina rear lights were fitted. The shape of the glasshouse was more successful, particularly the charismatic kink in the C-pillars.

The FT was unveiled on Bertone's stand at the 1966 Geneva Motor Show. The plan was to commence a production run, with distribution handled by Tarchini's sales organisation not only in Italy, while international sales were also mooted. Jaguar reportedly delivered seven chassis to Bertone but in the end only two FTs were ever finished. The Geneva prototype (chassis number 1B 78923) was metallic gold with a tan leather interior, and stayed in Italy with the Tarchini family. The second car (chassis A1F 25417) was built in 1967 for a customer in Madrid, Spain, originally painted pale green. Both cars survive today.

It could have been so different. Jaguar's senior management and engineering divisions evaluated the FT and Sir William Lyons was said to have thought highly of it. Jaguar's chief engineer, Norman Dewis, who tested it in May 1966, described its styling as "eye catching". Others were not so kind, however, with plenty of criticism being heaped on what was a somewhat heavy and non-Jaguar-esque design. Gandini himself was proud of his creation, stating in an interview that the FT was his favourite of the three Jaguar concepts he designed (the others being the Pirana and Ascot).

THIS PAGE: Almost Marcello Gandini's very first design ever was the 1966 Bertone FT, based on the Jaguar S-Type. OPPOSITE PAGE: Another Gandini design for Bertone: E-Type based Pirana.

PIRANA (BERTONE)

Every year during the late 1960s the *Daily Telegraph* presented a special styling exercise on its stand at the London Motor Show. For the 1967 event, the newspaper's magazine editor, John Anstey, commissioned a unique Jaguar coupe from Bertone, which was done with the full collaboration of Jaguar, which provided an E-Type 4.2-litre 2+2 (chassis 1E 50950) as a basis.

The brief was to create a usable grand tourer. Nuccio Bertone's lead designer on the project was Marcello Gandini, fresh from the triumph of his Lamborghini Miura. Gandini's shape, with its low nose and chopped Kamm tail, was clearly influenced by his Lamborghini Marzal show car, revealed seven months earlier at the 1967 Geneva Show. Overall the Pirana was shorter than the original E-Type, whose 2+2 wheelbase suited the car's grand touring role, while the Dunlop competition wheels widened the car's stance. The long, sleek bonnet and shallow-sloping tail were very well resolved. Gandini himself was not so enthusiastic, however, stating: "The Jaguar E-Type was not the best base to work on as the overhangs were very pronounced. So the request to translate the form and style of the Marzal to a car with altogether different proportions was not a good idea."

British technology abounded in the car, with such elements as a Smiths air conditioning unit (delivering cold air through an overhead distributor), Smiths radio/cassette (mounted in the centre console), Triplex Sundym heat-absorbing tinted safety glass with defrosting elements, and Connolly leather upholstery.

Starting in May 1967, Bertone built the Pirana in only five months, remarkable considering that the brief insisted the car be fully functional. It debuted at the October 1967 Earls Court Motor Show, featuring on the cover of the *Daily Telegraph Magazine* with the headline, "We have built the star of the Motor Show" which was undoubtedly true. The Pirana was also later shown at the Turin, Montreal and New York Motor Shows.

This one-off was eventually sold to a US customer in 1968, where it underwent a number of modifications, including being repainted British Racing Green from its original silver, and having extra seating added (it was originally a two-seater). It was subsequently restored back to its Earls Court Show spec and thankfully still exists today.

Pininfarina was courted by several British Leyland marques during the 1970s. The XJ12 PF of 1973 was done with Jaguar's blessing and assessed by the Browns Lane head office – but rejected.

XJ12 PF (PININFARINA)

Jaguar's new XJ6 saloon, launched in 1968, was almost universally hailed as a design masterpiece, and is undoubtedly one of the greatest four-door forms of all time. The XJ range reached a new zenith in 1972, when Jaguar belatedly launched the V12-engined XJ12.

Sergio Pininfarina obtained one of the earliest XJ12s and, with Jaguar's blessing, proceeded to create its own vision of a Jaguar saloon. Chief designer on the project was Paolo Martin. To update the XJ12 posed a challenge: how to marry a modern 1970s design ethic with traditional Jaguar cues. Martin's silhouette featured a low bonnet line, sleek body sides, belt-line kink, descending tail-line, slim roof pillars and a large glasshouse. In these respects, it did indeed honour Jaguar traditions. However, his flat surfacing and sharp lines were struck a very different tone. The bluff-fronted nose with its big rectangular headlamps and rather anonymous grille were not particularly successful; nor were the black impact bumpers front and rear. Particularities included a fluted panel behind the rear screen and raised rear wings that ended in 'peaks' above the taillights.

The XJ12 PF wasn't well received. One design critic called it "modish" and "lacking warmth", while Jaguar's senior body engineer Cyril Crouch described it as "an ugly looking brute". Another Jaguar designer, Colin Holtum, said: "What the Italians don't have is the Jaguar background. So we have found that, when we deal with outside people, they do a very professional product, but they don't produce a Jaguar."

The prototype was completed in 1973, ready for its debut at the 1973 London Motor Show. It then settled back at Jaguar HQ at Browns Lane, where it was assessed as a potential design for the forthcoming XJ40 (see page 189). Although Pininfarina's XJ12 PF was ultimately rejected, the Italian company was rewarded with the XJ Series 3 restyling job (page 189).

ASCOT (BERTONE)

With Jaguar actively seeking Italian design input in the 1970s, Bertone's creation of a new Jaguar-based four-seat coupe in 1977 was both strategic and impactful. The Ascot was based on a shortened version of the then-new XJ-S platform (the wheelbase was shrunk by about 200mm), using the Jaguar 5.3-litre V12 and automatic transmission. The Ascot was made of aluminium, making it much lighter than the donor XJ-S, while it was also shorter, wider and lower.

Bertone's design was entirely new for a Jaguar: a sharp-edged wedge of the type that Gandini had championed for Bertone with designs such as the Alfa Romeo Carabo, Ferrari Rainbow and Lamborghini Bravo. The low front end featured a leaping cat badge and a spoiler that looped around the front into the angular front wheelarches. The headlamps were pop-ups with raised extensions going backwards to form an 'H' shape with separate raised ducting for the V12 engine.

Gandini's signature geometric wheelarch shapes featured distinctive flares. The peculiar, hockey stick-shaped roof pillars and rear bumper were finished in dark grey, in contrast to the main body (originally painted white but later changed to gold). A full hatchback was another unique feature.

The interior of the right-hand drive prototype was trimmed in a mixture of tan leather and brown suede. A new flat dashboard housed XJ-S gauges, while the gear selector was also borrowed from the XJ-S. Two quintessentially 1970s items were a removable radio and a chunky car phone. Seen at the 1977 Turin Show, the Ascot was a pure concept and, although it was certainly driveable, it was never considered a candidate for production.

Sharp-suited Bertone Ascot of 1977 reclothed the Jaguar XJ-S platform with considerable aesthetic success. Another design by Marcello Gandini, it was destined to have no future in production form.

XJ SPIDER (PININFARINA)

Nominally Jaguar replaced its iconic E-Type with the XJ-S in 1975, but everyone recognised that the new car had moved away from the sporty feel of the 'E' and more towards the grand touring market. Almost immediately, designers started thinking about a true Jaguar sports car, including Pininfarina. Jaguar played ball, too, supplying the Italian company with one of its XJ-S development mules to pull apart and turn into the XJ Spider, which was built in under five months.

The styling was a joint effort by Leonardo Fioravanti, Sergio Pininfarina and Renzo Carli. The oval-shaped front air intake clearly referenced the Jaguar E-Type, as indeed did the curvaceous profile and swoopy belt-line. The rear end was perhaps overly long but at least that provided a big boot. In contrast to the E-Type's chrome-bumpered look, Pininfarina ensured that the front and rear ends were unimpeded by adornment. It had intended to make them both out of impact-absorbing polyurethane, but this ultimately proved too expensive and they were in fact formed from steel.

Pop-up double headlights were skilfully integrated into the front end. The slender lights to either side of the oval intake referenced the E-Type's slender bumpers, but the cut-off rear end was very different in style, featuring a full-width lighting panel. The donor car's GKN-made wheels were retained.

This was a full convertible, years before Jaguar would do its own soft-top XJ-S, featuring a fixed roll-over bar aft of the front seats; the fabric panel above the occupants' heads and the rear screen were both a removable for open-topped motoring. The two-seat interior was cleanly and simply styled with tan leather upholstery, while the fully digital dashboard was quite a novelty for 1978.

Pininfarina's XJ Spider was shorter, wider and lower than the donor XJ-S. Pininfarina's Lorenzo Ramaciotti thought that a production version would potentially be lighter than the XJ-S, too. Some criticised the XJ Spider's styling as being too 'American' but it was certainly very aerodynamic: when tested in Pininfarina's wind tunnel, it had a very impressive Cd figure of 0.36.

The XJ Spider debuted in October 1978 at the British Motor Show at Birmingham's NEC. It was originally painted British Racing Green but was soon repainted silver. It was generally well received. Jaguar's boss Sir John Egan certainly fell in love with it, while *Car* magazine called it, "The Jaguar the world's been waiting for". Some magazines reported that a production run was likely, while a few even drove the functional V12-engined prototype. Some customers even tried to put down speculative deposits. While Jaguar did put thought into developing the XJ Spider for production, sadly it never happened.

However, Pininfarina's XJ Spider clearly influenced Jaguar's own design team when, in 1980, the company initiated the development a true replacement for the E-Type, under the codenames XJ41 (coupe) and XJ42 (convertible) – not that this so-called 'F-Type' project would see production, either. Thankfully the sole XJ Spider prototype built still exists.

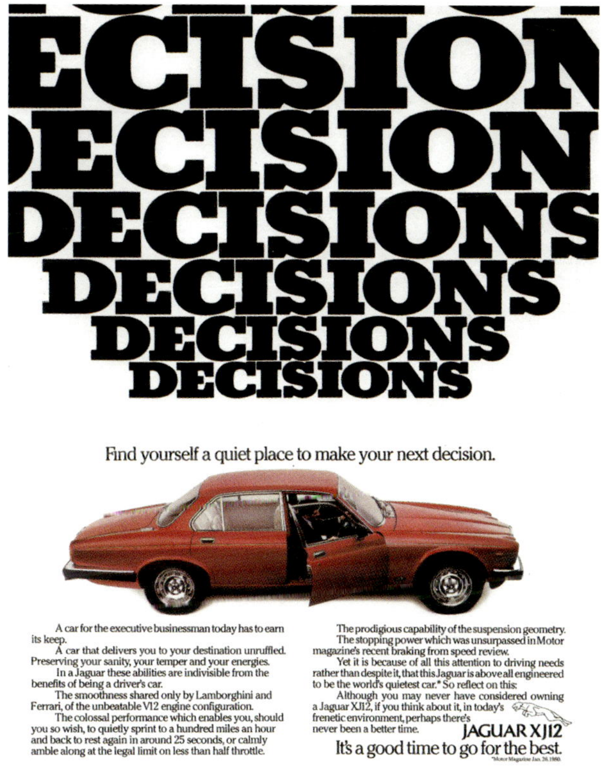

OPPOSITE PAGE: Exquisite XJ Spider of 1978 by Pininfarina. ABOVE LEFT: Pininfarina's XJ Series 3 evolution. ABOVE, TOP TO BOTTOM: XJ40 proposals by Pininfarina, Bertone and Italdesign.

XJ SERIES 3 (PININFARINA)

As work on the XJ40 project (see below) stalled in the mid-1970s, Jaguar wisely thought it was sensible to facelift the existing XJ, setting up the XJ50 (Series 3) programme. For this, it turned to Italy: Bertone and Pininfarina were each asked to provide proposals that would modernise the shape by altering virtually every panel on the car.

It was Pininfarina's proposal that pleased Jaguar. Under the supervision of Leonardo Fioravanti, Pininfarina managed to incorporate the extended wheelbase of the new S3 without disturbing the excellent proportions for which the XJ was famed. This was achieved by subtle means. The windscreen pillars were moved forwards at the base, the side glass was lengthened and made taller, the front quarterlights were deleted, the roof panel was made flatter and narrower, and the rear screen was less sharply inclined. Other changes included a simpler front grille, flush door handles and larger bumpers with rubber facings.

Overall the design was extremely well received and many regard the Series 3 as the prettiest of all Jaguar XJ models. The S3 lasted from March 1979 until November 1992, selling very well during that time.

XJ40 PROPOSALS (PININFARINA, BERTONE & ITALDESIGN)

Almost as soon as the original XJ had been launched in 1968, Jaguar started thinking about a successor: the XJ40. Originally due for release in 1977, its gestation ended up being long and drawn out; in fact, the XJ lasted for 18 years up until the XJ40 eventually arrived in 1986, a victim of British Leyland malaise and muddled planning.

Jaguar's design team initially came up with ideas, notably via chief stylist Doug Thorpe, in the early 1970s, but the controversial styling influence of the XJ-S pervaded many of its early proposals. When Pininfarina's XJ12 PF of 1973 was brought to Browns Lane for assessment alongside Jaguar's own efforts, Lord Stokes expressed a preference for the Italian design and arguably that opinion determined the look of the eventual production XJ40.

In 1974, Geoffrey Robinson was installed as Jaguar's Managing Director, having served several years as head of Innocenti in Turin. His Italian experiences gave him the confidence and enthusiasm to commission Italian design houses to submit new proposals for the XJ40. He duly approached Bertone and Italdesign that year, but their ideas were reportedly not well received at Browns Lane.

Two years later, in spring 1976, Bertone and Italdesign were asked to submit renewed proposals, but once again neither was accepted. The XJ40 would ultimately be a machine brewed in the West Midlands, although arguably its bluff profile drew on Pininfarina's 1973 XJ12 PF.

XJ-S SUCCESSOR (GHIA)

After Jaguar had dropped its XJ41 project (F-Type) in 1990, it then turned to a successor for the XJ-S – what would eventually become the XK8. The idea was to use the existing XJ-S platform but with all-new bodywork. Jaguar invited designs from four teams: two from Jaguar in the UK, one from Ford Design in Dearborn and one from Ghia in Italy.

Ghia's proposal was certainly distinctive, with an S-Type-style grille, circular headlamps and very rounded lines. However it was panned at Jaguar, where it was derisorily nicknamed "The Hoover". Reportedly Ghia's design was actually favoured by Ford's Board but when it was universally disliked in focus groups, Jaguar pursued its in-house 'X100' design instead.

Pietro Camardella of Pininfarina also created sketches of a so-called 'XJ-S 90' in 1990, believed to be an independent proposal for a Jaguar coupe of the 1990s, but this never amounted to anything.

FAR LEFT: XJ-S proposals by Ghia and Pininfarina. LEFT & BELOW: Giugiaro's Kensington. OPPOSITE PAGE: XJ220 was reworked by Pininfarina for Brunei, while the F-Type was initially scheduled to be manufactured in Italy.

KENSINGTON (ITALDESIGN)

The Kensington was Italdesign's vision of a future direction for Jaguar saloons. It was an entirely independent effort, without factory support; Giorgetto Giugiaro even went as far as buying a Jaguar himself to use as the basis (a Jaguar Sovereign V12 5.3-litre whose underpinnings were left untouched to result in a fully functional car).

Giugiaro has sometimes been criticised for not being sympathetic to the ethos of the marque on which he designs his concepts. Although he made a special effort to produce recognisably Jaguar elements, such as the grille and the glasshouse, the Kensington was still criticised in some quarters for not being sufficiently 'British'. One such incongruous element was the windscreen, which was set so far forward that it had to be removed if you wanted to take the engine out.

John Grant, managing director of Jaguar, adopted a positive view when interviewed by *Autocar & Motor* magazine: "Obviously I'm delighted that someone of the stature of Giugiaro chooses Jaguar. It's good to have some alternative input into our design thinking".

Debuting at the 1990 Geneva Show, the Kensington never did have any impact on future Jaguars, but some of its themes could be discerned in the later Lexus GS300 that Giugiaro designed.

XJ220 PININFARINA SPECIALE (PININFARINA/COGGIOLA)

We have already touched on the extraordinary car collection built up by Prince Jefri of Brunei in the chapters on Aston Martin and Bentley. Bespoke coachbuilt cars were a particular favourite and Pininfarina was called upon many times to design, and sometimes manufacture, some very special luxury cars for Brunei.

It is thought that Prince Jefri purchased no fewer than 20 examples of Jaguar's XJ220 supercar. Launched in production form in 1991, the XJ220 was more exotic than any other car at the time: aerospace-type bonded aluminium bodywork, Group C racing aerodynamics and racing-derived inboard suspension. With performance claims of 220mph (352km/h) top speed and 0-60mph in 3.5 seconds, it was comfortably the fastest road car on earth at the time.

In about 1995, Prince Jefri approached Pininfarina to restyle one of his XJ220s (thought to be chassis number 220889), at the same time reducing overall weight. Exactly what Pininfarina did has never been communicated officially, as the car was developed in strict secrecy, but among the visible changes were lighter fixed headlights in place of the original pop-up units; bigger front air inlets; a tapered cockpit; two-piece side windows; new full-width rear lights; a new rear spoiler; and a much reworked interior. The one-off was painted metallic dark green and the cabin was finished in black and green.

There were changes under the skin, too, including an F1 paddleshift gearbox, power steering, better cooling and revised electrics, all done in Italy by Italtecnica of Turin. And as with the Bentley B3 (see page 71), manufacture of the bodywork was sub-contracted out to a separate Turin-based coachbuilder, Coggiola.

F-TYPE (PININFARINA)

For decades, Jaguar had concocted and then abandoned plans to launch a spiritual successor to the E-Type, which would, logically enough, be called the F-Type. When an in-house designed concept car was revealed at the 2000 Detroit Auto Show to universally positive reviews, the project got the green light. Jaguar made bold plans to launch its new compact F-Type sports car in 2005 with a bonded and riveted aluminium chassis and a mid-mounted powertrain.

Working on a projected production run of 25,000 units a year, Jaguar intended to outsource manufacture of the F-Type to Pininfarina in Turin. The coachbuilder had even offered to share investment costs and was Jaguar's preferred partner in a contest with Valmet of Finland and Magna Steyr of Austria. Ultimately, however, budget cuts by Jaguar's parent company and Jaguar's pursuit of glory in Formula 1 drained the company of the resources that were required to bring the F-Type to production and the project had been canned by 2002.

X-TYPE ESTATE (PININFARINA)

As a compact saloon, Jaguar's X-Type was an entirely new departure for the marque when it was launched in 2001. Recognising that an estate body variant could boost X-Type sales substantially, Jaguar moved to add such a model. The in-house design – the very first Jaguar styled by its new design director, Ian Callum – was all-new from the B-pillars rearward, and stylistically it undoubtedly worked better than the X-Type saloon. While Pininfarina had no input in the car's styling, it did provide technical support in terms of body engineering, vehicle engineering and packaging. Paolo Garella was Pininfarina's programme manager for the project.

B99 (BERTONE)

After over three decades of having no association with the Jaguar marque, in 2011 Bertone once again produced a Jaguar concept car: the B99. Bertone's chief designer, Adrian Griffiths, and design director, Mike Robinson, met with Ian Callum and Julian Thompson of Jaguar at the 2010 Paris Show to let them know of their ideas, although the British marque would have no involvement officially.

The B99 was the result of a research project that Bertone dubbed 'Cats-to-Cars', as Griffiths commented: "We did lot of research on Jaguar, not just Britishness, but also the animal. It's a very quiet animal, it arrives with silence. Not like a Ferrari, a horse that arrives with lots of noise and vibration, but a Jaguar just arrives."

The eventual B99 was undoubtedly a fine design whose resolutely modern interpretation of Jaguar proportions was described by Bertone as "dynamic imbalance". The waistline was almost perfectly horizontal, subtly underlined by a feature line from the front wing to characteristic rear wing haunches and ending in a gently falling tail. The cabin was low (the car measured only 1350mm tall) and positioned well back, aft of a long bonnet, giving the B99 great poise. Chrome lower body lines and non-flared wheelarches gave the car a clean, classical feel.

The forward-leaning front grille and leaping cat mascot brought "slingshot" tension to the front end, accentuated by slender, horizontal headlamps – or as Griffiths put it: "The eyes are set high, giving us a look of high command. It's a regal look, nothing arrogant here, just a noble, confident look."

The four doors opened 'clap-hands' style, with the rear ones hinged at the back. The cabin featured leather, wood and polished aluminium and incorporated a wide instrument panel with a "concert piano feeling", said Bertone.

The powertrain was a Bertone-developed hybrid consisting of two electric motors driving the rear wheels plus a 1.4-litre range-extender petrol engine, total power amounting to 570hp.

The Jaguar B99 broke cover on Bertone's stand at the March 2011 Geneva Show, the name reflecting Bertone's 99th anniversary. The B99 received rave reviews and some speculated that it could be the next Jaguar X-Type but any such notion was soon quashed, as Jaguar's brand director, Adrian Hallmark, said: "We appreciate the fact that Jaguar is interesting enough for people to do a concept around. It's not that we are offended by it, or against it – it is just not for us."

As well as the B99 four-door saloon, Bertone also showed a B99 GT racing version at Geneva with a wider and lower body, revised aerodynamic parts and four-wheel drive courtesy of two extra electric motors up front, and peak power of 985hp.

ITALIAN COACHBUILT HEARSES & LIMOUSINES

British luxury saloons, in particular Jaguars, proved popular with Italian hearse coachbuilders in the 21st century. FT Autotrasformazioni of Ferentino (near Rome) made hearse coachwork on the Jaguar S-Type. Autotrasformazioni Pilato of Ponte della Priula (in the province of Treviso) started making Jaguar hearses in 2008, initially based on the XJ (called 'Queen') and later also on the XF ('Aurora'), new XJ ('Queen II') and F-Pace ('Luce'). Some of these hearses were enormous, measuring up to 6.25 metres long.

From 2013, Pilato also made a Jaguar XJ-based six-door limousine called the Imperial, and in 2017 Pilato became the only Italian coachbuilder to be awarded 'Approved Jaguar Converter' status. Biemme also made a range of Jaguar-based hearses, including an XF-based model with the bizarre name of 'Revenge'.

OPPOSITE PAGE: X-Type Estate and handsome Bertone B99. THIS PAGE, CLOCKWISE FROM TOP LEFT: Biemme XJ, Pilato Luce, Pilato Aurora, Pilato Queen II, Pilato Imperial, Biemme Revenge, Pilato XJ.

JENSEN

British Grand Touring, Italian Style

The Jensen brothers – Alan and Richard – started out building a one-off special in 1928. This led to a string of special-bodied cars made at their Birmingham base. Soon moving to West Bromwich, the business became known as Jensen Motors in 1936. Jensen's first post-war design was a luxurious saloon, the PW of 1946. In 1950 came the Interceptor and in 1953 the 541, which in various guises continued in production until 1962 when a new grand tourer, the C-V8, was unveiled powered by a 6.0-litre Chrysler V8 engine.

In 1966 a momentous decision was taken to follow in the footsteps of many other British luxury car makers and seek Italian design help for its new car, the Interceptor. This was styled by Touring and initially built in Italy by Vignale. A four-wheel drive variant, the FF, became the first ever grand touring car with all wheels driven. Ultimately the decision to use Italian help rather than stick with in-house talent hastened the departure of the founding Jensen brothers and the company's long-term designer Eric Neale.

In 1970 an American called Kjell Qvale took over the firm and within two years he had launched a new, cheaper sports car called the Jensen-Healey. As a result of troubled economic times, Jensen ceased trading in 1976. Several attempts were made to relaunch the Jensen marque, starting with a revived Interceptor in the 1980s. Then in 1998, another Jensen revival saw the unveiling of the S-V8 but by 2002 Jensen's story was over, despite a few attempts to revive the name since then.

INTERCEPTOR & FF (TOURING/VIGNALE)

Having made the charismatic but ungainly glassfibre-bodied C-V8 for some years, in 1965 Jensen turned its attentions to a replacement. The company's chief engineer and stylist, Eric Neale, came up with a design codenamed P66, which was duly presented as the Interceptor at the October 1965 Earls Court Motor Show. However, there was a split of opinion about the new car at management level: Neale and the Jensen brothers wanted to go ahead and make it, but deputy chief engineer Kevin Beattie and managing director Brian Owen regarded it as frumpy and old-fashioned and wanted to solicit design help from Italy. The latter pair's arguments ultimately prevailed and they duly visited Italy in late 1965 to scout three design houses for ideas: Ghia, Vignale and Touring.

It was Touring's submission – a shapely, handsome two-door fastback coupe penned by Federico Formenti – that was ultimately selected. Sadly Carrozzeria Touring was by this stage on a shaky financial footing: 1966 would be its final year of existence and it was in no position even to build the prototype for Jensen. Vignale was therefore tasked with making the prototype, which it duly completed in May 1966. Vignale altered Touring's design in several areas, for instance lowering the roof, altering the C-pillar shape to enlarge the rear quarter-lights, adding stainless steel sill trims and installing a cooling grille in each front wing. Easily the most striking element of the design, though, was the curved 'fishbowl' glass hatchback. This was virtually unique at the time and could even be

ABOVE: Jensen's engineer, Kevin Beattie, examining the Interceptor draughts from Italy that he was instrumental in orchestrating. RIGHT: Jensen's seminal Interceptor, seen here in convertible form.

KNH 921N

RIGHT: Fussy initial Interceptor P66 design by Eric Neale was dismissed in favour of Federico Formenti's iconic shape. In four-wheel drive FF guise, this was a truly pioneering GT car.

removed for the transportation of long objects, although the hatchback weighed a hefty 24kg.

Vignale was also tasked with building the bodywork of the first batch of production cars. Engineless chassis were sent over from Britain and returned back to the Jensen factory once they had been bodied in Turin using steel welded to a tubular framework. However, serious concerns were expressed over the quality of Vignale's work, with shoddy materials and poor workmanship being judged unacceptable. After as few as 60 cars had been built by Vignale, Jensen repatriated the manufacturing tools and jigs back to the UK in early 1967.

At the Interceptor's public debut at the October 1966 Earls Court Motor Show, it received widespread acclaim. From relative obscurity, Jensen really hit the jackpot with its new model. Despite its premium price – higher than an Aston Martin DB6 – it sold very well (over 1000 finding customers in the first three years) and seemed to have special appeal among musicians (owners included Ginger Baker, John Bonham and Cliff Richard). The 325hp 6.3-litre Chrysler V8 engine gave it real grand touring ability, as well as excellent performance: 135mph top speed and 0-60mph in 7.3 seconds. Using the old C-V8 separate chassis, however, with its rigid rear axle and semi-elliptic leaf springs, was hardly cutting edge. The 2+2 interior was plushly upholstered in leather and wood with Wilton carpeting. For a car measuring all of 4724mm long, it was perhaps surprising how restricted rear seat space was.

In October 1969 came the Interceptor II, which had a lightly revised front end and interior. Two years later, the MkIII introduced cast alloy wheels, vented disc brakes and restyled seats. The SP (Six Pack) of 1971 upped engine capacity and power to 7.2 litres and 385hp, making it the most powerful British car of the time, capable of 150mph. Alternative body styles were later added: convertible (1974) and notchback coupe (1975). Well over 6000 Interceptors had been made by the time production ceased in 1976.

A highly significant sister model to the Interceptor was

TOP: Vignale's one-off Nova was effectively the design it initially submitted for the Interceptor.
ABOVE: F-Type was designed in the UK by William Towns but was built in Italy.

the spectacular FF, which Jensen had asked Vignale to draw up alongside its revised Interceptor in 1966. FF stood for Ferguson Formula, the four-wheel drive system that made this car such a pioneer. Another highly advanced feature was Dunlop Maxaret anti-lock braking, a system originally designed for aircraft. The FF sat on wheelbase stretched by four inches over the Interceptor's and was easily identified by its double air vents in the front wings and its bonnet scoop. The FF was way ahead of its time and it took other manufacturers until the 1980s to realise the benefits of permanent four-wheel drive and anti-lock brakes. However, the FF was also exceedingly complex and not terribly reliable. A mere 320 examples were sold between 1966 and 1971, probably only 11 of which were made by Vignale in Italy before production devolved to the UK.

NOVA (VIGNALE)

Vignale had been one of the companies approached by Jensen in 1966 for ideas about its C-V8 replacement. Its design was declined in favour of Touring's but when Alfredo Vignale was approached to build the new Interceptor prototype, he also asked if he could have a special chassis on which to build a one-off, effectively to Vignale's rejected C-V8 design. Jensen duly shortened a chassis (number JM/EXP/117), fitted it with a Chrysler 6.2-litre V8 engine and four-speed manual transmission, and sent it to Vignale in October 1966.

Vignale's fastback coupe, realised in aluminium and glassfibre, was quite different to the Interceptor's, although it retained the concept of a framed curved glass tailgate. Since the engine mounts were lowered by 18mm, the bonnet line was lower by fully 30mm; the bonnet itself was a huge clamshell. Stainless steel bumpers front and rear were beautifully integrated into the shape of the car, while the front end featured electrically operated strakes over the headlights. The cabin shared much of the standard Interceptor's parts but was a strict two-seater.

The prototype was finished in February 1967, ready for its March 1967 debut at the Geneva Show, where its name was revealed: Nova. At Geneva it was shown painted in dark metallic green with a black roof and trimmed in two-tone beige and black. Immediately after the show, the rear end was altered to lose the curved glass tailgate in favour of a more conventional hatchback. The whole car was resprayed in cream paint and the cabin retrimmed in red leather, in which form the Nova appeared at the Turin Show in April 1967. It was subsequently sold to Jensen's distributor in France and the car survives in France to this day.

F-TYPE (COGGIOLA/INDESTOR)

A potential replacement for the Jensen Interceptor, called the F-Type, was designed in 1972 by the Aston Martin stylist, William Towns. He made a 4/10 scale model of the new car, which was then sent to Italy, where two little-known companies based in Turin – Indestor and Coggiola – collaborated to produce a full-size plaster mock-up. The plaster model was then returned to the UK, where Motor Panels used it to assemble four prototype bodyshells in steel. Ultimately, however, the F-Type never did replace the Interceptor.

JOWETT

Solid Basis For The *Carrozzerie*

Jowett was founded in 1901 by two brothers, Benjamin and William Jowett, alongside Arthur Lamb, and started making cars in Bradford, Yorkshire, in 1910. Its cars and commercial vehicles were always distinguished by their excellent engineering and robust quality. In the post-war period, Jowett's approach was an unusually brave one. Its Javelin of 1947 was a brand new saloon with an imaginatively engineered 1485cc flat-four engine boasting a power output of 50hp. Its unusually aerodynamic body had room for six people, thanks to the forward positioning of the engine, while other strengths included fine roadholding, good fuel economy and a top speed of over 80mph.

The Javelin was followed by an open sports tourer model, the Jupiter, in 1949. This was the brainchild of Leslie Johnson and had the distinction of a chassis designed by Eberan van Eberhorst of ERA, famous for his work on pre-war Auto Union racing cars. The tubular chassis carried an uprated (60hp) Javelin engine, transmission and suspension. The factory body was in aluminium with a nose section that hinged forward to reveal the flat-four engine. The Jupiter famously scored class victories at Le Mans from 1950 to 1952.

The Jupiter chassis was specifically designed to cater for the needs of independent coachbuilders – for instance, it ended forward of the rear axle to ease the creation of new rear shapes, while the rolling chassis were made with everything, even the electrics, already in place. Of the 899 Jupiters built, a remarkable one in ten had coachbuilt bodywork. Oddly, Jowett insisted on approving any new coachwork, although it's dubious that it ever actually did this. The first chassis-only Jupiters started shipping in August 1950, usually to small outfits in Britain, but also on the continent – including Italy. Jowett eventually ceased trading in 1955, mostly because of parts supply difficulties.

JUPITER COUPE (STABILIMENTI FARINA)

While the Jupiter chassis was being designed at ERA in 1949, the Jowett factory received a visit from a representative of the Italian *carrozzeria*, Stabilimenti Farina. It was hoped that Farina would make a body for the new chassis ready for display at the 1949 London Motor Show. That didn't happen but perhaps helps to explain why Stabilimenti Farina managed to secure the second Jupiter chassis ever made (number E0SA7R) in August 1950. To design its new bodywork, the coachbuilder engaged the services of Giovanni Michelotti, who had been Farina's chief stylist from 1936 to 1949 but had recently gone freelance.

Michelotti designed a coupe body around Jowett's tubular frame, somewhat resembling his earlier design for Farina on a Ferrari 166 chassis. It was cleverly engineered with many neat touches such as self-parking wipers, a spring-assisted door opening mechanism and a curious radio built into the rear wheelarch cover. Behind the two seats was a luggage space with a hinged panel to the boot – an early example of the ski flap.

ABOVE: Somewhat ungainlly drophead coupe bodywork by Ghia-Aigle was based on a Jowett chassis. RIGHT: Stabilimenti Farina produced this rather elegant-looking coupe. This is the last of four chassis rebodied by Farina in 1950-1951.

707 PL

707 PL

Work progressed quickly, so that Farina was able to show its new steel-bodied coupe in time for the October 1950 Paris Salon, and *Autocar* magazine was inspired to call it "superb". The maroon-painted two-seater coupe also appeared at the London Motor Show soon after and was subsequently registered in the UK. Following a crash in 1952, it was restored by HJ Mulliner and repainted white, whereupon it left for Singapore and then New Zealand before ultimately returning to Britain.

A second coupe, pretty much identical to the first, was then built on chassis E0SA33R for a customer in Chicago, USA. At a later stage this was fitted with a Ford V8 engine and automatic transmission.

A third Farina coupe (chassis 59) was ordered by the French racing driver, Marcel Becquart, who wanted to use it in the 1951 Le Mans race, but sadly the chassis arrived too late for this happen (Becquart was compensated with a Le Mans works drive in a standard Jowett Jupiter, in which he earned a class win). Farina having built the car during 1951, it was prepared for entry into the January 1952 Monte Carlo Rally, in which Becquart secured fifth place overall (the best ever result achieved by a Jowett in this race). He returned to the event in 1953 with the same car and was at one stage leading his class but was sadly forced to retire.

The fourth and final Farina Jupiter (chassis 109) was originally painted dark blue but by the time it was exhibited for the first time at the October 1951 Paris Salon, it had been repainted dove grey. The four Jupiters built by Farina – all of which still exist – differ only in small details such as grilles and embellishments. Their design is widely considered to be among the most attractive of all coachbuilt bodywork made for the Jupiter chassis.

JUPITER DROPHEAD COUPE & FIXED-HEAD COUPE (GHIA-AIGLE)

The Swiss-Italian coachbuilder Ghia-Aigle made its coachbuilding debut in 1949 with a rather odd estate car based on a Mercedes 170V. By 1951 it was doing a lot of coachwork on proprietary chassis with rather more harmonious designs, including on Jowett chassis.

Jowetts enjoyed a strong following in Switzerland and three chassis were bodied by Ghia-Aigle in all. It is possible that one of those was on a Javelin chassis but it is thought that probably all three were Jupiters.

Chassis 31, first seen at the March 1951 Geneva Show, was a Drophead Coupe. The design was rather dumpy and featured an odd-looking oval front grille with two smaller grilles beneath. The car was painted maroon with yellow wheels and a brown soft-top.

Chassis 56 was a Fixed Head Coupe first owned by the Geneva Jowett dealer, Henri Ziegler and later by an eccentric wine collector called Michel Dovaz. This car was painted green and featured a similarly unusual triple front grille. It is today the only known surviving Ghia-Aigle-bodied Jowett.

A third chassis (number unknown but believed to be Jupiter chassis 96) was a Coupe with a rather more conventional look and a single concave-shaped eggcrate front grille.

BELOW: Ghia-Aigle's third and final design on the Jupiter (seen in standard form in the bottom picture) featured a curious concave front grille.

LEA-FRANCIS

New Tricks For Old Master

The venerable Lea-Francis marque was founded in Coventry in 1895 by RH Lea and GI Francis. After making bicycles, the manufacture of cars began in 1903, initially under licence from Singer but then, from 1919, to Lea-Francis's own design. Its cars were always luxurious, sporting and expensive.

The only Lea-Francis model with any Italian connection was the Lynx, which has gone down in history as one of the greatest motoring lemons of all time. Launched at the 1960 London Motor Show, its Abbey Panels-built bodywork was shockingly ugly: an awkward front grille, bulbously bilious flanks and a brash colour scheme of violet paint and gold-plated brightwork. The engine was a 2.6-litre Ford Zephyr six, the gearbox Triumph TR3 in a tubular crossmember chassis. Three Lynxes were built, all of which survive.

According to author Barrie Price in his book, *The Lea-Francis Story*, one additional chassis was despatched to Italy in March 1962, the intention being to clothe it in a new body designed by the British-born but Italian-based Trevor Fiore. The coachbuilder cited by Price was Moretti although it seems more likely that the recipient was Fiore's constant collaborator, Fissore. The new model was to be called the Francesca and was envisaged in two body styles, sketches of which were released to the press in 1963. The first was a four-seater, two-door coupe in the fashion of the Gordon-Keeble GT. The second was an open-topped sports car with extraordinary exposed exhaust pipes emerging through the front wings and then snaking back into the side sills, which were to have featured a curious 'drilled' effect. The open-topped proposal provided a very strong foretaste of Fiore's forthcoming TVR Trident (see page 274).

Despite Lea-Francis claiming that it had orders for 1000 cars from the US, and that the cars were ready for production, the project was never more than mere conjecture. A shortage of funds caused the cancellation of the Francesca project and the sole, unclothed chassis eventually found its way from Italy to the USA.

Trevor Fiore designed both coupe and convertible versions of the Francesca, which would have been the polar opposite in terms of aesthetics to the rather 'challenging' Lynx (below)

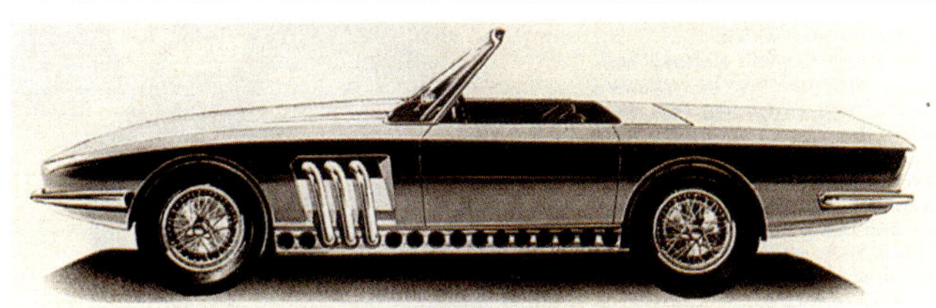

LOLA

Reclothed Racer

Founded in 1958 by Eric Broadley in Huntingdon, Cambridgeshire, Lola Cars elevated itself to become one of the pre-eminent names in race car engineering. From humble origins it eventually broke into Formula Junior, Formula 3, Formula 2 and Formula 1. Lola was also very big in sports car racing, notably with the T70 that was not only a superbly competitive machine but also one of the most handsome cars of its era.

Road cars were not part of Lola's milieu but when one man – a Canadian called Sidney Frank – approached Lola with the idea of building a one-off based on a T70 chassis, the ball started rolling. Frank had actually approached Aston Martin first but it wasn't interested; Lola was his second choice.

He then sought Italian design skills for the new body, approaching several *carrozzerie* but eventually appointing Edgardo Michelotti, who had recently taken over his late father's design company in Turin. Designer Tateo Uchida created the highly distinctive shape with an extremely low, forward-jutting nose that incorporated pop-up headlamps and rose sharply to a virtually straight-through waistline. The glasshouse was very generous considering the racing car basis, although what looked like rear three-quarter windows were in fact flying buttresses that flanked a tall engine cover. A large rear wing could be raised and lowered using a wiper motor. The doors opened upwards and forwards, butterfly-style, via hinges top and bottom of the windscreen pillars. All the bodywork was realised in aluminium except for the engine cover and bumpers, which were made of composites, but even so it emerged a tad weighty at 1350kg.

Part of the reason was that the right-hand drive cockpit was so plushly trimmed. It featured digital instrumentation and a gear lever mounted to the right of the driver, in true racing car style. Two small luggage areas were provided: one in the nose and the other in the right-hand sill (the left-hand sill carried the fuel tank).

The chassis was pretty much pure racing car. For the engine, a Morland-tuned Chevrolet 6.7-litre Can-Am V8 was sourced from Franco Sbarro, the iconoclastic Swiss car maker. This engine reputedly delivered 550hp in its carb-fed spec and the car was geared to achieve 214mph, although it is highly doubtful that it ever got anywhere close to this.

The one-off, sometimes referred to as the Lola Ultimo, was shown in mock-up guise at the Geneva Show in March 1981. It then took over a year for the car to reach running order. In this form, John Miles of *Autocar* magazine road-tested it in 1982, reporting that it offered "a feel and precision that one would expect in a race car". He added: "The rear [breaks] away more manageably than a Boxer's or even a Pantera's might" and that it "behaved with a docility that seemed to belie its obvious weight". The Michelotti Lola remained a one-off but as to its ultimate fate, sadly there is no information.

ABOVE: Michelotti-designed Lola made the cover of Autocar *magazine. ABOVE RIGHT: Lola T70 is seen here in handsome standard form. BELOW RIGHT: Highly dramatic one-off bodywork graced what was essentially a racing car chassis.*

ANTI-GLARE
LOLA

LOTUS

The Art & Science of Lightness

With good reason, many people have compared the talents and achievements of Anthony Colin Bruce Chapman with those of Enzo Ferrari. Chapman started life as a humble amateur racing driver and builder of home-made specials, starting in 1948 with a pre-war Austin 7-based sports car knocked up in a garage behind his girlfriend's house in London.

From such unassuming beginnings would emerge one of the world's greatest constructors of sports cars and a Formula 1 championship winner many times over. Chapman chose the name Lotus for his marque and on the road car side, Lotus started out making dual-purpose road/race cars like the Mark VI, XI and Seven. As Chapman's own taste in cars matured, so he started developing more and more sophisticated sports cars such as the Elan and Europa. By the early 1970s, he had completely abandoned his roots as a maker of sports cars that buyers were expected to build themselves at home, and was ready to challenge the likes of Porsche and Ferrari.

Chapman had a superb team of engineers and indeed designers within his company but he was always aware of Italian design talent (he was a regular visitor to the Geneva Motor Show). However, only one Lotus model would ever reach production that was designed by an Italian: the Lotus Esprit, which the prodigious Giorgetto Giugiaro designed as early as 1972. Several other Lotus models designed in Italy came close to making production but always just missed out.

Chapman passed away in 1982 and his company was sold to General Motors in 1986. Lotus would have one further connection with Italy in the form of corporate ownership. On 27 August 1993, General Motors sold Lotus for £30 million to the Italian businessman, Romano Artioli, who had recently revived Bugatti Automobili. This arrangement lasted a mere three years, however, as Bugatti's bankruptcy in 1995 forced Artioli to sell a majority share in Lotus to Proton, the Malaysian car manufacturer. Artioli stepped down as chairman at that point but continued as director of Lotus Special Projects until 1998. Perhaps Artioli's greatest achievement was bringing the Elise to production in 1995. Within 10 years this exceptional mid-engined sports car had sold more than 20,000 examples – the most popular Lotus of all time.

Italian design returned to Lotus in 2009, when the Italian-born stylist, Donato Coco, was appointed as Lotus's new Director of Design. He had previously been chief designer at Citroën, heading up the design teams that developed the Xsara, C3 and Picasso. From 2005 he had also worked with Ferrari, helping create cars like the 430 Scuderia, California, 599XX and the 458 Italia. Coco's role at Lotus was to design new concepts, which he did with alacrity – even if ultimately none of his creations enjoyed a production future.

ABOVE: Giorgetto Giugiaro and Colin Chapman alongside the prototype of the Esprit, a model that elevated Lotus to become a true rival for Porsche and which lasted in production for almost 28 years.

BUR 450S
UK·SPORTS·CARS

XI 1100 (GHIA-AIGLE)

Colin Chapman's Lotus XI (Eleven) was primarily a racing machine but could equally well be driven to competitive events. Three versions were offered: Sport (Ford sidevalve engine and live rear axle); Club (Coventry-Climax 1100 engine with 75hp and a live rear axle/coil springs); and Le Mans (Coventry-Climax power in 75, 83 or 100hp forms and a de Dion rear end).

Over its superb spaceframe chassis, Lotus normally built fabulously aerodynamic bodywork but one of its chassis – number 237, built in October 1956 – was sent to Switzerland for unique new bodywork. The chassis was to Le Mans spec and fitted with a Coventry-Climax 1100 engine. It arrived in February 1957 at Ghia-Aigle's works in Lugano, Switzerland, and within less than one month it was ready to make its debut at the March 1957 Geneva Motor Show – actually not quite ready, since the interior was unfinished and the roof missing.

Ghia-Aigle's Spider was designed with great flair by Giovanni Michelotti, featuring a long, low bonnet and an oval grille, at the ends of which were sited extremely low-set headlamps. At the rear end were small fins on the wings. The entire bodywork was realised in red glassfibre. Colin Chapman was present at the 1957 Geneva Show to inspect Ghia-Aigle's Spider but what he thought of it remained unrecorded.

Within six months (by September 1957), the car had been converted from a roadster into a coupe (or rather, fitted with a removable hardtop). The compact dimensions of the car forced Michelotti to design doors that cut into the roof to ease entry, with curved Plexiglas fitted to the sides and rear. The Ghia-Aigle XI was shown in this form at the 1958 Geneva Show and also competed in local hillclimbs. No further examples were made.

ELAN SS FASTBACK (FRUA)

The Elan's excellent steel backbone chassis, with its independent suspension and all-round disc brakes, could have formed the basis for many coachbuilt sports cars, but in fact only one was ever made. This came from the stable of Pietro Frua, whose Elan SS Fastback of 1964 was an undeniably handsome machine. There is some confusion over whether the Italian bodywork was commissioned by the Swiss Lotus importer, M D Perrin, or whether it was Colin Chapman himself who asked Frua to do it, with the possibility of series production in mind.

Whatever the truth, Elan chassis number 26/0341 was sent from Lotus HQ in Hethel to the Swiss Lotus importer, Holiday Cars Import of Geneva, in January 1964, on which Frua would create a new coupe body. The result was highly successful; the lines of his contemporaneous Maserati Mistral could be clearly discerned in his elegant creation. The low nose with cowled headlamps, appealing glasshouse design, vented rear quarter panels and slender bumpers lent the car an exotic feel, despite its compact dimensions. Its most striking aspect was the fastback rear end incorporating an opening glass tailgate.

While the regular Elan had a glassfibre body, Frua's two-seat coupe was realised in a mixture of steel and aluminium, a lightweight approach that added only 6kg to the overall weight, despite the large fastback roof.

The new car debuted on Frua's own stand at the Geneva Show of March 1964; it would also appear later that year at the Paris Salon. In a press release, plans were announced whereby Frua would produce bodies in series, cars then being built up at separate locations in Italy, Switzerland and Britain, but this never happened. The show car, which was painted red with an ivory interior and Rudge wire wheels, remained unique.

OPPOSITE PAGE: Michelotti designed this Lotus XI based car for Ghia-Aigle in 1957, initially in open form but soon converted to coupe. THIS PAGE: A touch of Maserati Mistral? Undoubtedly, since the 1964 Elan SS Fastback was designed by the same stylist, Pietro Frua.

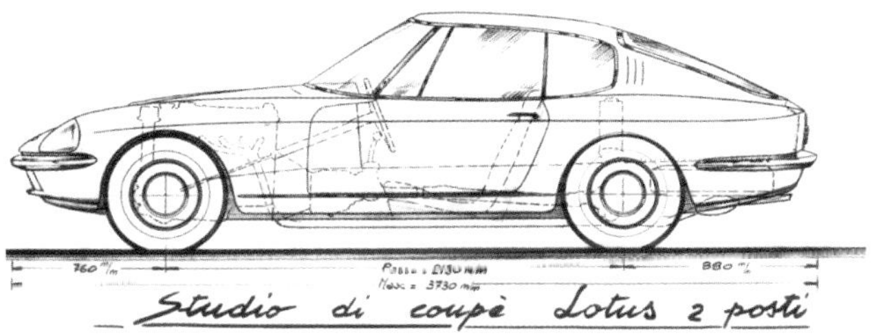

ESPRIT (ITALDESIGN)

Colin Chapman met Giorgetto Giugiaro at the March 1972 Geneva Motor Show, having gone on to the Italdesign stand to check out the great design master's Maserati Boomerang concept, which Chapman very much liked. After chatting together for some time, the pair formed the idea of creating a bold new Lotus concept car in time for a reveal at the November 1972 Turin Motor Show.

The basis was to be a modified Lotus Europa backbone chassis. Chapman had already begun planning an scaled-up replacement for the Europa under the project name M70 and this fitted in with this brief. Giugiaro himself referred to the project internally at Italdesign as 'Kiwi'. Despite the remarkably short time available, Giugiaro's Lotus Esprit concept was duly unveiled at the 1972 Turin Show.

Giugiaro excelled himself with the Esprit's design: a super-clean wedge that was enduringly simple and supremely balanced in every proportion. This was an early expression of Giugiaro's 'folder paper' design ethos, with plenty of straight lines – even the glass used for the screens was flat. The silver-painted prototype may have been a non-runner but the interior had already been fully developed for the car's debut.

So fundamentally right was Giugiaro's 1972 concept that, remarkably, it would emerge in production form at the October 1975 Paris Salon with almost no changes. It was tweaked only in respect of its aerodynamic qualities and some detailing to allow for Lotus's preferred method of injection moulding for the glassfibre body. Aerodynamic issues were the reason why Giugiaro's original large rear side windows were abandoned, while the inclination of the windscreen also had to be raised to meet American safety standards.

It's equally remarkable that the design would stand the test of time so long, still recognisable when the Esprit finally exited production in 2004. The unusual interior architecture was perhaps less appealing over the longer term and was revised as early as 1979.

For its day, the Esprit was state-of-the-art for a mid-engined sports car. In construction, it was classically Lotus: steel backbone chassis, all-independent suspension, all-round disc brakes and glassfibre bodywork. The engine was Lotus's brilliant

2.0-litre 16-valve four-cylinder '907' unit mounted amidships, while the five-speed gearbox was taken from the Citroen SM. The Esprit was not only a convincingly high-performance car for its day, but probably also the best-handling Lotus yet made.

The Esprit famously featured in the 1977 James Bond film *The Spy Who Loved Me*, in which Roger Moore's submarine Esprit was filmed emerging from the sea – fittingly enough given the Italian design connection – on a Sardinian beach.

Lotus kept abreast of the opposition with constant developments. The S2 of 1978 added an integrated front spoiler, the S2.2 of 1980 had an expanded 2.2-litre engine and a Turbo option. The S3 of 1981 added a wraparound front bumper, in which form it continued until 1987, when Lotus's in-house designer, Peter Stevens, effected a major restyle, smoothing off the lines to make the car more aerodynamic. There was another restyle in 1993, when the nose and rear wing were reshaped and the interior improved. The Esprit switched from four cylinders to eight in 1996 with an all-new twin-turbo V8 capable of 349hp.

Italians were involved with the Esprit later in its life, too. Romano Artioli, the industrialist behind the revival of Bugatti in the 1990s, acquired Lotus from General Motors in August 1993. Artioli's brother-in-law, the architect Giampaolo Benedini – who had reworked Marcello Gandini's original design for the Bugatti EB110 – was called in to make detail changes to the Esprit, giving birth to the GT3 of 1997.

Some 10,675 Esprits were built in all from 1976 to the very last example rolling off the production line on 20 February 2004, after almost 28 years in production – a remarkable feat for any car, let alone an exotic mid-engined sports car.

As an aside, Lotus also asked Giugiaro to propose a design for the interior of the new Elite, launched in 1974. His distinctive concept of a tall centre console with grouped controls was duly given the green light for production.

OPPOSITE PAGE: Simplicity and rectitude coalesced in the divine Esprit. James Bond emerged from a Sardinian beach in one. ABOVE: Italdesign advert shows how little Giugiaro's sketch was altered for production. BELOW: Shape stood test of time superbly.

ETNA (ITALDESIGN)

Following the 1970s Esprit, Giugiaro's next involvement with Lotus did not come until 1984, when the Etna was developed with Lotus as a potential successor to the Esprit. Italdesign took the existing Esprit chassis and extended its wheelbase by 70mm in order to accommodate a new Lotus V8 engine mounted amidships. Designed by Tony Rudd, this new Type 909 V8 engine was a 4.0-litre unit developing 335bhp – sadly a powerplant that would ultimately be stillborn. The active suspension system that Lotus had developed for its Formula 1 car was also due to make its debut in road-going form in the Etna, as well as other advanced features such as traction control, anti-lock brakes and active noise cancelling.

The wedge shape of the Etna was described by Italdesign as "aggressive, sophisticated and powerful", while it was also aerodynamic, with a claimed Cd of 0.29. The contrast between its upper and lower halves was emphasised by the use of thin, black-painted roof pillars, creating the impression of a transparent dome. The superb two-seat cabin featured leather and wood and an angled dashboard that looked and felt like it could easily have made production.

The Etna was unveiled at the 1984 Birmingham Motor Show. Despite being clearly earmarked for production, any prospect of the Etna reaching showrooms was scuppered when General Motors took Lotus over in 1986. Instead, the existing Esprit was simply warmed over for many years to come.

Italdesign's Etna remained a one-off. After being stored at Lotus's Hethel works, it came up for auction in 2001. The man who bought it, Olav Glasius, made the sensational discovery that the chassis Lotus had sent to Italdesign in 1984 actually had a Type 909 V8 engine fitted (one of only two ever made), having previously been hidden from view. The Etna was duly turned into a runner, while a new roof section was also made, since the original had blown off while the car was being trailered down the M1 motorway!

SALOON PROPOSAL (PININFARINA)

Just as Pininfarina was proposing that Ferrari should adopt its idea of the Pinin four-door saloon – a format that Maranello had always shied away from – by coincidence the very same idea was also being pursued for Lotus. Colin Chapman had approached Paolo Martin of Pininfarina as early as 1979 asking for a proposal for a four-door Lotus, as the Italian designer later recalled: "Chapman asked if I could design a four-door saloon based on a tubular backbone chassis with glassfibre bodywork. After some corrections, my sketches were approved in early 1980. Colin Chapman and Mike Kimberley then visited me to see the 1:4 scale model version." Paolo Martin's design looked something like an Aston Martin Lagonda, but his proposal never progressed beyond the scale model stage.

The idea of a four-door Lotus did not simply disappear, however. Four years later, on the occasion of the Etna's debut at the 1984 Motor Show, Lotus announced it was developing the Eminence, a large, six-seat saloon powered by the Type 909 4.0-litre V8 engine, with a targeted top speed of 160mph. Advanced features were to include a Kevlar-and-carbonfibre monocoque with an armour plating option and active suspension. Lotus released a sketch done by Harris Mann but the project did not progress beyond the drawing board, which was probably a wise move for Lotus.

X100 & ELAN M100 (CECOMP & ITALDESIGN)

In 1981, Lotus took advantage of a fresh collaboration with Toyota to start the development of a new entry-level sports car called the M90 – effectively a new, modern Elan. This 2+2 coupe/convertible was to be engineered around a mid-mounted Toyota engine. After Colin Chapman's death in 1982 and with new management in place, the project was renamed X100 and was somewhat reconfigured, while retaining the basic architecture intact. The X100's styling was done in house by Oliver Winterbottom, and his convertible design was built into a fully running prototype. Unbeknown to him, an alternative X100 proposal had also been designed by Peter Stevens, whose shape loosely recalled the Lotus Etna's (page 210). The Stevens prototype had an Italian connection, since it was built in Italy by CECOMP and delivered to Hethel for presentation in 1985. Stevens' car differed from the 'official' X100 in being a two-seater with a front engine and front-wheel drive.

The takeover of Lotus by General Motors in 1986 scuppered the X100 project, which – had it gone ahead – would have presented a potentially major competitor for Mazda's MX-5. As it was, the front-wheel drive Elan M100 – a more upmarket project entirely – was developed instead in double-quick time. Giugiaro was asked to present a design proposal for this new M100 Elan in 1986 but his effort – a smooth-edged but rather bland coupe – was ultimately was rejected in favour of Peter Stevens' design, which entered production in 1989.

OPPOSITE PAGE: 1984 Etna remained a one-off.
BELOW LEFT: Paolo Martin sketches for Pininfarina's Lotus four-door saloon.
BELOW: Italdesign's Elan M100 proposal (main pic) and the X100 built by CECOMP (inset).

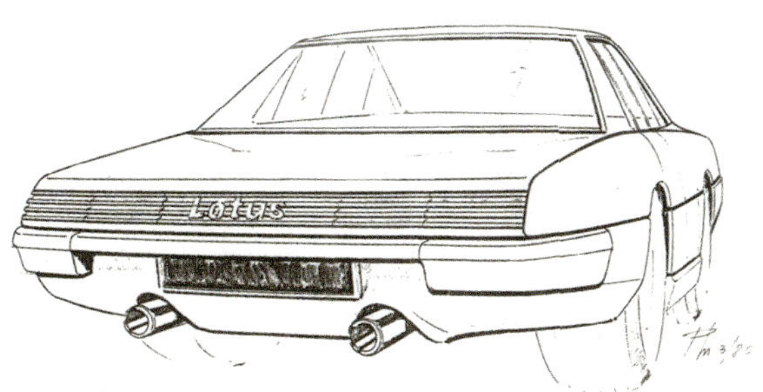

BULGARI (I.DE.A/PININFARINA)

Almost all examples of Italo-British cooperation concern British companies approaching Italian designers. The Bulgari car project was a rare example of the opposite being true. Gianni Bulgari's name is best known as one of Italy's most successful jewellers but if his plans had come to fruition, he would have become a car manufacturer too. He founded GB Automotive in October 1988 with a vision to make a car with the interior space of a people carrier but the compact footprint of a medium-size hatchback. His simple solution was to make his car wider than normal so that it could seat up to three people abreast. His first ideas were realised in Italy by Franco Mantegazza's design company, I.DE.A, but it was to Britain that he beat a path to fulfil his dreams – namely Lotus.

Lotus created a new separate chassis design, on to which a variety of different bodies could be fitted, from coupe to saloon to estate. Many different powertrains were considered; everything from a BMW four-cylinder to a Ferrari-Lancia 8.32 V8 were tried, but Lotus's then owner, General Motors, eventually installed its own 2.0-litre 16-valve engine.

The eventual body design was by Gianni Bulgari himself, aided by I.DE.A and latterly Pininfarina, and was strikingly similar to the Alfa Romeo 145 that would appear several years later. The proportions were short but wide and tall, the layout enabling a highly unconventional, patented five-seat cabin consisting of three staggered seats abreast up front and two skewed seats to the rear.

Lotus built a fully running prototype in 1990, which was widely pictured in the press at the time. By Bulgari's own admission, however, the exterior design – particularly the front end – was "too extreme". *Car* magazine, meanwhile, derided it as "a rakish delivery van". The radical concept was toned down back in Italy over the next few years, with a more conventional design gradually evolving, while Lotus Elan-based front suspension was also adopted. Despite bold talk of 5000 units a year being made, a lack of funds scuppered any production future for Bulgari's revolutionary car.

Inter-active styling: choose your own ending

SELF-SUPPORTING STEEL CHASSIS ALLOWS FOR HUGE DESIGN FREEDOM

When Lotus engineers came up with the idea of a self-supporting steel chassis for Bulgari's car, they simultaneously created huge design possibilities. Because the car's panels are not an integral part of the structure, they can be made from glassfibre, a much less expensive method than stamping out conventional steel panels. This technique also makes building a number of different bodystyles much less expensive. Such design freedom inspired Bulgari, with the help of design house IDEA, to come up with a stylish basic body style which could accommodate five different rear ends. Despite looking very different, only the upper rear decks have been changed – that's everything above the waistline and behind the central window pillar.

THIS PAGE: Peculiar does not begin to describe the Bulgari. Cabin could seat five people in a uniquely skewed manner. Car magazine's 1997 report shows adaptability of body design on Lotus's separate chassis. OPPOSITE PAGE: Bertone's Lotus Emotion was a hastily reimagined version of its Bugatti EB110 proposal (bottom right).

EMOTION (BERTONE)

The Lotus Esprit-based Emotion concept of 1991 has its origins in Bertone's pitch to design the forthcoming Bugatti EB110 supercar. Bertone was one of four design houses tasked with producing proposals and a Marc Deschamps-designed 1:1 scale model was duly built in clay in early 1990. However, Bertone was not destined to get the Bugatti design contract – it went to ex-Bertone man Marcello Gandini instead – so the *carrozzeria* simply repurposed its design and nonchalantly gave it 'Lotus Emotion' badging as a prospective new Esprit.

This mid-engined coupe was very successful, both conceptually and aesthetically. Its surfaces were clean, elegant and softly curved, in stark contrast to Giugiaro's original sharp-edged Esprit wedge. The Emotion was 270mm shorter than the Esprit at 4060mm, 70mm wider at 1900mm, and 70mm lower at 1080mm. Its waistline was almost horizontal, while deeply indented lower parts of the doors fed into engine air intakes on either side. There was an adjustable rear spoiler, too, but easily the most striking aspect of the design was the glasshouse, which wrapped around an ever-narrowing roof profile.

The underpinnings were – putatively at least – Lotus Esprit Turbo (2.2-litre four-cylinder engine with 264hp mounted amidships) and the car was claimed to do 0-62mph in 5.0 seconds and reach 170mph. However, the Emotion was never made into a functioning vehicle.

When it made its debut at the 1991 Detroit Show, Bertone said: "The rapport with Lotus is something new for Bertone. Emotion sets out to take a second look at the Lotus image and interpret it freely in a more modern key." The one and only Emotion returned to Bertone in Turin, where it was retained until Bertone went bankrupt in 2015, at which point it was sold at auction for the remarkable sum of €3,445,182.

CHRONOS (PININFARINA)

In 1990, General Motors ignited controversy when it launched the Lotus Carlton, a high-performance version of its humdrum four-door saloon. The storm surrounded the speed of a supposed family car: the Guinness Book of Records declared it the fastest saloon yet made, with a top speed of 177mph.

One year later, Pininfarina used the Lotus Carlton as a basis for its Chronos sports coupe – hard to discern because the Italian company had chopped 30cm out of the wheelbase. Pininfarina said of the car's voluptuous shape: "The essence of the design lies in the alternation of the ebb and flow of volumes at the base of the windscreen pillars, which lightens

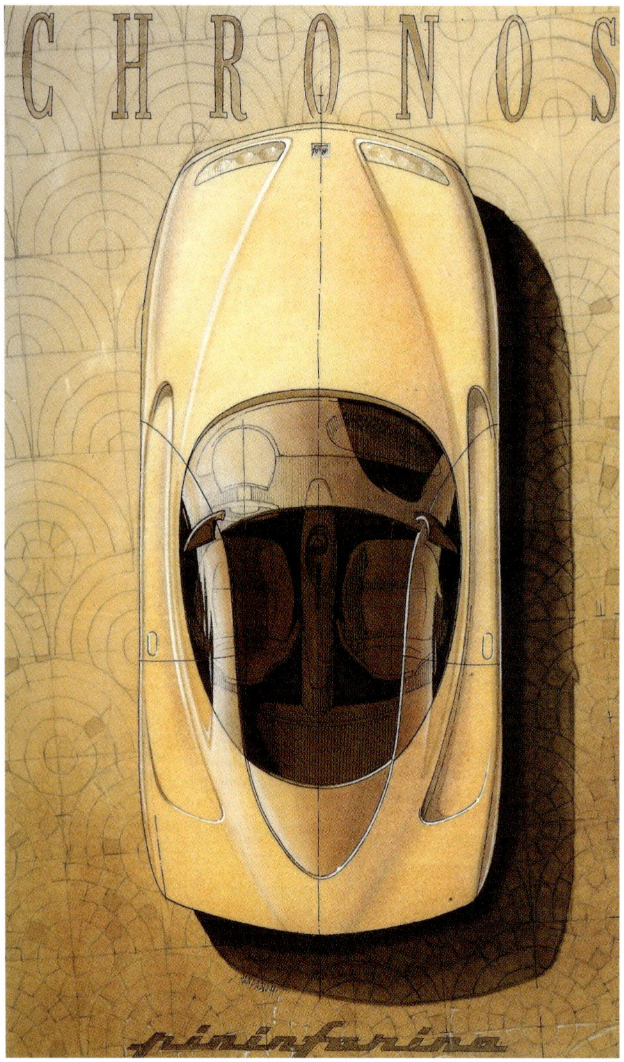

the whole design. The rear volume is low and short, supported by a waistline that rises compared to the side, generating lance-shaped windows." It was aerodynamic (Cd 0.29) and the two-seat interior was simple to the point of being austere.

Painted bright yellow, the composite-bodied prototype appeared at the 1991 Detroit and Geneva Shows. The project did not stall at being just a mere static motor show one-off; it was made fully functional with its Lotus-engineered 377hp 3.6-litre six-cylinder twin-turbo engine under the bonnet. Pininfarina harboured some hope that General Motors would produce the Chronos in series, but it didn't bite. In the end it's thought that Pininfarina eventually made a total of four examples of the Chronos: the yellow original plus three others in silver, black and blue.

ELISE & ELITE PROPOSALS (BREUER, I.DE.A, TJAARDA, ZAGATO)

With Lotus in Italian ownership in the early 1990s, it was perhaps no surprise that Italian design talent should be courted when it came to proposals for a 'new Lotus Seven'. Romano Artioli's brother-in-law, Giampaolo Benedini (who incidentally owned a Lotus 23) came up with the design brief for what would eventually become the Elise, and a whole host of designers were invited to tender for the styling job. Several of these were Italian, including Zagato, I.DE.A, Tjaarda Design and Paul Breuer.

Breuer later recalled: "The drawings were requested by Romano Artioli, owner at the time of Lotus and Bugatti, and the architect Benedini, who was responsible for design. I worked alone on the project, and although I was aware that there were proposals from other designers, I only knew about Zagato's. In fact it was my friend at Zagato, Ercole

Spada, who suggested that I make contact with Artioli. I received drawings of the chassis with some fixed points such as the windscreen. I did two proposals: one with English inspiration (Lotus Seven) and one with Italian inspiration."

In the end, the designer chosen for the Elise was not Italian but British: Julian Thompson. He did admit, however, to drawing inspiration for his Elise from a certain Italian machine that was very close to his heart: the Ducati motorbike. Launched at the Frankfurt Show in 1995, the Lotus Elise was named after Romano Artioli's granddaughter, Elisa Artioli.

Another project that Lotus asked designers to think about at the same time as the Elise was a 'new Elite' – essentially a sporting estate car for the 1990s, which was a highly unusual idea for the time. Among those who submitted design proposals were Ercole Spada of Zagato and Paul Breuer. Ultimately the project remained on the drawing board.

ENJOY (PININFARINA)

The Enjoy was a fascinating 21st century project by Pininfarina with Lotus as a technical partner. Lotus supplied the extruded aluminium chassis from the Elise, while Pininfarina created dramatic new bodywork, the intention being "to design a simple, practical, basic though dynamic barchetta that would be the ideal car for people who, in addition to wanting an enjoyable drive, also have a passion for racing."

The Elise chassis was substantially altered for the Enjoy, with a wider track fore and aft, and the front axle moved forwards to lengthen the wheelbase by 75mm. This enabled the weight to be shifted rearwards to improve turn-in, aided by Formula 1-style in-board suspension.

The Enjoy was conceived for both road and track

OPPOSITE PAGE: Lotus Carlton-based Pininfarina Chronos; Tom Tjaarda's sketches for the Elise and 'new Elite'. ABOVE: Elise proposals from Zagato (top) and Paul Breuer (middle and lower). RIGHT: Pininfarina's Elise-based Enjoy in its original open-wheel form (main pic) and in its later, more refined guise (inset).

use. Lotus's load-bearing chassis meant that the body panels did not form part of the car's structure, so the front and rear wings, complete with lights, could be easily detached by removing cotter pins, transforming the car into an open-wheeled car for track use (in which form its weight dropped to a mere 800kg).

At the front end, air was channelled through the suspension and on to side-mounted radiators that were deliberately made visible. Above a curvaceous panel behind the cabin sat two rollover bars that extended backwards to form fins on which the brake lights were fitted.

The doors opened in butterfly-wing fashion, while a rigid tonneau cover enclosed the passenger's side of the cabin, cleverly disappearing under the dashboard when not needed. A second tonneau protected the driver's side when parked. Instead of a windscreen there were two small deflectors in front of the cockpit. The minimalistic cabin featured seats and trim made from waterproof materials. The steering wheel was shaped to ease access to the cabin and incorporated a rev counter, while a second display was located on the facia. A compartment behind the cabin was designed to house helmets, gloves and tracksuits.

The prototype was powered by a 135hp 1.8-litre four-cylinder engine, as used in the Lotus Elise 135R. *Auto Express* road-tested the Enjoy in 2003, declaring that it offered "a seriously involving drive, pin-sharp steering and a responsive throttle. The ride is taut and the car feels stiffer than the standard Elise, which improves high-speed stability."

Following an unveiling at the March 2003 Geneva Show, Pininfarina announced that the Enjoy would enter production at a projected price of around £35,000. This would have been the first Pininfarina-branded production car since the Fiat 124 Spider-based Spidereuropa of the 1980s. Things moved on again in September 2003, when Pininfarina acquired the engineering, testing and prototype branches of the French car marque, Matra, and announced that Matra would manufacture the Enjoy.

A revised version of the Enjoy was then developed, still based on the Elise chassis but using new double wishbone suspension engineered by Matra and a change of powerplant to a 192hp Toyota engine, good for 0-62mph in 5.2 seconds. While the new Enjoy kept the removable-wing format, the body was substantially reshaped, notably at the front and rear ends, with a view to making it suitable for everyday use. The characteristic rear fins were repurposed as air extractors, between which luggage could be placed on a rack.

Matra also helped to develop the Enjoy's interior with the French luxury goods maker Louis Vuitton involved. In contrast to the 2003 model's minimalism, this was much more luxuriously trimmed in leather.

The Enjoy project was still 'live' in 2004, as Pininfarina announced it intended to produce 75 units to celebrate the 75th anniversary of the company in 2005, but sadly no production run ever did materialise.

'PARIS' CONCEPTS (DONATO COCO)

There is one final Italian sting in the Lotus tale: in 2009 Lotus appointed an Italian designer as its new Director of Design: Donato Coco, who had previously been with Citroën and Ferrari. He was very much given a 'thrown in at the deep end' assignment, being tasked with designing no fewer than five new concepts for Lotus within a mere 10 months, their launch scheduled for the 2010 Paris Show.

Coco certainly had a major impact at Lotus, as he recalled in an interview with Ashley Coates: "My first decision was to cancel the tea room – not very popular in England – and turn it into a virtual room with a big screen to visualise projects with optimal conditions. I rapidly grew the team of designers and modellers from 17 to 70 to be able to deliver this phenomenal plan."

The 'Paris five' were: Esprit, Elan, Eterne, Elite and new Elise. The cars presented at the show were not running prototypes but simple design concepts, acknowledged to be several years away from production. Lotus said that three different chassis configurations – small mid-engined, large mid-engined and front-engined – would be

required for this bold new range.

The Esprit was perhaps the most serious proposition, as work had already started on it beforehand. This would have used a Lexus ISF-derived 5.0-litre V8 with power of up to 620hp, good for 0-62mph in just over 3.0 seconds.

The Elan would have replaced the Lotus Evora, using a version of the Toyota-derived V6 with up to 450hp and the option of hybrid power. Made entirely of aluminium, it would have been a two-seat or 2+2 sports car.

The Elite would have been a front-engined 2+2 hardtop convertible with a hybrid electric/petrol V8 power system. The Eterne, meanwhile, would have been a four-door, four-seat version of the Elite, effectively a Porsche Panamera rival.

This quintet was ill-fated, however: not even one reached production. But when Coco was finally ousted from Lotus in 2014, praise was heaped on him by Lotus's CEO, Jean-Marc Gales, who said: "Donato leaves a legacy of a strong, motivated and talented team within Lotus Design."

CLOCKWISE FROM TOP LEFT: The five 'Paris' concepts from 2010 were the Elan, Eterne, Elise, Elite and Esprit. Most were simply speculative suggestions of future models rather than serious works-in-progress.

MINI

The Urbane Urbanite

Few car names have ever entered the English language in their own right; Mini is one of them. Alec Issigonis's original, ground-breaking concept was launched in 1959 as the Austin Se7en and Morris Mini-Minor. Discreetly buried in the latter's badge was the name by which the car be known for the rest of its life – Mini. In fact the 'Mini' name had such a strong identity that it became a brand in its own right in 1969. And when Rover's new owner BMW eventually sold the Rover brand on in 2000, the one thing it really wanted to keep was Mini.

BMW finally killed off the classic Mini in 2000 just one week after the September 2000 preview of the all-new Mini. Sales of the first-generation (R50) new Mini began in July 2001 and it was an instant hit. The second-generation (R56) followed in 2006 and the third generation (F55) in 2013. As well as the original hatchback body style, a whole raft of variations followed, from Convertible to Clubman estate, Roadster to Countryman SUV.

The story of Innocenti and Italian-modified classic Minis is told fully in the BMC chapter (page 74). Three Italian companies were involved with BMW-era Mini projects: Bertone (which built the 2006 Cooper S Works GP), Castagna (which offered several Mini-based variants independently) and Touring (which collaborated with BMW in designing the Mini Superleggera Vision of 2014).

COOPER S WORKS GP (BERTONE)

In 2006, just as BMW's first-generation 'new' Mini was about to be replaced by the Mk2 R56, a final flourish was the Mini Cooper S Works GP limited edition. This was built in Italy by Bertone, which secured the contract to make all 2000 units.

This was a very special car, one that *Autocar* magazine dubbed "the best version of the first Mini". Over and above the standard Cooper S Works, it got an 8hp boost in power, lowered suspension, styling tweaks, aerodynamic bumpers, red door mirrors and special graphics on the silver roof. 50kg was shaved off the weight thanks to aluminium suspension parts, special alloy wheels and a carbonfibre roof spoiler. The single biggest change was in the cabin: there were only two seats up front (Recaro race items), the rear ones being replaced by a strut brace. The asking price was £22,000 – way above the cost of a standard Mini – but that didn't stop demand being very high.

Bertone received bodies in white from the Mini plant in Oxford, and did the final assembly at its plant in Grugliasco near Turin. Why Bertone? Because Mini's parent company, BMW, had decided to compensate

ABOVE & LEFT: Bertone was tasked with assembling the Cooper S Works GP in Italy – the very last car Bertone built before its 2007 bankruptcy. OPPOSITE: Touring's stunningly beautiful Superleggera Vision was considered as an official Mini model.

MINI Superleggera
VISION

the Italian coachbuilder for prematurely ending its contract to build the BMW C1 motorcycle. The Mini GP was historic in one way: it was the very last car built by Bertone. Sadly the Grugliasco production line went silent after the Mini GP contract ended, and was one of the contributing factors to Bertone filing for bankruptcy in late 2007.

MINI ESTATES (CASTAGNA)

At the March 2004 Geneva Show, some three years in advance of Mini's own Clubman estate, Carrozzeria Castagna of Milan unveiled a trio of Mini estate cars. It chopped up a regular Mini hatch and added sheet metal to the rear end, lengthening the car by 250mm. The original Mini tailgate was cleverly retained but the bumper was new and Castagna fitted thick rear side windows (6mm versus 2.8mm) to help maintain rigidity. The conversion was offered commercially and you could choose from all sorts of customisation options, including specially reshaped seats, while a set of three Pellux suitcases was available as an extra.

Castagna also showed a 'Mini Woody' version which recalled the classic Mini Traveller, consisting of some 20 hand-carved wooden elements for the rear bodywork, plus the option of wood-framed instruments and door tops. The Woody even had wickerwork panels for the luggage compartment and a wicker hatbox.

The third model was the SUWagon which added a dash of SUV style. This consisted of extended wheelarch guards, bigger side skirts and a suspension system that could be raised or lowered.

Castagna's estate car conversions weren't cheap, starting at 10,000 euros, but some 30 were sold within 12 months. However, they were quickly rendered obsolete by Mini's own Clubman. Castagna caved in and at the 2008 Geneva Show announced its 'Woody Passion Kit' for the Clubman, essentially an exercise in stick-on nostalgia offered in a variety of wood finishes or carbonfibre.

MINI PICK-UPS (CASTAGNA)

Following Castagna's Mini estates, at the March 2005 Geneva it was the turn of its Mini pick-ups to shine. The Milanese coachbuilder launched two models: the Mini CrossUP and Mini Tender.

The CrossUP was described as an "easy-trek" machine – a pick-up/off-road mash-up. The extended pick-up section was clad in scratch-resistant material and included lockable compartments. As an option you could order four-wheel drive and hydraulic suspension to raise the ride height.

Alongside the CrossUP was the Mini Tender, an open-topped, open-sided pick-up designed to be hoisted on board yachts. Teak wood lined the pick-up bed, with added storage under the floor, while the interior trim was mostly in water-resistant neoprene.

OPPOSITE: Various iterations of Castagna's pick-up and estate offerings. BELOW: Castagna Tuning Concept and Clubman-based 'Woody Passion' kit. BOTTOM: Superleggera Vision two-seat cabin and low-slung side shot.

Castagna also offered a six-seater version based on the Mini Convertible and even an eight-seater whose wheelbase was lengthened by 500mm. Conversion prices started at around £13,500 and Castagna reported it had taken several orders.

MINI TUNING CONCEPT (CASTAGNA)

At the March 2006 Geneva Motor Show, Castagna presented its latest 'Tuning Concept' Mini with hybrid power. An electric motor was added at the rear, while the Mini's regular powertrain was retained intact to power the car on the open road or act as a generator to recharge the batteries. A range of 125 miles and a maximum speed of 87mph were claimed.

MINI SUPERLEGGERA VISION (TOURING)

Mini surprised everyone when, at the May 2014 Villa d'Este concours in Italy, it presented a new speedster concept: the Mini Superleggera Vision. This was a joint project between Mini and Carrozzeria Touring, with Mini design chief Anders Warming being joined by Touring's Louis de Fabribeckers. As a result, there were some Italian styling cues mixing it with traditional Mini tropes.

According to Warming, the idea was to create "a modern Riva power boat for the road, a proper Italian barchetta with a British soul". Louis de Fabribeckers added: "In this car all unnecessary equipment or decoration is sacrificed, as performance is gained through lightness and efficiency of the bodywork and interior. The Italian touch is in the proportions and waistline."

Some very clearly British details were evident, however, such as the Union Jack-themed rear LED lights and door brackets. The circular headlights and hexagonal grille were typically Mini, as were the bonnet stripes (three-dimensionally embossed with aluminium accents at their front ends).

The Superleggera had a more cab-rearward design than was typical for Mini, with a relatively long nose, while its wheelbase at 2520mm was 25mm more than the Mini hatch's. The bodywork was in aluminium and carbonfibre over an aluminium frame, the finished product measuring 4162mm long, 1964mm wide and 1209mm high. The mechanical power was electric.

The stripped-back cabin featured a big aluminium dashboard made out of a single sheet of metal, a touch-sensitive centre console, small circular dials and leather upholstery. A curious central fin on the bootlid incorporated a third brake light.

The car was presented as a two-seater speedster with no roof at all, although Mini said it planned to create a very simple manually-operated soft-top with a Perspex rear window.

BMW seriously considered launching the Superleggera roadster, as the head of the Mini brand, Peter Schwarzenbauer, said: "Does the Superleggera have potential? Absolutely. It could sharpen the brand. This car and the underlying engineering concept are significant in more ways than one." Sadly no production run ever did happen for the Mini Superleggera.

PANTHER

Flights of Fantasy

Panther was an extremely unusual car company. Founded in 1972 by Robert Jankel as Panther West Winds Ltd in Byfleet, Surrey, it epitomised the neo-classic movement with models such as the J72, De Ville and Lima. As a result, many people have derided Panther as a purveyor of vulgar and unseemly excess, but that belies the skill, artistry and quality that went into its cars, and ignores the ambition and originality of its non-neo-classic projects.

Jankel's unique offering to his wealthy customers was to produce exactly what they wanted in turnaround times that were unsurpassed in the industry. Projects included some extraordinary flights of fancy, such as the Jaguar-based Lazer buggy and the Six, a six-wheeled Cadillac-powered supercar.

Panther went into liquidation in 1979, whereupon it was bought by a Korean financier called Young C Kim, who launched the Kallista and the Solo mid-engined supercar, but Panther's time was definitively done by the 1990s.

There were three Panther projects with Italian connections. Following the 1972 J72 (a Jaguar SS pastiche), Panther's second ever project was the extraordinary Ferrari FF. In 1974, Swiss Ferrari dealer Willy Felber asked Jankel to create a Ferrari 125S-style body on a Ferrari 330 GTC chassis. This he did with painstaking quality, although it was not intended to be a replica. A square-tube frame supported the unstressed aluminium bodywork. A maximum speed of 160mph and a 0-60mph time of 4.5 seconds were quoted.

Debuting at the 1974 Geneva Motor Show, the FF was put on sale at the huge asking price of £13,500. While Felber declared he could source 330 GTC

TOP: Ferrari FF was designed for a Swiss client. At least one example was made in Italy by Michelotti. ABOVE & LEFT: Lancia D24 'replica' was based on Fulvia mechanicals. RIGHT: Astonishing Ferrari Daytona-based estate made for Luigi Chinetti. Photos by Matt Howell

chassis, these in fact proved rather elusive and only seven FFs were ever made up until 1975, including one built using Ferrari Daytona parts and painted metallic purple. At least one more Felber FF was built by the Italian coachbuilder Michelotti, which gives an additional Italian dimension to the Panther story.

In 1975 Panther received a commission from Lancia to create a replica of its 1954 D24 racer, which had triumphed in events such as the Targa Florio and Mille Miglia. The basis was Lancia's contemporary Fulvia with its 110hp 1.3-litre V4 engine. A weight of only 750kg ensured lively performance. The original plan was to make 100 examples as a limited edition in collaboration with Felber of Switzerland. Panther duly created a prototype with aluminium bodywork that vaguely recalled the D24's shape, although it must be said its front-wheel drive layout made the nose look out of proportion. This prototype was despatched on a transporter to Switzerland, where it was to make its debut at the March 1975 Geneva Show. Sadly, the car was badly damaged in transit and unsurprisingly Lancia was not amused; eventually the car found a buyer in Switzerland. Felber would later ask Giovanni Michelotti to design a second Lancia D24-inspired 'neo-classic' based on the Lancia Beta, although this had no connections with Panther.

Panther's only other Italian project – albeit obliquely – was the one-off Ferrari NART built for Luigi 'Coco' Chinetti Jr, the son of the US Ferrari importer and owner of the North American Racing Team (NART). This was a rebody of a Ferrari 365 GTB4 Daytona with very smooth shooting brake bodywork realised in aluminium by Panther in the UK. Unusually, the rear window was fixed; the luggage area was accessed via two gullwing-style glass panels to the sides. The interior was also new, albeit using Daytona instruments in a wooden dash. The V12 engine was turbocharged, leading to some wild claims: a power output of 600hp and a top speed of – ahem – 230mph.

RELIANT

Plastic Fantastic

Reliant was one of those peculiarly British companies that flourished filling niches that mainstream manufacturers could not – or simply did not want to – occupy. Alongside AC and Allard, Reliant had the unusual distinction of offering both economical three-wheelers and high-performance sports cars at the same time.

The history of Reliant stretches back to 1933, when Nottingham's Raleigh Cycle produced the Safety Seven, a cheap three-wheeler with a single front wheel on 'girder' forks. Raleigh's chief designer, Tom Williams, parted company with Raleigh in 1934, and proceeded to set up Reliant Engineering in Tamworth, Staffs in 1935 to make 7cwt delivery vans with three wheels. In post-war years, Reliant became the pre-eminent name in three-wheeled vehicles in Britain, producing as many as 195,000 over a 65-year period.

It was in 1961 that Reliant began making sports cars alongside its trikes, starting with the Sabre and followed in 1964 by the Scimitar GT. The Scimitar GTE of 1968 pioneered the concept of the sports estate with great success.

Reliant also engineered quite a few designs for companies abroad, among them Sabra in Israel and Otosan in Turkey. It was in the 1970s that Reliant first sought Italian design help when it approached Bertone for two abortive projects (the Otosan FW11 and the SE82, a potential replacement for the Scimitar GTE). However, it was to a different Italian design house – Michelotti – that Reliant turned for its new small sports car of the 1980s: the Scimitar SS1.

Financial problems eventually overcame the Reliant Motor Company in 1990. The marque was revived in 1991 by new owners, Beans Industries, but the receivers were called in again in 1994. Yet another new owner, Avonex, took over in 1995 but its tenure lasted less than 12 months. Jonathan Heynes (son of William Heynes of Jaguar fame) stepped in in 1996 but by 2001, the curtain had definitively fallen over Reliant.

FW11 (BERTONE)

In 1977, Reliant was tasked with developing a five-door hatchback for the Turkish car company, Otosan, which wanted a replacement for its ageing Ford-based Anadol A1/A2 (a saloon car that had originally been developed by Reliant and styled by Ogle). The new project was codenamed FW11.

For the styling, Bertone was approached with a brief to design a car that would be as simple as possible to manufacture. Marcello Gandini penned a very crisp five-door hatchback outline that looked fresh and surprisingly modern for the era – almost like a five-door version of Gandini's Jaguar Ascot coupe (see page 187).

Four prototypes were built with glassfibre bodywork over a rear-wheel drive platform that employed Ford running gear and engines. Two of

LEFT: FW11 was styled by Marcello Gandini. TOP: Hints of the future Citroen BX can be seen in the FW11, which was designed for Turkey. MIDDLE: Scimitar badges show how seriously the FW11 was considered as a Reliant model. ABOVE: SE82 coupe was a Gandini-styled proposal to replace the ageing Scimitar GTE.

the four prototypes were given Anadol badging and sent to Otosan in Turkey for evaluation, while the other two, which were Reliant-badged, remained in the UK.

After Otosan rolled back on the idea – it simply opted to facelift its existing Anadol instead – Reliant thought about making the FW11 itself. A prototype was shod with alloy wheels and Scimitar badges and fitted with a Ford 1.6-litre engine for display at the 1980 Motor Show in Birmingham, where it was presented as the Scimitar SE7. Ultimately, however, a five door hatchback was simply not the right direction for Reliant.

There is no doubt that in the FW11 profile could be seen a clear presage of the Citroën BX – not too surprising, perhaps, since Gandini also designed the BX (in 1978, with the production version arriving in 1982). Two of the four Reliant FW11 prototypes still exist today.

SE82 (BERTONE)

In 1978, Reliant asked Bertone to create a new two-door coupe as a direct replacement for the Scimitar GTE. The project was dubbed SE82, referring to the intended year of launch (1982). This would be one of Marcello Gandini's last designs for Bertone before he left the company in 1979.

A clay model was duly built in Italy and Reliant's engineering director, Ed Osmond, travelled over to Italy to see it in January 1979. Gandini said: "It was a fresh design, but keeping in mind that it needed to take a V8, and that the design could be simply altered to a sports estate too. What we proposed were two slightly different designs in one asymmetrical prototype." As well as a full-size prototype of the car, a full mock-up of the proposed interior was also built.

The resulting fastback coupe was slightly longer than the existing Reliant Scimitar GTE SE6, with seating for 2+2 – quite similar in format to the Alfa Romeo Alfetta GTV. The shape was angular but not, perhaps, Gandini's most successful.

It was intended that the SE82 would use a Rover 3.5-litre V8 engine and retail for £15,000. Reputedly Reliant spent over £100,000 with Bertone on the SE82's design and development. However, the company decided that this new model would never be profitable and scrapped its plans in March 1980; sadly the sole SE82 prototype was also scrapped.

SCIMITAR SS1 (MICHELOTTI)

Even while it was pursuing a potential replacement for the Scimitar GTE sports estate with Bertone, Reliant also investigated a very different direction with a smaller roadster. The low-cost open two-seater was codenamed 'Small Sports 1' (SS1 for short) and was intended as a modern rival for the MGB.

Despite the recent connections with Bertone,

Reliant's Managing Director, Ritchie Spencer, instead approached another Italian designer, Giovanni Michelotti in Turin, for the SS1. Michelotti duly sketched out the car's shape in 1978, one of his last designs before his sad death in 1980, whereupon the company passed to his son, Edgardo. Michelotti made a full-scale model and delivered it to Reliant.

Reliant designed its own new steel backbone chassis to a design that recalled the glory days of separate chassis. All the stresses would be taken by this main structure, leaving the body panels entirely unstressed. The chassis were manufactured in Germany by Thyssen.

Reliant turned away from its usual labour-intensive glassfibre in favour of cheaper-to-make bolt-on panels made of four different types: hand-laid polyester, cold-pressed polyester, reinforced reaction injection moulding (RRIM) and vacuum-assisted resin injection (VARI). This method of construction dictated some constraints for Michelotti, as the edges where there were bolts had to be hidden. The wheelarch blisters were a particularly fussy element, while another unusual

LEFT ABOVE: Cutaway shows how unstressed body panels were fixed on to chassis structure.
LEFT BELOW: The SS1 was great to drive and in Turbo form delivered punchy performance.
RIGHT: In 1990 William Towns restyled Michelotti's controversial original shape (seen below) to become the Scimitar SST.

feature was the flop-forward headlamps.

It took a long time for the Scimitar SS1 to be seen by the public (at the 1984 Birmingham Motor Show) and its design had perhaps already had its day; it was certainly poorly received. As Martin Buckley of *Classic & Sportscar* magazine opined, it was, "as awkward as a teenager with terminal acne… which just goes to prove that hiring a fancy Italian styling house doesn't guarantee good looks."

In 1990, Giles Chapman interviewed Reliant's marketing boss, Mike Bennett, for *Autocar* magazine, and he was candid about the design. "Michelotti died suddenly and his Japanese colleague [Tateo Uchida] finished off the car's design – it was overly fussy, and perhaps a little passé by then." Bennett also lamented the poor panel fit of early cars, which was down to the separate body panel construction method.

Given the criticisms, easily the most frustrating part of the Scimitar SS1 story was that the car actually drove extremely well. Road testers praised its confident handling, feelsome steering and comfortable ride. The original Ford CVH-engined versions had just 69hp in 1300 form and 96hp as the 1600. This weakness was addressed in 1986 when Reliant started fitting Nissan Silvia 1.8 Turbo engines with 135hp. The SS1 deserved to sell far better than it did: only 1507 were made from 1985 to 1990.

In 1988, US-based company Universal Motors asked Williams Towns to redesign the Scimitar SS1 to become – logically enough – the SS2. While this ultimately came to nothing, it did tempt Reliant to ask Towns for an official restyle in 1990. The resulting SST smoothed out the lumps and bumps of the original shape, and got rid of the multiplicity of body panels in favour of just three main mouldings. In 1992, Towns again restyled the SST to create the Scimitar Sabre, which limped on in production until 1995.

ROLLS-ROYCE

When Only The Best Will Do

Ask most people which car is the best in the world and Rolls-Royce will usually be cited. Set up in 1904 by Charles Rolls and Henry Royce, their express intention was to use superior engineering to cultivate the very best cars on sale. From a factory in Derby, they made exquisite models such as the 40/50 Silver Ghost and Phantom, leading Rolls-Royce to become the first choice of myriad members of royal families and captains of industry. When the company acquired Bentley in 1931, it became indisputably the world's leading maker of prestige motor cars. Car production moved from the original site in Derby to Crewe in 1946.

Rolls-Royce had also begun manufacturing engines for aircraft in 1914, a side of the business that would ultimately grow to be the dominant one. The immense cost of developing aero engines would also be the reason why, in 1971, the parent company was forced into liquidation. The car business remained profitable and was eventually acquired by Vickers in 1980, which kept control until 1998 when it sold out to new German owners: BMW. Production of Rolls-Royces at Crewe ceased in 2002 (when it became a Bentley-only line), as the company headquarters moved to a new factory in Goodwood, Sussex.

As a quintessentially upmarket British marque with exclusively separate chassis up until 1965, coachbuilt bodywork was the norm for many decades. While most were bodied in Britain by the likes of Park Ward, James Young and HJ Mulliner, a handful received coachwork by Italian *carrozzerie* such as Pinin Farina, Zagato, Ghia and Vignale.

In the unitary chassis era, coachbuilding went into sharp decline. Rolls-Royce effectively became its own coachbuilder, bit it beat a path to Pininfarina in Italy for the design of its Camargue coupe of 1975. That would be that for official Italian involvement with Rolls-Royce, except for the Corniche of 2000-2002, which was part-built in Italy.

PHANTOM (ZAGATO & GARAVINI)

Having established its reputation with the Silver Ghost, Rolls-Royce replaced it with a new model in 1925, called the 'New Phantom' (retrospectively dubbed the Phantom I). From its base in Derby, Rolls-Royce manufactured only the chassis and mechanicals; the bodywork was always made by independent coachbuilders to the customer's wishes. Most of these were British – the likes of Park Ward, Thrupp & Maberly, Mulliner and Hooper – but at least one Italian coachbuilder did make a body: Zagato. This was completed in 1928 to a stately four-door

LEFT: Zagato's stately 1928 bodywork on the Phantom chassis. ABOVE: Advert for Carrozzeria Garavini showcasing Rolls-Royce. RIGHT: Garguantuan dimensions of Frua's four-door convertible were explained by its Phantom VI basis.

FAR LEFT: Phantom II coachwork by Castagna. LEFT & SECOND ROW LEFT: Pinin Farina's Phantom II. SECOND ROW MIDDLE & RIGHT: Silver Dawn Coupe by Pinin Farina. THIRD ROW: Silver Dawn four-door saloon built by Ghia in 1952.

limousine design described as "of supreme elegance". It seems likely that this was the very first example of a British chassis bodied by an Italian coachbuilder, unless Carrozzeria Garavini of Turin got there first, which is possible since in September 1928 it completed a limousine de ville body on Phantom chassis number 97AL for Lady Becker.

PHANTOM II (CASTAGNA & PININ FARINA)

Another early example of an Italian-bodied Rolls-Royce came when an American, Mrs W Luden, ordered a Phantom II chassis from the factory, delivered in December 1932. She already owned an Isotta Fraschini with sedan laudaulet bodywork by Castagna. This sedate-looking body was removed and fitted to the new Phantom chassis in the US by the Brewster Body Company, which added new running boards.

Pinin Farina also built at least one body on a Phantom II. Chassis 20SK, which was built in 1934, was rebodied in 1935 by Pinin Farina into a limousine for Marquis Demetrio Imperiali di Francavilla. This was a four-door saloon with much more streamlined coachwork than was typical for Rolls-Royces of the period. Its quality was recognised when it secured the Grand Prix d'Honneur at the Monte Carlo Concours d'Elegance. This car was restored in the 21st century by Pavesi of Milan (bodywork) and Bosato of Turin (mechanicals) and was shown at the 2007 Turin Concours d'Elegance and at Villa d'Este in 2011. Confusion exists over whether a second Phantom II was made in 1937 by Pinin Farina, or whether it was merely the same car with minor changes such as a more steeply raked grille.

SILVER DAWN COUPE (PININ FARINA)

With a need for a smaller owner-driver model, notably for export markets, the Bentley MkVI was adapted in 1949 to create a closely related sister called the Rolls-Royce Silver Dawn. With standard Pressed Steel saloon bodywork, it looked very much like the MkVI, other than the flying lady mascot and a different facia. Under the skin, the 4257cc straight-six engine had a single carburettor and therefore less power (126hp) but a larger 4.6-litre engine was fitted from 1952.

Only 761 Dawns were made up until 1955, of

which only 64 were coachbuilt, and only three by non-British coachbuilders: Chapron, Ghia (see below) and Pinin Farina. The latter had already done some successful work on the Bentley MkVI chassis so it was a natural choice for a wealthy Milanese man, Commendatore Luigi Bressani, to commission – via the Italian Rolls-Royce agent, Mastorelli of Rome – a one-off based on the Silver Dawn.

In August 1950, a right-hand drive chassis (SCA43) was delivered to Pinin Farina at Corso Trapani in Turin. Farina's initial sketch was for a notchback two-door coupe but what it actually ended up building was a fastback – and quite an elegant one at that. The bodywork was realised in steel and was voluptuous for a Rolls-Royce, with particularly attractive shaping for the rear three-quarter windows. The Dawn's grille was unchanged and, while the bonnet was fresh, Pinin Farina kept Rolls-Royce's traditional centrally hinged format. Inside there was space for four passengers, the front ones sitting on a plainly trimmed split bench. The wood veneer dashboard and steering wheel were standard Silver Dawn.

Reputedly the car cost Bressani £10,000, which made it the most expensive car in the world when it made its debut at the April 1951 Turin Motor Show. It is thought that discussions were held between Rolls-Royce and Pinin Farina about the possibility of putting this coupe into production but these didn't progress far, since the costs were so prohibitive. The coupe remained a one-off, which thankfully survives to this day. The Pinin Farina Silver Dawn had resonances more than 60 years later, as Rolls-Royce referenced it as an influence in the design of its 2013 Wraith – however tenuous that may seem.

SILVER DAWN SALOON (GHIA)

At about the same time as it was creating new bodywork for the Silver Wraith (see below), Ghia also bodied a Rolls-Royce Silver Dawn to a similar style. Chassis LSHD22 was delivered in February 1952 to Ghia in Turin and, only four months later, it was ready for collection by its new owner, Contessa Ida Matarazzo.

This was a four-door, six-light saloon with clap-hands doors and no fixed B-pillars. In appearance it kept Rolls-Royce's upright stance but had an unusual swage line that looped around the front end, over the front wheelarches and along the sides of the car. In a departure from normal Rolls-Royce practice, the bonnet was hinged at the rear.

When the car appeared at the 1952 Villa Borghese Concours in Rome, it won the Gran Premio d'Onore. The car still exists in restored form and has been shown at modern concours events, including Villa d'Este.

SILVER WRAITH LIMOUSINE (GHIA)

Rolls-Royce re-entered production after World War Two in 1946 with the new Silver Wraith, initially for export only. It was made in chassis-only form, with coachbuilders creating their own ideas on top of what were fairly sedate underpinnings: a straight-six inlet-over-exhaust-valve engine (4.3 litres initially, then 4.6 from 1951 and 4.9 from 1954). Two chassis wheelbase lengths were provided: short (127 inches) and long (133 inches), the latter from 1951 onwards.

Chassis LWOF 48 was a 1951 left-hand drive short-wheelbase chassis supplied to Ghia in Italy, which bodied it in a fairly sober limousine style, similar to its contemporary Silver Dawn (above). The car was first shown at the Turin Show in 1952 and subsequently seen at a Concours event in Pincio.

There exists some confusion over who originally commissioned the car. It is widely presumed to have been King Farouk of Egypt, who was overthrown in the revolution of 1952 and was eventually exiled to Italy, but the eventual recipient of the car was the film director, Roberto Rossellini, who had long been a client of Ghia's.

SILVER WRAITH LIMOUSINE (VIGNALE)

One of the most extraordinary coachbuilt Rolls-Royces of all time has to be Vignale's unique Silver Wraith limousine. Few would ever call it handsome but there is no doubt how strong an impression it

BELOW: Formal-looking 1952 Silver Wraith Limousine by Ghia. LOWER THREE IMAGES: Vignale's eye-popping Limousine on the Silver Wraith always courted controversy.

makes on first acquaintance.

A long-wheelbase Silver Wraith chassis (LCLW14) was delivered to Vignale in 1954, the coachbuilder completing its work on the car in spring 1955. Giovanni Michelotti was tasked with designing the body to a very flamboyant style. While the gently bulging flanks were quite restrained, that could not be said of the front and rear ends. The Rolls-Royce grille was flanked by huge Lucas P100 headlamps, to each side of which sat hooded foglights in the front wings. Below all this was a gothic extravaganza of forward-thrusting chromework. The rear pillars were reverse-angled, which was a very innovative feature for the time, only predated by Dick Teague's 1953 Packard Balboa-X concept car. One big innovation was that the rear window could be retracted behind the rear seats. Overall, this immense behemoth was as imposing as it was eyebrow-raising.

Vignale's customer was Joseph Maschuch of New Jersey, who ordered some extremely opulent interior fittings. The front seats were electrically operated, while under the rear bench was a gold-plated toilet! The rear cabin – which was separated by a glass division – was also equipped with air conditioning, electric windows, a full bar, telephone and television. Even the under-bonnet area was special: the 4887cc straight-six engine block, cylinder head and many of the ancillaries were painted green, while other items were highly polished. The Vignale Silver Wraith survives today, having last been sold at auction in 2014 by Bonhams for $198,000 (£145,600).

SILVER SHADOW 'SCAPULA' (MICHELOTTI)

The Silver Shadow four-door saloon was launched in 1965, very much marking a new era for Rolls-Royce: this was its first model ever to have a unitary body/chassis. This construction method severely limited prospects for coachbuilders but there were two-door saloon versions made by

Mulliner Park Ward and James Young. A very rare example of a Silver Shadow modified abroad was a one-off made for Pierre Scapula, the famous collector of art, jewellery and cars, whose ideas for a more classically rendered Silver Shadow were realised by Giovanni Michelotti in about 1969. The whole nose section was extended forwards, including the grille, bumper and wings (the latter angled backwards at their leading edge). The front part of the glasshouse was kept unmodified but the C-pillars were extended back to create a fastback look. As well as spats over the rear wheels, other additions included new coachlines for the body flanks and chrome-covered sills.

CAMARGUE (PININFARINA)

Under the codename Project Delta, Rolls-Royce started making plans in the late 1960s for a new range-topping two-door coachbuilt car. While the Silver Shadow two-door saloon by Mulliner Park Ward looked pretty much the same as its four-door sister, the new car was intended to look very different. For this task, Rolls-Royce's boss David Plaistow turned to Italy.

LEFT: Michelotti's Silver Shadow for Parisian art collector Pierre Scapula. BELOW LEFT: Paolo Martin's original sketch for Camargue was done in 1970. RIGHT: Camargue might have been Bentley-badged, as seen in this sketch. BELOW: Production Camargue.

Bertone was considered for the job but Pininfarina was preferred, having recently designed a Bentley T Series based coupe (page 69). Sergio Pininfarina was so delighted to receive this commission that he reputedly moderated his usual fee, although it was agreed that the Italian designer would receive a royalty of £1 for every example built. The *carrozzeria* also insisted that any changes made by Crewe to its design should first be approved in Turin.

Paolo Martin started work on Project Delta as early as 1969 and by January 1970 had prepared four renderings for Rolls-Royce's consideration. At that stage it wasn't certain whether the new car would be badged as a Rolls-Royce or a Bentley (or indeed both), so versions were drawn with grilles for each.

Being based on the existing Silver Shadow floorpan, the shape had to work around the saloon's wheelbase, track and scuttle, which did impose some design restraints; for instance, the front end was higher than Pininfarina would have liked. This in turn meant that the original, sharp-edged shape on paper didn't translate as happily, proportionally speaking, as the Fiat 130 Coupe which Paolo Martin also designed at around the same time. The styling got a fairly lukewarm reception from many quarters – the bluff, vertical-sided lower half never sat happily with the more graceful upper half, and the squared arches looked clumsy; but there was no doubting its assertive presence on the road.

The design was originally going to have a black-coloured area just below the glasshouse but Rolls-Royce eventually decided against this as it thought the idea might date the car quickly; quirkily, the area set aside for this was still present, though, in an indented crease line.

The windscreen had a steep rake of some 60 degrees, which lent it a sporty look but made the top of the screen sit uncomfortably close to the driver. The drag coefficient of 0.423 was not exactly slippery but then the Camargue did have the widest grille of any model in the range. Two other historic 'firsts' for this model were that it was the first Rolls-Royce ever with curved side windows and the first to be designed to metric dimensions.

Pininfarina designed the interior, too, to a standard of elegance and comfort that few cars of the 1970s could match. The dashboard cleverly used Silver Shadow instruments in new square backings. The seats were unique to the Camargue, too, trimmed in special 'Nuella' leather. One innovation was split-level air conditioning, reputedly costing as much as a whole Mini to make, and with the cooling capacity of 30 refrigerators.

Befitting its Italian design, the Camargue was launched in Sicily in early 1975. Each Camargue took six months to make and it was very much a car for the super-rich, slotting in as the most expensive car on the market at the time: at £29,000 it was 50% more expensive than the Corniche convertible.

The 6.75-litre V8 engine had a little more power than the Silver Shadow (220hp, not that this figure was disclosed by the factory – that was judged unseemly), but even so this was no sports car, incapable of exceeding 120mph. Sharing the Shadow's hydraulic systems, brakes and self-levelling suspension, its ride was cosseting but the pitch and roll through corners could prove nauseating.

The Camargue was never a popular model: only 534 were sold from 1975 to 1986, most of those (390) to the USA, with 136 remaining in Britain and 75 going to Saudi Arabia.

PHANTOM VI CONVERTIBLES (FRUA)

If you were a head of state, or possibly a rock star like John Lennon, the Rolls-Royce Phantom VI was right at the top of your wish list from its launch in 1968. Here was the world's most expensive car, sold to special order with very formal limousine bodywork. Powered by a 6.2-litre V8 engine, this gargantuan machine measured 20ft long and weighed nearly three tonnes. Since it kept an old-school separate chassis, it was even possible to order completely bespoke coachwork – but of the 374 Phantom VI chassis made between 1968 and 1991, only two had special bodies, both done by Pietro Frua of Turin.

The first of these, a two-door convertible, was begun at the behest of Simon van Kempen, a Dutch diplomat living in Switzerland. Frua started work in February 1971 with design sketches, which were duly approved. The shape itself was almost naively simple, but Frua's stated aim was to shrink the car visually – which was sorely needed as the leviathan measured fully six metres long. Frua's initial design proposal had squared wheelarches but this was quickly changed to conventional round arches. The huge, imposing Rolls-Royce grille was retained but was visually diminished by a bumper that arced

TOP: Frua's first Phantom VI two-door convertible was absolutely immense. ABOVE & RIGHT: Even more imposing was Frua's four-door Phantom VI with a roof adaptable to multiple positions.

below it, and by rectangular headlamps and auxiliary lights that lent the front end a sharper-edged feel. The two-piece bonnet opened along its centre line, while huge numbers of electrical relays were required for the powered soft-top.

Chassis PRX4705 was delivered to Frua in 1971. The project was hardly straightforward: Frua spoke no English; no one at Rolls-Royce spoke Italian; and Frua was entirely unused to Rolls-Royce's strictly old-school imperial measurements, causing many headaches along the way. Rolls-Royce insisted on inspecting the completed car before giving its approval, a procedure that did not occur until late in 1973, almost three years after the project had started. Painted metallic green with a white interior and soft-top, it remained a one-off.

Frua was also approached about making a coupe version of this car, which he duly sketched, but sadly the arrival of the oil crisis in 1973 put a stop to the project before it got off the ground. However, one further coachbuilt Phantom VI (chassis PRX4643) would be created by Frua – the very last commission that Pietro Frua ever undertook. This was an enormous four-door convertible, with an overall length of 6.45 metres.

The original client was the British property developer Robert Buchanan-Michaelson but the car was still in build in 1977, when a new client, the Californian Rolls-Royce collector James Leake, took it on. Frua continued to work on the car with Rolls-Royce's assistance. Originally conceived as a sedanca de ville, it was reconfigured as a four-door 'All Weather Cabriolet'. The multi-position soft-top allowed for several configurations: sedanca de ville, landaulet or full convertible.

Sadly Pietro Frua knew he was reaching the end of his life and, unprepared to take the financial risks of completing the project, never finished the car before his death in 1983. The car went through the hands of several companies, ending up with Royle Cars of Darlington, England, which finally finished it off in 1992. The rear compartment was trimmed in walnut with sterling silver inlays and featured a silk-lined lady's vanity case, Davidoff cigar humidor, television, video player and cocktail cabinet. The car had the distinction of being displayed at the March 2003 Geneva Motor Show.

CORNICHE (PININFARINA/OPAC)

Following the commercial success of the Bentley Azure, Rolls-Royce decided to create a badge-engineered version called the Corniche – the first and only Roller to be created from a Bentley, rather than the other way around. Like the Azure, the project was farmed out to Pininfarina to manage the production side (the bodies were actually made by Opac of Turin). The Corniche was launched in 2000 and lasted just two years, some 384 being made in total.

BRUNEI SPECIAL PROJECTS (BERTONE/OPAC)

Prince Jefri of Brunei was probably the greatest buyer of new cars the world has ever known. He favoured luxury marques and owned about 600 different Rolls-Royces – indeed some say he probably single-handedly kept Rolls-Royce afloat during the 1990s. The prince also had a penchant for coachbuilt vehicles, and while most of these unique cars were Bentleys, he did also order several special-bodied Rolls-Royces.

The precise story of these cars is impossible to know fully, since the affairs of the Brunei royal family remained so secret. Even the names by which the cars were known is not clear. What is known is that at least two special Rolls-Royce creations had Italian input. The bodies in white for two projects were built by Opac, a coachbuilder based in Rivalta di Torino, while one project was designed by Bertone.

The Bertone project is the most interesting. It's been referred to variously as the Royale, Majestic, Phantom Majestic or Phantom VII, but let's refer to it here as the P200, its internal codename. We know Bertone had design input because images of it appeared in a Bertone brochure.

The P200's design was imposing indeed. The wheelbase was long, allowing plenty of space for the two rear passengers, but the overall look was quite sleek with its low, swept-back roofline. An elegant swage line began at the front wing tips and arced back in a classical style to the rear lights.

It is thought that six cars were made in total between 1995 and 1997. The specification appears to have evolved over time but all had a single-turbocharged, non-catalysed 6.75-litre V8 engine and the steering wheel on the right-hand side. The bodies were built by Opac, which referred to the cars as the 'Majestic'.

The second coachbuilt Rolls-Royce has variously been called the Majestic and Cloudesque (the latter as Opac referred to it) but it had an internal designation of P210. The design was more traditional, with a higher roofline and double headlights reminiscent of the classic Rolls-Royce Silver Cloud III's. Four examples were made, all in 1995, all right-hand drive and all with turbocharged 6.75-litre V8 engines. The bodies were made by Opac but final assembly appears to have taken place in France by Heuliez.

BELOW: Pininfarina-built Corniche. MIDDLE: P200 and P210 for Brunei. BOTTOM: Castagna Phantom Coupe. OPPOSITE BOTTOM: Pininfarina Hyperion.

COUPE ROYALE (CASTAGNA)

Castagna Milano announced that it would unveil a new Rolls-Royce Phantom-based 'Coupe Royale' at the 2008 Geneva Show. However, only digital images were released and it's thought that the car was never built. This might have something to do with the fact that Rolls-Royce itself chose to launch its own in-house fixed-head Phantom Coupe at the 2008 Geneva Show, so there was frankly little point in Castagna's effort. The idea was to slice up the four-door Phantom limousine and turn it into a two-door coupe but despite this, the rendering showed an almost unchanged look; only the front end was revised with LED and bi-xenon lights. Carbonfibre parts were also claimed to decrease overall weight and add a sportier look. Other changes were to include new "Italian style" cabin materials, 22-inch wheels, Brembo brakes and a tuned engine giving 72hp extra at 643hp.

HYPERION (PININFARINA)

A coachbuilt special based on Rolls-Royce's Phantom Drophead Coupe was announced by Pininfarina during the 2008 Monterey concours week. The Hyperion was a one-off named after the mythical Greek titan and built for the noted British car collector, Roland Hall, who reportedly paid £4 million for it.

The design (by Jason Castriota of Pininfarina) took inspiration not only from pre-war classic cars but also vintage boats. Classical themes were seen in strong lines flowing along the body's flanks, picked up again behind the rear wheelarches. The short rear end with its wood-lined tonneau cover recalled speedboat themes, hiding a new soft-top created by Pininfarina.

The windscreen was moved backwards by 400mm, the area in front of the windscreen now housing two compartments for hunting rifles, topped by wooden covers. The rearward shift of the cockpit left no room for rear seats; the Hyperion thereby became one of the world's largest ever two-seat cars.

The bodywork was realised entirely in carbonfibre, except for the rear-hinged doors, which were, highly unusually, crafted from solid wood. Inside, a Girard-Perregaux watch could be clipped into the centre of the dashboard. Rolls-Royce's Phantom Drophead Coupe mechanicals were left unchanged.

While the Hyperion remained a one-off, a somewhat similar exercise was apparently carried out by Pininfarina on a Rolls-Royce Phantom Drophead Coupe for a client in South Africa. This had its own unique bodywork to a different, but still classically inspired, design.

ITALIAN HEARSES

Rolls-Royces provided an ideal basis for Italy's buoyant hearse market. Among hearses built over the years was a Silver Shadow in the 1980s by Carrozzeria Casale (pictured below); a Silver Seraph hearse offered by Rolls-Royce dealer British Motors of Villafranca di Verona (actually built by Biemme); and Biemme conversions of the Silver Spirit and 21st century Phantom (pictured above).

ROOTES

Coventry's Climax

The Rootes brothers, William and Reginald, started out distributing and servicing cars. After making a lot of money this way, they decided to become manufacturers, a status they achieved in 1928 by purchasing a controlling stake in Hillman, the major marque based at Ryton-on-Dunsmore near Coventry. One year later they acquired Humber, followed in 1934 by Sunbeam and Talbot. To this burgeoning empire Singer was added in 1956.

In 1964, the US giant Chrysler took a significant shareholding in Rootes, although control remained in British hands. It took until 1967 for Chrysler to assume a majority shareholding and Rootes was rebranded as Chrysler UK in 1970. However, by 1978 Chrysler UK had been hived off to Peugeot and Renault.

The Rootes Group formed very strong links with one Italian design house in particular: Carrozzeria Touring. As early as 1959, the Milan-based coachbuilder was hired to enhance the Sunbeam Alpine. That led to a specific Italian-market GT car, the Sunbeam Venezia, a project that started in 1961 and reached the market two years later.

The relationship got even more serious when, on 23 October 1961, Touring signed an agreement with Rootes to assemble cars in a brand new factory being built in Nova Milanese. Two models were to be made there: the Sunbeam Alpine (with which Touring was already familiar) and the Hillman Super Minx. A contract was signed for up to four Alpines and ten Super Minxes per day to be made for the Italian market, and production duly began in 1962.

However, a strike at Touring in 1963 proved damaging to the company's fortunes, just as new tax laws in Italy punishing cars with larger engines came in, resulting in cutbacks in orders from marques like Lancia, Maserati and Lamborghini. That led to Touring's first brush with the receiver in March 1963 and it laid many workers off in 1964. Full receivership followed in March 1965, although the company did not finally cease trading until 31 December 1966.

SINGER SM1500 COUPE & CONVERTIBLE (GHIA-AIGLE)

Although first seen in 1947, production of Singer's bold new SM1500 saloon did not begin until June 1949. This was a rather robust machine with an equally forthright style – a full saloon that was hardly the last word in elegance.

Its chassis was used by the Swiss coachbuilder Ghia-Aigle to create a rather sportier machine with a design by Giovanni Michelotti. Singer's traditional character was exploited in the upright grille with smaller vents to each side. The most notable feature of the fastback design was its kicked-up rear wing feature, in effect a tailfin of the type that was then becoming popular in the USA. The car's first appearance came at the Salon de l'Automobile in Paris in October 1952, where it was shown in a dark colour. By the Geneva Show of March 1953, it was

ABOVE, TOP TO BOTTOM: Three different Singer SM1500s by Ghia-Aigle: 1952 coupe at '53 Geneva Show; 1954 coupe; 1954 convertible. OPPOSITE: Original Sunbeam Alpine rear wings were cut down by Touring.

sporting new two-tone paint.

A completely different Singer coupe was presented by Ghia-Aigle in 1954. Michelotti's hand had matured significantly in the intervening two years and his new design was much better resolved. The tailfins had gone, replaced by a clean new wing line. Up front was an oval grille in which were set a pair of foglights. The clean side profile was broken only by a character line above the rear wheelarch but overall the look was perhaps somewhat bland. That comment applied even more firmly to a final convertible version made on the Singer SM1500 chassis in 1954, which was smooth to the point of being anonymous.

The total number of Singers made by Ghia-Aigle is disputed; some sources state that six were built, others that it was as many as eight from 1952 to 1954 (seven coupes and a single convertible).

SUNBEAM ALPINE (TOURING)

Touring Superleggera is a name more associated with Aston Martin than Sunbeam, but the Rootes Group very much courted this venerable name. It started with the Sunbeam Alpine, a cleverly conceived sports car using nothing more exotic than the underpinnings of the Hillman Husky utility vehicle. Its sharply executed styling was an in-house job that featured tail fins – very much in vogue at the time of the car's launch in July 1959. When Rootes engineer Alec Caine attended the 1959 Turin Show, he approached the coachbuilder Touring of Milan asking it to lower the Alpine's pedals slightly, a modification which was incorporated into the Series II model of October 1960.

Alec Caine then returned to Italy with an Alpine so that Touring could increase boot capacity by moving the spare wheel and change the single fuel tank to two smaller tanks. These were adopted for the Series III Alpine of 1963, also offered in 'Grand Touring' coupe form with a Touring-inspired wooden dashboard and wood-rim steering wheel.

Touring also effected one substantial styling change by chopping down the outdated rear wings. The more handsome rear end was first shown at the Turin Show in October 1963. This revised wing shape would be adopted for UK-built Alpines but not until the Series IV of 1964, which also featured a new grille.

Touring's Carlo Felice Bianchi Anderloni later recalled: "[The Alpine] had really horrible rear wings that the Italian market would never accept. We were entrusted with restyling them and to submit a modified car to the make, for approval. As we received the approval from Brian Rootes, we were authorised to start assembly."

Touring agreed to manufacture the Alpine at a rate of up to four units per day, which started in June 1963 at the company's Nova Milanese factory, sales being aimed at the local market.

SUNBEAM VENEZIA (TOURING)

In spring 1960, the Rootes manager for Italy, George Carless – whose mother was Italian and father British – proposed the idea of producing a 2+2 sports coupe for the Italian market to Rootes' export sales director, Brian Rootes. There was enthusiasm for the project, leading Carless to approach Touring towards the end of 1960. At the time, the coachbuilder was already enjoying some collaboration with Rootes via the Sunbeam Alpine. Touring's Carlo Felice Bianchi Anderloni warmed to the idea as the new car would be perfect to make in his new factory being built at Nova Milanese.

Touring duly submitted a 1:10 scale model to Rootes in 1961. The styling was a joint effort by Anderloni, Federico Formenti and Aquilino Gilardi. Unquestionably it shared some similarities with Touring's Lancia Flaminia and Maserati 3500 GT, notably its clean rear wing shape and elegant glasshouse. However, the styling was compromised right from the outset by employing many Rootes parts, including the windscreen and quad headlamps from the Humber Sceptre, plus Hillman Super Minx rear lights. Mounting cancerous indicators above headlamps – later altered to become air intakes for the heating system – did the front end design no favours. Nor was it helped by the Sunbeam Rapier grille that made the car look like a neo-classic pastiche.

That was a shame because Touring built the car to a very high standard, using its famed 'superleggera' method of aluminium body panels over a tubular steel framework. This made the Venezia both stronger and lighter (by 50kg) than the car it was based on, the Humber Sceptre MkI, whose floorpan was used intact, including its suspension and 1592cc engine, although the latter was tuned to yield 88hp, while uprated front brakes and overdrive transmission were standard. By no stretch of the imagination was this a sports car, though, with a top speed of 100mph (Sunbeam actually claimed 108mph, rather optimistically).

The name Venezia was chosen by George Carless. After an initial unveiling in Milan, the car

Sunbeam's Venezia was launched in St Mark's Square in Venice in 1963 – the first time any car had been allowed into the historic centre of the city. What a shame that the car's aesthetic sensibilities failed to match those of the city nicknamed 'La Serenissima'.

was, appropriately enough, launched in Venice in September 1963 at a ceremony attended by the city's mayor and the British ambassador. A car was conveyed along the canals aboard a gondola to the Palazzo Ducale in St Mark's Square – the first time a car had ever been allowed to enter the square.

Sadly the Venezia was far too expensive to do well in Italy. While it would never be sold in Britain, Rootes did market it in continental European markets, again with scant success. The initial contract signed with Touring was to make 300 examples, but that was reduced in August 1963 to 250. In the end Rootes sent only 145 Sceptre chassis to Milan; Venezia chassis numbers appear to indicate that as many as 203 were made in all, some possibly using identical floorpans from the Super Minx. Touring ceased to exist in 1966 but the very last Venezias did not find buyers until 1968. Apart from one solitary right-hand drive example, all had the steering wheel mounted on the left.

Touring never got the chance to build its planned Venezia convertible, which Federico Formenti had speculatively penned. Also not realised was a proposal to mount a Ford V8 into the Venezia (something that Sunbeam had already done with its Tiger), since Chrysler's ever-closer involvement with Rootes ended any such plans. Rootes even considered the Venezia as the replacement for the Sunbeam Rapier but in the end opted for its own in-house fastback design.

HILLMAN SUPER MINX (TOURING)

In 1962, Touring began assembling the Hillman Super Minx saloon in Italy, using CKD (Complete Knocked Down) kits brought over in trucks from Britain. Most of the components were British-made but to keep local content high and avoid swingeing taxation, Touring sourced many items in Italy, such as the wheels, tyres, horns and batteries, while Touring produced its own seat structures, carpets, upholstery and glass. Aesthetically speaking, the Super Minx was entirely unaltered – complete with its then-trendy hooded headlamps, tailfins and wraparound screens – the only difference being 'Montaggio Carrozzeria Touring' badges on the doors and boot. The Touring-assembled Super Minx was sold in Italy and in Africa.

SALONE

IL MODELLO SUPER MINX MONTATO DALLA TOURING

LA HILLMAN MILANESE

Presentata fra le novità di Torino, verrà posta in vendita al prezzo di 1.418.000 lire - Nessuna modi-

CARATTERISTICHE TECNICHE

HILLMAN ZIMP (ZAGATO)

Having enjoyed a fruitful liaison with both Bristol and Aston Martin, Zagato of Milan thought it saw potential in selling a Zagato-designed car in Britain. The plan was to set up manufacturing in the UK, rather than Italy, a process that avoided hefty import duties imposed on foreign-built cars. A new company called British Zagato Ltd was duly formed, headed by Peter Thomas and Anthony Charles, and based in Kingston-upon-Thames.

This unique idea was sparked by the launch of the Hillman Imp in 1963, the Rootes Group's Scottish-built answer to the BMC Mini. Was it perhaps the rear-engined format that appealed to Zagato? After all, many Fiats, from 500 to 600 to 850, were all rear-engined and Zagato had successfully rebodied them all. Why not do something similar on the British equivalent? The very low-set engine presented plenty of opportunity to create an original new shape.

An early (May 1963) Imp was bought second-hand and despatched to Zagato in Milan, followed by two further brand new Imps which Peter Thomas and his wife drove personally to Milan. All three were transformed by Zagato in just nine months.

The design work was done by Ercole Spada, then still a young figure at Zagato. There were echoes, perhaps, of the Mini Gatto that Zagato had recently designed on the BMC Mini (see page 95). Overall, this was an extremely clean shape, razor-edged and free of adornments; there was no front grille at all, for instance. Despite being 150mm lower than the Imp, the glasshouse was just as generous, although some of the Imp's sharpness was perhaps lost. Indeed, in retrospect the shape could be criticised as being a little bland and anonymous.

Because Spada wanted to maintain a totally unbroken beltline around the car, he came up with

LEFT: 'The Milanese Hillman' was assembled by Carrozzeria Touring. ABOVE & RIGHT: Zagato's Hillman Zimp was a smart coupe styled by Ercole Spada. Headlamps featured moving 'eyebrows'. The Zimp very nearly reached production.

one highly unusual idea: little 'eyelids' that sat over the headlamps, which opened when the lights were switched on. The way these operated differed on the three cars built, opening either sideways or fore-and-aft.

Inside, there were new seats, the rear bench being foldable as per the Imp. There was a wood-rim steering wheel and elegant door handles, while the Imp instrument panel was mounted in a new leather-trimmed dashboard. All in all, the cabin had a real British-Italian flavour.

The bodywork was in aluminium, crimped and riveted to the floorpan. Overall the car weighed just 630kg, considerably less than the Imp. This, combined with better aerodynamics and a planned boost in engine power from 39hp to 46hp, meant an increase in top speed from 79mph to 87mph. However, despite cooling slots being designed into the rear panel, when Rootes tested the car, it discovered that it overheated.

Zagato unveiled its new car at the October 1964 Earls Court Motor Show, boldly named 'Zimp'. The plan was to market it as an upmarket, style-orientated, Italian-designed car for women. Just how upmarket? Well, Rootes evaluated the Zimp at its Ryton factory and estimated that it would likely sell for as much as £1200, way above the Imp's price of around £500.

British Zagato had made a gentlemen's agreement with Lord Rootes for the supply of Hillman Imps. However, 1964 was a time of great change at Rootes. In June, Chrysler bought into the company and soon installed new directors on the board. When Lord Rootes died in December 1964, he took with him the gentlemen's agreement. Ultimately the Zimp project died because it was vetoed by Rootes, which had its own plans for new Imp-based coupe models: it would make a prototype called the Asp – also stillborn – plus the Imp Californian and Sunbeam Stiletto, which reached the market in 1967. Thankfully all three Zimp prototypes made survive today.

LOMBARDI GRAND PRIX (FRANCIS LOMBARDI)

Francis Lombardi isn't one of the best known Italian coachbuilders but it was quite illustrious in its day. Founded by flying ace and aircraft constructor, Carlo Francesco Lombardi, it did good business in the post-WW2 years as a coachbuilder turning Fiats into limousines, estates and coupes. One of the latter was the Grand Prix, which debuted at the Geneva Show in March 1968. Its highly charismatic shape was the work of Giuseppe Rinaldi at the Lombardi works in Vercelli. The Grand Prix was a simple rebody of Fiat 850's Berlina platform using all-new steel bodywork.

The appeal of this little coupe was immediately recognised by a curious British-based Greek Cypriot character called Frixos Demetriou. This casino owner with the manners – and possibly interests – of a cartoon mafioso decided to set up a more respectable enterprise by importing cars from Italy in 1968. Alongside various Vignale-Fiats, he was particularly taken with the Francis Lombardi Grand Prix. He proceeded to offer the car in right-hand drive form at £1457 with a rear-mounted Fiat 843cc engine.

However, Demetriou's Queensway, London outfit did have plans to 'Anglicise' the Grand Prix by replacing the Fiat 850 underpinnings with the floorpan and running gear of a Hillman Imp Sport. This seemed to make sense as the cars were very alike, even if the Imp had a 50mm longer wheelbase, so some small changes would have been needed. Two plans were investigated: either

having the car fully built in Italy, or importing the rolling chassis/body only, leaving the trim and mechanical components to be added in the UK (a task that would have been done by Hillman Imp tuning specialist, Paul Emery Cars). The resulting car would have been about £200 cheaper than the Fiat-based machine, and the tuning potential of the Imp Sport engine was also very good.

It was reported in 1969 that Rootes had supplied two Imp platforms to Francis Lombardi in Turin but it's unknown whether either of these was actually finished. That could perhaps be because Demetriou had relocated to Cyprus, ending the Imp-engined project before it reached the market. In a bizarre final twist to the tale, Demetriou ended his days when a runaway tank squashed him flat in Cyprus.

HILLMAN HUNTER PAYKAN COUPE (MICHELOTTI)

The very last Italian-styled car to be done on a Rootes Group car – or more accurately Chrysler, which had by then bought the enterprise – was a highly unusual project. The Hillman Hunter (a car designed in-house by William Towns in 1966) was, from 1967 to 2005, manufactured under licence in Iran as the Paykan. A curious footnote to its story came in 1974, when an Iranian owner of a Paykan called Mr Samini drove his car all the way from Teheran to Turin. Here he asked Giovanni Michelotti to design a completely new one-off coupe body for it, which the Italian duly did, featuring the novelty of gullwing doors.

LEFT: Pretty Lombardi Grand Prix was at one stage scheduled to have Hillman Imp Sport running gear.
RIGHT: One-off gullwing coupe created in 1974 by Michelotti for an Iranian customer on a Paykan, itself derived from the Hillman Hunter.

ROVER

Vikings Seeking Roman Influence

With the image of a Viking longship heading straight towards you, Rover's badge has come to epitomise a very particular form of Britannic vigour. Its milieu was ever staid, upstanding cars designed for staid, upstanding buyers.

With roots stretching back to the 19th century as a bicycle maker, Rover started manufacturing cars in 1904. Since its Coventry factory was heavily bombed during World War Two, in the post-war aftermath it relocated to Solihull in the West Midlands. Rover also made the decision – in retrospect a very shrewd one – to enter production with a jeep-style off-road vehicle, the Land Rover, which ultimately became its most important sub-brand, easily outliving the parent marque.

While other car makers were turning to Italy for design inspiration – notably Rover's main rival, Triumph, whose reliance on Italian design was almost total – Rover ploughed a rigidly in-house design furrow. It was not always this way, though: Rover did court Pinin Farina for design input as early as 1951, ultimately without any lasting consequence. With only a few minor exceptions, Rover would never again return to Italian design.

Rover remained an independent car maker until a state-steered absorption by Leyland in 1967. In January 1968, Leyland merged with British Motor Holdings to form the British Leyland Motor Corporation (BLMC), meaning that Rover was now part of the same group as former arch-rival Triumph. There were tensions from the outset. For instance, when the successor to the Rover P6 was mooted, BLMC management rejected Rover's proposal and insisted that Triumph's Michelotti-designed Puma proposal be considered as an alternative. Perhaps as a result of this, there was also friction between Rover and Michelotti, with David Bache of Rover stating in an interview in 1976: "We still use Michelotti, but only as a prototype builder. We send him the designs and he builds them very quickly."

As other brands in the BL empire faded away, such as MG and Triumph, Rover increasingly assumed a role as the group's golden child. In 1982, BL was renamed the Austin Rover Group, while in 1986 it became simply Rover Group. In 1988, ownership passed to British Aerospace and then, in 1994, to BMW. The German company divested itself of what it called "the English patient" in 2000 to the Phoenix Consortium of executives. This set-up lasted until April 2005, when MG Rover ceased to exist and the Rover marque finally succumbed – although Land Rover continued to thrive.

P4 DROPHEAD COUPE & FIXED-HEAD COUPE (PININ FARINA)

The Rover 75 'P4', launched 1949, was a revolution for the company: a boldly styled full-width saloon which nevertheless retained the upright style that the marque was known for. One might even say 'upright' was the correct term for the sort of person to whom the P4 appealed, resulting in its affectionate nickname, the 'Auntie' Rover.

ABOVE: Rover P4 Drophead Coupe and fixed-head Coupe were quite influential designs by Pinin Farina. RIGHT: One of the final chapters in the MG Rover story was the XPower SV, a reimagined version of the Italian-engineered De Tomaso Mangusta.

XP03 WER

Its separate, and very sturdy, chassis designed by Gordon Bashford made it ideal for alternative body styles, a fact that Rover recognised early on. With an eye on expanding its range, in 1950 it commissioned Salmson-Tickford to design a drophead coupe (and also a fixed-head coupe) that retained as much as possible of the original bodywork intact. However Rover wasn't keen on Tickford's architecture and the design wasn't adopted.

Instead, Pinin Farina was courted, with the Wilks brothers who ran Rover at the time entering into negotiations as early as 1951. By the end of the year, a right-hand drive export Rover 75 chassis had been despatched to Italy, ready to be clothed with a drophead coupe body of Farina's own design.

For some reason it took almost two years for the car to be completed; it did not make its debut until the October 1953 Earls Court Show, finished in metallic bronze with a maroon hood. Here the Duke of Edinburgh was photographed admiring it; he even reputedly attempted to buy it. This perhaps sowed the seeds for the Duke's fateful recommendation of Pinin Farina to Leonard Lord of BMC in 1955 – but that is a different story, told in the chapter on BMC.

Motor magazine praised Pinin Farina's "beautifully sleek lines", adding that "Rover characteristics have been retained in the front-end styling but with subtle differences to achieve a perfect blend with the sweeping but dignified lines". There were some clear similarities with Farina's Lancia Aurelia. Characteristic features included bulging rear wing lines, frameless windows and chrome strips along the sills. The front grille was clearly Rover-esque but wider than the P4's. Overall the car measured 12in longer than the P4, giving it a long, sleek look.

The understated and tasteful cabin was also designed by Farina, with a body-colour metal dashboard housing familiar Rover dials. The upholstery was in beige leather, the front bench being asymmetrically split with an armrest. Two rear seats were also provided, plus luxuries like a heater, reading lamps and tinted sun visors.

The Wilks brothers asked HJ Mulliner to produce a replica of the DHC to establish the feasibility of a production run but the costs of tooling up were deemed too great. The public would never be offered a P4 convertible. Farina's DHC was eventually sold off to a private customer in 1955, with a Rover 90 engine fitted instead. After the car was shunted in 1963, it was slightly modified at the rear by the British coachbuilder Hooper.

A second Rover P4 chassis, this time a Rover 90, had also been sent to Farina during 1952 for fixed-head coupe bodywork to be fitted. This duplicated the DHC's look fairly closely but with a pillarless fixed roof and dark green metallic paint. This one-off coupe was sent to the Spanish Rover concessionaire in 1958 and converted to left-hand drive, but sadly it was seemingly scrapped after being crashed.

TOP: 2000 TCZ had an elegant profile. ABOVE RIGHT: Rover's David Bache talking with Gianni Zagato (in glasses). ABOVE & OPPOSITE: TCZ sketches done by Ercole Spada for Zagato. RIGHT: Standard Rover 2000 'P6'.

Some say that front end design of the Farina P4 directly influenced Rover's stylist David Bache when he came to design the P4 saloon's replacement. Although Bache himself has denied this, the P5's nose certainly bears striking similarities.

ROVER 2000 TCZ (ZAGATO)

In 1963, Rover's old 'Auntie' image was well and truly swept aside by the P6 2000. This smoothly styled, well-engineered saloon car was truly state-of-the-art at the time, something that was recognised when the new Rover won the inaugural Car of the Year Award.

In 1964, Zagato was approached by the UK-based Italian engineer, Vincenzo Piatti, who had already instigated the Mini Gatto project with Zagato (see page 95). The idea was to create a two-door coupe version of the new Rover 2000 TC P6 in collaboration with Rover.

Ercole Spada of Zagato was tasked with designing the new car, dubbed the 2000 TCZ. Some constraints were imposed on the design from the outset, since it retained the Rover P6 saloon's long wheelbase and bulky rear suspension. Spada elected to use one of his trademark design techniques – the coda tronca (truncated tail) – to shorten the car visually and improve aerodynamic performance. Some P6 design elements were echoed in Spada's shape, such as the roofline and nose; the standard Rover grille and double headlamps were retained but the bonnet line made a 'hood' for them.

It measured 4250mm long (280mm shorter than the 2000 saloon) and 1260mm tall (150mm lower). By using aluminium for the bodywork, some 172kg (380lb) of weight was saved versus the P6 saloon and a 120mph maximum speed was claimed. The four-seat cabin managed to retain good spaciousness and the rear seats had a split backrest so that they were individually foldable to increase luggage space. As per Spada's Lancia Fulvia Zagato and Alfa Romeo Giulia Zagato, the TCZ had a rear screen that could be electronically raised a couple of inches to improve cabin ventilation.

Although initially styled in 1964, the 2000 TCZ did not see the light of day for three years, when it was finally unveiled at the 1967 Geneva Motor Show (it also appeared at the Earls Court and Turin Shows later that year). The one and only prototype was made fully road-legal. It was apparently evaluated by Reliant as a possible new model, while some reports say that consideration was also given to it being made by Rover. David Bache of Rover also worked on a more conventional coupe version of the P6, potentially reviving the Alvis marque. However, no production run for either car ever materialised.

ROVER SD1 ESTATE (MICHELOTTI)

The Rover SD1, launched in 1976, is often cited as one of the most beautiful cars of the 1970s. It surely

TOP TO BOTTOM: Michelotti helped with Rover's abortive SD1 estate; Fissore's five-door Range Rover predated Rover's own; Bertone's proposal for the second-generation Range Rover; ill-fated CityRover.

owes at least some of its design inspiration to Italy, since its profile was quite clearly inspired by Palo Martin's Pininfarina BMC 1800 of 1967, and its sloping nose has more than a hint of Leonardo Fioravanti's Ferrari Daytona, too, with near-identical headlights and indicators, plus very similar indented swage lines along the body sides.

Michelotti claimed that there was a more direct link with Italy, too, as Rover investigated the possibility of making an estate body variant of its SD1 hatchback; designs by Michelotti dated September 1976 clearly show the SD1 estate. A clay buck was created by the Coventry-based coachbuilder, Carbodies, and two prototypes were built by British Leyland in 1976-1977. BL's chief Michael Edwardes used one as his personal car and the other was reputedly loaned to Prince Charles. The SD1 estate never saw production, though, and the project was definitively shelved in 1980. Both prototypes survive to this day.

ROVER SD2 (MICHELOTTI)

The SD2 project was a joint Rover/Triumph effort, to which Michelotti contributed. This is fully described in the Triumph chapter (page 272).

RANGE ROVER FIVE-DOOR (FISSORE)

Years before Land Rover offered a five-door version of its first-generation Range Rover, Swiss couturier Peter Monteverdi had already come up with the idea. In 1979, he approached Land Rover's Special Projects division and got an agreement to make a five-door conversion. This kept the wheelbase unaltered but new roof pillars were fabricated, the rear wings shortened and new rear doors made to curve around the rear wheelarches. The interior was much plusher and the rear seat was repositioned backwards to ease entry. Italian coachbuilder Fissore of Savigliano performed the conversion. It took around three months from the cars leaving the Solihull factory to emerge from Fissore fully finished.

Following a March 1980 debut at the Geneva Show, the five-door Range Rover went on sale in 1981, even being sold officially by selected Land Rover dealers. The model's shelf-life was curtailed by Land Rover's own official five-door model arriving in late 1981, and the last Monteverdi conversions were delivered in January 1983. An estimated 167 conversions were done in all.

RANGE ROVER SECOND GENERATION (BERTONE)

When it came to designing the second-generation Range Rover, which would eventually emerge in 1994, Land Rover began work in 1988 under the codename Project 38A. Land Rover's Styling Director, George Thomson, asked not only his in-house team but also three Italian companies – Pininfarina, Italdesign and Bertone – as well as UK-based John Heffernan and Ken Greenley, to produce proposals. Of these, only Bertone's design, developed by Marc Deschamps, was chosen to go forward against Solihull's own efforts, with a full-size clay model being built.

Bertone's design had many good ideas, such as a low nose and rear quarter glass that wrapped around the tailgate – described by Programme Director John Hall as "a tremendous styling feature". However, it quickly became clear in customer clinics that Bertone's design was simply not rugged enough, as one French interviewee opined: "It has lost its Wellington boots". The more conservative in-house design, codenamed Pegasus, was ultimately preferred.

ROVER CITYROVER (I.DE.A)

In 2003, Rover decided that it could offer a very cheap new small hatchback on the British market by rebadging the Indian-built Tata Indica as the CityRover. In this way, it introduced yet another Italian-designed model with British badging, since the Indica was originally designed in 1998 by the Italian *carrozzeria*, I.DE.A. Around 8600 CityRovers were sold before MG Rover entered liquidation in April 2005.

MG XPOWER SV (OPAC)

One curious final sting in MG Rover's story came in 2003, when the British company bought up the Italian supercar maker, Qvale. This operation was named after Kjell Qvale, who had founded British Motors in 1947 in San Francisco, importing the first Jaguars to the west coast of the USA. In 2000, Kjell's son Bruce assumed control of the De Tomaso Biguà project – a supercar designed by Marcello Gandini in 1996 – and renamed it the De Tomaso Mangusta. Some 284 cars were built between 2000 and 2002, before Qvale sold the rights to the Mangusta to the MG Rover Group.

After a major redesign, the Mangusta re-emerged as the ill-fated MG XPower SV. The chassis, suspension, engine and gearbox of the Mangusta were retained but the styling (by Peter Stevens) was all-new, and somewhat controversial.

While the materials for the carbonfibre body panels were supplied from the UK (by SP Systems), the car was essentially manufactured in Italy. A new company called MG X80 was set up in Modena to oversee the process. The chassis was made by Vaccari & Bosi of Modena (a company that boasted associations with Ferrari); the body panels were moulded by Belco Avia near Turin; and nearby coachbuilder Opac would then fit the bodywork on to the structure. The Italian connection could even be seen in many of the detail parts, such as Fiat Punto headlights and Fiat Coupé rear lights. Untrimmed and unpainted rolling units were shipped from Italy to the UK, where specialists finished the cars off for MG Rover.

Priced at £65,000, or £83,000 in uprated XPower SV-R form, it is thought that only 82 of these peculiar supercars were produced in total. When MG Rover went into administration in April 2005, one of the reasons cited was the high cost of developing the XPower SV.

BELOW: MG XPower SV was built in Italy by Opac along with various other Italian companies to a design penned by British stylist Peter Stevens.

STANDARD-TRIUMPH

A Triumph of High Standards

Triumph can trace its origins back to the nineteenth century, when it started out as a manufacturer of bicycles in Coventry. It moved into making motorcycles and, from 1923, cars as well. In an attempt to move upmarket, Triumph created its very own 'British Alfa Romeo' in the 1930s, with a straight-eight engined model that owed much to the Milanese marque's engineering ethos, while its two-seater sports bodywork was also very Alfa-esque. Even its name – Dolomite – referred to Italy, but only three examples were built.

In the aftermath of World War Two, during which Coventry had been heavily bombed (an ordeal that it shared, incidentally, with Turin), Triumph merged with Standard, another car firm based in Coventry. It was decided that Standard would produce mainstream family cars, while Triumph would move more upmarket, pursuing lucrative export markets with a range of new sports cars.

However, Triumph's early post-war efforts such as the Roadster were somewhat archaic in appearance and driving character. After failing to acquire Morgan, Triumph decided to enter the small sports car market in 1953. The resulting Triumph TR2 was designed by Walter Belgrove. While it was effective and good value, diktats from management to keep tooling costs down constrained Belgrove to come up with very simple panelwork over pre-existing parts borrowed from the Triumph Mayflower and Standard Vanguard.

It was clear that Triumph needed design help. Following Belgrove's departure from Triumph in 1955, the search for new talent began and eventually settled on an Italian: Giovanni Michelotti. This connection came about, somewhat unexpectedly, through Neville and Raymond Flower of Frisky (see page 154), who had approached Triumph's technical director, Harry Webster, asking to use Standard chassis for their new small car. When Webster asked Neville Flower about the Frisky's design, he was told this secret designer had promised to complete a prototype in fewer than three months. Webster asked if Flower could also have a prototype built for Triumph in the same time frame; when this duly transpired, he did some detective work and discovered that the coachbuilder was Vignale. Before long, Webster visited Vignale and met its star penman, Giovanni Michelotti.

Very quickly, Standard-Triumph arranged for Vignale to build a number of prototypes, all of which were designed by Michelotti, including facelifting the Standard Vanguard. When, in 1959, Michelotti decided to go fully independent, Standard-Triumph quickly negotiated a retainer for the designer.

Michelotti's first job after the Standard Vanguard tidy-up was the Triumph Herald. This distinctive range of small cars marked the beginning of a highly fruitful relationship with Triumph, the Italian designing such important models such as the TR4, Spitfire, GT6, 2000, 1300 and Stag.

Michelotti's ability to produce full-size prototypes from simple sketches within three to four months was unparalleled in the industry. Standard's managing director, Alick Dick, acknowledged this with fondness:

ABOVE: Harry Webster, Triumph's technical director, with sketches from Giovanni Michelotti, with whom he forged a strong personal friendship. RIGHT: Triumph Italia 2000 was one of the prettest cars of the late 1950s but was never marketed in Britain.

59TR

BELOW: Standard Vanguard (top) was lightly revised by Vignale (lower pics). OPPOSITE: Michelotti's original and revised sketches of the Zobo, the project that became the Triumph Herald, which was offered in saloon, coupe, convertible and estate guises.

"I have never met a stylist who was so capable of translating ideas on to a sheet of paper. Not only that, he interpreted your ideas as if he could read your mind, literally drawing the automobile that you described while you were watching him."

Harry Webster added: "He would start by drawing a one-eighth sketch in pencil, then a technical drawing, then a full-size drawing… He would draw this up in chalk so that he could modify the lines with a duster." Webster and Michelotti made a close team. Webster would drive out to Italy almost every other weekend to see his design touchstone. He declared: "We hit it off instantly… He and I became like brothers."

As with the whole British car industry in post-war years, Standard-Triumph underwent a number of upheavals. Strapped for cash, the company was circled by truck maker Leyland, resulting in a takeover in December 1960. Then in 1968 Leyland merged with British Motor Holdings to form the British Leyland Motor Corporation (BLMC). At this point the connection with Michelotti waned as Triumph's management was increasingly obliged to draw on in-house BLMC design resources. The Stag of 1970 would be the final production car that Michelotti designed, although he did continue to be asked for design proposals well into the 1970s, athough none reached production. The very last Triumph was built in 1984.

STANDARD VIGNALE VANGUARD (VIGNALE/MICHELOTTI)

Standard's all-new Vanguard Phase III of 1955 was a robust if heavy-handling large saloon car with a unitary chassis/body and a much more attractive shape – longer, lower and wider – than the outgoing Vanguard. However, it was still hardly the prettiest car on the market, so Italian help was called in to do a modest facelift in 1957.

This was done by Vignale – or more accurately by its chief stylist, Giovanni Michelotti, whom Standard's managing director, Alick Dick, had met at the 1957 Geneva Show. Michelotti styled a deeper windscreen and rear window; the taillights were new; and the front end shape was stronger, with more prominent headlamps, a more attractive grille and revised exterior trim.

Launched at the October 1958 London Motor Show, the new car was called the Vignale Vanguard and proudly sported Vignale's crossed-flag badges on its rear wings. Standard advertised it as "newly styled for tomorrow" and sold it in saloon, estate, van and utility (pick-up) body styles. There were also several alternative trims that lacked Vignale badging: the Sportsman, Ensign and Luxury Six. The Vignale Vanguard lasted three years in production, during which time 26,276 were made.

TRIUMPH HERALD & VITESSE (MICHELOTTI)

The 1950s 'Small Car' offered by Standard (variously badged as the Eight, Ten and Pennant) was typically British in look and feel: stolid, dumpy and overly fussy in its details. In short, it wasn't pretty and it wasn't exciting.

In 1956, Standard-Triumph embarked on a new project to replace the old Standard models, codenamed Zobo (the name of a Tibetan mountain ox), the intended launch date being 1958. Two problems faced the company at the time. Firstly, it had no steel pressing facilities of its own since its body supplier, Fisher & Ludlow, had become part of the British Motor Corporation and was now refusing to supply its rival. This major problem was cleverly swerved by sticking with the apparently antiquated idea of a separate chassis, rather than a monocoque.

The second problem was that the company's chief stylist, Walter Belgrove, had been sacked in the autumn of 1955. The task of overseeing the new project fell to the company's newly appointed head of engineering, Harry Webster, but here at least was a man with an eye for good design. When he received some initial styling proposals from the company's chosen third party designer, Leslie Moore of Mulliners in Coventry, he was disappointed to say the least. He later recalled: "What we finished up with was a mechanical bathtub on wheels. It looked dreadful."

Salvation came in the form of Webster's new-for-1957 contact, Giovanni Michelotti. At the same time that the Italian was presenting his sketches for the Standard Vanguard facelift, he was also asked to have a go at sorting out the Zobo project. A mock-up of what had been done so far was sent to Italy for fettling. Michelotti's brief was to alter the existing shape, rather than create a new design from scratch. He moved the headlamps, gave the windscreen extra wraparound, altered the roofline and got rid of the 'kick' in the waistline above the rear wheels. However, when Webster saw his efforts on 5 September 1957 on his way back from a holiday with his wife and children, he felt exasperated that he'd still been left with a 'bathtub'.

Webster later recalled: "I asked what he'd do given a clean sheet and in 20 minutes he'd drawn up the car we went on to make." It was that simple: Michelotti had sketched what would become the Herald Coupe, including its hooded headlamps, narrowing straight-through waistline accents and small rear fins. The very same night, Michelotti also drew up alternative body styles, including a saloon.

Webster took these drawings back with him to Britain, having obtained a promise from Michelotti that a prototype would be ready by the end of 1957. The designer's sketches were made into full-scale draughts and Michelotti kept his word: his prototype coupe, painted silver and black, was ready for delivery to Coventry on Christmas Eve. A saloon prototype followed in April 1958, while Michelotti also succeeded in spinning off other body styles such as a convertible, estate and van.

In contrast to the dumpy original Zobo, Michelotti's new shape was razor-edged. Notable was the very generous glasshouse, giving excellent visibility. Among the novelties of the Herald was a one-piece

front end that tilted forwards to allow access to the engine. The body panels simply bolted on to a separate chassis, which was by and large conventionally engineered. Although the suspension was all-independent, the rear end was unusual in having a single transverse leaf spring and swing axles, which resulted in sometimes wayward handling. Power came from a breathed-on 35hp Standard 948cc engine.

While conceived as a Standard, it was decided to badge the new car as a Triumph instead. The Triumph Herald was launched at the Albert Hall in London on 22 April 1959 to great acclaim, with Michelotti himself present to receive the plaudits.

A Herald 1200 version followed in 1961 with a bigger engine and an estate body option, also joined by an up-market 12/50. The 13/60 of 1967 gained a more powerful 1296cc engine and adopted a slanted Vitesse-style bonnet. Some 525,767 Heralds were made in all between 1959 and 1971, ranking it as a great success.

Michelotti also designed the Triumph Vitesse of 1962, which was essentially a Herald with a six-cylinder engine. Michelotti retained almost all the panels from the Herald unchanged, except for a new front end with a more angular shape and double headlamps. Under the skin the Vitesse benefited from a stronger chassis, front disc brakes and a very compact (1596cc) straight-six engine with 70hp (uprated in 1966 to 2.0 litres and 95hp). The Vitesse was made in saloon and convertible forms only, with production ending in 1971, by which time over 50,000 had been made.

TRIUMPH VITESSE 1600 GT (MICHELOTTI)

Having designed the Vitesse for Triumph in 1962, Michelotti – by now completely independent of Vignale – created an entirely fresh coupe concept based on the Vitesse chassis. The two-seat car looked quite unlike any other Triumph, or indeed any other Michelotti design. The front end had a reverse-angle grille and low-set, cowled oblong headlamps. The front wing line was raised above the largely flat bonnet, rising aft of the doors in a 'kink' before falling to the rear. Perhaps its most notable feature was a transparent panel in the roof immediately behind the windscreen, allowing a lot of light to enter the cabin – a pioneering piece of design. Launched at the March 1964 Geneva Show, the Vitesse 1600 GT remained a one-off.

TRIUMPH SPITFIRE (MICHELOTTI)

The idea for the Spitfire was hatched between Harry Webster and Giovanni Michelotti as a competitor for the Austin-Healey Sprite; in other words, a small sports car targeted at younger buyers. Work began on the new project in 1960 under the codename 'Bomb'.

To keep costs down, a shortened version of the Herald chassis was used. A chopped Herald chassis was duly sent to Michelotti, while a two-seater Herald test mule was built in Britain to develop the suspension. The Herald's chassis outriggers were removed to enable a much lower seating position in the Bomb, so low in fact that the driver could actually touch the ground in its eventual production form. Michelotti's original design lacked the distinctive low-door profile, as Webster later recalled: "I remember sitting in the wooden model in his little workshop in Italy and telling him it wasn't any good because when I put my arm over the door my fingers couldn't touch the ground. That's how the scoop in the door came about."

Michelotti's prototype was sent over to Coventry in October 1960 at a delicate moment for Standard-Triumph. After Leyland acquired the company in December 1960, all work immediately stopped on the Bomb and the prototype was covered up at the factory. It may well have been forgotten, too, had not Stanley Markland of Leyland asked to see what was hidden under the tarpaulin. He expressed such appreciation for what he saw that the Bomb project was revived in July 1961.

Very few changes were made to Michelotti's design in the eventual production car. Like the Herald, the bonnet was front-hinged and almost the whole front end tilted forwards for engine access. This was a highly accomplished design, with extremely well proportioned volumes, a long bonnet and charismatic wing lines. When asked, in an interview with the Italian journalist Clelia d'Onofrio, which of all his designs was his favourite, Michelotti replied that it was the Spitfire.

The Spitfire name was taken from the iconic fighter plane that had won the Battle of Britain in WW2. The new car was the undoubted star of the October 1962 Earls Court Motor Show where it debuted, before being shown one month later at the Turin Show. It was badged as the Spitfire 4, which Michelotti thought was perhaps because Triumph's management had chosen the fourth of his five design proposals, but in fact the numeral referred to the four-cylinder engine, which was a Herald unit tweaked to deliver 63hp – good enough for 0-60mph in 16.4 seconds and a top speed of 92mph.

Considering that it was essentially a Herald underneath and shared its tip-toe cornering stance, the Spitfire 4 did a creditable job of extracting true sporting character. Standard front brake discs were a boon, too, as was the improbably tight turning circle.

OPPOSITE: Vitesse 1600 GT was a 1964 one-off based on the Vitesse (inset). THIS PAGE: Spitfire was Michelotti's favourite of his designs for Triumph. Later MkIV (bottom and right, with Michelotti) looked especially crisp.

The Spitfire boasted a soft-top (an optional hardtop arrived in 1963), wind-up windows, external door locks and a comprehensively equipped cabin. The MkII model of 1965 added 4hp of power, a new grille and better upholstery. This was followed by the MkIII in 1967, whose higher bumpers were needed to satisfy American safety laws; other changes were a larger 1.3-litre engine, better brakes and a wood veneer facia.

For the MkIV of 1970, Michelotti was called upon to renew the styling front and rear. New one-piece front wings eliminated the old weld lines that had previously been covered by chrome strips. The headlight surrounds were now in body colour, the front grille was of black plastic and there were black plastic bumper under-riders. The wheelarches gained attractive flares, the door handles were now flush-mounted and the windscreen was raised by two inches. The biggest change, however, came at the rear, where a new 'Innsbruck Line' cut-off tail introduced a family resemblance with newer stablemates like the Stag and 2000. Other MkIV alterations were an all-synchromesh gearbox, higher final drive and improved suspension.

The final Spitfire 1500 (1974 to 1980) gained a larger engine but had only very minor cosmetic changes like decals on the bonnet and boot, and a black rear panel. Some 314,332 Spitfires were made in all, putting it into the top 10 best-selling sports cars of all time – a truly significant achievement.

TRIUMPH GT6 (MICHELOTTI)

With Pininfarina working on a new MGB GT fastback coupe, Triumph knew it had to develop a rival GT. In 1963, Harry Webster personally drove a well-worn Spitfire out to Italy to leave with Michelotti, asking him to create a new hardtop GT version. True to his reputation for fast work, Michelotti returned the completed 'Spitfire GT' prototype to Triumph by the end of the year. In the shape of this prototype was the basic outline of what would become the GT6, notably its fastback rear end and opening tailgate. The prototype's unique roof was used as the basis for making the glassfibre roofs that would grace Triumph's Spitfire racing contenders at Le Mans.

The prototype retained the 1147cc Spitfire engine. Beleaguered by extra weight, it didn't perform well so Triumph decided to fit the 1.6-litre six-cylinder engine from the Vitesse into the prototype – but even this 77hp unit wasn't really potent enough. Triumph eventually shoehorned in the 2.0-litre six from the Triumph 2000, tuned to deliver an exciting 95hp. This was mated to a new gearbox and a beefier back axle.

Stylistically, the GT6 was a triumph. The new fixed-head roofline, realised in steel, looked superb and was simple to adapt from the existing Spitfire shell. Incorporating a hinged rear window, it was even quite practical. The only other main change to the Spitfire shape was a new bonnet bulge to clear the six-cylinder engine.

The GT6 was launched to the market in October 1966. The Spitfire/Herald-derived running gear made the handling somewhat interesting at its limit, something that Triumph addressed with the 1968

LEFT: GT6 was a well resolved coupe development of the Spitfire. BELOW: This alternative GT6 proposal by Michelotti wore Leyland badges.

MkII, which received the Vitesse MkII's double wishbone rear suspension, as well as Spitfire-type raised bumpers, a power boost to 104hp, Rostyle wheels and a better cabin. The GT6 MkIII of 1970 shared Michelotti's Spitfire MkIV restyle, alongside a smooth bonnet, perforated disc wheels and reshaped rear quarter windows. The very last GT6s had Spitfire MkIV rear suspension. Some 40,926 GT6s were made in seven years, over half of which were exported to the USA.

Triumph TRs

TRIUMPH TR3 SPECIALE 'DREAM CAR' (VIGNALE/MICHELOTTI)

The TR3 Speciale marked the fateful moment when Triumph first used the services of Giovanni Michelotti – even though at the time it didn't even know his name. When, in late 1956, a man called Raymond Flower – one of the partners in the Frisky project (see page 154) – approached Standard-Triumph asking for permission to use its mechanicals in the new Frisky car, Harry Webster (technical director) and Martin Tustin (production director) asked how the new car would look. Flower responded that his designer had promised a prototype within three months. Impressed, Webster said that if he could build a car in such a short time frame, Triumph would also be interested in a sports car prototype (after all, Triumph's strong-selling TR3 sports car was looking a little antiquated by the late 1950s). Flower duly asked Michelotti to come up with some design proposals, which were then presented to Webster. Still without a clue who the designer was, Webster handed Flower a contract worth £3000 and a brand new TR3 chassis.

True to his word, within three months Flower successfully delivered the TR3-based sports car to Coventry. The people at Triumph were extremely impressed with it. The only clues they had to the car's origins were a little 'V' badge and the fact that the car had been delivered in a van that came from Turin. They managed to persuade the Italian delivery driver to reveal the origin of the car: the Vignale works. Within a very short time frame, Webster and Tustin had arranged to fly out to Turin to meet Alfredo Vignale. This meeting would have huge long-term consequences, for this marked the moment when they also met the car's designer for the first time: Giovanni Michelotti, who would go on to design a whole generation of Triumphs.

Michelotti's TR3 Speciale (also known as the 'Dream Car') hid its underpinnings very well. The design was American-influenced in terms of its conspicuous tailfins, ornate chromework, eggcrate front grille, U-shaped bumpers, bonnet scoop and forward-raked headlight shrouds. One curiosity was a Plexiglas half-height wind deflector behind the cabin that had to be removed before the soft-top could be deployed. This partly explained why the car was 90kg (200lb) heavier than the TR3. Press images also showed a detachable hardtop, although this appears to have been airbrushed in and may never actually have been built.

The cabin featured a new dashboard, wind-up

THIS PAGE: This TR3-based 'Dream Car' was the project that ignited Triumph's interest in Italian styling. Although it wore Vignale badges, it was designed by Giovanni Michelotti.

windows (the TR3 had mere floppy side curtains), radio (with electric aerial) and exotic upholstery in the form of black leather with cream piping and genuine leopard skin inserts.

The TR3 Speciale broke cover at the 1957 Geneva Motor Show, the very same show at which Michelotti's Vignale-badged Frisky prototype also made its debut. The one-off was then returned to the UK, where *The Autocar* tested it in 1958, reporting that it had a "very practical body as well as a very attractive one". The magazine also seemed to have some inside information about Triumph's plans for Michelotti when it said: "There is no doubt that even now the company is cooking up ideas and developing features to be incorporated progressively into TR3 successors." However, Triumph judged the Speciale to be too complex and costly as a direct TR3 replacement. After being driven for a while by Standard's managing director, Alick Dick, the prototype was sent back to Italy in January 1960, having been bought by the Italian Triumph importer, CESAC. It was re-registered in Turin but its current whereabouts are sadly unknown.

TRIUMPH ITALIA (VIGNALE/MICHELOTTI)

The Triumph Italia was the brainchild of Salvatore Ruffino, a Neapolitan who had, in 1957, acquired the rights to the Standard-Triumph concession for Italy. Selling the old-fashioned Triumph TR3A in a country blessed with beautiful coachwork at every turn, he was convinced that a more stylish version would be popular. Ruffino approached Zagato but he didn't like its proposal, so he then tried Giovanni Michelotti, whose Triumph TR3-based 'Dream Car' (see above) he had already seen.

Michelotti designed a smart TR3A-based coupe for Ruffino in 1958. The prototype was built by Carrozzeria Vignale and debuted at the November 1958 Turin Show on Vignale's stand, presented as the Triumph 2000 Italia. The prototype differed from eventual production cars in being bodied in

ABOVE: First Italia prototype had a 'droop snoot' that was unaerodynamic. BELOW & OPPOSITE: Definitive Italia design featured Maserati-esque lines.

aluminium, rather than steel, and having a smooth, sloping nose with faired-in headlights, but the rest of the shape was already set. This was a handsome car indeed, with clear echoes of the Maserati 3500 GT and an exceptionally clean shape with minimal brightwork.

Vignale built two further prototypes with new front-end styling, apparently because the aerodynamics of the original nose were poor. The production version of the Italia was duly revealed at the 1960 Turin Show. Standard-Triumph was fully on board with the new car, agreeing to supply rolling chassis to Vignale. The brochure described it as (translated): "The art of Italian coachbuilding, English sports car engineering". Mechanical changes over the Triumph TR3A were few: a front anti-roll bar, an extra leaf in each rear spring and stiffer dampers. Harry Webster used the first prototype as his own personal car, often driving it out to Italy to visit Michelotti.

Over the Triumph-supplied chassis, the Vignale works built the bodywork in steel. The wings were integral to the main bodyshell, which was both welded and bolted to the chassis. The interior seated 2+2 and was beautifully presented. All Italias had wire wheels and options included whitewall tyres, leather upholstery, overdrive, radio and Nardi steering wheel.

Autocar magazine tested the Italia in 1960; however it was disappointed by the performance of the 1991cc-engined 100bhp car, which failed to match its TR3 test results, reaching only 108mph. A retrospective road test by Mike McCarthy in 1994 also declared it to be very unrefined: "It looks so smooth and sweet and beautiful, how can it make such a din?"

Ruffino planned to make 1000 cars a year to sell in both continental Europe and the USA. The agreement reached between Triumph and Ruffino was that the Italia could be sold only in the 'Free Trade Area' of Europe, of which the UK was not a part, so no sales ever occurred in Britain. However, Triumph did bring some cars to the UK for evaluation as a possible replacement for the TR3. Finances ultimately scotched this notion: at a time when the Herald was being launched, cash was tight and tooling costs were judged to be prohibitive.

In other markets, the Italia's main problem was its exorbitant price (about the same as a Jaguar XK140). Another big issue was the launch of Triumph's new TR4 in 1961 with – guess what? – Michelotti styling and uncanny echoes of the Italia about it, including its bonnet bulge, body lines over the doors and rear end. The Italia's archaic TR3 underpinnings were feeling very old by then, too, so the larger 2138cc TR4 engine was adopted in an updated TR3B chassis as soon as possible. But it was all too late. The nail in the coffin was Standard-Triumph being taken over by Leyland Motors in 1961, and the supply of chassis coming to an abrupt end. It's thought that only 329 Italias were built up until March 1962, the last 30 or so with TR4 engines.

CONRERO-TRIUMPH TR (MICHELOTTI)

Triumph competed with some successes at the Le Mans 24 Hours race during the 1950s. In 1959 it fielded the TR3S at Le Mans, fitted with a new 2.0-litre engine dubbed the 'Sabrina', after the British actress Sabrina Sykes on account of its, ahem, curvaceous cam covers. Despite its healthy power output, the Sabrina engine proved unreliable in the race and competition success eluded the TR3S.

Triumph's response was to build the TRS, which had completely different bodywork to another Michelotti design, since his Zoom prototype (see below) was used as a buck to mould the TRS bodies in glassfibre. However, the TRS ended up being no lighter than the TR3S, nor was it particularly aerodynamic. As a result, the three TRSs entered in the 1960 24 Hours actually had slower lap times than the 1959 Triumphs.

So in 1961 Triumph turned to two Italian talents to develop a car with more competitive potential: Virgilio Conrero and Giovanni Michelotti. Conrero created a completely new multi-tubular steel chassis in a 'superleggera' style with a shorter wheelbase than the TRS racers. Conrero also fitted two twin-choke Weber carburettors to the Sabrina engine, resulting in a very healthy power output of 165hp, around 15hp more than the original.

Conrero was also accustomed to working with Michelotti. A Conrero-tuned Alfa Romeo Giulietta SVZ had previously been updated by Michelotti with an aerodynamic nose section that suggested its name – 'Goccia' (teardrop). At the time, Michelotti was busy experimenting in the wind tunnel at Turin Polytechnic and his studies there informed the streamlined shape for the new Conrero-Triumph. The nose featured headlamps and spotlights that were faired in; cooling ducts in the front wings were baffled with vanes; and very distinctive triple grilles on the left-side sill allowed heat to escape from the side-exit exhaust. The rounded rear end was fairly sharply cut-off, while the new interior was also designed by Michelotti.

With panelwork in aluminium, this was a very light machine that could perhaps have done well at the Le Mans 24 Hours, for which the one-off was prepared. However, it never raced there in 1962, as intended, since Triumph's competitions department had shut down in the meantime.

It is believed that three cars were ordered from Conrero but only one was actually completed, which was used on British roads by Harry Webster. It was also reputedly tested on the UK's M1 motorway at a speed of almost 150mph. The Conrero was subsequently exported to the USA but returned to Britain in the 1980s, where at the time of writing it is undergoing a restoration.

TRIUMPH ZOOM (VIGNALE/MICHELOTTI)

In 1959, the Triumph factory competitions department had developed the new Sabrina double overhead cam engine for that year's Le Mans 24 Hours. Triumph also thought about using this engine in a new upmarket, road-going sports car. Michelotti was called in to design the so-called 'Zoom', the prototype being hand-built in Turin in 1959 by Vignale.

OPPOSITE: Handsome Conrero TR never raced at Le Mans as intended. ABOVE LEFT: Zoom prototype was built as an intended upmarket sports car. ABOVE RIGHT: Zoom provided basis for TRS racers seen at Le Mans in 1960. ABOVE: Zest prefigured the TR4.

The Zoom used a TR3S chassis, whose wheelbase was six inches longer and track four inches wider than the TR3's. The overall shape was quite Maserati-like, with upright flanks, a waistline kink in the doors and front wheelarch profiles that slanted to the rear. The front end had a compact, low-set grille flanked by minor lights, with headlights mounted on the front wings.

Two Zoom prototypes were made, one with a soft-top and the other with a novel hardtop that had a removable centre panel – the so-called 'Surrey top' that would eventually be used on the TR4. The hardtop prototype was also notable for its cooling vents in the front wings.

Unfortunately the Triumph Zoom did not proceed, as planned, to the production road car stage. The complexity and cost of the Sabrina engine ultimately doomed the whole project. One of Michelotti's prototypes survives to this day.

The Zoom did, in a way, have its moment of glory, since the prototype was used as the buck for the new bodywork of Triumph's TRS racers that ran at Le Mans in 1960 and 1961. Four cars were built, all with glassfibre bodywork that duplicated Michelotti's Zoom, based on modified TR3S underpinnings. At the first Le Mans outing in 1960, three cars raced, finishing 15th, 18th and 19th, although they were unclassified because they did not reach the minimum distance required. Triumph returned with the TRS in 1961 and had much better results: the trio finished 9th, 11th and 15th overall – enough for Triumph to take the Manufacturer's Team Prize.

TRIUMPH ZEST (MICHELOTTI)

'Zest' was the codename given by Triumph to its TR3 replacement, work on which started in 1958. Following the positive reception that Michelotti's Triumph TR3 Speciale 'Dream Car' of 1957 had received, he was the natural choice to style Triumph's new TR.

Michelotti's initial attempt was much less flamboyant than his Dream Car concept. The nose was completely new: lower, with a smaller oblate grille, conventional bumper and headlamps set into scooped nacelles. The rear fins were greatly toned down and the door aperture was angled backwards at its leading edge.

The first Zest prototype was ready by 1959.

LEFT & BELOW: TR4 in convertible and hardtop forms. BOTTOM: TR5 PI brochure. OPPOSITE: So-called TR4B was a Michelotti update proposal.

However, by then the Zoom project was in full swing and this deflected the Zest's progress. By the time Zoom had been canned, attitudes at Triumph had changed somewhat. Alick Dick said he wanted to move away from Michelotti's previously feline lines, commenting: "I challenged him to produce me a masculine car, brutish and muscular, which is what I wanted for the TR4."

By 1960, Michelotti had designed two new bodies, one of which had a hardtop. Already many of the seeds of what would become the TR4 were evident: the headlights mounted within the front grille below distinctive 'eyebrows'; the raised, thrusting wing line; and the waistline kink in the doors. There were the remnants of rear fins, too. All in all, it was every bit as masculine as Dick had ordered. It got even more brutish with a hump in the right-hand side of the bonnet that, it was realised at a late stage, was required to clear the engine.

TRIUMPH TR4, TR5 & TR250 (MICHELOTTI)

The last of Michelotti's Zest designs formed the basis of the new TR4. Overall the car was longer, lower, wider and heavier than the TR3, but not all traces of the TR3's styling were abandoned.

Overriders were kept on the front bumper, for instance, and while the full-width front grille was all-new, the prominent round headlamps certainly echoed the old TR3's, albeit now topped by distinctive 'eyebrows' that extended back into the bonnet. The bonnet was hinged at the front and featured a hump on the right-hand side to clear the carburettor, while the wheelarches were flared to clear the wider track of the chassis. Brightwork was relatively restrained, with narrow stainless steel strips along the top of the wings, front and rear.

As well as the open roadster TR4 with its removable vinyl soft-top, Triumph took up Michelotti's novel idea for an optional 'Surrey' roof. This consisted of a bolt-on metal rear section with a large wraparound rear window, supplemented by a removable vinyl centre roof (which could in turn be replaced with a metal top). This idea would soon be borrowed by other car companies – notably Porsche – and has become better known as the 'Targa' roof.

Underneath, the TR4 was essentially an updated version of the TR3 chassis, now fitted with rack-and-pinion steering and servo-assisted brakes. Inside it was more comfortable and practical, despite retaining TR3 seats and instruments. Winding windows and proper cockpit ventilation were quite sophisticated for the time.

The initial idea was to revive the Triumph Dolomite name for the new model but the more obvious name TR4 was chosen for the August 1961 launch. The TR4 received regular updates throughout its life, most notably in 1964 when the TR4A adopted independent rear suspension; it was recognisable by its front wing-mounted sidelights. Up until 1967, almost 70,000 TR4s were made.

In 1967, the TR4 evolved into the TR5 PI, which retained the same styling but was notable for being the first ever British production car to have fuel injection, using a Triumph 2000-derived 2.5-litre six-cylinder engine. Bigger brakes and stiffer rear suspension also featured. The American-market TR250 used twin carburettors instead of fuel injection, dropping its power from 150hp to 104hp; its bonnet-mounted racing stripes were, therefore, a somewhat ironic addition. The TR5 ducked out of production in 1968.

TRIUMPH TR4B (MICHELOTTI)

A facelift of the TR4 was considered soon after its launch. Triumph had installed a six-cylinder Vanguard engine into a TR4 chassis (number X684) which was road-registered in January 1963 as 6206 VC. This car was delivered in 1965 to Turin for Michelotti to perform a restyle. This project is often referred to as the 'Zest' but since this label can get very confusing (the codename was used for so many different TR proposals), the author has selected the term 'TR4B' instead.

The transformation was almost total. Only the swage lines and kinks in the doors identified it as a TR4; the rest was quite new, and marked a return to more feminine lines. The grille was reduced to a narrow full-width slot with horizontal bars, to the sides of which were wraparound minor lights. The headlights were positioned right at the tips of the front wings and the bonnet was smoothed out. Michelotti would later update the front end – it's thought in 1966 – by adopting more aerodynamic pop-up headlamps. Ultimately this proposal never reached production.

When it came to replacing the TR5 with the TR6, Michelotti was so swamped with other work for companies like DAF and Mazda that Triumph was forced to send its prototype to Karmann in Germany to perform the update, which featured reshaped front and rear ends. Interestingly, Triumph internal documents referred to the German company as "Karmann Ghia" and sometimes even just "Ghia", but there was never any Italian involvement in the TR6's design.

TRIUMPH
TVT 990G

Fury

TRIUMPH FURY (MICHELOTTI)

Triumph pursued a separate-chassis policy for its cars for far longer than most of its rivals. Only with the 2000 of 1963 did it enter the modern era of monocoque body/chassis design. All of Triumph's sports cars in the 1960s – TR4/5/6, Spitfire and GT6 – had a separate chassis but that would have changed if the Fury had made production, for here was Triumph's first ever monocoque sports car.

The Fury was conceived as a potential replacement for the TR4. In November 1964, Giovanni Michelotti was called in to do the styling work, creating a shape of great elegance and dynamism, somewhat resembling an enlarged Spitfire. The front end was marked by a smooth nose, gently curved wings and then-novel pop-up headlights. Two half-bumpers with overriders partially obscured a wide grille composed of horizontal slats, while the Kamm tail was Triumph 2000-inspired and featured vertical light clusters.

Underneath, the Fury used the Triumph 2000's basic monocoque structure, MacPherson strut front and trailing arm rear suspension, and six-cylinder engine. There were apparently putative plans to fit the Fury with a V8 engine and to adopt MacPherson struts at the rear end as well as the front, but that never happened.

The Fury represented a great opportunity to modernise and raise the profile of Triumph's sports car offering but sadly the cost of development and tooling scuppered any production future. Instead Triumph stuck to its separate chassis policy and the TR4 was merely evolved lightly to become the TR5. Luckily the Fury prototype still exists in the UK.

Although it looked a bit like a Spitfire, the Fury was all-new and based on a monocoque chassis. To the right, Harry Webster stands next to the styling buck.

THIS PAGE: TR5 Ginevra was a stop-gap for 1968 Geneva Show. OPPOSITE: Stag proposals and final production version.

TRIUMPH TR5 GINEVRA (MICHELOTTI)

Giovanni Michelotti had booked a stand at the March 1968 Geneva Show, where he fully expected to present his new Triumph Stag proposal. When Triumph HQ vetoed the idea, Michelotti suddenly had a gap to fill on his stand. He asked Triumph for a chassis on which to build a show car; Triumph agreed and sent him a 1967 TR5 prototype chassis (X760).

The shape that Michelotti came up with – in just two weeks – was heavily influenced by his earlier Triumph Fury. The side profile was remarkably similar and the sloping wheelarch shapes also recalled the Fury. However, there were many differences, particularly at the front and rear ends. The chiselled, forward-slanting nose was five inches longer than the TR5's and featured a full-width bumper and four headlights. The tail end treatment was also a flatter affair than the Fury's, and the fuel tank was moved forwards by four inches to boost luggage space. Meanwhile the 'coke bottle' side profile was emphasised by rather heavy-handed trim strips. Overall, the car was longer and wider than the TR5 on which it was based. Inside, TR5 instruments were mounted in a unique dashboard.

After the car's debut at the March 1968 Geneva Show (giving it its name, the 'TR5 Ginevra'), it was tested on the roads of Turin. Triumph had neither the funds nor the enthusiasm to pursue this car as a new model, settling instead merely to facelift the TR5 to create the TR6. Eventually, the Ginevra was sold to a private Swiss customer in 1971; thankfully it survives to this day.

TRIUMPH STAG (MICHELOTTI)

The idea for the Stag was very firmly Michelotti's. The Italian had plans to create a new concept car based on a shortened version of an old Triumph 2000 hack that Harry Webster at Triumph had despatched to him in June 1965, the intention being that the design study would appear at the upcoming Turin Show.

When Webster saw the proposal, he recognised its potential immediately, as he later recalled: "I thought it was so good I said, 'You're not putting that in. I'm having it'." Webster admitted that Michelotti wasn't exactly happy about this intervention but at least it meant that the design made production. The project was very much liked by Triumph's management: the board approved it in June 1966, by which time it already been given the codename 'Stag'.

The original plan was to use the existing 2.5-litre straight-six and develop a new V8 to be added further down the line. The first running Stag prototype was ready in 1967 with just such a 2.5-litre engine fitted. However, somewhat fatefully the decision was taken to pursue a V8-only policy. Since Triumph's engineers ruled out the idea of using Rover's V8, even though it was perfectly viable (rivalries were still intense between the two newly merged marques), there was a lengthy gestation period during which Triumph developed its own all-new V8, which significantly delayed the Stag's production debut. The eventual 3.0-litre V8 engine was a development of the Saab/Triumph 1854cc 'four' and proved smooth if not very powerful (developing a modest 145hp). Reliability would, however, become a very thorny problem, as the engine suffered from major overheating issues.

Michelotti's convertible four-seater concept was highly unusual for the time; indeed very few European car makers ever produced anything like it. Unitary construction was a first for a sporting Triumph and the T-bar roof added much-needed rigidity. A body-coloured removable hardtop was a popular option, and later adopted as standard equipment.

The Stag was launched to ecstatic press reviews in June 1970. However it was beleaguered by reliability problems and sales were also impacted by the early 1970s oil crisis. As a result, a mere 25,939 Stags were made up until 1977, well shy of the initial plan to make 12,000 per year.

Michelotti also came up with a number of design proposals for a fixed-roof coupe version of the Stag, and in 1970 converted two prototype Stag shells into GT6-style coupes. Triumph decided to adopt and adapt this design, making a working 'Stag Fastback' prototype. However, despite an intended production run, no fixed-roof Stag ever did reach the market. Luckily the prototype still survives.

STANDARD ZEBU (MICHELOTTI)

Standard had been one of the first British companies to come to market with an Italian-styled car, the Vignale Vanguard of 1958. But the Vanguard was looking a little old-fashioned by the end of the decade and so its replacement – codenamed Zebu – was set in motion.

The initial design work was done in-house, featuring a characteristic backward-slanting rear window, but when Standard found out that Ford's forthcoming Anglia 105E would have precisely this 'reverse-rake' design, a more conventional approach was taken, but even this was soon dropped. Instead, Michelotti's widely-liked Herald design was simply expanded by the UK team, suitably widened and lengthened. This did not impress the management, so Giovanni Michelotti was asked to come up with a completely fresh design. However, as likely tooling costs escalated, Zebu was cancelled at the end of 1960. In its place would come project 'Barb' which emerged as the Triumph 2000 (see below).

TRIUMPH 2000 & 2500 (MICHELOTTI)

Following the cancellation of project Zebu, a new large car project was set up by Harry Webster, codenamed 'Barb', based on a new unitary body/chassis. In April 1961, Giovanni Michelotti was given the job of styling it and, true to form, he took a mere three months to produce a full-scale model in wood. The shape was widely liked at Coventry, and even if some minor tweaks were made in-house, Michelotti's proposal was adopted virtually unchanged.

The new car would not be sold as a Standard (the very last Standard-badged car was made in May 1963) but as a Triumph. Arch-rival Rover announced its new 'P6' 2000 model in October 1963. In response, Triumph revealed its own 2000 just one week later, and although it wouldn't actually enter production until January 1964, it stole a march on the Rover by undercutting it on price.

Jaguar's Chairman William Lyons commented at the time: "I think the new Triumph 2000 is going to be a winner. I had a good look at it at the show and was very impressed." Police forces were also impressed, ordering many for traffic duties.

The old Standard Vanguard donated most of the mechanical side but a star of the new car was its 1998cc twin-carb six-cylinder engine, turning it into an easy 100mph cruiser. Other highlights included synchromesh on all four gears, servo-assisted front disc brakes, all-independent suspension and optional overdrive or automatic transmission.

The Triumph 2000 platform formed the basis of a proposed Michelotti convertible version in 1965 – this would ultimately turn into the Triumph Stag. Another proposal from 1964 was a GT fastback estate; while this fastback was vetoed by management, a more practical estate version did reach production for the 1966 model year, and very attractive it looked, too. Another boon came in 1968, when Triumph installed a detuned TR5 fuel-injected 2.5-litre engine into the 2000 hull, conjuring up a true executive express in the 2.5 PI, identified by its black vinyl C-pillars and Rostyle wheel trims.

In 1967 Michelotti was asked to work on a

facelifted 2000/2.5PI under the codename 'Innsbruck'. This would take its styling cues from the forthcoming Stag. The eventual MkII of 1969 benefited from an appealing restyle front and rear, which lengthened both ends, as well as new wheel trims and a full-width wooden dashboard. The estate was pensioned off in 1975 and the very last saloon was made in 1977.

TRIUMPH 1300, 1500, TOLEDO & DOLOMITE (MICHELOTTI)

This compact saloon started out in 1962, under the codename 'Ajax', as an intended replacement for the initially poor-selling Herald. However, as the Herald's popularity steadily increased, so the need for a replacement diminished and Ajax was repurposed – effectively becoming Britain's answer to BMW's successful small saloon car range. There is another parallel in this comparison: stylist Giovanni Michelotti, who had started working for BMW in the 1950s and had also been consulted for the design of BMW's 'Neue Klasse' cars, from the 1500 to the 2002.

What Michelotti designed can be seen as a downsized version of his Triumph 2000. As ever, he worked quickly and efficiently. The new 1300 was launched in September 1965 as Triumph's first (and indeed only) front-wheel drive car (although somewhat perversely the later 1500TC, Toledo and Dolomite all switched to rear-wheel drive). The constraints of the new format, including a rather tall engine/gearbox (borrowed from the Herald), gave the car a more upright look than the 2000, but overall the shape was very well balanced. The front end was clearly an iteration of the 2000's look but with single headlamps. At the rear was a cut-off tail, while the trailing edge of the roof featured a prominent lip.

In 1970 the larger-engined 1500 arrived with a Michelotti facelift. The nose was upgraded with a new grille and four headlamps, while the tail was lengthened to improve versatility and, happily, give it a more balanced look. A cheaper model, named Toledo, had single rectangular headlamps and kept the old-style short rear end.

OPPOSITE PAGE: Standard's 'Zebu' prototype was axed in favour of 'Barb' – what would become Triumph's 2000/2500 large saloon range. ABOVE: Triumph 1300, Toledo and Dolomite were highly successful.

Fulfilling the model's sporting saloon role was an attractive new version in 1971: the Dolomite 1850, fitted with a new 'slant-four' 1854cc overhead cam engine. The Italianate name revived a Triumph badge of pre-war years and seemed apt given the new car's Italian design. The Toledo would also be renamed Dolomite in 1976.

By then, the Dolomite range had been significantly extended by a new Sprint model, launched in 1973. Its 127hp 16-valve 1998cc engine was very advanced for 1973, giving it superb performance. Meanwhile alloy wheels were a first for a British mass-production car, while a vinyl roof and front spoiler bolstered its upmarket theme.

The Dolomite range lasted until 1980 as the last of the old-style 'traditional' Triumphs, and the factories at Canley and Speke that made these models closed when they were axed. The Michelotti-designed Triumph SD2 (see below) never made production as a replacement – the 1981 Honda-based Triumph Acclaim performed that role instead.

TRIUMPH SD2 (MICHELOTTI/PININFARINA)

Following the Rover SD1 saloon, BL's 'Specialist Division 2' (SD2) project was initiated as an intended mid-1970s replacement for the Toledo/Dolomite. With a chassis based on the forthcoming Triumph TR7, it was a joint Rover/Triumph project that would have been made at the Solihull factory.

As with so many BL endeavours, the design was farmed out to competitive tender, with an in-house team headed by David Bache put up against alternatives from Michelotti and Pininfarina. Designs were duly submitted in 1972 for appraisal.

Pininfarina's design had crispness and modernity in its favour, with a stubby tail and a short boot lid. Michelotti's was really little more than a subtle facelift of the existing Dolomite – the cabin was left completely untouched, for instance – and therefore judged to be too conservative.

That was not an adjective you can bandy about the SD2 design that was preferred by management: the in-house effort, a controversial affair with a prominent swage line, semi-covered rear wheelarches and a rather heavy overall feel. Running prototypes were built but ultimately the SD2 programme was canned in 1977, probably fortuitously.

TRIUMPH PUMA (MICHELOTTI)

Triumph was already, by the mid-1960s, thinking about a replacement for the 2000/2500. The project proceeded under the codename Puma, with several designers approached to come up with proposals. Michelotti's was liked best: an attractively sharp-edged four-door saloon that boasted a long nose and a three-box profile. Engineered by Harry Webster, the Puma was intended to be powered by a development of the 2000/2500 straight-six engine, as well as Triumph's new V8. The underpinnings would have been carried over from the 2000/2500, except for a new five-speed gearbox. In the end, the merger of Triumph with British Leyland forced the Puma into competition with what would eventually

become the Rover SD1, and its development was halted in December 1970. However, some engineering elements of the Puma made their way into the Rover SD1 of 1976. Meanwhile, the Puma was developed in short-wheelbase form into the Lynx coupe (see below).

TRIUMPH LYNX & BULLET (MICHELOTTI)

At the end of the 1960s, BLMC had investigated a new mid-engined sports car under the project name ADO21. This in-house design may have looked good but it was deemed too expensive to put into production and was shelved in 1970.

A more realistic pair of sports car projects, also in development at the end of the 1960s, was eventually preferred: the Bullet and Lynx. 'Bullet' was a putative TR6 replacement with a Stag-style targa roof; the 'Lynx' codename was used on more than one vehicle project but at its conception in 1969 it was a 2+2 coupe intended to replace the GT6 in 1972. The Lynx had a longer wheelbase than the Bullet and a version with four seats and four doors was even created.

There is some dispute over exactly who did the design work but it was almost certainly a collaboration between Canley and Turin. David Bache was quoted in 1976 as saying: "We still use Michelotti but only as a prototype builder" – a contention later refuted by the Michelotti family as "a little white lie".

Whatever the story, the Lynx and Bullet were conceived as fairly cheap sports cars to be powered by a development of the Dolomite four-cylinder engine and using a live rear axle. However, management judged that such cars would be too expensive and not distinguished enough to replace the Midget and Spitfire. Moving the project upmarket and fitting Triumph's straight-six engine was a possibility; the Rover V8 was also considered, as the project was reimagined as a possible replacement for the MGB GT V8.

Ultimately the looks of the Bullet and Lynx were simply not liked by management. The new Triumph sports car for the 1970s would instead be Harris Mann's TR7. Incidentally, since Triumph was swamped with work when it came to building the TR7 convertible prototype, Michelotti was asked to build it in Italy. The same Italian designer was later approached to come up with a proposal for an MG-badged version of the Triumph TR7 but the MG TR7 never reached the market.

OPPOSITE: Michelotti's prototypes for the SD2, Puma and Lynx. BELOW: 'Bullet' with British Leyland's Spen King. RIGHT: Broadside was a Triumph TR7 restyle.

TRIUMPH BROADSIDE (MICHELOTTI)

The Lynx codename was also used on a new, in-house project: a larger version of Harris Mann's TR7, with its wheelbase extended by 12 inches. Although the front end bore a clear resemblance to the TR7's, the sides and rear end were quite different. This 'Lynx 2' evolved into the Triumph Broadside project, a coupe and convertible pairing that was started in 1979 under the project code RT061, and intended to replace the TR7, MGB and MG Midget in one fell swoop.

With David Bache's in-house design team fully occupied, Michelotti was approached towards the end of 1979 to restyle the existing Broadside pairing. An ailing Giovanni Michelotti asked his son Edgardo to do this work, and it ended up with a sleeker and more distinctive front end. This was, however, to be Michelotti's very last design for Triumph, as Giovanni Michelotti passed away in early 1980. For its part, BL was facing a multitude of challenges at the time and Broadside was canned along with many other projects then in development.

TVR

Made in Blackpool

TVR is the only car company in the world to have the peculiar distinction of being named after someone called Trevor. Blackpool-based Trevor Wilkinson founded an engineering and vehicle servicing business called Trevcar Motors in 1946, soon renaming it TVR Engineering as a contraction of his forename. Having made a series of one-off sports cars, he started offering chassis commercially in 1953, leading to the very first full TVR model: the Sports Saloon of 1954. Bolstered by early interest in the marque from the USA, TVR developed its first truly significant sports car, the very popular Grantura of 1957.

Keith Aitchison and Bryan Hopton acquired a controlling stake in TVR in 1961 and an increasingly side-lined Trevor Wilkinson felt he had to resign in 1962. By October 1962, financial troubles had forced TVR into receivership. TVR returned to production under the auspices of Grantura Engineering but by 1965 another financial collapse had brought yet another change of ownership: Arthur Lilley and his son Martin took control, forming TVR Engineering.

TVR developed a string of models based on the Grantura throughout the 1960s, among them the V8-powered Griffith and Tuscan. However, the Blackpool marque had even greater ambitions: a plan to produce an upmarket sports car to rival Jaguar and Aston Martin. This was the Trident, designed by Trevor Fiore – who could trace Italian descent – and the prototypes of which were built in Italy by Fissore. Ultimately, however, the Trident ended up not being badged as a TVR but made by an ex-TVR dealer called Bill Last.

TVR also formed plans to launch a quite different Fissore-built model, the Tina of 1968, but these came to naught. That would be the end of the road for TVR's Italian chapter. The company survived for far longer than most of its contemporaries. After a string of Grantura-based models, TVR produced its new 'M' series line from 1972 onwards, followed by the so-called 'Wedge' era (1980-1991) and, under Peter Wheeler's ownership, an increasingly ambitious line of models. TVR lurched through a series of crises in the 21st century and, at the time of writing, was undergoing yet another restructure in an attempt to restart production.

TRIDENT (FISSORE/FIORE)

TVR's plan to move upmarket led its managers, in early 1963, to meet up with a little-known designer called Trevor Frost in a pub near Blackpool (since Frost had an Italian mother, he chose the professional name Trevor Fiore). Reputedly he sketched his ideas out on a pub table napkin and these received a warm welcome at TVR. Fiore was quite possibly influenced by his abortive design for the Lea-Francis Francesca (see page 201).

Despite TVR's enthusiasm for the project, however, a shortage of cash delayed matters until late 1964. When the money finally materialised, Fiore used a contact in Italy, Carrozzeria Fissore of Savigliano, to build two prototypes to his design on TVR's Grantura/Griffith chassis. Fissore duly

ABOVE: Trevor Fiore poses by the TVR Trident prototype he designed; it was built in Italy by Fissore. RIGHT: Striking shape was a pioneer of the wedge school of design. Swivelling headlights were a novelty.

1 NEH

1
NEH

completed the pair, both left-hand drive coupes with 4.7-litre Ford V8s, just in time for a debut at the March 1965 Geneva Show.

Here was a pioneering example of the 'wedge' shape, a precursor of a school of design that would flourish in the late 1960s and 1970s. Fiore's design solution for overcoming the challenges of a short wheelbase and bulky V8 engine was to create a series of geometric lines around a strong beltline. The bonnet slanted upwards front the front and fell away to each side. The door profiles and rear end pinched the shape elegantly in, while the shallow fastback roof allowed for a generous full-length rear screen. A great novelty was flush-fitting headlamp units that swivelled when switched on.

Fissore's prototypes were built entirely in steel, except for the bonnet which was in aluminium. This marked a novel approach for TVR, since all its previous models had been made of glassfibre. Fissore incorporated quite a few locally-made components, including Alfa Romeo rear lights, Fiat front lights and Alfa Romeo switchgear in the cabin. The Dunlop wire wheels were a resolutely British touch, however.

The new TVR Trident was extremely well received. *Style Auto* magazine, for instance, described it as

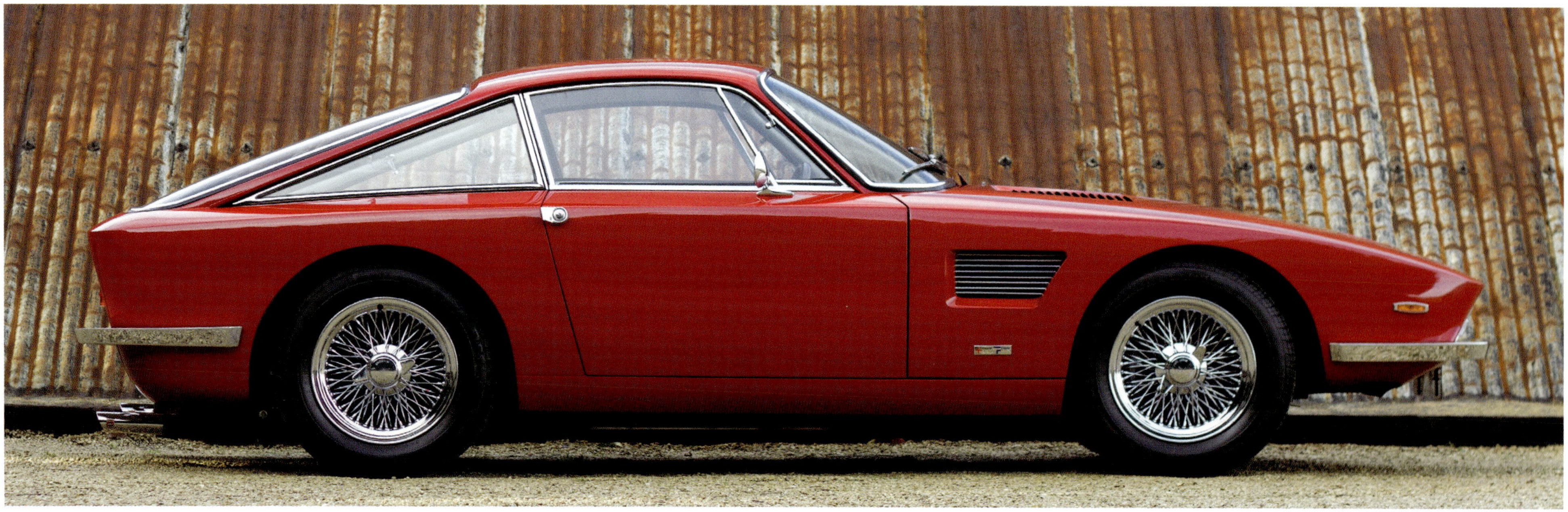

OPPOSITE PAGE: Fissore was credited with the Trident's styling in TVR literature but it was actually by Trevor Fiore; he also designed a convertible, one of which was built by Fissore. ABOVE: Rear design was well resolved.

"one of the masterpieces" of the Geneva show and the *Daily Mail* was moved to ask, "Is this the most beautiful car in the world?" TVR reputedly took orders worth more than £150,000 at the show.

TVR asked Fissore to build two more Tridents, a coupe and a convertible, to use for development testing. However, TVR's increasingly dire financial situation had overtaken matters by August 1965, as it went bankrupt before it could take delivery of Fissore's new prototypes. Into this uncertain scenario, a Suffolk TVR dealer, Bill Last, asked Fissore about obtaining the rights to the Trident. Duly procuring these rights, he commissioned Fissore to reconfigure the car to his own wishes.

In the meantime, the TVR marque was acquired by another TVR dealer, Arthur Lilley and his son Martin. Discovering Bill Last's involvement with the Trident project, a convoluted legal battle ensued. Ultimately the Trident would not be made as a TVR, although Fissore did hand over its third and fourth prototypes to the Lilleys, the Trident convertible becoming Martin Lilley's personal car for several years.

Instead the Trident reached production via a new enterprise created by Bill Last – Trident Cars, based in Suffolk – and the model was renamed the Trident Clipper. Trident signed a contract with Fissore for it to build a new prototype convertible, whose first showing duly occurred at the January 1966 London Racing Car Show. This would be the final contact Trident Cars had with Fissore.

It took a full year for the production Clipper to be shown, now in coupe form, at the 1967 London

Racing Car Show. The styling was lightly revised by Trevor Fiore, losing some of the original TVR's design purity. The longer wheelbase – now 7ft 6in – didn't help its proportions and the awkwardness was exacerbated by a switch to fixed headlights. The bodywork was also now in glassfibre, not steel.

V8 power was retained in the form of Ford's 4.7-litre unit, making the car something of a brute to drive. The claimed maximum speed was 150mph and 0-60mph took only 5.0 seconds. Typical of many British specialist cars of the time, it was sold both as a complete car and in kit form, the latter priced at £1923.

In 1968, Trident switched to a lengthened Triumph TR6 chassis. From 1971, a Chrysler 5.6-litre V8 became standard, and from 1976, a Ford 5.0-litre V8. A second model named Venturer was offered from 1969, fitted with a Ford 3.0-litre V6 engine. As the Tycoon, Triumph 2.5 fuel-injected power could also be ordered. Trident made an attempt to improve on its clumsy headlight arrangement with rectangular units, not altogether successfully.

Despite its appeal, the Trident was never a popular car. Trident shut its doors in 1974 and while there was an attempted revival in 1976, it didn't last long. While some sources say that 135 Tridents were made during its 11-year lifespan from 1966 to 1977, it's thought that a more accurate figure is around the 85 mark.

ABOVE: Trident made production as a standalone marque with a modified design, including fixed headlamps. This is a 1967 Clipper with V8 power. BELOW LEFT: Cabin had a brawny, sporty feel to it.

TINA (FISSORE/FIORE)

When the Lilleys, who had acquired TVR in 1965, found out that they had lost the rights to the Trident, they faced a future seemingly looking resolutely backwards with the ageing TVR Grantura/Griffith the only model in its line-up. As a riposte, Fissore was approached about a completely new model, which was initially planned to be based on the BMC 1800, but instead Fissore and Fiore persuaded TVR to pursue a new small sports car based on the Rootes Sunbeam Imp Sport floorpan.

Trevor Fiore once again took up his pen. Stylistically his new car recalled, albeit faintly, some aspects of the Trident, with its low nose and simple waistline arc from front to rear. Fiore's first prototype featured oblong headlamps mounted behind Perspex fairings in a gently sloping nose. The steel bodyshell was built by Fissore in Savigliano using a Sunbeam Imp Sport floorpan, engine and transmission. Also clearly recognisable from the Imp were its wheels.

The new car was christened Tina, after the daughter of the legendary racing driver Gerry Marshall, who was a business associate of Martin Lilley's. The debut of the new 2+2 convertible was in November 1966 at the Turin Show. It took until the October 1967 Earls Court Show for the Tina to make its UK debut, when the convertible was joined by a new fastback coupe version. The front end of the original convertible had now been restyled, since the previous version would not have been road-legal. Gone was the sloping nose, replaced by a bluff, forward-thrusting profile. The coupe featured rectangular headlamps, while the convertible had twin circular headlamps.

The Tina was very compact, measuring just 3658mm long, and also lightweight at only 711kg. TVR claimed that, with a completely unmodified Sunbeam Imp Sport 51hp 875cc engine mounted in the tail, a top speed of over 100mph was possible.

TVR announced that production of the Tina Coupe and Tina Spyder would begin in early 1968, with prices starting at £998. The intention was to make production bodies in glassfibre over the steel Imp floorpan, with manufacture contracted out – Rootes, Jensen and Aston-Martin were all approached about this, but with no success. After having spent around £15,000 on development, TVR decided to cut its losses and abandoned the project.

CLOCKWISE FROM TOP: 1967 Earls Court Show saw restyled Tina Spyder and new Coupe; Fiore sketch; open-top Tina as originally shown had sloping nose and faired-in headlamps; Tina used an Imp Sport engine in the rear.

VAUXHALL

General Motors' British Outpost

Founded as an engineering company, Vauxhall began making cars in 1903. In 1925 it was bought by the American car giant, General Motors, to become GM's outpost in Britain. For decades, Vauxhall produced its own home-designed range of models but it increasingly devolved to making the same products as its sister operation, Opel of Germany. As a domestic-focused brand, Vauxhall rarely involved itself with Italian designers. Only one Vauxhall was specifically designed by an Italian: Vignale's Viva HA De Luxe. Other than that, Bertone manufactured three generations, and designed two generations, of two-door Vauxhall/Opel Astras.

VIVA DE LUXE (VIGNALE)

Vauxhall launched its Viva HA in 1963. In 1965, Vignale built a little-known 'Viva De Luxe' prototype. While superficially this looked very much like the British-designed Viva, in fact it had almost entirely different bodywork. The wing profiles front and rear were new and more rounded, with a unique bonnet and boot lid, the overall effect being to smooth out the original design. The front end also differed in shape, with a new front grille, while the bumpers front and rear were different, too, as were the lights. The rear side windows were altered, the C-pillars had false vents in, the fuel filler was in a different place and extra chromework was added. The dashboard was more luxurious, too. Overall it looked more elegant than the original Viva, justifying its 'De Luxe' tag. What purpose Vignale's prototype served is not known.

LEFT: Vignale Viva De Luxe had almost entirely new bodywork to UK producton Viva (pic inset). ABOVE, TOP TO BOTTOM: Astra T85 Convertible was built by Bertone in Italy; the Italian company also designed the Astra F Convertible; and the G Coupe and Convertible.

ASTRA CONVERTIBLE T85 (BERTONE)

The second-generation (T85) Vauxhall Astra was launched in 1984 and immediately won the 1985 European Car of the Year award. Initially a convertible model wasn't in the product plan but with drop-top versions of the Ford Escort and VW Golf proving so popular, GM made a quick decision to go head-to-head with them.

Vauxhall presented a convertible Astra at the October 1986 NEC Motor Show. The two-door bodyshell was strengthened in the floorpan and pillars and a roll-over bar was fitted above the front passengers. Initially the roof was manually operated but later it was also available with electric operation. As well as an entry-level 1.6 (82hp) model, there was a 2.0-litre GTE version (115hp), priced at £9686 and £11,599 respectively.

Despite explicit hints in brochures that it had Italian styling – "the flair and expertise of international stylists and coachbuilders Bertone are obviously present" – the Astra Convertible was in fact designed in-house and merely built in Italy by Bertone at Grugliasco near Turin. Some 6764 examples were made there from January 1987 to 1993.

ASTRA CONVERTIBLE F (BERTONE)

The third-generation Vauxhall Astra (T92 or 'F') debuted in September 1991 in hatchback, saloon and estate body styles. The old Mk2 Convertible continued in production at Bertone until 1993, when the new-generation Convertible came on stream. This was not only built by Bertone in Italy but this time also designed by the Turin carrozzeria.

The new design was much cleaner since the roll-over bar was dispensed with. Bertone designed a soft-top that could be stowed behind the rear seats, which were therefore sited further forwards than the regular Astra and made legroom tighter, despite the Convertible using the long-wheelbase saloon platform as a basis.

At launch in June 1993, the Convertible had a 2.0-litre engine only; 1.6-litre and 1.8-litre options followed in 1994. The Convertible got a facelift in 1995 before exiting production in 1999.

ASTRA COUPE & CONVERTIBLE G (BERTONE)

The fourth-generation Astra G was launched in 1998, once again in hatchback, saloon and estate forms. In 2000 came the Astra Coupe with almost entirely new panelwork that had the distinction of being designed and built by Bertone; it even had little Bertone badges fitted to attest to the fact.

The Coupe was 15mm longer than the regular Astra and had lowered and stiffened suspension tuned by Lotus. Entered in the British Touring Car Championship (BTCC) from 2001 to 2004, the Coupe famously won each of these seasons. Approximately 90,000 Coupes were produced between 2000 and mid-2005.

Based on the Coupe was a second Bertone model, the Astra Convertible, launched at the 2001 Geneva Show. This was the handsomest Astra yet, with clean lines and no separate tonneau cover. Instead, the soft-top folded away electronically (via a cabin switch or remote control) under a metal cover behind the seats.

When Astra Convertible production ended in 2005, it was Bertone's last remaining production model – indeed it was almost the last car ever made in series by Bertone (the Mini GP was actually the very last). Production of the next open-roof Astra, the hard-roof TwinTop of 2006, was diverted to Opel's plant in Antwerp, Belgium. Arrivederci Italia.

Bodies of Work: Italy's *Carrozzerie*

ALLEMANO

Carrozzeria Allemano was founded by Serafino Allemano in Via Orto Botanico, Turin, in 1927. Like many *carrozzerie*, he started out simply doing repairs but soon started beating panels for other more established coachbuilders. It was in 1935 that his first full coachbuilt body was prroduced. At the end of World War Two, he occupied a warehouse in Via Pietro Cossa to restart production of bodywork.

Although he was not a designer himself, Allemano hired talented stylists such as such as Giovanni Michelotti, Pietro Frua and Franco Scaglione, whose designs were notable for their simplicity. Allemano embraced enveloping shapes with vertical flanks that became de rigueur after the war. Aerodynamics were enthusiastically embraced in the post-1960 Scaglione era.

Mostly it was Fiat chassis that were clothed but Allemano was the very first coachbuilder to create a road-going body on a Ferrari chassis (with the Ferrari 166 of 1948). Allemano also clothed Maserati A6G/54s with bodies designed by Giovanni Michelotti, while several Abarths were also rebodied.

Allemano's fame spread abroad, too. In France, Jean Rédélé got Allemano to design his 1953 precursor to the Alpine, while various Panhards were Allemano-bodied, too. The Japanese also came knocking: the Prince Skyline was built by Allemano. As for British chassis, Allemano worked on only three: an Aston Martin DB2/4 in 1953, a Jaguar XK140 in 1956 and a Jaguar XK150 in 1958.

Aston Martin DB2/4 by Allemano

Allemano's decision to keep things cottage industry-sized and production numbers exclusive left the company exposed to the downturn in upmarket coachbuilt cars that occured in the 1960s and its prices were simply too high to contend with its more industrialised competitors. As a result, Allemano close its doors in 1965.

INDEX OF BRITISH-ITALIAN MODELS

Aston Martin DB2/4 Berlinetta *(p35)*
Jaguar XK140 Coupe *(p173)*
Jaguar XK150 Coupe *(p179)*

ARES

Ares Design was set up in 2014 by Danny Bahar (ex of Ferrari and Lotus) as a modern Italian coachbuilder. From its base in Modena, it offered a range of special-bodied cars, including – from 2018 – a two-door coupe version of the Bentley Mulsanne four-door saloon.

INDEX OF BRITISH-ITALIAN MODELS

Bentley Mulsanne Coupe *(p73)*

BERTONE

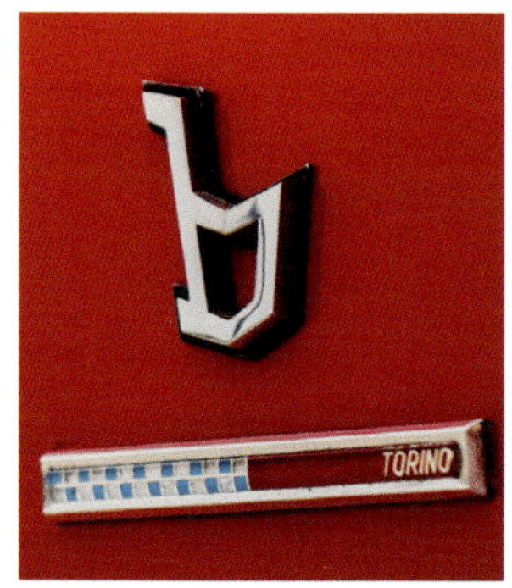

Without question, Bertone ranks right up alongside Pininfarina as one of the greatest design houses of all time. Its history stretches back to 1912 when Giovanni Bertone founded a *carrozzeria* at Borgo San Paolo, Turin. In 1921 he started to produce his first complete bodies based on the likes of Fiat, Ansaldo, Diatto, Lancia and Itala. Designer Mario Revelli di Beaumont became Bertone's star stylist, with a strong aesthetic viewpoint and many innovations, such as transparent roof panels and panoramic windscreens.

Aston Martin DB2/4 Spider by Bertone

Bertone's great days began in the 1950s and it became the first port of call for numerous manufacturers seeking the right design for their new products. Giovanni's son Giuseppe 'Nuccio' Bertone steered the company through its greatest era. He had a propensity for spotting brilliant young talent, and such great names as Giovanni Michelotti, Franco Scaglione, Marcello Gandini, Giorgetto Giugiaro and Marc Deschamps all saw very productive spells working for Bertone.

Bertone was also a pioneer of the idea of the 'show car' or 'concept car', especially his so-called "wicked children" – pure dream cars like the Alfa Romeo BAT series of the 1950s designed by Franco Scaglione. Bertone was equally at the forefront of the haute couture special body industry in the 1950s. In addition to bodying domestic Alfa Romeos and Maseratis, Bertone did coachbuilt bodywork on many British chassis including Jaguar, Aston Martin, MG and Bristol, the latter for American importer Wacky Arnolt.

But a major change was coming. After Bertone's Scaglione designed the sensational 1955 Alfa Romeo Giulietta Sprint, the company stepped up to the role of car assembler as well, leading a new and modern factory being built at Grugliasco in 1959. It was at this point that Bertone hired a young Giorgetto Giugiaro, who created a string of exceptional cars, almost the first of which, in 1960, was for a British company, Gordon-Keeble.

Following Giugiaro's departure in 1965, another genius was hired in the form of Marcello Gandini, whose exceptional hand was responsible for some dramatic concept cars, such as the Lamborghini Marzal and Alfa Romeo Carabo, while he was also responsible for production icons like the Lamborghini Miura and Countach, Lancia Stratos road/rally car and Ferrari Dino 308 GT4.

Bertone also maintained a major manufacturing arm, for instance building the Fiat X1/9, Ritmo Cabriolet and Punto Cabriolet. Collaborations outside Italy included Citroën (BX, ZX, XM, Xantia), Volvo (780), Skoda (Favorit) and Opel/Vauxhall (Astra convertible).

Nuccio Bertone died in 1997 but left behind him a design and manufacturing empire of great repute and impressive size, employing 1500 staff at the time of his death. Nuccio had had the sense to split the design studio from the industrial side. The latter fluttered out of existence in 2007, after the end of the line for the very last car built by Bertone – ironically a British one, the Mini GP. The Grugliasco factory eventually deferred to the Fiat empire.

After some turmoil in the design studio side, Nuccio's widow Lilli Bertone eventually stepped in and appointed Scotsman David Wilkie to head up the design studio – a Royal College of Art graduate and ex-Ghia employee who styled the Aston Martin Vanquish-based Aston Martin Jet II. Bertone was declared bankrupt in 2014, although the name was revived as a general design consultancy that exists to this day.

INDEX OF BRITISH-ITALIAN MODELS

Aston Martin DB2/4 Spider *(p32)*
Aston Martin DB2/4 Drophead Coupe *(p33)*
Aston Martin DB2/4 DHC 'Indiana' *(p34)*
Aston Martin DB2/4 Berlinetta *(p34)*
Aston Martin DB4 GT Jet *(p44)*
Aston Martin Jet II *(p62)*
Aston Martin Jet 2+2 *(p63)*
Bentley R-Type Continental Saloon *(p68)*
Bristol Arnolt *(p121)*
Ford Zodiac Mk2 proposal *(p142)*
Gordon-Keeble GK1 *(p156)*
Healey Cabriolet *(p160)*
Innocenti Mini *(p114)*
Jaguar Ascot *(p187)*
Jaguar B99 *(p192)*
Jaguar FT *(p184)*
Jaguar Pirana *(p185)*
Jaguar XJ Series 3 proposal *(p189)*
Jaguar XJ40 proposal *(p189)*
Jaguar XK150 XKE *(p177)*
Lotus Emotion *(p213)*
MG TD Arnolt Coupe *(p81)*
MG TD Arnolt Convertible *(p81)*
Mini Cooper S Works GP *(p218)*
Mini VIP *(p94)*
Range Rover proposal *(p250)*
Reliant FW11 *(p224)*
Reliant Scimitar SE82 *(p225)*
Riley RM Drophead Convertible *(p84)*
Rolls-Royce P200 *(p236)*
Vauxhall Astra Convertible T85 *(p283)*
Vauxhall Astra Convertible F *(p283)*
Vauxhall Astra Convertible & Coupe G *(p283)*

BIEMME

Biemme grew out of a Padova-based funeral business run by Massimo Battistella, whose transformations of cars into hearses became a proper business in 1991. Its work included hearses based on such British prestige marques as Jaguar and Rolls-Royce.

INDEX OF BRITISH-ITALIAN MODELS

Jaguar XF Revenge *(p193)*
Rolls-Royce Silver Seraph hearse *(p237)*
Rolls-Royce Phantom hearse *(p237)*

BOANO

Mario Felice Boano started life at Stabilimenti Farina as a technician, which properly describes his talent; he was not really a designer as such. From 1944, Boano became the joint owner of Carrozzeria Ghia but within a decade, he had been ousted from the company by Luigi Segre. In 1953, Boano duly founded Carrozzeria Boano in Turin, along with his son Paolo, his son-in-law Ezio Ellena and Giampaolo Luciano Pollo.

Boano's principal hired design talents were Giovanni Michelotti and Sergio Sartorelli. Boano made several interesting bodies on the likes of the Alfa Romeo 1900, 2000 and 6C 3000 but he also importantly collaborated with Carlo Abarth. Boano did work on Lancias, Fiats and more, and took over production of the Ferrari 250 GT from Pinin Farina. However, the only Boano built on a British chassis was designed by an American, Raymond Loewy, who made a one-off on a Jaguar XK140 in 1955.

Carrozzeria Boano came to an end in 1957, when Gianni Agnelli asked Mario Felice Boano to head up the nascent Fiat Centro Stile in-house design department. Boano's Via Collegno works were renamed Carrozzeria Ellena, a name that survived until 1966, although Ellena was never involved with any British projects.

INDEX OF BRITISH-ITALIAN MODELS

Jaguar XK140 Coupe *(p173)*

Jaguar XK140 by Boano

BONESCHI

Carrozzeria Boneschi was once one of the stars of Italian coachbuilt couture. Founded in Cambiago near Milan, at the end of World War I, its founder, Giovanni Boneschi, concentrated on prestige coachwork for upmarket chassis such as the Lancia Lambda, Dilambda, Astura and Aprilia, as well as the Alfa Romeo 6C 2500, mostly designed by Count Mario Revelli di Beaumont. The coachbuilder was even thought good enough for official government commissions.

After WW2, Boneschi turned its attentions to making special bodies for various Alfa Romeos and Lancias, designed by the likes of Giovanni Michelotti, John Cornolò and Carlo Rossi. In 1957 the company signed a deal with Alfa Romeo to transform Giuliettas into Giardinetta estate cars. In 1960 it launched coachbuilt Alfa Romeo 2600s with coupe or cabriolet bodywork, while in 1961, it returned to the Lancia stable with a Flaminia-based convertible styled by industrial designer and architect, Rodolfo Bonetto, who was very much a self-taught stylist. The only design on a British base was the Innocenti Morris IM3 designed especially for a factory visit by the Duke of Edinburgh.

By the early 1960s, high-class coachwork was in terminal decline and the *carrozzeria* was forced to turn its attention to making buses, trucks and armoured vehicles, even sinking as low as making sanitary fittings. Boneschi was eventually swallowed up by Carrozzeria Savio of Turin.

INDEX OF BRITISH-ITALIAN MODELS

Innocenti Morris IM3 *(p111)*

BONIOLO

Boniolo Advanced Design was founded in 1975 by Francesco Boniolo, who did work for a number of car companies as well as producing a string of little-known concept cars.

The first coachbuilt Boniolo was a shooting brake based on an Aston Martin Vanquish, built in cooperation with a coachbuilder called Quality Cars, based near Vigonza.

INDEX OF BRITISH-ITALIAN MODELS

Aston Martin Vanquish EG *(p63)*

Aston Martin Vanquish EG by Boniolo

BREUER

paul breuer designer

Belgian-born Paul Breuer arrived in Turin in 1966, where he was hired as a designer by OSI. When OSI was absorbed by Fiat Centro Stile in 1968, Breuer famously styled the 128 Coupe. In 1972, he transferred to Ford's short-lived studio near Turin, which was soon absorbed by Ghia. In 1978, he became chief designer at Open Design, run by Aldo Sessano. In 1986, he opened his own independent studio and was called on to propose some designs for Lotus in the 1990s. He remains active in Italy.

INDEX OF BRITISH-ITALIAN MODELS

Lotus Elise & Elite proposals *(p214)*

CASALE

Carrozzeria Fratelli Casale & Meneghetti was founded in 1919 in Bassano del Grappa by Carlo Casale, Ippolito Casale and Domenico Meneghetti, making special bodies on such chassis as OM, Fiat, Ansaldo and Lancia. The business was continued post-war by Carlo's children: Dario, Danilo, Dino and Dina. Only a few special bodies were made up until 1999 when the business closed.

INDEX OF BRITISH-ITALIAN MODELS
Rolls-Royce Silver Shadow hearse *(p237)*

CASTAGNA

Carrozzeria Castagna – which means 'chestnut' in Italian – once claimed itself to be the biggest coachbuilder in Italy, with staff totalling 400 in pre-WW2 years, when Castagna's work included trimming the coaches of the Orient Express train and building one-off bodywork on superior chassis such as Daimler, Alfa Romeo and Lancia, as well as Rolls-Royce. In post-war years, Castagna's fortunes waned and by 1960 it had closed its doors.

Almost four decades later, architect Gioacchino Acampora thought the Castagna name had enough cachet to be revived. His first effort was a controversial Alfa Romeo-based sports car shown at the Geneva Motor Show in 1995. Castagna returned the following decade with various coachbuilt Fiat 500s and – of more interest in the context of this book – BMW Minis, starting with estate car conversions in 2004. It also proposed coachbuilt Bentley and Rolls-Royce models in the 21st century, although these were never made in reality. Carrozzeria Castagna Milano survives to this day.

INDEX OF BRITISH-ITALIAN MODELS
Bentley Continental Shooting Brake *(p72)*
MG Y-Type *(p79)*
Mini CrossUP *(p220)*
Mini SUWagon *(p220)*
Mini Wagon *(p220)*
Mini Woody *(p220)*
Mini Tender *(p220)*
Mini Tuning Concept *(p221)*
Rolls-Royce Coupe Royale *(p236)*
Rolls-Royce Phantom II Sedanca *(p230)*

CATTELAN

Fratelli Cattelan was a coachbuilder based in Udine. Cattelan's heyday as a coachbuilder was prior to World War Two, but it was still operating after the war, mostly making bodywork for commercial vehicles and light buses. One Austin-Healey 100 was rebodied for an American pilot by this outfit. Cattelan closed its workshops in 1970.

INDEX OF BRITISH-ITALIAN MODELS
Austin-Healey 100 *(p84)*

Rolls-Royce Coupe Royale by Castagna

Austin-Healey 100 by Cattelan

CECOMP

CECOMP (which stands for Centro Esperienze Costruzione Modelli e Prototipi) was founded in 1978 by ex-Fiat Design man, Giovanni Forneris, in La Loggia, Turin. Its speciality was building prototypes and mock-ups for car manufacturers, the only British one being Lotus for its X100 project. CECOMP continues in existence at the time of writing as a design, prototyping and manufacturing operation.

INDEX OF BRITISH-ITALIAN MODELS
Lotus X100 *(p211)*

COGGIOLA

Sergio Coggiola made his name at Carrozzeria Ghia in Turin, where he was head of the prototype shop. He founded his own design and coachbuilding company, Carrozziere Coggiola, in 1966 in Orbassano on the outskirts of Turin.

While it never designed any cars for British car makers, it did build one prototype for Jensen (the F-Type of 1972). In the 1990s it also manufactured several Pininfarina designs for the Sultan of Brunei, including Aston Martins, Bentleys and Jaguars. Sergio Coggiola died in 1989 but his company survived in new ownership well into the 21st century.

INDEX OF BRITISH-ITALIAN MODELS
Aston Martin AM3 *(p60)*
Aston Martin AM4 *(p60)*
Bentley B2 *(p71)*
Bentley B3 *(p71)*
Bentley Spectre *(p71)*
Bentley Phoenix *(p71)*
Jaguar XJ220 Speciale *(p191)*
Jensen F-Type *(p197)*

DROGO/CARROZZERIA SPORTS CARS

Carrozzeria Sports Cars was founded in Modena in 1960 by ex-Formula 1 driver, Piero Drogo and is often referred to simply as 'Drogo'. His partners included Otello Benedetti, Mario Allegretti and Lino Marchesini. The company specialised in making racing car bodywork, for instance for Serenissima and Bizzarrini, but especially on Ferrari chassis (the most famous being the legendary Ferrari 250 'Breadvan').

However Drogo also bodied a few road-going cars too. Some of Drogo's designs were extraordinarily beautiful and dramatic. Others, particularly in later years, were brutal in their angularity, and that included its only design on a British basis, a Jaguar E-Type. The company shut down in 1971.

INDEX OF BRITISH-ITALIAN MODELS

Jaguar E-Type *(p182)*

F&F Design Studio

F&F

F&F Design Studio was founded in Turin in 1995 by the Italian architect and design specialist, Fulvio Fantolino, who also taught at the Istituto Europeo di Design (IED), coordinating the transportation design department, which included projects with Jaguar and McLaren. F&F was responsible for the instrumentation and interior of the Fiat Grande Punto and Lancia Ypsilon but started a link with the British automotive industry through Kamkorp, the company behind the revived Bristol and Frazer Nash marques.

Bristol Bullet by F&F

INDEX OF BRITISH-ITALIAN MODELS

Bristol Bullet *(p128)*
Bristol Fighter Sport Coupe *(p128)*
Bristol Blenheim *(p129)*
Bristol Hot Rod *(p129)*
Frazer Nash Perdana *(p153)*
Metrocab Taxi *(p153)*

FIORE

The name Fiore is Italian, and although Trevor Fiore was born Trevor Frost in Britain, he did indeed have Italian parentage on his mother's side (one of his grandfathers was a Milanese watchmaker). He worked at Standard's design studio for six years from 1956. He then set up independently and quickly moved to Paris, where he adopted the Italian surname Fiore. He established a good working relationship with Fissore of Milan in the mid-1960s, using his connections with British companies such as Elva and TVR to get Fissore to build up several of his designs. In 1975 he set up his own short-lived studio and coachbuilding company in the south of Italy (Naples) before returning to Turin. In 1980 he joined Citroën to become director of its advanced studio.

INDEX OF BRITISH-ITALIAN MODELS

Daimler Roadster proposal *(p131)*
Elva-BMW GT160 *(p136)*
Jaguar S-Type proposal *(p183)*
Lea-Francis Francesca *(p201)*
TVR Tina *(p279)*
TVR Trident *(p274)*

Elva-BMW GT160 by Fiore

FISSORE

Carrozzeria Fissore was set up in 1921 at Savigliano in Piedmont when four brothers – Bernardo, Antonio, Giovanni and Costanzo Fissore – took over the Montaldi horse-drawn cart factory. They started making special bodies for Fiats, designed by Mario Fissore, Bernardo's eldest son, and later Mario's brother Sergio.

Postwar efforts included small estate car conversions, mostly 'woodies', with designs by Mario de Revelli Beaumont. From 1950, Fissore used the newly freelance Giovanni Michelotti to design its cars, mostly on Fiat chassis. Possibly Fissore's best known project was the OSCA 1500/1600 coupe, made from 1959 onwards. The Italian Auto Union importer also got Fissore to design new DKW 1000 SP coupes and spiders, styled by Giovanni Michelotti, which ended up being produced in Brazil by DKW-Vemag.

Fissore collaborated with several British manufacturers through the auspices of UK-born Trevor Fiore, who was the design talent behind three projects that were realised in Italy by Fissore: the Elva-BMW GT160 (1964), TVR Trident (1965) and TVR Tina (1968).

Fissore also built the first De Tomaso Vallelunga cars, while there were international cooperations with the likes of Mitsubishi in Japan and, from 1966, Swiss manufacturer Peter Monteverdi, including V8-powered grand tourers and the Hai mid-engined supercar.

In 1968 ownership of Fissore passed to the founder's sons, who in the following year forged an alliance with the designer Aldo Sessano. Commercial success awaited the Scout, a Fiat 127-based off-road/leisure vehicle from 1971 on. Fissore even built the Fiat 130 'Popemobile' for Pope John Paul II's visit to Poland.

Swiss car maker Peter Monteverdi took control of Fissore in the 1970s, since the Italian company was designing most of his cars at the time. When Monteverdi ceased trading in 1984, Fissore closed its doors too.

INDEX OF BRITISH-ITALIAN MODELS

Elva-BMW GT160 *(p136)*
Lea-Francis Francesca *(p201)*
Range Rover five-door *(p270)*
TVR Tina *(p279)*
TVR Trident *(p274)*

FORD OF ITALY

In September 1969, Ford set up a styling studio in Italy, in a small town called Bruino near Turin. This was essentially a way for Ford to get styling input from the world capital of car design, essentially creating a new hub to propose ideas alongside Dearborn in the US, Cologne in Germany and Dunton in the UK. To head the studio, Ford poached Filippo Sapino from Pininfarina. In his words, "We were respectfully left to work on our own". Sapino was joined in 1970 by Ercole Spada, ex of Zagato. The GT70 prototype was pretty much the only output of the Italian studio that was ever revealed publicly. The Bruino outpost was closed down in July 1973 because Ford had by then bought Ghia, to which Sapino and Spada were immediately transferred.

INDEX OF BRITISH-ITALIAN MODELS

GT70 *(p147)*

TVR Trident by Fissore

Ford GT70 by Ford of Italy

FRANCIS LOMBARDI

Francis Lombardi isn't one of the best-known Italian coachbuilders but it was quite illustrious in its day. Founded by flying ace and aircraft constructor, Carlo Francesco Lombardi, he did good business in the post-WW2 years as a coachbuilder, based in Vercelli, turning Fiats into limousines, estates and coupes. Giuseppe Rinaldi styled one of Francis Lombardi's best-known cars, the Grand Prix, which was at one stage set to use Hillman Imp mechanicals. The company was liquidated in 1976.

INDEX OF BRITISH-ITALIAN MODELS

Grand Prix Hillman Imp *(p244)*

AC 428 by Frua

FRUA

Pietro Frua is a name that should undoubtedly shine brighter in the pantheon of *carrozzieri*. However, his predilection for staying out of the limelight muted more widespread appeciation of his talents; and he was prodigiously talented. He was less interested in fantasy than some of his contemporaries – he called that school of design "pop singers' screams" – and preferred, in his own words, the attributes of "comfort, practicality and sobriety".

Frua was born in June 1913 in Piedmont and started out aged 17 as an apprentice draughtsman at Stabilimenti Farina. It he was chosen to replace 'Pinin' Farina as head of design, and it was he who trained a young apprentice called Giovanni Michelotti in 1936, but the following year Frua was fired. He went to another coachbuilder, Viberti, but decided to go freelance in 1944, occupying a warehouse in Via Giovanni da Verrazzano in Turin.

He started to produce coachbuilt cars from 1947, initially on the Fiat 1100, Lancia Astura and Lancia Aprilia. His low-winged, full-width 'pontoon' designs were much sought after and he was soon working with prestigious manufacturers like Maserati, OSCA and Nardi. He employed a young Sergio Coggiola, who would later found his own *carrozzeria.*

Abroad, Pietro Frua started working with French manufacturers DB and Dubois and also began collaborating with Ghia from the mid-1950s. By 1957, Luigi Segre, the owner of Ghia, had bought out the Frua workshop and all its employees, while Pietro Frua became Ghia's chief designer. His convertible design on Renault Dauphine mechanicals reached production as the Floride. However, unaware that this was happening, Frua also created a Dauphine convertible for Ghia-Aigle, upsetting both Renault and Segre; the courts even became involved.

Frua was soon back as a freelancer, opening a new studio – called Studio Tecnica Pietro Frua – in Via Villa Glori in Moncalieri, Turin and started making bodywork on various Fiats for Viotti.

He also courted foreign interest, including the Lloyd Alexander and Arabella coupes in Germany; Italsuisse Studebaker Lark and Bossaert Citroën DS Gété.

Frua's seminal 1962 Maserati 5000 GT for the Aga Khan established a style that would be used in other Maseratis, including the Quattroporte and Mistral, and several Glas models such as the 1700 saloon and Glas 1300/1700 GT. When, in 1966, BMW took over Glas, Frua tried his hand at a succession of BMW concept cars but sadly these never reached production.

In 1965 Frua's studio moved to Via Papa Giovanni XXIII in Moncalieri, from where he designed exotic machines for Monteverdi, Ligier and Momo. He also designed concepts on the Opel Diplomat, Porsche 914/6 and Citroën SM. Latterly Pietro Frua worked as a freelance designer; he died in 1983.

Frua's work on British cars was substantial. He famously designed the AC 428, while he also did various designs on British Fords from the 1950s onwards, including Anglia, Zephyr and Escort. His 1964 Lotus Elan coupe was an exercise in elegance. More controversially, he occasionally accepted customer commissions that lacked his usual good taste, such as a Jaguar E-Type with awkward front and rear restyling and two extraordinary Rolls-Royce Phantom VI convertibles.

Although he continued working, more or less as a one-man band, into the 1980s, Pietro Frua died of cancer in June 1983, a few weeks after his 70th birthday.

INDEX OF BRITISH-ITALIAN MODELS

AC 428 *(p22)*
AC 429 *(p25)*
Ford Anglia Spider *(p143)*
Ford Escort Mexico Coupe *(p146)*
Ford Escort Monte Carlo GT *(p146)*
Ford Zephyr Mk3 *(p142)*
Jaguar E-Type *(p181)*
Jaguar S-Type Coupe *(p183)*
Lotus Elan SS Fastback *(p206)*
MGA EX205/2 *(p83)*
Rolls-Royce Phantom VI Convertible 2-dr *(p234)*
Rolls-Royce Phantom VI Convertible 4-dr *(p234)*

Rolls-Royce Phantom VI Cabriolet by Frua

FT

FT Autotrasformazioni was named after its founders, Massimiliano Frezza and Stephane Torbi. Based near Rome, it specialised in hearse coachwork from 2001 to the present day.

INDEX OF BRITISH-ITALIAN MODELS

Jaguar S-Type hearse *(p193)*

GARAVINI

Eusebio Garavini set up shop as a coachbuilder in Turin in 1908, specialising in ambulances, buses and luxury bodies for Alfa Romeo, Bugatti, Fiat, Isotta Fraschini, Itala and OM, as well as Rolls-Royce. In 1947 Aldo Garavini took over the business on his father's death, concentrating on buses. The business closed in 1958.

INDEX OF BRITISH-ITALIAN MODELS

Rolls-Royce Phantom *(p228)*

GHIA

It is perhaps a sad reflection that, for many people, Ghia is merely a posh trim level on humdrum Fords, a situation that stemmed from Ford's 1973 acquisition of Carrozzeria Ghia. However, Ghia's history is every bit as illustrious as the best of Italy's coachbuilders.

Giacinto Ghia established the firm in 1915 in Turin, specialising in bespoke coachwork for high quality Italian chassis, in which it was extremely successful, notably crafting some very fine aluminium panelwork. Count Mario Revelli di Beaumont's design input from the late 1920s on was especially noteworthy.

When Giacinto Ghia died in 1944, his will handed control jointly to his brother, George Alberti, and to Marco Felice Boano. By 1947 Alberti had retired, leaving Boano in full control. Ghia's Naples-born engineering chief, Luigi Segre, emerged as man of such importance to the business that he was given a large quantity of shares in the company. Eventually tensions between Boano and Segre reached a head in 1953, and Boano was ousted from Carrozzeria Ghia as Segre took charge.

Fruitful collaborations were established with names such as Lambretta (scooters), Ducati (motorcycles) and the Chrysler Corporation in the USA, the latter a relationship that led to Ghia building many of Chrysler's concept cars in the 1950s. In terms of both outlook and style, Carrozzeria Ghia represented something of a cultural crossroads. Design inputs spanned Virgil Exner (chief designer at Chrysler), Giovanni Michelotti and Giovanni Savonuzzi. Some very important car designs, including the Chrysler K310, Fiat 8V Supersonic and Volkswagen Karmann-Ghia were Ghia products of the 1950s.

Ghia pursued some extraordinary design avenues, particularly in terms of streamlining. The Gilda, created in a wind tunnel at Turin Polytechnic, was a radically-befinned device, while the Nibbio record breaker reached 100mph on 350cc. Ghia also made 'Jolly' beach cars and manufactured its own range of sports cars with the Dual-Ghia Firebomb, L6.4, 450 SS and 1500.

Talent was inexorably drawn to Ghia. Pietro Frua was head of design from 1957 to 1960; Tom Tjaarda was another (famous for his 1959 Ghia Selene and 1970 De Tomaso Pantera), while the brilliant Giorgetto Giugiaro left Bertone to join Ghia in 1965, designing not only exceptional production cars like the Maserati Ghibli and Iso Fidia but also concepts like the Maserati Simun, De Tomaso Pampero and Oldsmobile Toronado Thor.

After Segre's death in 1963, ownership of Ghia eventually passed to Ramfis Trujillo, the son of the Dominican dictator, who soon sold Ghia on to Alessandro de Tomaso, who at the time owned rival coachbuilder Vignale. In 1970, De Tomaso sold Ghia on to Ford, mid-way through creating the De Tomaso Pantera.

Innocenti Coupe & Spider by Ghia

Filippo Sapino became Ghia's design director from 1973, at which point the *carrozzeria* was firmly seen as the European styling and prototype wing of Ford's global organisation. Ghia's concept cars in this phase were usually based on European Fords, while it also did its own take on the mid-engined AC 3000 ME.

The Aston Martin marque was bought by Ford in 1991, so it was natural for Ghia to have some input here, tackling design work for the Lagonda brand in 1993 with its Lagonda Vignale. In the 1990s, Ghia's styling team then was essentially British – brothers Ian and Moray Callum, plus David Wilkie and Sally Wilson – although Finnish designer Taru Lahti made a big impression with designs such as the radical Ghia Focus concept of 1992.

Jaguar XK120 Supersonic by Ghia

Gradually, Ghia lost its role as a design hub, switching to a mere prototype-building facility. Its last real project was the StreetKa of 2003, at which point Ford closed Ghia down – although the Ghia badge persisted on upmarket Fords right up until 2010 in the UK, and as late as 2013 in some other markets.

INDEX OF BRITISH-ITALIAN MODELS

AC Shelby Cobra Spider GT *(p20)*
AC Willment Cobra Supersonic Coupe *(p21)*
AC-Ghia 3000 ME *(p25)*
AC Ford/Lincoln Quicksilver *(p26)*
Armstrong Siddeley Whitley Two-Door *(p28)*
Aston Martin DB2/4 Mark II Supersonic *(p36)*
Ford RS200 *(p148)*
Innocenti Spider & Coupé *(p108)*
Jaguar XK120 Supersonic *(p170)*
Jaguar XK140 Coupe *(p172)*
Jaguar XJ-S proposal *(p190)*
Lagonda Vignale *(p59)*
Rolls-Royce Silver Dawn Saloon *(p231)*
Rolls-Royce Silver Wraith Limousine *(p231)*

GHIA-AIGLE & ITALSUISSE

Aigle is a small town in Switzerland, which immediately opens up the question, why is that of relevance to a book about Italian design? There is a reason: which is that Carrozzeria Ghia of Turin was persuaded in 1948 to lend its name to an enterprise over the border in Switzerland. This was Mario Felice Boano's idea, but he quickly became tired of the Ghia-Aigle set-up and it became entirely Swiss-owned from 1953. In 1955, the operation relocated from Aigle to Lugano, but by 1958 it was back in Aigle again. Ghia-Aigle's course as a coachbuilder was run soon after, and it returned to trading as a body repair shop.

In its time, Ghia-Aigle produced a string of special coachwork designed by Ghia's talented Italian heroes: Mario Felice Boano in the early years, Pietro Frua at the end, but for most of the time it was Giovanni Michelotti. The latter would frequently travel over the Gran San Bernardo pass to Switzerland in his Topolino.

Jowett Jupiter Convertible by Ghia-Aigle

Ghia-Aigle bodied all sorts of chassis, from Mercedes-Benz to Bugatti, but it frequently turned to British-manufactured chassis, such as AC, Bristol, Austin-Healey, Jowett, MG, Riley, Singer and, in particular, Jaguar.

A minor spin-off of Ghia-Aigle was Italsuisse, a company formed in 1959 when one of Ghia-Aigle's directors, Adriano Guglielmetti, set up his own independent bodyshop in Geneva. He employed Pietro Frua's design services on several projects of which, however, only one was British-based: an extraordinary disfigurement of the Jaguar E-Type.

INDEX OF BRITISH-ITALIAN MODELS

AC Aceca ***(p18)***
Aston Martin DB2 Drophead Coupe ***(p32)***
Austin-Healey Sprite ***(p85)***
Bristol 401 Coupe ***(p121)***
Daimler Regency Coupe ***(p130)***
Jaguar E-Type ***(p181)***
Jaguar MkVII Coupe & Cabriolet ***(p167)***
Jaguar XK120 ***(p169)***
Jaguar XK140 Coupe ***(p174)***
Jaguar XK150 Coupe ***(p178)***
Jowett Jupiter Coupe & Convertible ***(p200)***
Lotus Eleven 1100 ***(p206)***
MG TD Convertible ***(p81)***
MG TD Coupe ***(p81)***
Singer SM1500 Coupe & Convertible ***(p238)***

I.DE.A

I.DE.A is not a well-known name outside Italy but it had a significant role in Italian car design during the 1980s, 1990s and 2000s. I.DE.A stood for Institute of Development in Automotive Engineering and was set up in 1978 by Franco Mantegazza, an ex-Volkswagen and Magneti Marelli employee. From a base in Turin, I.DE.A designed such iconic cars as the 1988 Fiat Tipo, 1992 Alfa Romeo 155, 1994 Lancia Kappa and 2008 Tata Nano. Apart from some marginal work for Lotus, the main reason for I.DE.A's appearance in this book is its 1998 design for the Indian company Tata, the Indica, which was developed to become the City Rover, an ignominious project that symbolised the teetering end-of-days era at MG Rover.

INDEX OF BRITISH-ITALIAN MODELS

Lotus Bulgari ***(p212)***
Lotus Elise proposal ***(p214)***
Rover CityRover ***(p250)***

Rover CityRover by I.DE.A

INDESTOR

Founded in 1971 by ex-OSI CEO, Giacomo Bianco, Indestor (Industrial Design Torino) was a short-lived outfit, lasting only until 1975. Its output was pretty meagre but one of its projects was the construction of the Jensen F-Type prototype in 1972.

Index of British-Italian Models

Jensen F-Type ***(p197)***

Jensen F-Type by Indestor

GIUGIARO

ITALDESIGN

Giorgetto Giugiaro was born on 14 August 1938 into a family of artists and musicians in Garessio (Cuneo). While his vocation was artistic, he was also a gifted at technical drawing, and perfectly suited to car design. In June 1955, his end-of-year school exhibition was noticed by Dante Giacosa, Fiat's head of design, and aged just 17, Giugiaro joined Fiat, first in its Ufficio Pubblicazioni Tecniche (Office of Technical Publications), then the Studi Stilistici Vetture Speciali (Special Car Styling Department) headed by Fabio Luigi Rapi.

In 1959, Nuccio Bertone paid Giugiaro, while on military service, to design what became the Alfa Romeo 2000 Sprint. He then joined Bertone, where he learnt valuable technical, industrial and commercial lessons, and became Bertone's youngest ever head of design.

In 1965 he left Bertone to head up Ghia but didn't get on well with its new owner, Alessandro de Tomaso. Within three years his confidence had grown sufficiently for him to set up his own design consultancy: on 7 February 1968, he founded Ital Style.

He quickly joined forces with ex-Fiat designer and engineer, Aldo Mantovani, forming a new company, Studi Industriali Realizzazione Prototipi in Turin. Shortly after came a new name: Italdesign.

Italdesign's very first showpiece was the well received 1968 Bizzarrini Manta supercar, quickly followed by such dramatic designs as the Alfa Romeo Iguana and Caimano, VW-Porsche Tapiro, Karmann Cheetah and Maserati Boomerang.

Italdesign offered not only styling but all the services needed to bring a design to production, and soon manufacturers were flocking to his door. It was not just cars but all sorts of objects, from the Nikon F1 camera to pasta and glass 'bubbles' on fizzy water bottles. The enterprise was so successful that huge new premises were built in Moncalieri in the 1970s.

Giugiaro's design impact on mass-produced cars was huge, including the VW Golf Mk1, Alfa Romeo Alfasud, Alfa Romeo Alfetta GTV, Lancia Delta, Fiat Panda and Fiat Uno. Sports cars interested him less but he still produced icons like the Maserati Bora and BMW M1.

His visions were also conceptual. Giugiaro surprised everyone with his plain and functional Alfa Romeo Taxi created for the Museum of Modern Art in New York, while the Lancia Megagamma of 1978 invented the Multi Purpose Vehicle (MPV) form. Some of the most admirable dream cars have also arisen from Giugiaro's pen and he has been highly influential in setting future trends. Most of Giugiaro's work was notable for its exceptional cleanliness of line and for proportions that were unmatched in the

DeLorean DMC-12 by Italdesign

industry. He was also inspired by a sense of honesty in his work, as he once commented: "As a designer I think it's important to have the consistency between the content that the appearance of a car promises and the content that it actually provides."

Work for British companies was never as significant as for those of other countries, such as VW, Hyundai and Isuzu. In 1972, Giugiaro styled the Esprit for Lotus, a very successful and long-lived design, while he would follow that up with another Lotus, the 1984 Etna, which at one stage looked like having a production future. Another highly admired design was the 1990 Jaguar Kensington. The ignominious Morris Ital, meanwhile, continues to haunt Giugiaro to this day, even though he had no design input in the car.

The 1991 BMW Nazca M12 marked the entrance of Fabrizio Giugiaro, Giorgetto's son, to the Italdesign fold, and in 1999 the company name changed to Italdesign-Giugiaro. It was Fabrizio who suggested the exposed external structure of the 2001 Aston Martin Twenty Twenty. When the management at Aston Martin viewed the car, they said that perhaps the style could be understood in 2020, hence the Twenty Twenty name was born.

In May 2010, 90.1% of the share capital of Italdesign-Giugiaro was acquired by the Volkswagen Group. Giorgetto remained with the company until selling his remaining stake in 2015. He then joined his son, Fabrizio, to form a new independent *carrozzeria*, GFG Style, in Moncalieri, Turin.

Frazer Nash Namir by Italdesign-Giugiaro

Aston Martin Twenty Twenty by Italdesign

INDEX OF BRITISH-ITALIAN MODELS

Aston Martin Twenty Twenty ***(p61)***
DeLorean DMC-12 ***(p132)***
Frazer Nash Namir ***(p152)***
Jaguar Kensington ***(p190)***
Jaguar XJ40 proposal ***(p189)***
Lotus Elan M100 proposal ***(p211)***
Lotus Esprit ***(p208)***
Lotus Etna ***(p210)***
Morris Ital ***(p104)***

MICHELOTTI

Giovanni Michelotti's impact on car design, not just in Italy but throughout the whole world, should not be underestimated. That's partly because of sheer numbers – he famously penned as many as 1200 designs in his lifetime – but also because his work was so widely appreciated among internationally, from the UK to Japan. He was very much *not* the archetypal flamboyant, egocentric stylist; in contrast he was a true workaholic with a natural talent that came easily to him. He was also famed for the speed of his work and the excellent value he provided, endearing him to many major clients.

Michelotti was born in Turin in 1921 and took his first job as an apprentice at the Stabilimenti Farina coachworks in 1936, at the age of just 15. First under Pietro Frua, then Francesco Martinengo and Count Mario Revelli di Beaumont, he learned his art quickly and assiduously. During World War Two, he worked on armoured vehicles and trucks for Stabilimenti Farina, but left in 1946 to set up on his own. Arguably this made him the world's first true freelance car designer.

However, his light was mostly kept under the proverbial bushel because, unlike many designers who set up studios under their own name, he mostly worked incognito and his designs largely remained unattributed until many years later. He worked for a multitude of different companies: Balbo, Bertone, Boano, Fissore, Francis Lombardi, Monterosa, Monviso, Savio, Scioneri and Vignale – in fact, virtually every Italian *carrozzeria* except for Pinin Farina. Easily the most important of these collaborations was with Vignale, while Ghia-Aigle in Switzerland was another significant client, lasting from 1949 to 1957. His designs were not always classically beautiful, like those of say Pinin Farina, but were quirkily individualistic.

After designing a huge number of production and coachbuilt cars for marques as diverse as Lancia and Ferrari, in 1959 he decided to become a coachbuilder in his own right, creating cars under his own name. He hired a small but talented team and founded Carrozzeria Michelotti. It would be 1960 before Michelotti was ready for his first show, which was actually in Paris, since he didn't have the minimum of 50 employees required to join ANFIA, the trade body, membership of which was required to exhibit at Turin (a rule that Michelotti would not comply with until 1972). His first design of the new era, Fiat-Osca 1600 S Coupe, is often seen as the template on which the Lancia Fulvia Coupe was designed.

Michelotti gradually expanded, opening his own factory in Orbassano on the outskirts of Turin to manufacture cars in series, such as the Shellette beach car, while he also rebodied several Ferraris for Luigi Chinetti.

He was a truly international player. He was fundamental to BMW's post-war success, first with the 700, then BMW's seminal 1800 'Mittelklasse' range and then the pioneering '02' Touring hatchback. He was also in the vanguard of European design talent drawn on by Japan in the early 1960s, working for companies like Hino and Prince.

Among his coachbuilt designs on British chassis were the Conrero-Triumph TR, Jaguar Le Mans (based on a D-Type), Triumph Vitesse 1600 GT and Triumph TR5 Ginevra.

But it is his work for Standard-Triumph that is the

Triumph Fury by Michelotti

Triumph TR4 by Michelotti

most celebrated. This liaison came about as a result of designing the Frisky for Raymond Flower. When Flower approached Harry Webster of Standard Cars about using Standard mechanicals for the Frisky, Webster saw Michelotti's work and eventually tracked him down. A close friendship quickly evolved, as Webster stated: "He was a lovely man. Quite frankly, the board of Triumph thought the sun shone out of his backside… He was great entertainment; everyone would crowd around while he did thumbnail sketches on his napkin."

Between 1957 and the late 1970s, Michelotti produced dozens of designs for Standard-Triumph, many of which has the distinction of becoming much loved production cars. From popular saloons like the Triumph Herald to sports car icons like the Triumph TR4, Spitfire and Stag, Michelotti's work was recognised internationally for its high standards.

Michelotti encapsulated the mutual feeling of respect and collaboration between Britain and Italy better than any other designer. He was a great Anglophile and loved spending time in Britain. Giovanni Michelotti's very last design was for a British company – the Reliant Scimitar SS1. Sadly he succumbed to illness in 1980, aged just 59. The company was assumed by his son, Edgardo, who had started working alongside his father at the start of the 1970s, and who kept it going until 1991.

INDEX OF BRITISH-ITALIAN MODELS

Armstrong Siddeley Sapphire 234 Saloon *(p29)*
Austin Apache & Victoria *(p90)*
BLMC Condor (ADO68/28) *(p104)*
BLMC Ladybird (ADO74) *(p98)*
BMC Calypso (ADO70) *(p97)*
Ferguson R5 *(p139)*
Ford Anglia Torino *(p144)*
Frisky *(p154)*
Hillman Hunter Paykan Coupe *(p245)*
Innocenti Austin I4 proposal *(p111)*
Innocenti Mini proposal *(p114)*
Jaguar XK140 SE Coupe *(p175)*
Jaguar D-Type Le Mans *(p180)*
Leyland P76 *(p102)*
Leyland P82 *(p103)*
Leyland-Crompton Electric *(p99)*
Lola Ultimo *(p202)*
MGB facelift *(p100)*
Morris Marina proposal (ADO28) *(p104)*
Morris Spiagetta *(p98)*
Panther Ferrari FF *(p222)*
Reliant Scimitar SS1 *(p225)*
Rolls-Royce Silver Shadow 'Scapula' *(p232)*
Rover SD1 Estate *(p249)*
Rover/Triumph SD2 *(p250 & p272)*
Standard Vanguard Vignale *(p254)*
Standard Zebu *(p270)*
Triumph 1300/1500 *(p271)*
Triumph 2000/2500 *(p270)*
Triumph Broadside *(p273)*
Triumph Bullet *(p273)*
Triumph Conrero-Triumph TR *(p262)*
Triumph Dolomite *(p271)*
Triumph Fury *(p266)*
Triumph GT6 *(p258)*
Triumph Herald *(p254)*
Triumph Italia *(p260)*
Triumph Lynx *(p273)*
Triumph Puma *(p272)*
Triumph Spitfire *(p256)*
Triumph Stag *(p268)*
Triumph Toledo *(p271)*
Triumph TR3 Speciale 'Dream Car' *(p259)*
Triumph TR4 *(p264)*
Triumph TR4B *(p265)*
Triumph TR5 & TR250 *(p264)*
Triumph TR5 Ginevra *(p268)*
Triumph Vitesse *(p254)*
Triumph Vitesse 1600 GT *(p256)*
Triumph Zest *(p263)*
Triumph Zoom *(p262)*

Triumph Herald by Michelotti

Triumph Lynx saloon prototype by Michelotti

MONVISO

Stabilimento Monviso of Turin was one of Italy's lesser-known coachbuilders that made special bodywork on Fiat 1100 chassis under the name Stella Alpina. Monviso used an MG TF chassis for its Everest model of 1954. Ghia, which commissioned many of the cars built by Monviso, took the company over in 1955.

INDEX OF BRITISH-ITALIAN MODELS

MG TF Everest ***(p83)***

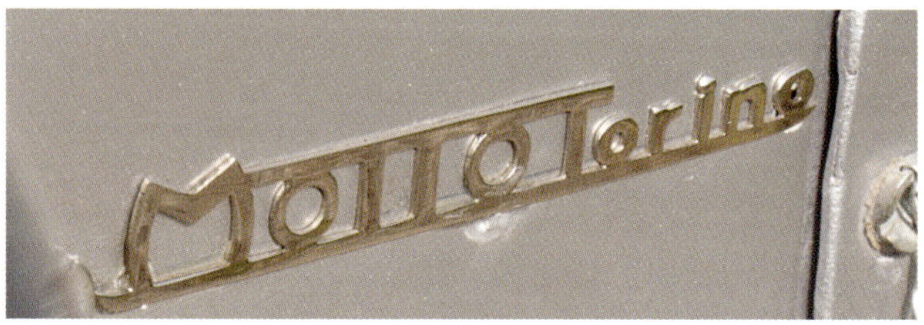

MOTTO

Rocco Motto was born just north of Turin in 1904 and began work at a very young age in a bodyshop called Viarengo & Filipponi. Aged 21, he joined Carrozzeria Maggiora but left in 1930 to set up his own workshop in Turin. Here he made bare bodies for the likes of Lancia, Stabilimenti Farina, Bertone and Ghia. He was soon joined by his brothers, Ernesto and Clemente, and made his first complete car, a Siata, in 1938.

After World War 2, the name Ca-Mo (an acronym of Carrozzeria Motto) was often used. Motto formed a close relationship with Fiat's chief designer Dante Giacosa, who asked Rocco to do the bodywork for such projects as the Cisitalia D46, Cisitalia 202 and Fiat 1100S. Thereafter Motto worked mostly for private racing clients and minnow manufacturers like Nardi, Bandini and Ermini. It was at this time that Motto did its first bodies on British chassis, including an MG TD and a Jaguar XK120. His reputation grew and he built the bodies for such significant cars as the Siata 208S and Porsche 356 Carrera GTL Abarth. Rocco Motto stopped building bodywork for cars in 1965, instead concentrating on caravans, trailers and industrial vehicles.

INDEX OF BRITISH-ITALIAN MODELS

Austin-Healey 100 ***(p84)***
Frazer Nash Le Mans ***(p152)***
Jaguar XK120 Barchetta ***(p169)***
Jaguar XK150 Coupe ***(p176)***
MG-Gilco ***(p79)***
MG TD Barchetta ***(p79)***

OPAC

Opac was formed in 1986 by Pierangelo Sacco and Giuliano Feroldi in Rivalta di Torino. Its main activity was making bodies in white for limited production cars. It collaborated not only with Italian design houses like Pininfarina, Bertone and Zagato, but also with major manufacturers such as Maserati, Alfa Romeo and Lamborghini. Bodies in white were also made for some British car makers, such as Aston Martin, Bentley, MG-Rover and Rolls-Royce. Notable was Opac's behind-the-scenes work on many of the special cars made in Italy for Prince Jefri of Brunei, among them several Rolls-Royces. Opac also developed and manufactured components, in particular soft-tops and hard-tops for convertibles. The company is still flourishing at the time of writing.

INDEX OF BRITISH-ITALIAN MODELS

Aston Martin V8 Vantage Zagato ***(p47)***
Aston Martin DB7 Zagato ***(p50)***
Bentley Azure ***(p71)***
MG XPower SV ***(p251)***
Rolls-Royce Corniche ***(p235)***
Rolls-Royce P200 ***(p236)***
Rolls-Royce P210 ***(p236)***

OSI

Carrozzeria OSI was intimately linked with Ghia, since it was founded by Luigi Segre, the owner of Carrozzeria Ghia, who wanted to establish a production hub. In 1959 Segre had a former armaments factory next to Ghia's Turin premises rebuilt and here set up Officine Stampaggi Industriali (OSI) in partnership with Arrigo Olivetti of alloy wheel manufacturer, Fergat.

OSI quickly acquired contracts to build cars such as the Innocenti Spider, Fiat 2300S and Fiat 1300/1500 estate, and by 1963 had 600 employees and was making 50 cars a day. After Segre died in 1963, Olivetti took control of the company, which was separated from Ghia. Giovanni Michelotti was used extensively during this time, including for the Ford Anglia Torino which OSI put into production.

OSI attracted some talented designers to work for it, including Sergio Sartorelli, Werner Hölbl and Paul Breuer. After making cars such as the Alfa Romeo 2600 De Luxe and Ford 20M TS Coupe, OSI's fortunes declined. It closed its design centre in December 1967 and the following year Sartorelli asked Dante Giacosa if Fiat Centro Stile would absorb OSI, which it duly did.

INDEX OF BRITISH-ITALIAN MODELS

Ford Anglia Torino ***(p144)***
Innocenti Spider & Coupé ***(p108)***

Ford Anglia Torino by OSI

PILATO

Autotrasformazioni Pilato was based in Ponte della Priula, in the province of Treviso. Its speciality was conversions of luxury cars into limousines and hearses, including Jaguars.

INDEX OF BRITISH-ITALIAN MODELS

Jaguar F-Pace Luce *(p193)*
Jaguar XF Aurora *(p193)*
Jaguar XJ Imperial *(p193)*
Jaguar XJ Queen *(p193)*
Jaguar XJ Queen II *(p193)*

PININ FARINA
PININFARINA

At only 5ft tall, Giovanni Battista Farina's nickname of Pinin – which means 'kid' in the dialect of Piedmont – was perfectly fitting. Born in Turin on 2 November 1893, he was the last male of 11 children. Aged just 12, he joined his brothers in the Stabilimenti Farina body shop in Turin, where he excelled as a designer.

Following a spell in the USA, Pinin's desire to innovate fell out of in line with Stabilimenti Farina's conservative thinking, so in 1928 he left by mutual consent to found his own enterprise: Carrozzeria Pinin Farina in Corso Trapani, Turin. He received financial assistance from both family members and Vincenzo Lancia, founder of the Lancia marque. His chosen badge – a little blue 'f' with a crown on top – came to signify the mark of genius.

His reputation quickly grew and he secured a lot of custom from wealthy clients, establishing a large manufacturing facility. He was particularly interested in aerodynamic research, with many radical ideas put into practice, including inclined windscreens and changing classic vertical radiator grilles to low horizontal ones.

By 1939, Carrozzeria Pinin Farina had 500 employees and was making 800 bodies per year. After the war, individual commissions continued to come in, including many on high-class British chassis such as Bentley, Bristol and Rolls-Royce.

However, one car changed everything: the Cisitalia 202. Here was a true turning point in automotive design: a car with aerodynamics and aesthetics in perfect harmony thanks to the its bonnet, front wings and waistline forming a single line with smooth flanks and softly curving side windows – all pioneering features. It was quickly recognised as a masterpiece, finding space in the New York Museum of Modern Art. Custom quickly flocked to Pinin Farina and major manufacturers asked for designs from him: Lancia with the Aurelia GT and Alfa Romeo with its 1900 Convertible and Sprint Coupe. From 1952, Ferrari also began to use Pinin Farina almost exclusively for its factory bodywork.

Pinin Farina pioneered the move among Italian *carrozzerie* towards mass production, notably with the 1955 Alfa Romeo Giulietta Spider. A huge new factory was built in Grugliasco, just outside Turin, for this purpose.

At the same time, the company continued to espouse a philosophy of unmatched purity and conceptual originality in design. Its creations were united by themes of flowing shapes and perfect proportions. In contrast to the geometric shapes espoused by so many other design houses, Farina was inspired by organic forms, from the female body to the way snow is sculpted by winds. Indeed, the company was one of the first in the world to install a wind tunnel. Some extraordinary shapes emerged over the years, such as the extreme Ferrari-based Modulo of 1970.

Many of the talented individuals at Pinin Farina were never lauded in period, such as Franco Martinengo and Francesco Salomone in the immediate post-war years, followed by luminaries such as Aldo Brovarone, Paolo Martin, Filippo Sapino, Leonardo Fioravanti and Diego Ottina.

In 1956, a contract was signed with BMC that led to Pinin Farina designing a whole tranche of family cars from the Austin A40 to the Wolseley 6/99. This relationship lasted well into the 1960s with such projects as ADO16 (the Austin/Morris 1100) and even an MG (the MGB GT fastback). While Pininfarina was asked to tender for design work after this, the only further production design it did was Jaguar's XJ Series 3 of 1979.

Battista maintained strong connections with Britain. For instance, in 1954 he was declared a 'Royal Designer for Industry' by the Royal Society of Arts (of which Queen Elizabeth was president). Farina later recalled: "I had the honour of being presented to her. When Queen Elizabeth came to Turin in 1961… [she] called me by my name and proceeded to ask me many questions."

In 1961, five years before his death, Battista Farina officially changed his surname to Pininfarina, at which point the company name also changed from Pinin Farina to Pininfarina (one word) and control of the company passed to his son, Sergio, along with his son-in-law Renzo Carli. Sergio would go on to become a Member of the European Parliament and was made an Italian life senator in 2005.

In the 1970s, Pininfarina went on to cooperate with other British marques, notably designing the Camargue coupe for Rolls-Royce, a company with which Pininfarina would reprise relations in the

Austin A40 by Pinin Farina

Jaguar XJ Spider by Pininfarina

1990s with the Bentley Azure. In the 1990s Pininfarina also made numerous special-bodied cars for the Brunei royal family, among them Jaguars, Aston Martins and Bentleys. It also worked on Lotus chassis with the Chronos and Enjoy.

In 2006, Sergio Pininfarina's son Andrea was appointed chairman and his other son Paolo vice-chairman. Two years later, Andrea was fatally injured in an accident, leading to Paolo ascending to the presidency. This was at a time of great economic turmoil that saw Pininfarina's production operations terminally affected (the last car was made at its factory in October 2011). Pininfarina remained active in design terms, however, and in 2015 was bought out by the Indian car maker, Mahindra. In 2018, Automobili Pininfarina announced that it would return as a car manufacturer with the Battista supercar.

INDEX OF BRITISH-ITALIAN MODELS

Aston Martin AM3 ***(p60)***
Aston Martin AM4 ***(p60)***
Austin A40 ***(p86 & p107)***
Austin-Healey 3000 GT 'Firrere' ***(p85)***
Bentley Azure ***(p71)***
Bentley B2 ***(p71)***
Bentley B3 ***(p71)***
Bentley MkVI Coupe ***(p67)***
Bentley MkVI Cresta ***(p64)***
Bentley MkVI Drophead Coupe & Coupe ***(p66)***
Bentley Phoenix ***(p71)***
Bentley R-Type Continental ***(p67)***
Bentley Spectre ***(p71)***
Bentley T Coupe Speciale ***(p69)***
BL ADO88 Mini replacement ***(p98)***
BMC ADO9: Austin A55 MkII & A60, MG Magnette MkIII & MkIV, Morris Oxford V & VI, Riley 4/68 & 4/72, Wolseley 15/60 & 16/60 ***(p86)***
BMC ADO16: Morris 1100/1300, Austin 1100/1300, MG 1100/1300, Riley Kestrel, Vanden Plas Princess, Wolseley 1100/1300 ***(p89, 90 & 111)***
BMC ADO17: Austin 1800/2200, Morris 1800/2200, Wolseley 18/85 & Six ***(p90)***
BMC ADO37: Vanden Plas Princess 3-Litre
BMC ADO53: Austin A99 & A110 Westminster, Wolseley 6/99 & 6/110 ***(p88)***
BMC ADO66: Vanden Plas 4-Litre R ***(p88)***
BMC 9X ***(p97)***
BMC 1100 Berlina Aerodinamica ***(p93)***
BMC 1800 Berlina Aerodinamica ***(p92)***
Bristol 400 Cabriolet ***(p118)***
Bristol 401 Drophead Convertible ***(p120)***
Healey Nash-Healey ***(p160)***
Jaguar F-Type ***(p191)***
Jaguar MkVII Saloon & Coupe ***(p167)***
Jaguar XK120 SE Coupe ***(p171)***
Jaguar XJ12 PF ***(p186)***
Jaguar XJ40 proposal ***(p189)***
Jaguar XJ220 Speciale ***(p191)***
Jaguar XJ Series 3 ***(p189)***
Jaguar XJ Spider ***(p188)***
Jaguar X-Type Estate ***(p192)***
Lotus Bulgari ***(p212)***
Lotus Chronos ***(p214)***
Lotus Enjoy ***(p215)***
Lotus Saloon ***(p211)***
MGB GT ***(p99)***
MG EX234 ***(p100)***
MGF ***(p105)***
MG Mini Sports Car (ADO34/ADO35) ***(p96)***
Morris Marina proposal (ADO28) ***(p104)***
Rolls-Royce Camargue ***(p232)***
Rolls-Royce Corniche ***(p235)***
Rolls-Royce Hyperion ***(p237)***
Rolls-Royce Phantom II Limousine ***(p230)***
Rolls-Royce Silver Dawn Coupe ***(p230)***
Rover P4 Drophead & Fixed-Head Coupe ***(p246)***
Rover/Triumph SD2 ***(p250 & p272)***

SCHIARETTI

One of Italy's innumerable metal fabricators who occasionally made bodywork was Virgilio Schiaretti, based in Parma. His only contribution of note was an MG TD rebodied for an American soldier in 1956.

INDEX OF BRITISH-ITALIAN MODELS

MG TD ***(p79)***

SIBONA-BASANO

Carrozzeria Sibona-Basano was founded in Turin in 1957 by the Sibona brothers (Pietro and Giovanni) along with Walter Basano. This outfit made the bodywork for a number of companies including Abarth, as well as designing its own cars from 1963 on. The only project to have any UK connections was the Virgil Exner-designed Mercer Cobra that was based on a stretched AC Cobra 289 chassis.

INDEX OF BRITISH-ITALIAN MODELS

AC Mercer Cobra ***(p21)***

STABILIMENTI FARINA

Say the name Farina to most car people and they will think only of Pinin Farina. But there was another coachbuilder called Farina, founded by Pinin's brother Giovanni Carlo Farina and called Stabilimenti Farina.

Giovanni Carlo Farina was just 12 years old when he became an apprentice at Carrozzeria Alessio in 1896. After 10 years there, he departed to found his own workshop, Stabilimenti Farina, in Corso Tortona in Turin supplying many other local coachbuilders and doing its own work on various chassis. With design input from his talented brother, 'Pinin' Farina, the company soon became a trusted partner of Giovanni Agnelli, Fiat's boss.

Experience in aviation during Word War 1 informed the firm's deployment of lightweight construction methods. In 1919, the company developed a technique for eliminating wooden framework entirely from its bodywork. Among the patents that it applied for were powered sunroofs, adjustable dampers and hydraulic brakes. Increasingly, Stabilimenti Farina received commissions from wealthy clientele for tailor-made cars, with notable work on chassis such as Itala, Lancia, Alfa Romeo and Isotta Fraschini.

In 1930, Giovanni 'Pinin' Farina departed to found his own coachbuilding company, Carrozzeria Pinin Farina. Stabilimenti Farina continued in business, drawing on the design talents of Count Revelli di Beaumont as well as hiring a very young Pietro Frua, a brilliant designer and engineer.

The company became known for its ground-breaking aerodynamic techniques, with innovations like enclosed wheels and inclined windscreens. Frua left in 1937 and was effectively replaced by Giovanni Michelotti, aged just 17 when he took over as technical director. Alfredo Vignale (also later to found his own *carrozzeria*) was the works manager.

Following WW2, Giovanni Farina passed control to his sons Attilio and Nino, who cleaved to the old ways of doing things, something that hastened Michelotti's departure from the company soon after the war's end. While Stabilimenti Farina's quality was never in question, innovation certainly took a back seat. The *carrozzeria* closed its doors in 1953.

INDEX OF BRITISH-ITALIAN MODELS

Jaguar MkVII Meteor & Golden Arrow *(p166)*
Jaguar XK120 Flying Jaguar *(p169)*
Jowett Jupiter Coupe *(p198)*

TJAARDA

Born in 1934 as Stevens Thompson Tjaarda van Starkenberg, Tom Tjaarda designed more than 80 cars over a five-decade working lifespan. The American dearly wanted to work in Italy and leapt at the offer of a job with Ghia in 1958, where he designed the Innocenti 950 Spider.

He moved to Pininfarina in 1961 and here created two Ferraris (the 330GT 2+2 and 365 California) as well as the Fiat 124 Spider. He then rejoined Ghia, where he designed the seminal De Tomaso Pantera in 1970.

When Ghia was sold to Ford, Tjaarda stayed on as design chief, notably shaping the first-generation Fiesta. After a spell at Fiat, he moved to Rayton-Fissore in 1981 and then, in 1984, he went freelance, initially as Dimensione Design and then as Tjaarda Design.

The only British marques he designed for – and then only as proposals – were Aston Martin Lagonda and Lotus. Tjaarda passed away in 2017.

INDEX OF BRITISH-ITALIAN MODELS

Aston Martin Lagonda Coupe proposal *(p50)*
Innocenti Spider & Coupe *(p108)*
Lotus Elise & Elite proposals *(p214)*

TOURING

Felice Bianchi Anderloni trained as a lawyer but chose a profession in the brave new world of automobiles, as a director at Isotta Fraschini. Together with Gaetano Ponzoni, Anderloni purchased a controlling interest in the Milanese coachbuilder, Carrozzeria Falco (owned by Vittorio Ascari, brother of racing driver Antonio Ascari), which was soon renamed Carrozzeria Touring.

The company rebodied fine Italian chassis such as Alfa Romeo, Isotta Fraschini, Lancias and OM, and earned a reputation for understated elegance and an impeccable finish. A licence was acquired to make Weymann patented bodywork (a type of artificial leather stretched over a wooden frame), beginning a long obsession with lightness, as well as aerodynamic forms. Racing cars widely used Touring bodies, notably Alfa Romeos, which won almost every Mille Miglia of the 1930s.

In 1937 came the biggest innovation in Touring's history: the patented 'superleggera' (superlight)

Aston Martin DB5 by Touring

construction method of thin aluminium body panels attached to a framework of steel tubes. So significant was this event that the word superleggera was incorporated into a new name for the company: Carrozzeria Touring Superleggera. Another advance was widespread use of a new material, Plexiglas, that permitted curved windows and even – with another Touring patent applied – the Aerlux roof.

Anderloni's son Carlo joined the company in 1944 and four years later took over at the helm following his father's death. A new and visionary designer called Federico Formenti was hired, and despite being largely unknown (even in retrospect), his impact was enormous. One of his first jobs was designing the seminal Ferrari 166 MM Barchetta of 1948. Very quickly, Touring became the primary coachbuilder of Ferraris, as well as collaborating with Alfa Romeo for its 1949 6C 2500 SS Villa d'Este.

Carlo Felice Bianchi Anderloni realised that the market for bespoke bodywork for wealthy individuals was fast disappearing, and henceforth clients would increasingly be large businesses. He forged relations with companies like Bristol, for which he developed the 401 with superleggera bodywork. But easily the most important link to a British company was Aston Martin. This relationship started when David Brown, owner of Aston Martin, saw and liked Touring's 1956 Aston Martin DB2/4 convertible. Brown soon entrusted Anderloni with the development of the new DB4, styled by Formenti, a seminal model that was quickly followed by the Lagonda Rapide, DB5 and DB6.

Another fateful liaison with a British company – Rootes – occurred in 1959, when Touring restyled the Sunbeam Alpine and then created its very own Sunbeam, the Venezia, which reached the market in 1963. In October 1961, Touring also signed a deal to assemble Rootes cars in a brand new factory at Nova Milanese. A combination of industrial unrest in Italy, new tax rules for large-engined cars and financial overstretching with the Rootes contract ultimately led to the company being wound up for good in 1966. The very last car designed by Touring was for a new British client, Jensen, for which Formenti designed the Interceptor. Carlo Felice Bianchi Anderloni went on to become head of styling at Alfa Romeo, eventually passing away in August 2003.

In 2006 the Touring Superleggera name was revived to make special-bodied luxury conversions for an upmarket clientele. Based in Milan, right next to the Zagato works, the new Touring operation converted various Maserati, Alfa Romeo and Bentley models, as well as collaborating with BMW for a Mini concept in 2014. The coachbuilder remains in robust health at the time of writing.

Sunbeam Venezia by Touring

INDEX OF BRITISH-ITALIAN MODELS

Aston Martin DB2/4 Mark II Spider *(p37)*
Aston Martin DB4 *(p38)*
Aston Martin DB5 *(p40)*
Aston Martin DB6 *(p41)*
Aston Martin DBS C *(p42)*
Bentley Continental Flying Star *(p72)*
Bristol 401 *(p119)*
Frazer Nash 2000 Spyder *(p150)*
Hillman Super Minx *(p242)*
Jensen Interceptor & FF *(p194)*
Lagonda Rapide *(p42)*
Mini Superleggera Vision *(p221)*
Sunbeam Alpine *(p239)*
Sunbeam Venezia *(p240)*

Jensen FF by Touring

VIGNALE

Alfredo Vignale – the fifth of seven brothers – started working as a car panel beater in Turin in 1924 aged just 11. Employed by Ferrero & Morandi, he worked on sub-contracted bodywork for Pinin Farina. This led to Pinin's brother, Giovanni Farina, offering Vignale the role of foreman at Stabilimenti Farina.

In 1947 Piero Dusio of Cisitalia asked Vignale to make the body for his 202 Berlinetta, a difficult job that was so well rewarded that he was able to fund starting up his own company in Turin: Carrozzeria Vignale. The first Vignale car arrived in 1948: a rebodied Fiat Topolino. The British magazine *The Autocar* published a photo of the car, incorrectly attributing it to Farina, but the misunderstanding was quickly clarified and got Vignale some good publicity.

A strong and lasting collaboration was formed with Giovanni Michelotti from 1948 on. By 1950 he was bodying Ferraris and was soon working for American clients such as Briggs Cunningham and Bill Frick. He also bodied a British chassis – a Rolls-Royce Silver Wraith – for Joseph Maschuch of New Jersey in 1955. By this time, Vignale had already bodied Aston Martin and Riley chassis.

In 1957, Carrozzeria Vignale won a contract to build the Lancia Appia Convertible, requiring a new factory in 1959 in Grugliasco, close to Fiat's Mirafiori plant. This enabled Vignale to manufacture many other models such as the Triumph Italia, Maserati 3500 Spider and Lancia Flavia Convertible.

Vignale was instrumental in setting up Giovanni Michelotti to pursue a highly productive career designing cars for Standard-Triumph in Britain. Vignale had made a prototype microcar for Frisky in 1957, leading to Harry Webster of Standard-Triumph to visit the company, which at the time was using Michelotti as its designer. The collaboration started with the Vignale-badged Standard Vanguard of 1958, followed by building several Michelotti-designed Triumph prototypes, ultimately giving Michelotti the impetus to set up his own *carrozzeria*.

Triumph Italia by Vignale

A further British collaboration arrived in 1966, when Vignale stepped in to build the Touring-designed Jensen Interceptor. Vignale also made its own Jensen Nova prototype in 1967. Another tangential British connection was the official UK importer of Vignale cars, Frixos Demetriou, who sold quite a few Vignale-bodied Fiats in the UK, including the Eveline, Samantha and Gamine.

Alfredo Vignale tragically died in a car accident in 1969, just one week after Alessandro de Tomaso had taken control of the coachbuilder. De Tomaso also owned Ghia, which he sold along with Vignale to Ford in 1970. Vignale ceased to exist as a design and coachbuilding entity at that point but the name was later used on some Ford/Ghia prototypes, including the 1993 Lagonda. In 2013, Ford announced that the 'Vignale' name would be adopted as an upmarket trim level, a scenario that continues to this day.

INDEX OF BRITISH-ITALIAN MODELS

Aston Martin DB2/4 Coupe *(p35)*
Aston Martin DB3 *(p37)*
Frisky *(p154)*
Jensen Interceptor & FF *(p194)*
Jensen Nova *(p197)*
MG TD *(p82)*
Riley RM Sports Saloon *(p84)*
Rolls-Royce Silver Wraith Limousine *(p231)*
Standard Vignale Vanguard *(p254)*
Triumph Italia *(p260)*
Triumph TR3 Speciale 'Dream Car' *(p259)*
Triumph Zoom *(p262)*
Vauxhall Viva De Luxe *(p282)*

VIOTTI

Viotti was founded in Turin in 1921 as Viotti & Tolfo, reformed in 1930 after liquidation as Carrozzeria Viotti. It made its name making special bodies for Fiat, Alfa Romeo and Lancia chassis. It was a notable user of the lightweight 'Clairalpax' construction method and in pre-war years formed a strong design partnership with Mario Revelli di Beaumont.

In 1946, the company moved to a new factory in Corso Bramante in Turin but by 1949 had been reformed as Carrozziere Esercizio Stabilimenti Viotti.

On the death of its founder, Vittorino Viotti, in 1956, control of the company passed to Francesco Viotti. From 1957, Pietro Frua was used as a stylist, followed by Rodolfo Bonetto. The company closed for good in 1964.
It restricted its work on British chassis to two marques: Bentley and Bristol.

INDEX OF BRITISH-ITALIAN MODELS

Bentley 3-Litre *(p64)*
Bristol 407 Convertible *(p126)*

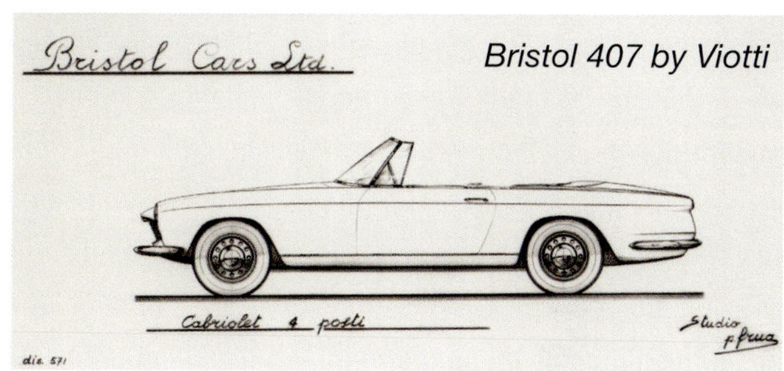

Bristol 407 by Viotti

ZAGATO

Ugo Zagato was born on 25 June 1890 in Gavello in the province of Rovigo (north eastern Italy). Having learnt the craft of metal processing, he founded his own coachbuilding company in Milan in 1919, making Zagato one of Italy's oldest coachbuilders. Zagato scored a coup in winning the contract to make the bodywork for the Alfa Romeo RL, while the Alfa Romeo 6C 1750 GS Zagato was a zenith of aesthetics, light weight, low drag and high speed.

Bristol 406S Zagato

Zagato's first work on a British chassis was a Rolls-Royce Phantom in 1928. Then the first of several partnerships with British financiers came via an English-born benefactor, Teresa Johnson Giorgi, who was Zagato's major shareholder from 1935 to 1938.

After the war, Ugo's son Elio joined the company and Fabio Luigi Rapi became a new styling consultant. This fresh partnership produced the 'Panoramica' concept of transparent Plexiglas curving into the roof to allow extra light into the cabin and enhance visibility (an MG Y-Type was so clothed). This original thinking typified Zagato's non-conformist approach to design. Another uniquely characteristic Zagato novelty was the 'double bubble' roof, originally conceived in the 1950s to clear the heads of passengers in very low bodies, but it quickly became an unmistakeable trademark. A passion for lightness also brought much racing success to Zagato-bodied cars.

In 1955, the second of Ugo's sons, Gianni Zagato, joined the company. Another significant Zagato appointment was Ercole Spada to a design role in 1960. Spada quickly penned a string of highly significant sports cars for the likes of Alfa Romeo and Lancia but also notably for Bristol (on the 406 and 407) and Aston Martin (the glorious DB4 GTZ). While Touring was Aston Martin's chief Italian designer, arguably Zagato's lightweight DB4 GT remains one of the most iconic cars in motoring history, even though only 19 examples were built.

Aston Martin Vanquish Roadster Zagato

Aston Martin Vanquish Zagato

Rover 2000 TCZ by Zagato

In 1962, the company transferred to a larger factory in Terrazzano di Rho, a suburb of Milan, where it remains to the this day. In 1970 Giuseppe Mittino replaced Ercole Spada as design chief, just as the era of coachbuilding was in the throes of terminal decline. Zagato sought to establish new business liaisons with the likes of Rover and Volvo and even started making an electric car (the Zele). The Bristol 412 was a rare example of a Zagato design in the 1970s reaching production, although the Milan factory was employed to assemble vehicles for third parties, like the Lancia Beta Spider and Maserati Biturbo Spider.

Zagato's fortunes were revived in the 1980s with the Aston Martin Vantage V8 Zagato project. The Italian company's finances remained perilous, however, resulting in Aston Martin taking a 50% stake in Zagato in July 1986 to get the V8 Vantage Zagato built, an arrangement that would last only until May 1987. Zagato did get to build further production models like the Alfa Romeo SZ, Lancia Hyena and Nissan Autech Stelvio but the factory ceased making cars in the early 1990s. Reformed in 1994 as SZ Design, a new generation family member, Andrea Zagato, was now at the helm, reorienting Zagato as a design consultancy with prototyping facilities.

Andrea Zagato successfully revived the link with Aston Martin with a new series of Aston Martin Zagato specials, starting in 2002 with the DB7 GT Zagato. Many more Aston Martins followed – and continue to emerge to this day. Zagato also created the Bentley GTZ of 2007, while the Perana Z-One of 2009 morphed into the AC 378 GT.

Another British company would also become involved with Zagato when, in 2011, CPP Manufacturing of Coventry bought the Italian design house for more than £6 million; on CPP going bust in 2012, ownership passed to another UK firm, Envisage. Zagato continued to co-create cars with Aston Martin that were actually built in the UK.

Zagato continues to thrive creating '*fuoriserie*' (low-production) designs at high prices, and it's a curious fact that the most valuable examples of many car marques happen, by and large, to wear Zagato badges. Its legacy is a huge and broad spread of bold, iconoclastic cars that are unlike those of any other coachbuilder.

INDEX OF BRITISH-ITALIAN MODELS

AC 378 GT *(p26)*
AC Ace-Bristol *(p18)*
Aston Martin DB4 GT Zagato *(p45)*
Aston Martin DB4 GT Zagato Sanction II *(p46)*
Aston Martin DB4 GT Zagato Sanction III *(p47)*
Aston Martin DB4 GT Zagato Continuation *(p47)*
Aston Martin DB7 Zagato *(p50)*
Aston Martin DB9 Spyder Zagato Centennial *(p55)*
Aston Martin DB AR1 Zagato *(p52)*
Aston Martin DBS Coupe Zagato Centennial *(p54)*
Aston Martin DBS GT Zagato Centenary *(p57)*
Aston Martin V8 Vantage Zagato *(p47)*
Aston Martin V8 Volante Zagato *(p48)*
Aston Martin V12 Zagato Heritage Coupe & Speedster *(p58)*
Aston Martin V12 Zagato *(p53)*
Aston Martin Vanquish Roadster Zagato *(p53)*
Aston Martin Vanquish Zagato Coupe *(p55)*
Aston Martin Vanquish Zagato Shooting Brake *(p57)*
Aston Martin Vanquish Zagato Speedster *(p57)*
Aston Martin Vanquish Zagato Volante *(p56)*
Aston Martin Virage Shooting Brake Zagato Centennial *(p55)*
Bentley Continental GTZ *(p72)*
Bristol 406 GT Zagato *(p123)*
Bristol 406S Zagato *(p124)*
Bristol 407 GT Zagato *(p125)*
Bristol 412 *(p126)*
Hillman Zimp *(p242)*
Jaguar XK140 Coupe *(p174)*
Jaguar XK150 SE *(p176)*
Lagonda Rapide *(p50)*
Lotus Elise proposal *(p214)*
MG Y-Type Panoramica *(p78)*
Mini Gatto (Mini Cat) *(p95)*
Rolls-Royce Phantom *(p228)*
Rover 2000 TCZ *(p248)*